Contents

Preface

I am a poet who is also a pastor, theologian, and teacher. I am fascinated by public worship in its varied forms, teach and practice worship design, and am interested in what people sing, especially when they sing together. Grafted into a hymn-singing tradition, and glad of it, I recognize the need for a variety of styles in congregational song. I have come to appreciate musical styles formerly unknown or foreign to me, and to accept as valid styles that offend me theologically, or aesthetically leave me cold.

I write with pastors and seminarians particularly in mind, but also lay worship leaders, musicians, people who enjoy singing in church, people who consider themselves unmusical, and people who care about the words they say or sing. I hope this book will be especially useful to churches that traditionally emphasize congregational singing, especially hymn singing. I write as an Englishman in a North American context, with an eye to other parts of the English-speaking world.

I hope this will prove to be an accessible and practical book, which pastors, ordinands, seminarians, musicians on-site or in training, and other worship leaders can draw on directly for their work. References and comment are footnoted on the page, for ease of access. For economy, they mostly give the author's last name and part of the title: complete references are in the Bibliography. As is now widely customary, I use the neutrally descriptive year-date abbreviations B.C.E. and C.E. ("Before the Common Era" and "Common Era") in place of "Before Christ" and "Anno Domini."

Many people have helped to make this book possible. Among many churches and seminaries I give particular thanks to Garrett-Evangelical Theological Seminary (Evanston, Illinois) for inviting me to teach in their summer school; to Lancaster Seminary, Pennsylvania (Lecture and Workshop, 1998); Louisville Presbyterian Seminary (Greenhoe Lectures, 1998); Seminary of the Southwest (Scholars in Residence, 1995); Trinity College, Melbourne, Australia (Frank Woods Fellowship and Marshall Memorial Lecture, 1999), the Baptist Theological Seminary, Richmond, Virginia (Cousins Lectures, 1999); and the Episcopal parish of St. Michael and All Angels, Stone Mountain, Georgia (Retreat and Workshop, 1996). Gordon and Ellie Clifford helped me at a crucial time by giving me the use of their cottage at Flying Pond, Maine. George and Nancy Shorney hosted me on many visits to Hope Publishing Company (Carol Stream, Illinois) and for a visit to a Seeker Service at the Community Church of Willow Creek. At Westminster John Knox Press, Stephanie Egnotovich encouraged the writing of this book, waited patiently for me to finish, and gave indispensable help in its evaluation; the promotion and production teams have been unfailingly courteous, professional, and helpful. My partner in marriage and partner in ministry, Revd Susan Heafield, has given essential ongoing feedback and encouragement.

Finally, here is a list of resources I have found especially useful. A complete listing is in the Bibliography.

Works of Reference

Espy, Willard R. *Words to Rhyme With, For Poets and Song Writers.* Part 1 is a primer of prosody (verse writing) with witty, clear examples. Part 2 is the rhyming dictionary (using American pronunciation).

Watson, Richard, and Kenneth Trickett, eds. *Companion to "Hymns and Psalms."* Well informed.

Young, Carlton R. *Companion to the United Methodist Hymnal.* A gold mine of information, plus enjoyable strong opinions.

Historical

Foley, Edward. *Foundations of Christian Music: The Music of Pre-Constantinian Christianity.* Short, and in the best sense scholarly.

————. *From Age to Age: How Christians Celebrated the Eucharist.* Well written, beautifully illustrated.

Hustad, Donald P. *Jubilate II: Church Music in Worship and Renewal.* Major work from a great ecumenical evangelical.

Marshall, Madeleine Forell, and Janet Todd. *English Congregational Hymns in the Eighteenth Century.* Careful historical study of Watts, Wesley, and their forebears and successors.

Routley, Erik. *A Panorama of Christian Hymnody.* A wide range of examples (text only) from all ages, conveniently under one cover, with many Routleyesque flashes of insight.

Stackhouse, Rochelle. *The Language of the Psalms in Worship: American Revisions of Watts's Psalter.* Title describes it: a well-researched case study.

Westermeyer, Paul. *Te Deum: The Church and Music—A Textbook, a Reference, a History, an Essay.* An excellent introductory history.

White, Susan J. *Christian Worship and Technological Change.* Focuses on the technological issues behind, and around, lyrics and music.

Wilson-Dickson, Andrew. *The Story of Christian Music: From Gregorian Chant to Black Gospel. An Authoritative Illustrated Guide to All the Major Traditions of Music for Worship.* Beautifully illustrated, comprehensive.

Congregational Singing / Contemporary Worship

Clark, Linda J. *Music in Churches: Nourishing Your Congregation's Musical Life.* Findings of a New England congregational survey.

Collins, Dori Erwin, and Scott C. Weidler. *Sound Decisions: Evaluating Contemporary Music for Lutheran Worship.* Good example of how a particular tradition draws on its theological resources to give new possibilities a thoughtful, critical welcome.

Farlee, Robert Buckley, ed. *Leading the Church's Song.* Foreword by Paul Westermeyer, and articles by various authors on Techniques for Leading, Chant, Northern European, North American, African American, Contemporary, Latino, African, and Asian types of congregational song; plus a CD (in a pocket on the inside back cover) with 56 short musical examples, listed on the inside back pages. An invaluable resource.

Parker, Alice. *Melodious Accord: Good Singing in Church.* Sound, and practical, from someone who can teach any group of people how to sing.

Sample, Tex. *The Spectacle of Worship in a Wired World: Electronic Culture and the Gathered People of God.* Pioneering exploration of how popular music (sound as beat) integrates with the visual and dramatic in electronic culture.

Hymnody

Castle, Brian. *Sing a New Song to the Lord: The Power and Potential of Hymns.* Readably surveys hymnody, and raises probing sociopolitical questions.

Hollander, John. *Rhyme's Reason.* Short, pithy treatise on prosody.

Polman, Bert, Marilyn Kay Stulken, and James R. Sydnor, eds. *Amazing Grace: Hymn Texts for Devotional Use.* Good selection of hymns, in poetic form.

Reynolds, William J., and Milburn Price. *A Survey of Christian Hymnody.* Covers the ground well, with a range of words-and-music examples at the back.

Watson, J. R. *The English Hymn: A Critical and Historical Study.* On hymns as works of literature: a major work of scholarship and appreciation.

Young, Carlton R. *My Great Redeemer's Praise: An Introduction to Christian Hymns.* Twelve essays on all aspects of hymnody, ranging from informational to provocative—worth reading and keeping.

Music

Jourdain, Robert. *Music, the Brain, and Ecstasy: How Music Captures Our Imagination*. Recent, comprehensive survey, from the physics of sound waves to music's inspirational power.

Meyer, Leonard. *Meaning and Emotion in Music*. A classic work, combining philosophy and psychology with illuminating analysis of many musical examples.

Rock, Judith, and Norman Mealy. *Performer as Priest and Prophet: Restoring the Intuitive in Worship through Music and Dance*. Not only music, but other worship arts.

Storr, Anthony. *Music and the Mind*. Readable, informative, from a noted psychiatrist and skilled communicator.

Westermeyer, Paul. *The Church Musician*. For church musicians, and all who need to know what it takes to make one.

List of Abbreviations

Bibles

KJV	*King James Version*
NEB	*New English Bible*
NIB	*New Interpreter's Bible*
NRSV	*New Revised Standard Version*
REB	*Revised English Bible*

Hymnals

BOP	*Book of Praise*
H&P	*Hymns and Psalms* (Methodist, U.K.)
HCS	*A New Hymnal for Colleges and Schools*
NCH	*New Century Hymnal*
PH	*The Presbyterian Hymnal*
R&S	*Rejoice and Sing*
SBH	*Baptist Hymnal* (Southern Baptist)
TCH	*The Chalice Hymnal*
UMH	*United Methodist Hymnal*
VU	*Voices United*

Other

BCP	*Book of Common Prayer*

Chapter One

"Through All the Changing Scenes of Life": Glimpses of Congregational Song

Through all the changing scenes of life,
    in trouble and in joy,
the praises of my God shall still
    my heart and tongue employ.
        —From Psalm 34, Nahum Tate
and Nicholas Brady, *New Version,* 1696

"Whoever sings [to God, in worship], prays twice." The epigram suggests that when we sing a praise and prayer instead of simply speaking it, we add something important to the utterance.[1]

This book considers the music and words of congregational song. Though the words we sing are only part of the experience of singing, they deserve critical attention, because they either enlarge and develop Christian faith, or distort and diminish it. In the latter part of the book, I study the lyrics of different kinds of congregational song, especially choruses (Taizé or evangelical), hymns, chant, and ritual song. I urge pastors, musicians and worshipers in hymn-singing traditions to capitalize on their heritage by using hymn lyrics as poetry; explain why hymn lyrics get altered over time; and show how hymn lyrics do theology.

The first part of the book looks at the music of congregational song. Because I am an amateur musician, and have in mind readers who may not see themselves as musical, I discuss music not from a technical standpoint, but to explore the power of music in worship and the

---

1. Attributed to Augustine of Hippo, 354–430 C.E.

1

importance of congregational song in the life of a congregation. I claim that evangelical necessity calls people in hymn-singing traditions to give a critical welcome to "contemporary worship music." I explore why the subject is difficult to discuss, respond to some objections, and ask "Why welcome?" and "How critical?"

My major claim is that congregational song is an indispensable part of Christian public worship. By "congregational song" I mean anything that a worshiping congregation sings, not as presentation or performance to someone else, but as a vehicle for its encounter with God. I aim to show that congregational song has been a distinctive part of Christian worship from the beginning; that song can do what speech cannot; and that congregational song is theologically important: a matter of vital interest to pastors, worshipers, and educators, as well as musicians and the musically minded. I look at how different songs function in worship, and how best to foster strong congregational singing.

To set the scene for what follows, here are some glimpses or "video clips" of congregational song in different places and times. My glimpses come with cautionary notes. To begin with, they are approximations. When we look back at congregational song, even in the recent past, it is possible to guess, but probably impossible to know, how people experienced the act of singing. As we reach through time, the music people sang and how they sang it recede into uncertainty. From earliest times, what survives is only the words people sang.

My glimpses are not a history of congregational song. History is not my field, and the tracing of cause, effect, and development over the centuries is excellently done by others.[2]

Nor are my glimpses comprehensive. Comprehensive coverage would include glimpses of today's congregational song in India, China, Indonesia, the Philippines, the rest of Asia, the Middle East, Africa, Central and South America, Eastern Europe, and the Pacific; historical portraits of Coptic, Ethiopian, Moravian, Mennonite, and Orthodox traditions; black gospel; Shakers and Campbellites; nineteenth-century urbanites who could read music off the page and were irked by Moody and Sankey, and many others. Details of dialogue and description are invented; I aim to be plausible within boundaries set by sources of information.

---

2. I draw, in particular, on Foley, *From Age to Age* and *Foundations of Christian Music;* Westermeyer, *Te Deum;* and Wilson-Dickson, *The Story of Christian Music.*

Begin by calling to mind the congregational singing we each know best today. Perhaps it is the ritual song of Roman Catholic, Lutheran, and Episcopal/Anglican Communion liturgies, including the Kyrie ("Lord have mercy, Christ have mercy, Lord have mercy"), the Sanctus ("Holy, holy, holy!"), and memorial acclamations ("Christ has died. Christ is risen. Christ will come again"). Perhaps it is the classic hymn repertoire, and its recent outpouring. Or metrical psalmody. Or psalms and canticles chanted, Gregorian or Anglican fashion. Or psalms and hymns sung responsorially (cantor and congregation). Or "evangelical" choruses repeated or sung in sequence. Or candlelit Taizé worship songs. Or the driving beat of "contemporary worship music." Or the mind-and-body involvement of African, African American, and charismatic song.

Call to mind also our present-day culture, where (for many of us) group singing is rarely done except in church, and some of our best-remembered songs may be the jingles in commercials.[3] Recall how, for many of us, music is instantly available, through earphones and amplifiers, in automobiles and living rooms, stored in the latest recording media or downloaded from the Internet. Music is also often unavoidable: in grocery stores and shopping malls, as we wait on the telephone, and in dentists' waiting rooms.

To travel back in time, we mentally divest ourselves of today's culture. We take off our headsets; turn off the stereo, TV, and radio; put down our cell phone; and shut the door on Web browsers and e-mail. We enter a world where visual stimuli are less frenetic; mass media diminish and disappear; transport slows from train to horseback and sailing ship; and news media are first print-based; then handwritten; finally spoken and memorized.

In the world of the past, sound is neither recorded nor amplified; and music cannot be retrieved once it has been played or sung. Concert halls fade and vanish, and high-quality instrumental music is for ordinary people a rare and memorable experience: at church festivals and fairs, or through the kitchen doors of stately homes.[4] Vocal music is a different matter. People sing together several times a week: for pleasure and love in homes and taverns; for courage to face invasion and battle; at

---

3. Westermeyer, "The Future of Congregational Song," pp. 4–9.

4. "Any musical sound, no matter how crudely performed, must have been as delicious as the meats and candies enjoyed only on festive days" (Jourdain, *Music, the Brain, and Ecstasy*, p. 239).

rites of passage from cradle to grave; to bless divine presence in daily routines; and wherever people do hard, repetitive work together—on board ship, in factories and fields, or at the digging of a well.

As we begin our journey, our guidebook reminds us that the cultures we visit do not see themselves as impoverished, much less inferior, in relation to our own. They cannot possibly see themselves that way: our culture does not yet exist for them, and if it did, they might regard us unfavorably, or see our musical life as impoverished. To enter past cultures sympathetically we must divest ourselves of notions of cultural superiority and try to see the world through other people's eyes, listen through their ears, and walk in their shoes.

Our guiding questions are: "What did people sing congregationally in worship?" and "How did people experience the songs they sang?"

Let the journey begin.

London, England: 1970 C.E.

Midday Mass at a joint meeting of two Roman Catholic commissions: "Justice and Peace," and "Mission."[5] Mass is held in a late-nineteenth-century church, marbled, pillared, cavernous, and resplendent. Protestants are present: observers from counterpart committees, and from an ecumenical committee cosponsored by the commissions. Pressing concerns of international justice and peace have brought Protestants and Catholics together. Common action on economic development is easier than common agreement on doctrine.

For some non-Catholics, it is their first visit to a Roman Catholic Mass. They enter cautiously. Centuries of antagonism and suspicion have only recently begun to dissipate.

The Mass is in English—a decade earlier it would have been in Latin, but the Second Vatican Council has dramatically altered the Catholic liturgical landscape. Protestant visitors show a determined lack of surprise at its familiarity: with few exceptions, the dreaded Mass is similar to the Word and Table liturgies of their own traditions.

After centuries of liturgical silence, Catholics have recovered their voice in word and song. Congregational singing is led by a cantor, supported by a magnificent pipe organ. A Gelineau psalm is announced:

---

5. This account is from personal recollection. Protestant is a shorthand description: Anglicans categorize themselves as both Protestant and Catholic.

the cantor sings the verses, all sing the refrain. One or two hymns are included: Wesley, Watts, and others have entered the Catholic repertoire. The congregation sings "Glory be to God on high," "Lord have mercy," and "Holy, holy, holy." To visitors, the texts are familiar, but the musical settings are new. Bishop Mahon presides, speaking the printed liturgy as if each word were freshly minted. Then he quietly springs a surprise: official rules are waived, and all are invited to take Communion. His tone conveys that this is for him a hope, not simply a concession. "The gifts of God for the people of God," he proclaims. "Come, all is ready." At the table of division, Protestant and Catholic come unexpectedly together, and say a united "Amen" to the post-Communion prayer. Thanksgiving spills into song: the concluding hymn is heartfelt and full-voiced.

England: 1873 C.E.

A city, London perhaps.[6] Mr. Moody and Mr. Sankey have hired a vast exhibition hall for their latest revival meeting. During the past month, "Moody and Sankey" have become as familiar as Gilbert and Sullivan will be before long. Their methods are controversial, and their fame has spread: through newspaper articles, letters to newspapers, posters, leaflets, and word of mouth. People arrive mostly by train or on foot; a few have carriages or hansom cabs. The hall is crowded. Dark-suited ushers move up and down, carrying long wooden wands for identification. High on the platform, visible to all, are Mr. Moody, standing at the rail, and Mr. Sankey, sitting at a desk beside him. A choir sits behind them.

The hall is bare and functional. Someone has strung a few scripture texts between two of the high iron pillars, but they are barely readable. People arrive, talk, wave to one another, and call out to friends. The atmosphere is boisterous. "Is this really a religious service?" someone asks.

Mr. Sankey swivels in his seat and signals to the choir. They stand. Mr. Sankey faces the crowd, leans forward at his desk, and reedy organ music sounds through the hall. Evidently the "desk" is the portable organ described in newspaper articles. The choir sings. The audience quietens. Singing continues. For a full half hour, Mr. Sankey alternates

---

6. Hustad, *Jubilate II*, pp. 234–37; Wilhoit, " 'Sing Me a Sankey' "; Wilson-Dickson, *The Story of Christian Music*, pp. 138–39, 200.

choir songs, his own solos, and songs with refrains for the audience to join in. Because he is playing as well as singing, he uses few hand signals. His eyes, head, and bearded chin keep time and give direction. A solo singer in worship is a novelty—some are offended; many are spellbound.

Mr. Sankey's solo style is magnetic. Sometimes he prays before singing a solo, asking God to touch the hearts of those who listen. Often he pauses at the end of a phrase, to make sure the meaning has struck home. The songs sound modern: like the music-hall songs his audience knows so well. His method of teaching is old-fashioned. For decades, literate Christians have been taught to read music and sing in four-part harmony off the printed page. By contrast, Mr. Sankey teaches line by line, or phrase by phrase. Choruses to the hymns are easily held in memory. Anyone can sing them, and everyone does. Few in the audience have Mr. Sankey's printed songbooks. Many cannot afford them, and most cannot read, or cannot read well.

As the singing continues, the bare surroundings are forgotten. The audience is caught up in the fervor of revival. Singing alternates with prayers and scripture readings. Mr. Moody preaches. Amplification is far in the future. His voice carries easily, and fills the hall, though some older listeners strain to hear. Mr. Moody is less polished, less theological, less emotional, and less long-winded than earlier evangelists. His convictions carry conviction, his stories touch people's hearts, and people are visibly moved. As the choir sings, many come forward in response to his invitation.

The meeting would normally now be finished. But Mr. Moody senses that people are not ready to leave. "Shall we sing another song to the Lord tonight?" Mr. Moody asks. A thousand voices thunder, "Yes!" "What shall we sing?" cries Mr. Moody. Within seconds, a muttering begins, rapidly turning into a chant: "Hold the fort, hold the fort, hold the fort!"

Mr. Sankey grimaces. The song has become almost too popular. Its spiritual meaning is so easily lost. Finally, he nods his head in acceptance. The clamor hushes. Mr. Sankey summarizes the message of the song: Just as General Sherman, during the American Civil War, signaled to a beleaguered garrison that help was on the way, so Jesus Christ, our heavenly commander, will come to our aid in temptation, if only we resolve to "hold the fort." The song resounds through the hall. Some know it entirely by heart. Everyone knows the recurring refrain:

> Fierce and long the battle rages,
>   but our help is near;
> onward comes our great Commander,
>   cheer, my comrades, cheer!
> *"Hold the fort, for I am coming!"*
> *Jesus signals still;*
> *Wave the answer back to heaven,*
> *"By thy grace, we will!"*[7]

As the song ends, Mr. Sankey declares that souls can still be saved tonight. He sings his most famous solo, "The Ninety and Nine." It tells of a lost sheep, and Christ's determination to find it and bring it home. The listeners identify themselves with the one who is lost, yet found, and hear Christ rejoice at finding them. Even men weep, as the words strike home:

> But none of the ransomed ever knew
> how dark was the night that the Lord passed through
> ere he found his sheep that was lost.
> . . . .
> There arose a cry to the gate of heaven,
> "Rejoice! I have found my sheep!"
> And the angels echoed around the throne,
> "Rejoice, for the Lord brings back his own."[8]

South Carolina: 1862 C.E.

At a plantation on St. Helena Island, African American slaves gather in the praise house, a wooden building used for worship.[9] They arrive

---

7. "Hold the Fort" was written and composed in 1870, by P. P. Bliss, at Rockford, Illinois. Text and music appear in several places, including *Sacred Songs and Solos,* no. 669. The text, with the story of its composition, is in Whittle, *Memoirs,* pp. 68–70.

8. Poem by Elizabeth C. Clephane, music by Sankey, *Sacred Songs and Solos,* no. 97.

9. Spencer, *Protest and Praise,* pp. 142–51; Wilson-Dickson, *The Story of Christian Music,* p. 194. Spencer shows that all the musical ingredients imperative to African religion are present in the ring-shout: corporate song, percussive rhythm manifested in bodily accompaniment, and dancing, which together result in several of the worshipers "getting the power" or being "filled with the Spirit." The percussive mode of shouting was a rhythmic stimulant, while the nonpercussive mode of swaying was a rhythmic calmative. In both states the enslaved were temporarily able to find relief from the troubles of the world. The choice of "I'm Gonna Sing When the Spirit Says Sing" is mine, to illustrate the coded resistance in many slave songs.

slowly, in twos and threes; many look tired and careworn. The meeting begins with songs and prayers. "Some are hurting," cries the pastor. "Some are burdened, Lord! Some of your children are sore dismayed!" The congregation responds, fervently: "Yes, Lord!" "Yes, Jesus Lord!" "Lord Jesus, hear our prayer!" The pastor preaches, and the congregation responds, line by line, with calls and cries hovering between speech and song.

As the sermon ends, willing hands push the benches back against the side walls, and everyone, young and old, stands in the middle of the floor. Someone begins a spiritual, "I'm gonna sing when the Spirit says sing, and obey the Spirit of the Lord." The people begin to move, slowly at first, walking and shuffling in a ring, singing and clapping as they go. Because dancing is frowned upon, the worshipers shuffle and jerk their way forward, their feet barely leaving the floor. If a slave owner sees them, they are swaying, not dancing. Because drums have long been forbidden, their bodies become rhythm instruments: swaying, stomping, clapping, slapping the knees are ways of beating time.

In the "ring-shout," or "holy dance," song and dance are one, in the wholehearted praise of singing bodies. Dance it is, even if called a shuffle. Without dance, how can the Spirit come upon the dancers? As the Spirit moves, so worshipers must be in movement. Without the Spirit's movement, how can there be prophesying, revelation, and healing—Christianized essentials of African traditional religion?

The pace quickens, as worshipers vent their frustrations, fears, and longings. The stress and humiliation of enslavement are eased. In song, rhythm, and movement, the enslaved find temporary freedom. The pace quickens, the song intensifies: "I'm gonna sing *when the Spirit says sing*," as if to say, "And no-one's gonna stop me." The feet shuffle, the ring moves faster and faster, the floor shakes. As singers get out of breath, they sit on the benches, recover, and boost the dancers by singing, clapping, and stamping. For twenty minutes, half an hour, or longer, the shout continues; everyone is caught up in the song.

Finally, the pastor raises his hand. Movement slows and stops. Everyone is still. The pastor prays and gives a benediction. The worshipers file out of the praise house, smiling and talking, heads held high: God's chosen, Spirit-blessed. For a moment, and for eternity, they have found God's freedom.

Plymouth, England: 1746 C.E.

On the outskirts of this busy seaport and naval dockyard, at eleven o'clock in the forenoon, Charles Wesley is preaching in the open air.[10] He rode into town yesterday, on horseback, and tomorrow will ride on. In the past five years he has ridden hundreds of miles, to Nottingham, Sheffield, Leeds, and Wakefield, to Bristol and Cardiff, through Devon and Cornwall. Some know of him through printed reports, others by word of mouth. He and his brother are variously regarded as godly men, compassionate evangelists, unseemly enthusiasts, and disturbers of the peace.

As Mr. Wesley speaks, his powerful voice carries easily across the crowd, above the cries of street vendors, drunkards, and children at play, almost as far as the ships of the line whose masts rise at the end of a distant street.

A group of off-duty sailors, half tipsy with the daily ration of rum, are cat-calling and jostling at the edge of the crowd. As the preacher proclaims God's love, they have a different kind of love in mind. One of them starts up an obscene parody of the popular ballad "Nancy Dawson," and others join in. Preacher and singers vocally oppose each other. The preacher's words compete with a ribald version of a popular song, whose bouncy tune sounds like a cross between "I Saw Three Ships Come Sailing In" and "Here We Go Round the Mulberry Bush."

Finally, Mr. Wesley stops, holds up his hand, and waits till the sailors finish their song. "Brethren, I like your music well," he calls to them. "But if ye are minded to come again this evening I'll give you better words to sing."

The sailors drop their clamor and wander off, arguing among themselves. The service ends, and Mr. Wesley retires to a friend's house. He calls for pen and paper, and begins to write. Food and drink are forgotten. Within hours, he has written new words for the sailors' tune. Friends help him make handwritten copies.

That evening Charles Wesley preaches again. Word of the confrontation has gotten around. A huge crowd gathers. Some of the sailors return, less tipsy than before. Mr. Wesley leads in prayer and song. He preaches

---

10. The text and anecdote that follow are from Young, *Music of the Heart*, pp. 170–71, and Leaver, "Hymnody and the Reality of God." For the full text of Wesley's song, see the Appendix at the end of this book.

the dread seriousness of sin and the joyful news of salvation. He carries conviction to many, as much by his evident love for them as by his eloquence. Some stay hostile or indifferent; some shake and weep; others wipe tears from their eyes. Mr. Wesley looks out over the crowd and spreads his arms wide to the sailors. He contrasts the peril of being lost with God's desire for their happiness. "Happiness is the end of your being," he cries. "But being merry is not the same as being happy. None but a Christian is happy, none but a real inward Christian. I promised you a better song," he calls. "Take it, and join your hearts with ours." The new song is passed around. Mr. Wesley leads the singing:

> Listed into the Cause of Sin,
>   Why should a Good be Evil?
> Musick, alas! Too long has been
>   Prest to obey the Devil.

In other words, music has been, like the sailors, enlisted ("listed"), but in the service of the wrong navy—sin, instead of grace. It has been forcibly enrolled, or impressed ("prest") into the devil's service. Some of the sailors listen more keenly. Mr. Wesley is speaking directly to them. He knows that many were beaten and abducted by Press Gangs, whose royal warrant authorized them to roam through towns and villages, capturing young men for naval service.

The new song calls, not for conscripts, but for gospel volunteers who will recover "innocent sound" as they give music employment "in virtue's cause," and "rescue [its] holy pleasure." To the tune they know well, he invites them to sing a better song: "Come, let us try if Jesu's love/will not as well inspire us." If our hearts are tuned to sing, he asks, "is there a subject greater?":

> JESUS the Soul of Musick is;
>   His is the Noblest Passion;
> JESUS'S Name is Joy and Peace,
>   Happiness and Salvation:
> JESUS'S Name the dead can raise,
>   Shew us our Sins forgiven,
> Fill us with all the Life of Grace,
>   Carry us up to Heaven.

By the end of the song, everyone is singing. The sound of five hundred voices singing "lustily and with good courage" resounds through

Plymouth streets. On the steps of a nearby church, a frock-coated clergyman shakes his head disapprovingly. "Methodists! Tavern songs!" he mutters, and hurries inside.

England and New England: 1742 C.E.

A village church in an English country parish.[11] The parish priest is saying Matins for his congregation of artisans, agricultural laborers, and domestic servants. Local gentry no longer give leadership and financial support. The worshipers are impoverished and mostly illiterate. The church is in walking distance of their cottages. Few can venture beyond the village, except for daylong excursions, on foot, to the market town fifteen miles away. They live in isolation from the rapidly developing commerce and industry of the cities. The Wesleyan revival has hardly begun, and has not yet reached them.

The church is centuries old, a mixture of Early English and Perpendicular. Inside, its once brightly decorated walls are whitewashed and bare: a legacy of the Puritan revolution, a century ago, when medieval statues were pulled down, stained-glass windows destroyed, and wall paintings covered over.

The congregation wants to sing its beloved metrical psalms. The priest yields, unwillingly. Metrical psalms have no official place in Anglican liturgy, and educated clerics cannot abide the way they are sung. They are, however, the only church music people know and can join in.

Someone stands up to lead the psalm. He sings the first line, slowly, to convey its meaning and establish the tune:[12]

---

11. Names and places in what follows are accurate, as is the issue between Jonathan Edwards and the Northampton congregation. Other details are a fictional reconstruction based on Bishop, *Isaac Watts' Hymns and Spiritual Songs*, p. xxii; Leaver, "The Failure That Succeeded," esp. p. 29; Routley, *Panorama*, pp. 16–17; Westermeyer, *Te Deum*, pp. 108, 205, 248–51, 261; and Wilson-Dickson, *The Story of Christian Music*, pp. 101–4.

12. "Psalm 18, the Third Part," from Sternhold and Hopkins, *The Whole Book of Psalmes*. Urban parishes were acquiring Tate and Brady's *New Version* (1696), but Sternhold and Hopkins was the mainstay of country parishes into the nineteenth century. In its original spelling and format, the complete stanza reads:

But evermore I have respect	to his law and decree:
His statutes and commandment I	cast not away from me.
But pure and clean, and uncorrupt	appeared before his face:
and did refrain from wickedness,	and sin in every case.

"But evermore I have respect"

The congregation sings it back, enthusiastically, and even more slowly. The sound is raucous, nasal. But the people smile and sing from the heart: this is their music, and they love to sing.

"But e——ver——more I ha——ve re——spe——ct"

This single line has taken nearly half a minute. The song leader then sings the next line:

"to his law and decree:"

The congregation sings it back. Bolder voices embellish the melody, or try homespun harmonies. To a trained ear, the noise is displeasing. From within, it is the whole heart offered to God, and an expression of social identity.

"to—— hi——i——s la——w and decre——e,"

The song leader is warming up. He shuts his eyes, and sings, with some embellishments:

"His statutes and commandment I"

The congregation roars back, untroubled by a line that stops in mid-sentence:

"His sta——a——tutes and comma——a——andment I——"

Finally, after several minutes, half of the first stanza comes to completion, as the leader sings:

"cast not away from me," and the people respond,
    triumphantly:
"ca——s——st, ca——st, not a——a—way fro——o—m m—e."[13]

* * *

<hr>

13. In England, "lining out" was instituted during the short-lived Cromwellian revolution. The 1644 (Puritan) *Directory of Public Worship* decreed that "in singing of psalms, the voice is to be tunably and gravely ordered; but the chief care must be to sing with understanding." All who could read were to have books, but because many

In First Church, Northampton, Massachusetts, Jonathan Edwards preaches at morning worship.[14] The building is plain and unadorned, with benches, a central pulpit, and clear-glass windows letting in the light. The worship order is as plain as the architecture: opening prayer, scripture readings, prayers, sermon, blessing, interspersed with songs sung by the congregation. Everyone has a book where the words of the songs are printed, and they sing each song straight through to a familiar tune. The previous minister, Solomon Stoddard, introduced "regular singing," decades ago, in place of lining out. This congregation's singing is tuneful, vigorous, and committed. The Great Awakening is sweeping New England and has enlivened the First Church congregation. Pastor Edwards is a major instrument of the wider revival. Two weeks ago, he returned from a long preaching tour and found that in his absence, the church had bought copies of Dr. Isaac Watts's *Hymns and Spiritual Songs* and has been singing them in place of their traditional metrical psalms.[15] Pastor Edwards is happy to sing Dr. Watts's new hymns, but not at the cost of abandoning metrical psalmody. A compromise has been agreed: both books will from now on be used. In this literate community, words are as important as music. Pastor Edwards preaches on Galatians 6:14: "God forbid that I should glory, save in the cross of our Lord Jesus Christ, by which the world has been crucified to me and I to the world." People listen intently, intellectually fed and emotionally moved. Then the whole congregation stands and sings, for the first time, Dr. Watts's new hymn for the ordinance of the Lord's Supper:

---

could not read it was decreed that "the minister, or some other fit person . . . do read the psalm, line by line, before the singing thereof." Though the monarchy, and the Anglican Church, were restored in 1660, the practice of lining out continued. Like others, Isaac Watts catered to it by using rhyme (to aid memorization); unlike some of his predecessors, he usually ensured that each line made sense on its own, even when it was grammatically part of a longer sentence.

14. Jonathan Edwards (1703–58) served at First Church, Northampton, for many years, first as assistant to Solomon Stoddard, then as pastor after Stoddard's death in 1729. From about 1734, his preaching stimulated the "Great Awakening" in New England. Isaac Watts (1674–1748) grew up in Southampton, England, and wrote his first hymn at the age of nineteen. His many publications include *Hymns and Spiritual Songs* (1707) and *The Psalms of David, Imitated in the Language of the New Testament* (1719).

15. Possibly the *Bay Psalm Book* (Massachusetts, 1640), but I have no information on this point.

When I survey the wondrous cross
   on which the Prince of glory died,
my richest gain I count but loss,
   and pour contempt on all my pride.
. . . . .'. . . . . ,.
Were the whole realm of nature mine,
   that were a present far too small;
love so amazing, so divine,
   demands my soul, my life, my all.

Berlin, Germany: 1659 C.E.

It is a cold Christmas morning in the Church of St. Nicholas (Niko-laikirche).[16] Church and city have survived more than half a lifetime of civil war, invasion, battle, looting, and destruction, ending only a decade ago.[17] Only the youngest in today's congregation are untouched by the war. Cities, towns, villages and farms are still in ruins; hundreds were killed and wounded; thousands fled to other parts of Europe, or to America. The economy will take a century to recover.

Though science and art are elsewhere in decline, Lutheran churches preserve a rich musical tradition. One of the Nikolaikirche's deacons, Paul Gerhardt, is a noted hymn writer, working closely with the cantor, composer Johann Crüger. Today is Christmas Day. Worship will appeal to eye and ear, proclaim the gospel, and chase away the miseries of life's daily struggle.

The Nikolaikirche is a fitting "stage" for the festival: Gothic, with a soaring roof, and four hundred years of history. There are no competing events. Today the church will be full.

Many are already here, to worship or lead the worship. Beneath the pulpit are a group of tradesmen and craftsmen, the Collegium

---

16. Based on Gerhardt's account in Wilson-Dickson, *The Story of Christian Music*, p. 89. Paul Gerhardt (1607–76) was a deacon at the Nikolaikirche. His hymn lyrics include *O Jesu Christ, mein schönstes Licht* ("Jesus, Thy Boundless Love to Me"), *O Haupt voll Blut und Wunden* ("O Sacred Head, Sore Wounded"), and the Christmas hymn *Fröhlich soll mein Herze springen* ("All My Heart This Night Rejoices"). He worked closely with composer Johann Crüger (1598–1662), who was cantor at the Nikolaikirche from 1622 until his death (Young, *Companion to the United Methodist Hymnal*, p. 737; see also Reynolds and Price, *Survey*, pp. 22–24).

17. The "Thirty Years War" (1618–48), actually a series of wars between Catholics and Protestants, which led to successive interventions by Denmark, Sweden, and France.

Musicum, with violins and woodwind instruments, grouped round a movable pipe organ. Nearby are a male quartet and a military band with trumpets, snare drums, and kettledrums. In the gallery are a schoolboy choir on one side and a mixed-voice choir on the other.

Candles are lit. From the high organ, a soaring prelude fills the church. All are hushed and expectant. The organ signals the first chorale; people open their books, their lips, and their hearts; the church fills with song. In Lutheran theology, music is one of God's greatest gifts. Instrumental music is treasured in public worship, and new hymns are written, because the Bible calls us to sing a new song. In words and music, congregational hymns proclaim the gospel. Martin Luther set the tone, a century earlier, with bold, confident, joyful hymns. Others have followed in his footsteps.[18]

The service proceeds, led by three robed clergy standing at the altar. In this part of Germany the liturgy is still sung in Latin, by the choirs and schoolchildren. It is time for the first scripture reading. All eyes turn to the pulpit, where a college student stands, dressed as an angel with large, white wings. He sings an Old Testament prophecy, accompanied by the Collegium Musicum.

The main doors open. A teacher leads a procession of girls, dressed as angels. As they walk in procession to the high altar, one of the ministers chants a "Gloria," answered by the military band with trumpet fanfares and drumrolls.

The girls reach the altar and face the congregation. Their teacher— in the role of an angel—sings the first stanza of Martin Luther's Christmas hymn, written originally for a children's pageant:

From heaven high I come to earth . . .[19]

The girls sing the second stanza, in two-part counterpoint, while the third stanza is sung as a five-part motet by the gallery choir, accompanied by the organ.

The sermon is followed by a lively Te Deum, led by the instrumentalists, then a Latin anthem from the schoolboys. From the organ loft a nativity scene is presented, and boys imitate the sounds of farm

---

18. For example, Paul Speratus (1484–1551), Nicolaus Hermann (ca. 1480–1561), Philipp Nicolai (1556–1608), Martin Rinkart (1586–1649), Johann Franck (1618–77), Johann Heermann (1585–1667), and of course Paul Gerhardt and Johann Crüger.

19. "*Vom Himmel Hoch.*" For the full German text (fifteen stanzas) and Roland Bainton's translation, see Routley, *Panorama*, p. 3.

animals in the stable at Bethlehem. In response, choir and congregation sing a hymn. As they sing, a Christmas star revolves high above, on the front of the organ. The three Wise Men are represented by wooden puppets; they bow before the Christ-child in the cradle. A boy soprano sings "In dulci jubilo," and Father Christmas walks down the center aisle, with a sackful of gifts for the children. Finally, all sing "Puer natus est in Bethlehem" ("A boy is born in Bethlehem"). Christmas has fully come.

York, England: 1644 C.E.

Sunday: a service of Morning Prayer in the great cathedral of York Minster.[20] Wartime. York is a Royalist city, besieged for the past eleven weeks by the Parliamentarian army. The city is crowded with refugees from the countryside. They fill the vast cathedral. Before the sermon, according to local custom, a metrical psalm is sung, led by the choir and accompanied by the organ. The organ sounds a few introductory phrases. Choir and congregation begin to sing. Stress and anxiety drive the song, and make the singers more fervent. Some know the psalm by heart, others read from a printed page. They sing with heart and voice; they sing for dear life. The sound swells up and out, filling the nave. Tension is eased, and hope momentarily recovered.

Geneva, Switzerland: 1558 C.E.

Sunday morning worship, led by one of the city's pastors, Jean Cauvin (John Calvin).[21] Geneva is a cosmopolitan city, a center of commerce and industry on a major trade route. It has a population of

---

20. From a contemporary report by Thomas Mace, in Wilson-Dickson, *The Story of Christian Music,* p. 101. Mace was a staunch Royalist, so his account is not objective. Within a matter of months, York Minster was closed and stripped of its paintings, organ, and statues. Lining out replaced uninterrupted song.

21. Bouwsma, *Calvin,* pp. 29 and 126–27; various Web pages; Westermeyer, *Te Deum,* 153–63; and Wilson-Dickson, *The Story of Christian Music,* p. 66. John Calvin (1509–64) supported the textual work of Clement Marot (ca. 1496–1544) and Theodore Beza (1529–1605), and the musical work of Louis Bourgeois (ca. 1510–60) in producing the Genevan Psalter. I have, perhaps inaccurately, installed Bourgeois as song leader. The Genevan Psalter went through several editions, of which the 1551 edition was especially influential. It reached its final form in 1562. "Calvin" is the Latin rendering of French "Cauvin"; "John" is the English form of "Jean." Calvin preached from Ephesians on Sundays throughout 1558 and 1559.

thirteen thousand people, five monasteries, and more than five hundred church officials.

Calvin has preached more than a hundred and seventy sermons a year since being invited to return to Geneva in 1541. Early each morning (seven A.M. in winter, six A.M. at other times) he preaches from the Old Testament. This afternoon he will preach on the psalms. This Sunday he begins a two-year series on Paul's letter to the Ephesians. Now forty-nine years old, he suffers from recurrent migraine, gout, and bladder stones. Sometimes he has to be carried to church. Though he now has unquestioned authority in the affairs of church and city, he claims no special privileges, and lives like any other pastor.

The church is plain and unadorned, the service dignified and simple: prayers, readings, preaching, and singing. For Calvin, congregational song is a type of prayer. Music was created to tell and proclaim the praise of God, and for mutual edification. It has "a secret and almost incredible power to move hearts in one way or another." Singing in church is an ancient tradition, but to use music rightly we need holy and honest songs. God provides the words for our song (the Psalms of David) and must be worshiped only in ways appointed in his Word. If the Bible does not say, "Do this," it should not be done. Christ and the apostles sang, but did not use musical instruments. Thus, instruments are excluded from worship. Music in church must have weight and majesty. But because it is music for the people's song, it must be simple. Because we worship the sovereign God, it must be modest. These qualities are best achieved by the unison congregational singing of unaccompanied voices. Psalms are sung in metrical verse, because their ancient music has been lost.

The service begins with prayer, and a familiar psalm:

> Vous qui la ter-re habitez,
> chantez tout haut à Dieu, chantez:
> servez à Dieu, joyeus-e-ment,
> venez devant lui gai-e-ment.
> ("All people that on earth do dwell,
> sing out to God with cheerful voice.
> Him serve with mirth; his praise forth tell;
> come ye before him and rejoice!")[22]

---

22. Theodore Beza, 1551, with William Kethe's translation (Routley, *Panorama,* pp. 6–7), slightly corrected ("Sing out" renders "*tout haut,*" and Beza says "God" not "the Lord").

Today, Monsieur Bourgeois leads the singing, from the 1554 edition of the Genevan Psalter, which he himself prepared. Some of his tunes have echoes of plainsong; others draw on popular "secular" songs. All are crafted for ease of singing by the congregation. They use one note per syllable, dotted notes are rare, lines begin and end with long notes, and the psalms are sung in unison, without instrumental accompaniment. In spite of these restrictions, their simplicity and directness make them strong and memorable.

The service continues: scripture reading, psalm, prayer, sermon. Calvin begins by quoting his text, the first three verses of the first chapter of Ephesians: "Paul, an apostle of Jesus Christ by the will of God, to all you holy and faithful ones in Jesus Christ which are at Ephesus. Grace be to you and peace from God our Father, and from the Lord Jesus Christ. Blessed be the God and Father of our Lord Jesus Christ, who has blessed us with all spiritual blessings in heavenly things in Christ." He summarizes his message, then gives the text a verse-by-verse exposition. Though not free from mistakes and inconsistencies, the Bible is the Word of God, and speaks directly to us. The preacher therefore scrutinizes every phrase, to hear what God is saying through it. Though Paul wrote to particular places, such as Ephesus, God intended that his letters should "serve not only for one time alone, but for ever, and in general for the whole church." The spiritual blessings brought to us by Christ "are so excellent that we must surely be extremely unthankful if we scurry to and fro like people who are never at rest or contented." We must be vigilant, because the devil "strives ceaselessly to turn us to evil" and "entangle us in new curiosities." To Calvin and his congregation, sin, temptation, and the devil are serious threats to life. Yet his overall message is good news: "Christ has so well provided for his church that if we know how to use the gifts of grace he offers us, we shall have full and perfect happiness."

Calvin's preaching is lucid, rational, and meticulous, with flashes of passion and eloquence. He speaks for forty minutes or more; some minds wander; but mostly, people listen. To older worshipers, hearing the Bible read in French is still a relatively novel experience. To have it explained so clearly is empowering and uplifting. Sometimes Calvin repeats a particular turn of phrase: "Be that as it may," he says, more than once. Occasionally he gets attention with a colloquialism, satirizing those busybodies who pretend that they have the Holy Spirit *en leur manche* ("at their beck and call," literally "in their sleeve"). Like most preaching, his rhetoric is better heard than read:

> For if anyone asks us why we are found in this world,
> why God has such a care for us,
> why his goodness feeds and cherishes us,
> and finally why he, as it were,
> dazzles us with the great number of benefits he bestows upon us,
> it is in order
> that we should yield some acknowledgement of them to him.
> But now, when God blesses us, is it simply in words?
> No! No!
> But it is a filling of us
> and a bestowing of all things upon us that we want,
> as far as is needful.
> Therefore let us understand that
> in Jesus Christ
> we obtain all that is necessary
> for our salvation and for our happiness.

Calvin ends by urging his hearers to fall down before the majesty of God, acknowledging their faults and praying for true repentance. Let us aim to find in Jesus Christ all we need, he exclaims,

> not for one day,
> or for a mere brief moment,
> but continually and steadfastly to our life's end.
> And may it please God
> to grant this grace
> not only to us
> but also to all peoples.

The service ends with prayer, and a concluding psalm. Worshipers file quietly out of the church, and walk home. That evening, many of them will take out their pocket psalters and sing the same psalms in harmony, in counterpoint, with instrumental accompaniment, or as motets. Church and home are part of a unified worldview: plain singing in church is balanced by polyphonic song at home.[23]

---

23. Louis Bourgeois composed polyphonic settings of his tunes. As early as 1551, Claude Goudimel (ca. 1505–72) wrote motetlike settings for some of them. The title page of Goudimel's 1565 harmonized psalter explained it was not for singing in church, but for glorifying God at home.

Northern Germany: 1451 C.E.

Easter Sunday in a lofty Gothic church.[24] Flying buttresses carry the eye upward to rooftop and heavenbound spire, visible from miles away, and from every part of town. Inside, high-arched windows flood the nave with light, that daily, mysterious mediator of divine presence. Colorful murals show Christ risen in glory; the feeding of the multitude; and souls cast into hellfire. Statues of saints, apostles, and martyrs proclaim their presence and prayers. On a large crucifix, Christ hangs in timeless agony. Our Lady looks down serenely, her arms beckoning and blessing. High above is the ordered beauty of a fan-vaulted roof. Today, a festival Mass will be sung by the choir, as the priest intones some parts and speaks others privately and silently.

A year ago, in Mainz, Johannes Gutenberg combined the techniques of winepress, die-stamping, and wood-block engraving to create his movable-type printing press. Within the next few months, literate and illiterate alike will see their first fly sheet or pamphlet and marvel at the possibility of spreading thoughts, news, stories, and rumors far and wide in accurately reproduced, identical copies. In fifteen years' time the first German Bible will be printed and sold. Within forty years there will be more than a thousand public presses in Germany alone, and hundreds more in monasteries and wealthy homes. In fifty years time, printed sheet music will allow composers to hear each other's work at a distance, making old and new music rapidly available to singers and instrumentalists.[25]

Today, however, as for many years to come, Mass is celebrated in the sacred, time-honored way. The priest mumbles or whispers from his leather-bound, scribe-copied, illuminated Missal. The choir chants or sings from scribe-copied, leather-bound cantatories and antiphonaries. The people neither read nor speak. On Friday, they joined in the sorrowful songs of the passion play. Next week, they will sing together on pilgrimage.[26] At Sunday Mass, they are silent. Six

---

24. See Foley, *From Age to Age*, pp. 91–102; Reynolds and Price, *A Survey of Christian Hymnody*, pp. 17–19; Westermeyer, *Te Deum*, pp. 106–8 and 112–26; White, *Christian Worship and Technological Change*, pp. 40–49.

25. 1450: Gutenberg's press starts production; 1466: first German Bible, seventeen years before Luther's birth (biblical literacy begins well before the Reformation); by 1490, Germany has a thousand or more public presses; 1501: first printed sheet music.

26. Elsewhere in Europe, people sing carols and other vernacular Christian songs. In Germany, these include German versions of *cantiones* (songs with folk or dance tunes, often part of liturgical dramas) and German translations of Latin hymns.

hundred years earlier, Charlemagne had made alliance with the pope and decreed universal use of the Church of Rome's liturgy. Franks and Germans alike found themselves following Mass in a foreign language—Latin. In the past three hundred years music has dramatically developed: from a line of chanted melody to melody over a sustained bass note (drone); from melody and drone to organum (singing in parallel fourths or fifths); and from organum to polyphony, where different groups of voices sing different melodic lines, interweaving with each other. To a time-traveling ear, it sounds ancient and medieval; to people of the time, it is rich and wondrous, far beyond the scope of untrained singers, with words now doubly unintelligible.[27] In its many melodic lines, one above another, polyphonic music mirrors the soaring vaults and repetitive patterns of Gothic space. Music and architecture declare the holiness of God, evoking awe and/or exceeding comprehension.

Mass begins. Procession, music, incense, vestments. Priest and choir have seats and stalls; ordinary people stand, pray silently, listen, and look. The Kyrie, Credo, Sanctus, Benedictus, and Agnus Dei, in olden times sung by the people, are beautifully elaborated by the choir. The priest stands, kneels, and genuflects at the high altar; the people watch from a safe distance. The bread and wine are holy; it is dangerous to get too near. Unworthy people shrink from the risk of touching holy ground. Receiving the wine at Communion has long been unthinkable. Receiving the bread is so terrifying that church authorities have to enforce yearly reception.

At Mass elsewhere in Europe, the people are intent and watchful, but silent. Germany has a different tradition. Today, as on other high days, a short song is sung by all. The choir leads off, accompanied by the organ, and the congregation sings, from memory, the popular *Leise,* "Christ ist erstanden":

> Christ is arisen
> from the grave's dark prison.
> We now rejoice with gladness;
> Christ will end all sadness.
> Lord have mercy. Alleluia! Alleluia! Alleluia!
> We now rejoice with gladness;

---

27. "Doubly," because it was both polyphonic and in a foreign language; "ancient and medieval" if the time-traveler is attuned to Western (rather than, say, Indonesian, Arabian, or Indian) music.

Christ will end all sadness.
Lord have mercy.[28]

The song ends. The service proceeds. All eyes are now on the priest. In front of the altar, facing east, away from the people, he silently prays while the choir sings the Sanctus and the Benedictus. Slowly, with reverence, he lifts the consecrated host, raises it, and for a long moment holds it high. A thousand faces gaze enraptured, making visual communion, knowing that seeing the consecrated host can even save their sight. The host is lowered, the choir sings, the priest takes Communion, some worshipers risk receiving the bread. The Mass is ended. "Ite, Missa est," the priest declares.

Outside the church, a man hums a snatch of the Kyrie, often heard, easily memorized. A family group walking home sing a macaronic carol—German mixed with fragments of liturgical Latin. A four-year-old girl sings a fragment from the *Leise*: "Christ will end all sadness, Lord have mercy, Alleluia!" Parents smile, and join the song.

Cluny and Le Thoronet, France: 1200 C.E.

In darkness, hours before dawn, torches flicker in the cloisters of the monastery of the Order of St. Benedict at Cluny.[29] The monks walk in procession, singing as they go. Today, as on every other day of the week, they will spend six hours in prayer, five doing manual work, and four studying scripture.

The monks are processing to Matins. They belong to what their founder called a "school for the Lord's service, in which we hope to order nothing harsh or rigorous." Their daily ration is a pound of bread, a pint of wine, two cooked vegetables, and fruit in season. Meat

28. By 1450, pipe organs were well developed and common enough for us to guess their use at this point. *Leisen* were German versions of Latin songs called "sequences," inserted in the liturgy, perhaps originating as lyrics to help memorize the music of the final, greatly elaborated "a" of the "Alleluia." The word *Leise* comes from "Kyrieleis" (*Kyrie eleison*, "Lord, have mercy"), which concluded these short songs. For the English version of *Christ ist erstanden* (translating the twelfth-century Easter sequence *Victimae paschali laude*) and an arrangement of its original music, see Reynolds and Price, *A Survey of Christian Hymnody*, p. 182, example 19.

29. Main sources are the *New Harvard Dictionary of Music*, s.v. "Neume," "Notation"; Routley, *Panorama*, pp. 55–71; Westermeyer, *Te Deum*, pp. 130–31; and Wilson-Dickson, *The Story of Christian Music*, p. 33.

is reserved for those who are frail or unwell. Silence is urged at all times, except when it is necessary to speak.

Today, as always, the six hours of prayer are spread between eight services of worship, the Divine Office, which punctuate the day. The members of this faith community will meet more often for worship than for meals, and spend more time at prayer than at agricultural labor. An hour or two after Matins ("morning"), they will gather at dawn for Lauds ("praises"), then for Prime ("first"—meaning the first hour) at about six A.M. At around nine A.M. they will assemble again for Terce ("third [hour]"), then at midday for Sext ("sixth [hour]"), three P.M. for None ("ninth [hour]"), and six P.M. for Vespers ("evening"). Finally, at the end of the day, they will meet once more for Compline ("completion").

Community life is austere, but worship demands the best that human art can give. Though worship at the Lesser Hours (Prime, Terce, Sext, and None) is short and unadorned, the longer services, and the Mass, have ceremonial and extended song. There are three churches in or near the monastery, and the monks often move in procession between them. As in Europe's three thousand other Benedictine monasteries, the Divine Office draws heavily on the biblical psalms, so that the whole cycle of one hundred and fifty psalms is sung, in Latin, every week. Matins begin with a chanted greeting and response: "Dominus vobiscum" ("May the Lord be with you [all]"); "Et cum spiritu tuo" ("And with you yourself"—literally, "and with your spirit"). A hymn is sung:

> Nocte surgentes vigilemus omnes,
> semper in psalmis meditemur, atque
> viribus totis Domino cantamus dulciter hymnos.
> ("Waking in darkness, vigilant and watchful,
> guided by psalms that frame our meditation,
> singing with strength, we praise, in hymns of gladness, God our
>   creator.")[30]

Following this, prayers are intoned, and psalms and scriptures chanted. The time-traveling ear recognizes the sound of Gregorian

---

30. First stanza of a hymn attributed to Gregory the Great (ca. 540–604), my translation. For the Latin text, see Routley, *Panorama*, p. 61, example no. 144. For complete translations, compare *New Century Hymnal* #90, with Percy Dearmer (Routley, *Panorama*, p. 61, and many hymnals). I picture the monks singing this hymn, or one like it.

chant, akin to, but in subtle ways different from, its later (nineteenth-century) interpretation. It is sung, of course, as a melodic line, without instrumental accompaniment or part-song harmonization. Older brothers have sung the chants so often that they are stored in memory. New arrivals learn them by ear, and refresh their memory from melodic contour marks (*neumes*) above the hand-scribed text in their breviaries. In time, these or similar markings will evolve into music notation. The chants exist in a tension between frugality and creativity. As befits the austerity of community life, the monks aspire to sing a "plain song," without ornament or decoration. In worshiping God, however, creative minds will always aspire to do more and soar higher. From its beginnings nine hundred years earlier, the monastic move-ment has lived with a similar paradox: austerity, hard work, and com-munity solidarity recurrently lead to capital accumulation, comfort, and corruption, followed by revolt, reform, and a return to simplicity.[31]

The Cistercian Abbey at Le Thoronet is the product of one such revolt. It is an offshoot of the Cistercian communities of Cîteaux and Clairvaux, founded in 1112 and 1118 in reaction against the liturgical splendors of Cluny. The White Monks[32] aim to follow Benedict's rule more exactly than their Cluny counterparts. They settle on unproductive land, drain swamps, clear forests, and irrigate terraced hillsides. Silence is kept more strictly, but their daily routine is similar. Their liturgical practice is different. Chapel walls are whitewashed and bare; against the trend of the times, but prefiguring Reformation emphases, they forbid painting, sculpture, furnishings, and crucifixes. Even rhymed Latin hymns are too elaborate. The Cistercians value sound over sight, and words over ceremonial actions. Their chapel at Le Thoronet is a simple stone vault, constructed as "geometry in the service of prayer," with per-fect acoustics for corporate singing. "Hearing is superior to vision," said Bernard of Clairvaux, "and will restore vision to us."[33]

---

31. Cluny was founded in 910 C.E. by William the Pious (William III), Duke of Aquitaine. Benedict of Nursia, Italy (ca. 480–ca. 530), the order's founder, reorga-nized the monastic movement with a rule widely followed since. Monasticism origi-nated as a revolt against the wealth and comfort of church life in the years following the Emperor Constantine's edict (310 C.E.) recognizing Christianity as the Roman Empire's official religion. There were, apparently, three churches at, or associated with, Cluny. My processional descriptions are speculation.

32. They wore white habits. "Cistercian" is derived from "Cîteaux," their first home (probably then pronounced "Cisteaux").

33. Bernard of Clairvaux (1090–1153) was a key figure in the Cistercian movement. In 1114 he joined the community at Cîteaux, then founded Clairvaux, at the request

Rome: 452 C.E.

Sunday morning. The first gleams of sunrise glance off the stone walls of the basilica, a large rectangular building with a low-pitched, tiled roof.[34] Its walls are a line of Roman arches, each housing two . clear glass windows, one above the other, each window subdivided into small square panes. At the eastern end, a semicircular extension (the apse) bulges outward, also with arches and windows.

In former times, a basilica (Greek: "king's hall") was a Roman government building, built to the same plan, but with an apse at both ends. Entering from the middle of one of the long side walls, the visitor found an interior with subdivided spaces for government offices, library, and law courts. At each end, the deeply recessed alcoves of the apses housed a sacrificial altar. Behind each altar, flush with the alcove wall, were tribunal benches for judges and assessors, also used for royal audiences and other state functions.

For nearly a century, Christianity has been the official state religion of the Roman Empire. Toleration, followed by recognition, has dramatically altered Christian lifestyles.[35] From being a risky and sometimes fatal faith choice, Christianity has become the advantageous religion to profess. Bishops are receiving state honors and wearing the insignia of civil magistrates. Gradually, Christian identity is becoming more and more an accident of birth, and less and less the result of conversion. In towns and cities, spectacular buildings for worship are being constructed. Amateurism in liturgical leadership is becoming less and less acceptable. In the Egyptian desert, the monastic movement has begun, reacting against the temptations of material comfort.

---

of his abbot, in 1118. He is sometimes credited as the author of two Latin poems, "Dulcis Jesus memoria" and "Salve caput cruentatum," from which derive the English hymns "Jesus the Very Thought of Thee" (Edward Caswall) and "O Sacred Head, Sore Wounded" (Robert Bridges). "Salve caput cruentatum" is also the source of Paul Gerhardt's hymn, "O Haupt voll Blut und Wunden" (rendered by J. W. Alexander as "O Sacred Head, Now Wounded"). See Routley, *Panorama*, pp. 71 and 88–89.

34. Foley, *From Age to Age*, pp. 43–46.

35. In 313 Christianity was recognized and given special privileges by Constantine (d. 337), following his victory (in 312) over his coruler, Maxentius. Constantine gained control of the whole empire, and moved its capital to Byzantium (renamed Constantinople). In 380, Theodosius made Christianity the official state religion.

In the western part of the empire, basilicas have become the preferred style of building for Christian worship.[36] In Christian basilicas,
side entrances are absent or secondary, because one of the apses is
replaced by a straight wall housing a main entrance. The interior is
now a large space, with a long central aisle, sometimes flanked by
columns, leading to the apse. Before Constantine, Christian house
churches had room for fifty, seventy, or at most a hundred people.
Basilicas can accommodate a thousand or more.

As the sun peeps above the rooftops, the first worshipers arrive. A
grandfather comes with his granddaughter. An entire household walks
in orderly procession. Women and children carry bread for the
Eucharist, baked before dawn. Off-duty soldiers, civil officials, and
merchants mingle with laborers, slaves, and artisans.

In the east, Constantinople is flourishing. Here, in the west, Rome
is in decline. From northern and eastern Europe, successive population movements have brought tidal waves of invasion and displace-
ment to Gaul, Britain, Spain, and North Africa. Forty years ago, in the
year 410, the Ostrogoths and Visigoths, a confederation of Germanic
tribes, had invaded the empire. The Visigoths roared into Italy, plundered Rome, and moved on to Spain. The latest invaders are the Huns,
a warlike, mobile people from east of the River Volga. They have
defeated the Alani and driven the Ostrogoths out of their recently settled lands. Two months ago they reached the gates of Rome. But it was
Pope Leo, not the emperor, Valentinian, who met them. Unarmed
and unaided, Leo led a small party of clergy, wealthy merchants, and
civic officials, and walked into Attila's camp. They negotiated and
reached an agreement: the city would pay tribute, and Attila and his
army would withdraw northward. Attila has kept the agreement, and
the Huns are crossing the border out of Italy. Today's Eucharist is, in
part, a celebration of deliverance.[37]

Inside the basilica, crowds gather. Women and girls stand on one
side of the aisle, men and boys on the other. Wooden barriers keep the
aisle clear. The bishop's throne is in the apse. The movable, wooden
altar table is at the front of the apse, so that people can gather round

---

36. Eastern churches were more often modeled on *martyria* ("martyries," buildings with a central plan, for rites and remembrances of Christian martyrs). See Foley,
From Age to Age, pp. 47–48.

37. Leo the Great was bishop of Rome from 440 until his death in 461. His meeting with Attila is historical; a celebratory Eucharist is plausible, but speculative; Leo's
entourage is guesswork.

it for Communion. Nearby is the ambo, a wooden platform from which the scriptures will be read.

Hymns are sung and litanies chanted. Whispers run through the crowd: Pope Leo has arrived. The grand procession gathers at the main door as singers lead the entrance song, "Introibo ad altare Dei" ("I will go to the altar of God"). The song alternates between the congregation and a choir of boys and men. Led by an incense bearer, seven torchbearers, subdeacons and deacons, the procession moves slowly forward. A book of the Gospels is carried with reverence, a reminder of the days when people risked their lives to protect Christian writings from seizure and destruction. Bishop Leo comes last, greeting and blessing the crowd. He has always been loved and respected, but today his courage is honored. Men and women reach out to touch his robe. Some cry out a blessing.

The service continues. In a large building, the intimate song-speech of house church leadership is necessarily replaced by voice-projected cantillation. Prayer and readings are intoned, so that everyone can hear. The choir leads and the people sing a variety of responses, including "Kyrie eleison; Christe eleison; Kyrie eleison" (Greek: "Lord/Christ/Lord, have mercy"), recently imported from the East. Singers memorize their songs, because there is no way of notating the music. To a time-traveling ear, the chants sound foreign, remote.

Bread is collected from the congregation, taken to the table, blessed, and distributed. Everyone receives bread and wine. A hymn is sung. It has short stanzas, easily memorized, each with the same poetic meter, to the tune of a popular, "secular" song. People enjoy singing it, but here, in the evolving Roman liturgy, hymns have no set, obvious place; there is no guarantee that they will continue to be sung.[38]

Jerusalem: 400 C.E.

Sunday, before dawn, at the church of St. James.[39] In the flickering light of torches, a crowd gathers in front of the doors, waiting for

---

38. Latin hymnody remained peripheral to the Eucharist; Greek hymnody became part of it. From this point in time backward, there is no way of knowing how chants and hymns sounded. In later years, altars were made out of stone, and distanced from the people by removal into the apse; women were barred from the sanctuary; and the congregation sang less and less at Mass. Hymns, carols, and other Christian songs flourished on other occasions.

39. Approximate year, from an account by Egeria (or Etheria), a Spanish nun, in Wilson-Dickson, *The Story of Christian Music*, p. 30. Worship moves between two churches, the "Great Church" and another, which I call "St. James" for identification.

Matins to begin. Priests and deacons gather with them, and begin to sing. The people sing with them: antiphons and short hymns, memorized or quickly learned. Monks arrive from a nearby monastery.

At cockcrow, the bishop arrives and enters the church. The doors are opened, and the crowd streams into the sanctuary, brightly lit by torches and oil lamps. The priest chants a psalm, and the congregation sings in response. A prayer follows, and more psalms are sung. Two or three people enter, carrying censers; the sweet smell of incense fills the church. The bishop walks forward, toward the congregation, and chants the Gospel reading, which recounts Christ's death and resurrection. People listen intently. The story has extraordinary power, because in this culture, hearing is believing. The bishop's voice rises and falls, or stays on one note, following the meaning of the words. Listeners respond with sighs, gasps, and tears.

Priests and deacons join the bishop. Everyone sings hymns, as the bishop is led to the foot of a large cross. A psalm is chanted, with the congregation singing in response. The bishop prays aloud, then blesses and dismisses the congregation.

Accompanied by priests, monks, and deacons, the bishop leaves the church, stopping repeatedly as people come forward to kiss his hand. Then he goes home. The monks return to the sanctuary. They sing psalms and antiphons till daybreak. Some of the laity go home to sleep. Others stay in church.

Sunrise. Crowds gather at the Great Church of Constantine, built on the hill of Golgotha. Psalms are sung, and sermons preached, in a service lasting till ten in the morning. Converts under instruction are then dismissed with a blessing. The bishop and monks form a procession, and walk from the Great Church back to St. James, singing hymns as they go. A crowd of baptized Christians follows, singing.

In the church of St. James, hymns are sung, thanksgiving offered, and all the baptized receive Communion. The service ends with hymns and songs.

Milan, Italy: 386 C.E.

It is the week before Easter. The Basilica Portiana, occupied by Bishop Ambrose's unarmed supporters, is surrounded by imperial troops sent by the teenage emperor Valentinian III.[40] In the Basilica

---

40. *Ambrose: École Initiative Web-Page* (Ivor J. Davidson, 1999); Routley, *Panorama*, pp. 56–59; Westermeyer, *Te Deum*, pp. 82–83.

Nova, his cathedral, Bishop Ambrose is keeping vigil with clergy, lay supporters, and catechumens (adults receiving Christian instruction). One of the catechumens is Augustine, who will later become Bishop of Hippo in North Africa and write major works of theology and spirituality.

The sit-in and blockade arise from a bitter conflict between two Christian theologies, intertwined with political maneuvering. Arians, named after their chief theologian, Arius, argue that God's Word in Jesus Christ is not eternal, but created by God. They are opposed by Trinitarians, whose viewpoint eventually won: They believe that God's Word in Christ is eternally divine.

Ambrose is a key player in the struggle. Born into a ruling Roman family, he had practiced law till being appointed governor of the Aemilia Liguria region, centered on Milan. When the Arian bishop of Milan died, both sides had agreed on Ambrose as the best choice for bishop, even though he was still only a catechumen. Ambrose had accepted, and been rapidly baptized and ordained. He wears simple clothing; prays regularly, especially at night; preaches, studies, and writes; and speaks up for the poor and oppressed. In his struggle against Arianism, he combines determination with political skill, and refuses to compromise.

In the name of religious toleration, Ambrose's opponents have long been agitating for basilicas staffed by Arian priests. The Empress Justina, mother of the young Valentinian, has powerful allies and is strongly pro-Arian. A year ago she orchestrated her son's demand that Ambrose surrender the Basilica Portiana so that the imperial court's liturgy could be conducted by Arian clergy. Rumor has it that Ambrose persuaded his supporters to threaten a riot if the basilica was seized. Be that as it may, the court backed down, and the sequestration order was withdrawn.

Three months ago, however, the dispute flared up again. On January 23 the emperor promulgated a law mandating freedom of worship for Arians. Last week, Ambrose received fresh orders to hand over a church for Arian-led worship. At first, the authorities named his own cathedral, the Basilica Nova. Then the emperor demanded, instead, the original target, the Basilica Portiana, and sent troops to seize it. Ambrose declared that no bishop could surrender God's property. So his supporters are staging a sit-in; soldiers patrol outside.

In solidarity with the occupants of the threatened basilica, Ambrose and his congregation keep vigil day and night in the Basilica Nova. To keep the initiative, pass the time, and boost morale, Ambrose teaches the Eastern practice of antiphonal singing, then some of his own hymns. "The church hums with the prayer of entire people," he says. "It is like the washing of waves, and the singing of psalms is like the crashing of breakers."

The days pass slowly. Tension is high. If the troops move in, there will be bloodshed, even civil war. Each evening, as the shadows lengthen and light fades, the people sing psalms to each other, across the aisle of the Basilica Nova, then join their voices in one of the bishop's hymns:

> Creator of the earth and sky,
> you spread the shining stars on high
> and clothe the day with robes of light;
> with peaceful sleep now bless this night:
>   let rest repair the harassed mind,
>   and sorrow's heavy load unbind,
>   until, refreshed from weariness,
>   we rise in thankful wakefulness.
>
> Day sinks; we thank you for your gift;
> night comes, as now again we lift
> our prayers and vows and hymns, for night
> can never take us from your sight:
>   then let our inmost hearts acclaim,
>   the Love our tuneful voices name:
>   to you we cling, to you we call,
>   great God, presiding over all.
>
> As darkness gently closes day,
> and shadows thicken on our way,
> let faith no darkness know, that night
> from faith's clear beam may borrow light:
>   be still, each heaven-born mind and will;
>   depart, all thoughts and deeds of ill;
>   let faith its watch unwearied keep
>   as mind and body mend with sleep.
>
> From night's delusions keep us free,
> in dreams your glory let us see;
> let no invading harm draw near,
> and keep us safe from foe and fear.
>   Blest Trinity, to you we pray;
>   defend us now by night and day,

Eternal Father, Equal Son
and Holy Spirit, Three in One.[41]

Easter approaches. Perhaps the soldiers are reluctant to kill other Christians on Good Friday. Perhaps the court cannot risk civil war. New orders come down the chain of command, and the troops withdraw. In the weeks that follow, Ambrose maintains his position, by a combination of stubbornness and adroit maneuvering. Milan's basilicas stay Trinitarian.

Antioch, Syria: 200 C.E.

Early on Sunday, the first day of the week, a man walks through busy streets and arrives at a house on the edge of town.[42] The house is shaped as a large oblong, with tiled roofs and windowless external walls. The visitor knocks on the door and is admitted. "Greetings, my dear bishop," says Timotheus, his host. "Greetings to you, Timotheus, in the name of Christ Jesus," Apelles replies. He follows Timotheus through the atrium (a partially covered courtyard surrounded by family rooms), into the peristyle, a larger, open courtyard. Beyond the peristyle is a walled garden, planted with flowers, bushes, and herbs. The whole house faces inward. Light reaches interior rooms through peristyle and atrium; external walls shield the household from street noises, thieves, and prying eyes.

From letters and visitors, Timotheus and his wife Junia know that in some towns Christian assemblies are now buying houses specifically for worship. Perhaps the assembly that meets in their home will one day outgrow it and do likewise. For the present, Junia and Timotheus are glad that their home is large enough, and private enough, for the Lord's Day meeting.

---

41. Charles Bigg's 1905 translation of *Deus creator omnium*, which I have reworked stylistically but not retranslated. In his treatise on music (ca. 389) Augustine quotes Ambrose's hymn as an example of poetic meter. In his *Confessions* (ca. 410) he tells how it comforted him after his mother's funeral. The original has eight four-line stanzas.

42. Foley, *Foundations of Christian Music*, pp. 94–97, and *From Age to Age*, pp. 25–42; esp. pp. 41–42; Reynolds and Price, *A Survey of Christian Hymnody*, p. 6. My description is speculative: the extent of manumission is perhaps optimistic; Apelles' election and livelihood are hopefully plausible but cannot be vouched for. Community song is not perceived as a "special" activity: contemporary lists of church offices never mention musicians or cantors.

In ones and twos, members and guests arrive. Servants greet them, offering oil for anointing and water for footwashing, a courtesy given to Apelles as he sits on a bench in the peristyle. All but three of the household staff are free servants. Since their conversion eight years ago, Junia and Timotheus have quietly manumitted most of their slaves. Of the three remaining slaves, one will be manumitted later this year and the other two have declined; they are in failing health, and know they will be cared for.

Six years previously, the assembly in Timotheus's house elected Apelles as its bishop. His livelihood comes partly from their support, but mostly from his work as a professional scribe, copying manuscripts, preparing legal documents, or writing letters at a client's dictation.

When all are gathered in the peristyle, Apelles stands and greets them in the name of the Lord Jesus. He welcomes friends and strangers. Guests are introduced by the member who invited them, and welcomed by others. Though persecution is intermittent, it is important to know who the newcomers are, and test their trustworthiness. There is a warm welcome for Epaenetus, who has brought greetings and letters from assemblies farther north. Apelles reads the letters. Hearing is believing, and as he speaks the stories of healing, imprisonment, and martyrdom come vividly alive, prompting sighs, applause, spontaneous prayers, and acclamations: Alleluia! Marana tha! (Come, Lord!). Yesous Christos Kyrios! (Jesus Christ [not Caesar] is Lord!). Apelles leads the assembly in prayer. Miriam, one of the household servants, is the community's chief prophet. She recites stories of Jesus, Peter, Martha, and Paul, and calls everyone to faith, hope, love, and prayer. As she gives her utterance, hovering between speech and song, the hearers respond with a series of cries and acclamations. When she finishes, there is a series of whispered amens. One of the women begins to sing from the Odes of Solomon, a new collection of Christian hymns. The song is short. Everyone listens, and chants the concluding acclamation:

> I extended my hands
> and hallowed my Lord,
> for the expansion of my hands
> is his sign,
> and my extension
> is the upright cross:
> Alleluia![43]

---

43. *Odes of Solomon* (Palestine or Syria, 2d century), Ode 27, trans. James Charlesworth.

Apelles now calls forward two women and a man who have received instruction and are ready for baptism. Everyone gathers around the pool in the atrium as the reborn are baptized.

After the baptism, those not yet baptized are embraced, blessed, and invited to return. They leave, and a servant locks the outer door. The baptized believers gather once more in the peristyle, in the bright morning sun. They pray for one another, for other assemblies, and for people in need. Some of the men leave the peristyle and return carrying a table. Junia brings bread and wine. Gifts of money and food are collected and brought forward. Apelles gives thanks over all the gifts. He breaks the bread, and Junia and Timotheus help him share bread and wine with all who are present. The names of absent members are recorded, so that sanctified bread and wine can be taken to their homes. Money gifts and food gifts are collected by the appointed deacons for distribution to poorer members of the assembly. Someone begins a song, and others join in. Prayers and song continue, until finally the meeting is over, and people go home.

Cenchrae, Greece: 55 C.E.

Friday evening, at the house of Philologos.[44] One by one, members of a Christian society arrive for prayer, praise, God's life-changing word, and a holy meal. They include Jewish members of the local synagogue, and Gentiles: God-fearing synagogue-supporters or former worshipers of Hermes, Diana, and other pagan divinities.

The Christ-believers come from every social station. They include former prostitutes, a city official, laborers, scribes, and destitute widows; a tinsmith, a glassblower, and a baker; a blind mother, a one-armed ex-soldier, and an amputee carried by friends; women, men, and children; free citizens and household slaves. Few are wealthy or of noble birth. Wealthier members bring food: milk, cheese, olives,

---

44. Psalm 118; Romans 16:1–2; 1 Corinthians 1; 2; 7; and 10—15; 1 Timothy 3:16; Foley, *Foundations of Christian Music,* pp. 1–24, and *From Age to Age,* p. 14. Phoebe was a leader of the Christian society in Cenchrae, near Corinth. She probably funded Paul's missionary journeys, and may well have traveled to Rome with Paul's letter. This speculative reconstruction tries to capture the ecstatic, charismatic nature of early Christian worship. Early "songs" were probably more like shouts. The "psalms, hymns, and spiritual songs" of Colossians 3:16 cannot reliably be interpreted by reading back later meanings; there is no consensus about the extent of "Christ hymns" in New Testament writings; and the psalms of David were not sung in Christian worship till much later.

fish, bread, grapes, and wine. Their gifts are put on a table, to be shared later at the community meal. One of the widows brings a flat, round barley loaf for the breaking of bread.

A woman enters, smiling at their surprised faces. Phoebe has returned from a four-month journey to Rome. Paul's letter has been safely delivered, and she brings good news. There are shouts of welcome, greetings, embraces.

As the hubbub subsides, Nereus raises his right hand. Everyone listens, knowing that the Spirit of God has blessed him with gifts of leadership. He welcomes them all in the name of the Lord Jesus; there are answering cries of "Amen!" and "Peace be with you." Then he asks Phoebe to bring news of her journey.

Though Greek culture values sight, for most people hearing is believing. Because words are too important to be merely said, Phoebe does not "speak," but recites the account of her journey, using the attention-getting cadence of other Christian proclaimers. The effect is more like that of an auctioneer than a rabbi or wisdom teacher, and the whole company responds, standing, clapping, swaying, shouting amens and alleluias.

When Phoebe finishes, there is shouting, stomping, and prolonged applause. As people take their seats, abuzz with excitement, the prophet Callista stands in the middle of the room. She song-speaks quietly, but with ecstatic intensity. She declares that Phoebe, like Paul, has been traveling in the name of Jesus. The Spirit has blessed sister Phoebe's journey, for the Lord Jesus is risen and alive, and his Spirit is moving among us. As she prophesies, there are sighs, wordless cries, and alleluias. A babble of sound cascades through the room. The tinsmith is speaking in tongues. When he subsides, exhausted, a neighbor interprets, falling rapidly into rhythmic chant. At the end, there is a tidal wave of acclamation:

> Beloved sisters, beloved brothers,
> great is the mystery of our faith,
> great is the power of Jesus:
> revealed in flesh,
> vindicated in spirit,
> seen by angels,
> proclaimed to the nations,
> taken up in glory.
> Alleluia!
> *Alleluia! Alleluia!*

"The Lord is coming soon!"
Marana tha. Hosanna. Alleluia!

As the clamor again subsides, Philologos walks forward, carrying the scroll of Psalms. He chants a psalm of David. These are God's ancient words. Alive with wisdom and power, they proclaim the victory of Christ crucified:

> I shall not die, but I shall live,
>   and recount the deeds of the LORD. . . .
> Open to me the gates of righteousness,
>   that I may enter through them
>   and give thanks to the LORD. . . .
> I thank you that you have answered me
>   and have become my salvation.
> The stone that the builders rejected
>   has become the chief cornerstone.
> This is the LORD's doing;
>   it is marvelous in our eyes.
> This is the day that the LORD has made;
>   let us rejoice and be glad in it.

Suddenly, there is movement at the far end of the room. One of Philologos's slaves is standing. He stammers, never having prophesied before. But he is filled with the Spirit, and cannot stay silent: "The day, the day, that the Lord has made! The Lord was raised on the first day of the week. That is the Lord's Day, the day that the Lord has made. Brothers and sisters, let us break bread on the Lord's Day—the day, the day, that the Lord has made!"

The newfound prophet gets a mixed response: "Amen!" "Alleluia!" "Not so, not so!" Nereus waits for silence, then directs two of the believers to pray daily and test the spirits, to hear if this is, indeed, the Lord's new command.

Tables are set. Food and drink are shared. For some, it is the only food they will get today. Prayers follow, for believers who are ill, inquirers receiving instruction, widows and orphans in need.

Nereus then chants the story of the Supper, and others join in. The story is familiar, part of the teaching memorized before baptism:

> The Lord Jesus,
> on the night he was betrayed
> took a loaf of bread,
> and when he had given thanks,

> he broke it and said,
> "This is my body that is for you.
> Do this in remembrance of me."
> In the same way
> he took the cup after supper, saying,
> "This cup is the new covenant in my blood.
> Do this, as often as you drink it,
> in remembrance of me."

More cries, more prophecies. A woman shouts, wide-eyed: "Listen to the Lord Jesus. Listen to the Lord. You cannot drink the cup of the Lord and the cup of demons. You cannot partake of the table of the Lord and the table of demons."

"Let us discern the Lord's body," says Nereus. "Let us eat and drink with joy. For this is indeed the supper of our Lord. And every time we eat this bread and drink the cup, we proclaim the Lord's death until he comes. Marana tha—Come, Lord Jesus!" He begins the blessing chant, and everyone responds:

> The blessing-cup we bless,
> is it not a sharing
> in the blood of Christ?
> The given-bread we break,
> is it not a sharing
> in the body of Christ?
> *Because there is one bread,*
> *we who are many*
> *are one body,*
> *for we all share one bread.*

The barley bread is broken and passed around. Red wine is poured into a tall glass cup. Left undiluted, it would be too potent, so water is added, reducing it to manageable strength. The cup also is passed round. Believers eat and drink, sigh or moan, or rock to and fro, chanting prayers and acclamations. Prayers are offered, and Nereus signals the concluding blessing:

> Beloved in the Lord,
> may the grace of the Lord Jesus Christ,
> the love of God,
> and the communion of the Holy Spirit,
> be with you all.
> *Amen! Alleluia! Amen!*

In and around Jerusalem: 4 B.C.E.

Jerusalem. The Temple Mount towers above the city.[45] Within its walls is the new Temple, built sixteen years ago, a gift of King Herod the Great, who died last month. Construction work on its surroundings will take another sixty years.

The Temple is about the same size as its earliest predecessor, Solomon's Temple, built nine hundred years ago and destroyed by the Babylonians in 587. It looks more magnificent than either Solomon's Temple or its postexilic successor, the Temple of Zerubbabel, partly on account of its elegant Greco-Roman colonnades, and partly because the Temple Mount is larger, with massive retaining walls. Within the walls, visiting pilgrims find a vast enclosure, largely taken up by the outermost court of the Temple, the Court of the Gentiles, which all can enter. In the Court of the Gentiles, money changers convert unclean, idol-bearing pagan coinage into coins acceptable to the Temple treasury. Vendors sell doves and other sacrificial animals.

Beyond the Court of the Gentiles are the inner courts. Together they form an oblong, facing east. At the western end, beyond a ten-foot high marble fence with posted warnings of death to Gentile trespassers, five steps lead upward into the Court of the Women, open to Jewish women, children, and men. Within it are five chests to receive Temple offerings. Beyond it is the Court of Israel, open only to Jewish men; just inside its entrance is the altar, on which daily sacrifices are offered. The Court of the Priests is five steps higher, and surrounds the Temple proper.

Within the Temple is the sanctuary, and beyond it the Holy of Holies, shrouded in darkness, which only the high priest may enter, with fear and trembling, only once every year, on the Day of Atonement. Here, as in all ancient Temples, the sanctuary is not an assembly

---

45. Deuteronomy 6:4–9; Acts 21:28; Foley, *From Age to Age*, pp. 11–15, and *Foundations of Christian Music*, pp. 6–37; Wilson-Dickson, *The Story of Christian Music*, pp. 18–23; Gary A. Anderson, "Introduction to Israelite Religion," and John J. Collins, "Introduction to Early Jewish Religion," NIB, vol. 1 (1994); and Pheme Perkins, "Mark," NIB, vol. 8 (1995). The absence or near-absence of congregational song in this era of Temple worship, and the reasons for it, are speculative. Among recent reconstructions of Herod's Temple, Leen Ritmeyer's plan includes a three-dimensional sketch (NIB, vol. 8, p. 662). There is no consensus as to how the music sounded. To contemporaries, its tones and scales were no doubt familiar and probably magnificent. To modern ears Temple music would probably sound remote, and synagogue chant might, or might not, sound "musical."

hall for worshipers, but a "beth-El," or house of divinity. No one imagines that God literally lives here. Nonetheless, God's holy Name dwells in the Holy of Holies, and the surrounding courts put human impurities progressively at a distance from that fearsome, holy place.

In Temple worship, the Name is revered and honored, in the only way culturally possible, with actions and materials showing reverence for the One who ranks higher than the highest human ruler. Thus, as befits the King of all kings, the Temple has a large staff of court servants, dressed in fine robes (the priests); secluded, finely paneled rooms (equivalent to throne room and audience chambers); the best that music can offer; and sumptuous daily banquets (sacrifices, oblations, and the firstfruits of harvested food).

To this courthouse of the Most Holy Name come crowds of pilgrims daily, bearing gifts. The disparity between human offerings and divine blessings creates and sustains creaturely awe and gratitude. When their first boy is born, the parents sacrifice two doves, yet God has given them the infinitely more precious gift of a child.

Animal sacrifice is a messy business; obviously, the Temple must be radically distanced from the meat market. Solemn ritual goes part of the way, but it is music, perhaps, that evokes the necessary sense of wonder, excitement, and sublimity. The Temple has a large staff of professional musicians. There are never less than twelve adult male singers present, and never less than twelve instrumentalists (also male). On high holy days each group can number twenty or more. Singers train for years, until they know the music by heart. There are few, if any, soloists: group singing and ensemble playing are the norm. Most of the orchestral players have string instruments: several play a small lyre; some pluck a large, ten-stringed lyre. Others play a double-pipe *halil*, two or more *hazozerah* (silver trumpets), a *tof* (a shallow, round-frame drum), a *sistrum* with its tinkling bells, and various types of cymbal. Apart from dramatic flourishes and trumpet calls, there is no independent instrumental music. The orchestra's purpose is to accompany the singers. In olden times, ordinary worshipers sang an occasional psalm response or hallelujah. Nowadays, this is rarely if ever feasible: Jerusalem's regular attenders are swamped by the daily flow of pilgrims, from Judea, Galilee, the farthest reaches of empire, and beyond.

Today, as every day, hundreds of pilgrims throng the courtyards; many wait patiently to offer sacrifice. Trumpets play a fanfare and hubbub hushes into silence; in the vast crowd, no one talks or whispers. The rituals of sacrifice begin. Accompanied by the orchestra, the Levitical choir sings from the Court of the Women. Village dwellers have never heard such music. Even city dwellers are caught up in the song, for this is no theatrical drama or pagan show, but a song of praise to one most holy God, maker of heaven and earth. In the line of people waiting to offer sacrifice is a young couple. The father carries two turtledoves. The mother cradles their firstborn infant son. They call him Yeshua ("Deliverer").

Some days later, in a nearby town, a synagogue congregation gathers for Sabbath prayer, summoned by the braying call of the shofar, a ram's horn sounded by blowing into its wider end. The synagogue interior is simple: shrines for the Torah scrolls, windows, a reader's desk, seats for synagogue elders and the teacher of the day, and benches for the congregation: women on one side, men on the other.

From the ancient prophets, the congregation knows that God is near to every Jew, and that they may all approach God in prayer, privately or publicly, by day or by night. Here, in sharp contrast with the Temple, there are no professional worship leaders or musicians. No instruments are heard after the initial call to prayer on the shofar. Volunteers lead the service. The reader and expositor is an "emissary of the people" (*sheliach tsibbur*) chosen by the head of the synagogue. The sounds of worship migrate back and forth between what later centuries call "speech" and "song." In this intensely oral culture, writing is an aid to memory, a prompt for the song-spoken word. All words have impact, and chanted speech can divide spirit from flesh and reach the innermost heart. Words are never merely "spoken": to read Torah without chanted tunes would be shocking, disrespectful—and unintelligible. Though the written text is fixed, it becomes meaningful only by the proper grouping of words, clauses, and subclauses in chanted recitation.

The service begins. From his seat in the middle of the congregation an appointed leader raises his voice and declaims: "She-ma-' Y'Is-ra-el, Adho-nai—elo-he—nu." The congregation song-chants in response, "Adho-nai—ech-adh—":

Hear, O Israel, Adonai   *Adonai alone.*
     is our God:
You shall love Adonai your   *with all your heart,*
     God: and with all your soul: *and with all your strength. . . . .*
Bind [these words] as a sign   *fix them as an emblem on your*
     on your hand: *forehead,*
write them on the doorposts   *and on your gates.*
     of your house:

Following the Shema, all stand for the eighteen benedictions, chanted in the same way. All sit, and the synagogue leader chooses today's *sheliach tsibbur,* a visitor from Jerusalem. He stands, calls for one of the Torah scrolls, and walks to the reading desk. The *hazzan* (assistant) hands him the scroll. He unrolls it, and chants a passage from Exodus, following the chant marks above the text. He translates the Hebrew text into Aramaic, so that everyone can understand it, rolls up the scroll, hands it back to the *hazzan,* then sits to give his exposition. This too is in song-speech: measured and prayerful; sometimes touched with passion, joy, or sorrow; never declamatory or ecstatic. He ends, to a chorus of amens, stands, and walks back to his seat in the congregation. From her place in the congregation, a woman chants a psalm,[46] and the congregation responds with "Amen." Finally, the head of the synagogue stands and gives the blessing.

Jerusalem: 197 B.C.E.

Yom Kippur: the Day of Atonement.[47] Priests and people are fasting from sundown to sundown. In the Temple of Zerubbabel, the high priest, Simon ben-Onias, leads the ritual of a day so important that it is often simply called *Yoma,* the Day.

Under Simon's twenty-two-year leadership Judah has enjoyed growing stability and security. The Temple has been repaired and fortified, with high double walls. A cistern has been hollowed out of the rock, to store drinking water against a siege.

Since the restoration of land, city, and Temple at the end of the Babylonian exile, Judah (or Judea) has been a minor province of successive empires: Persia, Egypt, and most recently the Seleucid Empire of Antiochus III, centered in Syria. A year ago, Antiochus decisively defeated the Egyptian king, Ptolemy V. The Jerusalemites then cap-

---

46. On female leadership in this era of synagogue worship, see Foley, *Foundations,* p. 50 and note 22, p. 60.

47. Leviticus 16; Numbers 6:24–26; 1 Kings 22:11; Psalm 103; Psalm 136; Sirach 50:1–24; Walter C. Kaiser, "Leviticus" (NIB, vol. 1, 1994); James L. Crenshaw, "Sirach" (NIB, vol. 5, 1997). The Temple of Zerubbabel was completed in 515 B.C.E. Simon II was high priest from 219 to 196. Antiochus III ruled from 223 to 187. Judean security was soon followed by repression, eventually triggering the Maccabean revolt. My use of Numbers 6:4–26 is plausible but speculative; the use of Psalms 103 and 136 is poetic fancy: the former is at least theologically appropriate; the latter suggests how congregational song may have functioned in Temple worship.

tured Ptolemy's garrison and welcomed Antiochus's troops. In response, Antiochus issued a decree exempting Temple personnel and building materials from taxation, emancipating slaves, reducing the people's taxes, subsidizing Temple sacrifices, and confirming the validity of Jewish law.

Today is the culmination of forty days of penance, self-examination, and spiritual cleansing, culminating in Rôsh Ha-shânâh, the Jewish New Year. The worshipers have confessed their individual wrongdoing and shameful impurity, and lamented Israel's corporate failure to do justice, love kindness, and walk humbly with God. Whether in public or private, they chant their prayers aloud. Even personal prayers are not a private matter, but a social utterance.

Today, on this holiest of days, all sins—blasphemy alone excepted—will be forgiven and removed. Ritual acts go hand in hand with chanted confession, the climactic pronouncement of atonement, and the high priest's once-a-year utterance of God's holy Name.

The power of speech-chanted words cannot be overestimated. Despite the influence of Hellenistic culture, so visual and rational, speech and hearing are Israel's primary mode of communication. The chanted word is as powerful now as in the days of King Josiah, four and a half centuries ago, when the king was so shaken by Shaphan's declamation of a newly found Law scroll that he wept and tore his clothes in penitence. Then, as now, visions of God are granted so that God's word can be heard and believed. To open someone's ear is to give understanding. To hear someone means taking notice and acting accordingly, as in the summons *"Hear,* O Israel!" which entails acts of loving obedience.

In the Temple of Zerubbabel, the ritual of Yom Kippur is approaching its climax. Psalms and songs accompany most of the action. The high priest began by bringing a bull for his own sin offering, and receiving from the people the ram of burnt offering and a pair of goats for their sin offering. He cast lots over the goats, to determine which will live, and which be sacrificed.

Next, Simon ben Onias withdrew inside the Temple sanctuary, to divest himself of the "golden garments," his richly ornamented robes of office. He clothed himself, instead, in the white linen shirt, shorts, sash and turban of an ordinary priest. Thus, when he enters the Holy of Holies on behalf of the people, he does so as a humble servant, even though he alone may approach the holiness of God.

After sacrificing the bull as a sin offering for himself and his sons,

Simon ben-Onias entered the Holy Place for the first time to sprinkle the bull's blood, dropping a handful of incense on the hot coals of his censer, so that sweet-smelling smoke could protect him from the unseen presence of God. Emerging again from the sanctuary, he sacrificed one of the goats, and is now again in the Holy Place, sprinkling its blood for the sins of the people.

Finally, Simon again comes out of the sanctuary into the courtyard. He places both hands on the head of the live goat, and in sorrowful chant confesses all the sins and wickedness of Israel, sacramentally transferring them to the goat. His action does not effect the removal of sin in a magical, mechanical way, but gives God's forgiveness material form and essential dramatization. The fate of the two goats demonstrates that all Israel's sins are now forgiven and forgotten. A man especially chosen for the task leads the "escape-goat" on its long walk to the wilderness, where it will be released. As it disappears from view, trumpets blare, the full orchestra plays, and the Temple singers stand in two groups, facing each other, filling the courtyard with joyful, antiphonal song:

> Bless Adonai, O my soul,
> *and all that is within me,*
> *bless his holy name,*
> who forgives all your iniquity,
> *who heals all your diseases,*
> who redeems your life from the Pit,
> *who crowns you with steadfast love and mercy.*
> Adonai is merciful and gracious,
> *slow to anger and abounding in steadfast love.*
> He does not deal with us according to our sins,
> *nor repay us according to our iniquities.*
> For as the heavens are high above the earth,
> *so great is his steadfast love toward those who fear him;*
> as far as the east is from the west,
> *so far he removes our transgressions from us.*

As the choir sings, Simon again disappears behind the sanctuary curtain. The psalm ends, the curtain is pulled aside, and there he stands, clad once more in resplendent, ceremonial robes. The effect is spectacular. A high-ranking scribe will later describe him as looking like the sun, a rainbow, or a vessel of hammered gold.

Advancing to the altar, Simon receives sacrificial portions from the priests, completes the sacrificial ritual, takes a proffered wine cup, and pours a drink offering over the base of the altar. The priests shout in cho-

rus, and trumpeters blow a fanfare. Like a rippling wave, the people fall
to their knees and bow their heads to the ground. Prayers are chanted.
The worshipers stand for a psalm of thanksgiving. This time the song
flows between choir and congregation, who sing the familiar refrain:

O give thanks to Adonai, for he is good:	*for his steadfast love endures forever.*
O give thanks to the God of gods:	*for his steadfast love endures forever;*
who by understanding made the heavens:	*for his steadfast love endures forever;*
who divided the Red Sea in two:	*for his steadfast love endures forever;*
and made Israel pass through the midst of it:	*for his steadfast love endures forever;*
but overthrew Pharaoh and his army in the Red Sea:	*for his steadfast love endures forever;*
who remembered us in our low estate:	*for his steadfast love endures forever;*
and rescued us from our foes:	*for his steadfast love endures forever.*

Finally, Simon raises his hands in blessing. In city street and Temple court there is silence, broken only by the bleating of the distant
goat. Throughout the year, and throughout today's ritual, the name of
God has been reverently avoided. Priests, choir, and people say, not
the name itself, but "Adonai," meaning "chief" or "governor." Today,
for one moment, because Israel's sins and impurities are forgiven and
forgotten, the high priest can safely sing God's own, true name:

> May *Yahweh* bless you and keep you;
> May *Yahweh* make his face shine upon you, and be gracious to
>   you;
> May *Yahweh* lift up his countenance upon you, and give you
>   peace.

Overcome and awestruck, priests and people fall on their knees and
bow to the ground. They have heard God's very Name, the Name they
dare not say aloud. They begin a chant, murmuring, swelling, then fading into silence:

> *Bles-sed be the Name, bles-sed be the Name,*
> *bles-sed be the Name of the glory,*

bles-sed be the Name of the glory of his kingdom,
for ever and ever, for ever and ever.
Amen! Amen! Amen!

Israel: 1100 B.C.E.

At the shrine of Yahweh, Israel's God, local tribes gather for celebration.[48] Against heavy odds, their warriors have returned victorious. Three weeks ago, summoned by one of Israel's spirit-filled leaders ("judges"), shepherds and farmers put down their crooks and sickles, picked up their swords, and mustered to fight a Philistine invasion. Sent out with songs and blessings, they ambushed the enemy in a narrow valley where Philistine chariots had no room to maneuver. They took lives, prisoners, and plunder, and drove Philistine remnants back to the coastal plain.

Returning home, the battle-weary men were met by groups of women from their villages with victory songs praising their courage and success. If the battle had gone the other way, these same women would have been raped, killed, or driven into the hills; they would have seen their meager possessions plundered, children and parents killed or wounded, fields burned, and homes destroyed.

At the shrine of Yahweh, the women sing again. Hand-clapping and foot-stomping, with pipe and hand-drum accompaniment, they dance before the men, singing:

> Sing to Yahweh,
> he has gloriously triumphed;
> horse and rider
> he has thrown into the sea.

As the dance goes faster and faster, the song is sung repeatedly, over and over again. Caught up in the music, the onlookers join in. Finally, the men themselves join the song, lifting high the spoils of war.

Attributed to Miriam the prophet, the victory song is already ancient, handed down orally over generations. Longer versions tell the whole story: how Israelites escaping from Egypt were pursued and nearly overrun by Egyptian forces, then miraculously saved by Yahweh's command over wind and sea.

---

48. Exodus 15:20–21; 1 Samuel 18: 4–7; Walter Brueggemann, "Exodus," NIB, vol. 1 (1994); Martin Noth, *Exodus*, in loc. The song's use in holy war celebrations, or more generalized worship, is plausible, but speculative.

Short though it may be, the ancient song sets the tone for Israel's recollection of its national story. Like longer psalms on this theme, it begins
with a summons, "Sing to Yahweh"—itself an act of praise. Like other
psalms, it recalls specific events, especially the exodus, when Yahweh
overcame the invincible power of Egyptian oppression. Henceforth,
forever, Israel will worship the only divinity who lifts the downtrodden
and rescues the oppressed. The song connects past and present. The
recent victory is also a defeat of superior forces bent on plunder and
conquest. If Israel ever becomes a powerful nation, Miriam's song, and
its holy war theology, could be misused to justify aggression. Even so, it
contains a subversive memory. Prophets will one day proclaim that God
overthrows every kind of domination—especially in Israel.

Israel: 1200 B.C.E.

At the edge of a field, men and women gather round a notch in the
hillside.[49] It is a wellspring, long disused, covered with thornbushes
and choked with earth and stones. As a signal for work to begin, the
village elders lift their rods of office and ceremonially tap them on the
ground, chanting an old divine promise:

> Gather the people together,
> and I will give them water.

Chanting in regular rhythm, men hack at the bushes, dig out the
stones, and fling the earth aside. Women and children cart away the
debris in their hands, or in baskets. As they dig, lift and heave, and
carry, they all keep time by singing:

> Spring up, O well ! Spring up, O well !
> Sing to it now! Sing to it now!
> the well that the leaders sank,
> the well that the nobles dug,
> with the scepter, the rod, and the staff.

For three hours and more, the villagers sing as they dig, lift, heave,
and carry. Finally, the well mouth is clear. Water appears, first a patch

---

49. Numbers 21:16–18; Thomas B. Dozeman, "Numbers," NIB, vol. 2 (1998).
Because the song the people sing is of unknown age, the date given here is guesswork.
I have adapted the NRSV so as to give English rhythms to the song.

of moisture, then a trickle, then a steady stream. The old spring is flow-ing again.

Once more, the villagers sing the Song of the Well.

Is it worship?

How could it be anything else?

Chapter Two

"Rescue the Holy Pleasure": Why Congregational Song Is Indispensable

Who on the part of God will rise,
 innocent sound recover,
. . . .
music in virtue's cause retain,
 rescue the holy pleasure?
                    —Charles Wesley

Charles Wesley invited sailors and Methodists to "rescue the holy pleasure"[1] of singing together. In eighteenth-century England, communal song was a normal part of everyday life. Wesley needed to rescue, not the act of singing together, but the "innocent sound" of Christian song.

For many today, the question is not what to sing but whether to sing at all. "Let those refuse to sing who never knew our God," said Isaac Watts. Many people know God quite well and refuse to sing. Some say they cannot; others cannot see why they should.

"I'm a pastor, and that's a musical problem; I'll pass it to my music director." Not quite. What if strong congregational singing not only encourages and inspires, but helps form our spirituality and shape our theology? If so, it is of great importance, not only to congregations and music leaders, but to pastors.

I believe that congregational song is an indispensable part of Christian public worship. By "public worship" I mean the assembly of

---

1. Part of the lyric written in Plymouth, 1746. See pp. 9–11. For the full text, see the Appendix at the end of this book.

47

Christian people, from Baptist to Catholic, for the purpose of honoring, praising, and, hopefully, encountering God, whether their worship be "liturgical," "spontaneous," or in between. By "indispensable" I mean two steps down from "essential" but three floors higher than "optional." Nonhearing congregations can worship without song, and hearers can worship together without singing together, as Quakers do mostly, and others do occasionally. But though we don't have to sing in order to worship, it helps immeasurably if we do. In a "seeker service," whose unchurched audience comes to look and listen, but not yet to worship, it may be appropriate to use performance songs with little or no participation.[2] But when we assemble for worship, congregational song is in most circumstances indispensable.

By "congregational song" I mean anything sung by a group of people assembled to worship God, not as a presentation to some other group, but as a vehicle for their worship. The content, musical style, and liturgical function of such songs can be quite varied, but if it is group singing, community singing, it is congregational song. I aim to show that congregational song, because it is liturgically indispensable, should be the professional preoccupation not merely of musicians, but of pastors and lay worship leaders. I write as a pastor, theologian, and amateur musician, with people who see themselves as "unmusical" very much in mind.

Congregational Song in the Past

In early cultures, singing together was a taken-for-granted aspect of being together.[3] The earliest music was probably vocal, with or without instrumental support, and evolved to strengthen community bonding and resolve conflicts.[4] Independent instrumental music is a later development.

There are differences, of course, between ancient singing and today's understanding of congregational song. As my "glimpses" indicate (see Chapter 1), religion permeated every activity. In ancient

---

2. As argued, for example, by Kallestad, *Entertainment Evangelism.*

3. And still today, in many parts of the world.

4. Jourdain, *Music, the Brain, and Ecstasy,* pp. 306–8; Storr, *Music and the Mind,* pp. 16–19. The earliest surviving instruments are prehistoric bone flutes. In one part of France, Cro-Magnon caves with the most paintings are also the most resonant, suggesting that they were chosen as sites for religious ceremonies involving song. In oral cultures, song is also a storehouse of knowledge.

Israel, a well-digging song, or a war song, was by definition also a worship song. Speech and song were less clearly distinguished than they are now. Public utterance was closer to chanting than speaking. Ancient Greek poetry, for example, was probably chanted, moving between the ground note of the poem and a note above it, probably a fourth or a fifth. This is what the Greeks called "music."[5] First-century synagogue worship migrated between speech and song. By contrast, first-century Christian worship "song" was probably closer to a ring-shout than to a cathedral choir. Then, as now, what counts as "musical" is culturally specific and culturally determined. If we knew what it sounded like, a well-digging chant, a Temple psalm response, or an early Christian "hymn" might, or might not, sound "musical" to us. Even so, they were corporate, congregational song.

With those provisos, it is fair to say that in Judaism and Christianity congregational song has ancient roots. On the night when he was arrested, Jesus and his disciples sang a hymn (probably one of the psalms associated with Passover) before they "went out to the Mount of Olives" (Mark 14:26). Paul and Silas sang in prison (Acts 16:25). New Testament writings contain fragments of what may have been congregational songs.[6] The book of Revelation depicts a series of worship spectaculars, in which people of every tribe, tongue, and nation sing eternal praise to God: this suggests that corporate singing was familiar to, and important to, the author. For several centuries, congregational singing was part of Sunday worship, in both the Eastern and the Western church.

Throughout Christian history, congregational song has rebounded from trends that diminished it and survived attempts to suppress it. In the Western church, for reasons sketched in Chapter 1, it declined and almost vanished from Sunday worship (Mass) during the Middle Ages. Ordinary people still sang, however, in the street, on pilgrimage, at liturgical dramas, and on other occasions. During the same period of

---

5. Storr, *Music and the Mind*, pp. 14–15. A dactylic poem was probably sounded using, say, the notes GCC, GCC (or GDD, GDD) with no extra emphasis on the G. (In English, a dactyl has one loud and two soft syllables, e.g., "*El*-ean-or *Roo*-se-velt.") The accents on written Greek, (ˊ, ˋ, and ˆ) indicated a rising, falling, or up-and-down pitch on a particular syllable.

6. Possible fragments include Ephesians 5:14b; 1 Timothy 2:5; 1 Timothy 3:16b; and 2 Timothy 2:11–13. There is, however, no consensus on this question. For contrasting views, see Foley, *Foundations of Christian Music*, p. 67, and Mountain, articles in *The Hymn* (see Bibliography).

history, thousands of congregations sang vigorously, several times a day. The monastic movement was vigorous and widespread, and its communities were, by definition, congregations. It is impossible to conceive of monasticism without corporate song. In the 1960s, not long after the Second Vatican Council, a Benedictine monastery in the south of France asked for help. Its members were listless, fatigued, and mildly (though not clinically) depressed.Though there was some anxiety about the Council's reforms, the members' physical symptoms had no obvious cause. Asked whether they had in any way changed their routine, they replied that they had eliminated several hours of Latin Gregorian chant. They were advised to reinstate it; when they did so, their health and morale rapidly improved.[7]

For most strands of Protestantism, congregational song was recovered and reinvigorated by the Reformation. Though Lutherans and Calvinists had different views of what should be sung, and how (see Chapter 1), the singing of hymns or metrical psalms was vigorously promoted. There is anecdotal evidence that the freedom to sing corporately was enjoyed and appreciated. Visiting London in 1560, the Anglican bishop of Salisbury, John Jewel, describes the rapid spread of congregational psalm singing after its introduction in one small church. Churches nearby followed suit, and churches in distant towns heard of the new worship style and joined in. In central London, Jewel writes, "You may sometimes see at St. Paul's Cross, after the service, six thousand persons, old and young, of both sexes, all singing together and praising God."[8]

In one branch of the Reformation, congregational singing was temporarily silenced. Paradoxically, one of the "silencers" was an accomplished musician. In sixteenth-century Zurich, Reformer Ulrich Zwingli composed music, sang, and played a variety of instruments. On his reading of the Bible, however, he believed that congregational singing was unwarranted, so banned singing and instrumental music in church.[9] The ban was short-lived: at the end of the century, Zurich congregations were again singing psalms.

Similarly, in sixteenth-century England early Baptists and Congregationalists (Brownists) opposed "singing with conjoint [united] voices," believing that the Spirit was quenched when "mediated" (fil-

7. Campbell, *The Mozart Effect*, pp. 103–4.
8. Westermeyer, *Te Deum*, p. 180.
9. See ibid., pp. 149–53.

tered) through someone else's words and music. Within decades, Particular Baptist Benjamin Keach wrote *The Breach Repair'd in God's Worship* (London, 1691), the "breach" being, as he put it, "the lost and neglected ordinance of singing Psalms, Hymns, and Spiritual Songs."[10] Keach was persuasive: Baptists and Congregationalists soon became known for their singing.

Congregational song has sometimes been silenced by persecution. For centuries, Irish Catholics met for Mass in secret, not daring to sing, and internalized mute observance as distinctively Catholic, over against the boisterous hymn singing of the dominant Protestantism.[11] More often, however, the people's song has flourished in the face of opposition. Vigorous community singing has been the hallmark of Christian renewal movements, including early Methodism, Pentecostalism, American camp meetings, and the Salvation Army.[12] New songs, sung by all, are important means of building faith and identity. African Americans, Anabaptists, Mennonites, and Moravians have sometimes literally sung for dear life. Peace and protest movements know the necessity of community song.

Congregational Song in Trouble

Go to a Pentecostal service next Sunday, and you'll find a congregation standing, clapping, swaying to the beat, and singing twenty to thirty minutes of praise songs. African American congregations have a similar level of participation. Mennonite, Moravian, Church of the Brethren, and Church of Christ congregations cherish their heritage of congregational part-song, though nowadays they worry about losing it.

Worry they well might, for congregational song is in trouble. Social mobility in North America has drastically reduced the number of times a group of people can feel a "natural" or "given" sense of community easily expressed in song, except in Irish pubs, at baseball games, and in moments of national or community crisis. Individualism and the quest for privacy make us less inclined to join a group and sing along with it. With less experience of enjoyable singing, people lose confidence, and draw back from joining in. When we move to a new town, we visit

---

10. See Westermeyer, "The Future of Congregational Song."

11. For the effects of this experience on American Catholicism, see Day, *Why Catholics Can't Sing*.

12. See Hustad, *Jubilate II*, pp. 157–58.

churches that used to have a different set of "well-known hymns" from ours but have lost them because their members, too, are on the move. If we join a church that sings new hymns, choruses, or praise songs, it's probably a different selection from the new songs we sang in our previous congregation: the abundance of new material is exciting (because it shows the Holy Spirit creatively at work) and frustrating (because there's no common stock on which to draw). As already indicated, our most common musical memory today may be of the jingles in commercials.[13] Engaging and amusing as they may be, they are designed to sell products, not express our deepest joy, sorrow, faith, hope, and love. Many, indeed, shortchange us with counterfeit solutions to human needs.

Popular music today is soloistic. For my parents' generation, born in the early years of the twentieth century, popular song included music-hall numbers where the soloist sang trite, forgettable verses whose primary purpose was to permit at least three repetitions of the refrains the audience wanted to sing. Nowadays, though fans sing along at concerts, popular songs are not generally geared to audience participation. The best are good to hear but often hard to sing, because they come from the composer's personal vision and the singer's performance style and lack the aural cues, repetition, and "catchiness" essential for group singing.

Through television, a singer or group can reach millions of people over vast distances. Opportunities to be at a live performance are keenly sought by fans, but the main emphasis is on studio-recorded CDs, DVDs, and videos, marketed for people to play in their homes or cars, or through earphones. Live music is no longer the norm, so our role as listeners is reinforced.

Studio recording demands a high level of professionalism, with retakes, multitracking, mixes, and fine-tunings. The result is excellence in sound and presentation, irrespective of aesthetic quality. Karaoke singing is fun, and live performance goes in and out of fashion, depending on whether it is seen as "real" or imperfect compared with studio sound. But in general, studio sound has become normative, as it is lip-synched in videos, TV appearances, and even sometimes in "live" concerts. The result for many is "electronic discouragement,"[14] as the quality of recorded sound persuades us that our own voice has little value.

---

13. Westermeyer, "The Future of Congregational Song," pp. 4–9. See also Chapter 1, above.

14. Martin Josman, executive director of the National Choral Council in Manhattan, quoted by Calta, "Singing in Groups Becoming a Thing of the Past."

Most popular music today is delivered through high amplification. Audiences expect a thumping, throbbing, enveloping, sometimes ear-damaging sound. The knock-on effect is that, in other contexts, such as church worship, singers and instrumentalists often crank up the volume unnecessarily and diminish their personal connection with the congregation. The microphone takes over, whether or not it is needed, and whether or not there is a live musician in our midst. "So the sound is bigger than life, and the person who makes it is regarded as bigger than life."[15] If that person then tries to encourage audience participation without dropping the volume, the amplified voice overwhelms the communal voice and discourages the participation that was sought. Few singers of popular music know how to enable group singing, because their training, skills, and disposition are focused on performance.

So congregational song is in trouble, nowadays not because authority frowns on it, but because our culture undermines it, through social mobility, performance-oriented popular music, electronic discouragement, and overamplification.[16] One result, as composer Alice Parker records from conversations with public-school music teachers, is that many children come to school with no musical background except music videos and TV advertisements. "They have never heard an adult they know well sing for pure pleasure; have never sung around the house." Their idea of music is shaped by electronic music, soloistic styles, high volume, and instant gratification. Thus, at primary age levels "children cannot match pitches; singing with their own age group without accompaniment is unheard-of"; they have no folk or community repertoire, and the idea of music as a disposable extra is reinforced by after-school rehearsals, budget cuts, and lack of community support. At community colleges, students commute from home, without living-on-campus time to develop the skills of amateur choral singing. Because Alice Parker aims to develop teaching techniques to cope with these changes, she asks how teachers can work with college students "who want to sing but have no realization that reading music is a skill that takes practice."[17] To

---

15. Westermeyer, "The Future of Congregational Song."

16. Anecdotal conclusion, but from many reports and experiences. I don't know how far the health of congregational song in mainstream churches has been quantified. Clark's study, *Music in Churches*, has mixed findings and is limited to 24 congregations (Episcopal and United Methodist) in three New England states.

17. Parker, "Mus. Ed. 2001." She also asks what can be done for postgraduate music composition students "who can write music only for the academic community on the computer?"(!)

transpose her concerns into a church setting, how can children, youth, and adults in today's congregations learn the basics of music and rediscover the joy of congregational song?

A prior question is, "Why should they?"—to which there are two answers. Congregational song does important things that speech alone cannot do, and its distinguishing marks have theological implications.

"I Love That Awful Hymn"

In trying to understand what song can do that speech cannot, a good starting point is an age-old conundrum: Why do people sometimes love to sing hymns cluttered with archaic language and defective theology? The question is often asked, especially by clergy, and assumes that the meaning of a sung hymn derives completely from the meaning of its text. "From such a perspective it is quite puzzling that erroneous texts can continue to be wholeheartedly sung by intelligent and articulate people who—if pressed—would candidly admit that they did not really believe them!"[18]

Perhaps, however, the meaning conveyed and expressed in singing a congregational song is more than, or even other than, the meaning of its lyric. What happens, then, when words are sung? Does the music merely decorate and embroider them? Or, at the other extreme, does it drown and engulf them? Is the truth somewhere in between? How, in any case, can we account for the appeal of a tune, or describe it? Nor surprisingly, these and similar questions have generated a vast literature and competing theories. I shall look for explanations that make sense to me; however, my account is necessarily partial. First, some groundwork.

Speech and Song

If I say "Hello," my voice probably changes pitch between the two syllables, or even within the same syllable. The pitch, loudness, and relative length of the syllables change according to the kind of "hello" I am saying: delighted, surprised, astounded, disappointed, sad, puzzled, suspicious, bored, friendly, angry—a simple "hello" has many vocal permutations.

---

18. Cole, "Hymns and Meaning." In developing this section, Cole's discussion has been especially helpful.

If I sing "Hel-lo," my vocal sounds lengthen and become more consistent. If I use more than one note, my changes of pitch become deliberate, measured, and often cover a wider range.[19] If (for example) my "hel-lo" has two notes forming a major third, each note has a continuous sound called a "tone." By contrast with sound-as-noise and the variable sounds of speech, tones are separable units with constant sound-wave forms which can be repeated and reproduced. In recognizing musical tones, the brain is necessarily less exacting than scientific instruments, and "categorizes" a range of sounds as a single identity. In Western culture, for example, vocal and instrumental "sounds of the frequencies 438, 440, and 442 cycles per second are all heard as an instance of the note A."[20]

Speech and song (or more broadly, language and vocal or instrumental music) have important similarities. The brain treats musical and spoken phrases similarly, suspending comprehension until the phrase can be taken as a whole. Both speech and music are understood through repeated exposure. Both are long, highly organized streams of sound without equivalent in the natural world. Both are acquired, and can be used, without formal training: the overwhelming majority of people can generate sentences and melodies without being trained in the rules of grammar or music.[21] Both are experienced as conveying "meaning": there is a degree of "linguistic" meaning even in nonverbal vocal sound. If two people conduct a conversation by humming, with closed lips and without using words, much can be conveyed, such as: "I am tired," "I am happy," or even "I love you."[22]

Still, music and language also have marked differences. Words have relatively "fixed" meanings. The noun "giraffe" has a limited range of possible meanings, even in metaphorical uses. A musical note, however, has no wordlike, "dictionary" meaning. A D-flat can be described in terms of its frequency, or its timbre on different instruments; it does not mean "sadness," "milepost," "sausages," or anything else specifically

---

19. Ordinary English speech has frequent pitch changes, even within a syllable. In relaxed speech, the maximum variations are about a fifth (Storr, *Music and the Mind*, pp. 14–15).

20. Jourdain, *Music, the Brain, and Ecstasy*, p. 336. I use "instrument(al)" for convenience, to describe musical instruments other than the human voice.

21. Ibid., p. 275.

22. Storr, *Music and the Mind*, p. 71. I assume this holds good even if the speakers cannot see each other, so that facial and body language cues are screened out; Storr does not clarify this, however.

linguistic. In one context, it can be an entire "statement"; in another, merely part of a longer musical figure. In European and many other languages, linguistic sequences are usually invariable: changing the word order changes the meaning. "Hickory, dickory, dock, / the mouse ran up the clock" has a different meaning from "Dock, dickory, hickory, / the clock ran up the mouse." But a melody can be turned one way or another, and played in different keys and at different speeds, without ceasing to be recognizable. Within quite wide limits, language is translatable. A speech in Chinese can usually be adequately translated into English; though a poem presents more difficulty, it can be recognizably rendered. But a Beethoven symphony cannot be "translated" into Chinese or Balinese traditional music.[23]

Music and Culture

Though some musical relationships are universally recognized, music is not "a universal language."[24] If I sound middle C on a piano, and then the Cs above and below it, the overwhelming majority of human ears will hear these three distinct sounds as the same note. The octave, in other words, is universal, and two intervals within it, the fourth and the fifth, are universally—or almost universally—treated as stable, focal tones, toward which other terms of a given musical system tend to move, or return. But different cultures differ markedly in how they divide the scale; whether they use full tones, half tones, or quarter tones; whether a singer steps, slides, or hovers between them, and so on. Though Western and Indonesian music both tend to return to their starting point, "a brain acculturated to Indonesian music does not categorize scales and harmonic intervals as [Westerners] do."[25] Because music is deeply rooted in human nature, yet not closely connected with the external world, "different cultures create different musics, just as they create different languages."[26] No one type of music is more deeply rooted in the nature of things than any other.[27]

---

23. Jourdain, *Music, the Brain, and Ecstasy,* p. 275. I have exemplified and elaborated his discussion.

24. For this section, see, in particular, Jourdain, *Music, the Brain, and Ecstasy,* pp. 66–79, 255; Meyer, *Meaning and Emotion in Music,* pp. 46, 62–63, 151; and Storr, *Music and the Mind,* pp. 51–64.

25. Jourdain, *Music, the Brain, and Ecstasy,* p. 255.

26. Storr, *Music and the Mind,* p. 49.

27. Ibid., p. 63.

In different cultures, the same sound can have different meanings and create different expectations. Thus, "the language and dialect of music are many. They vary from culture to culture, from epoch to epoch within the same culture and even within a single epoch and culture."[28]

Meaning in Music

Whatever music is understood to mean, then, is likely to be culturally specific. A given piece of music affects its hearers through learned conventions of melody, harmony, and rhythm. In a given culture, certain musical elements imply other elements and nudge the mind toward particular anticipations. Without such nonverbal anticipations any musical event would be equally probable, and we would always be in the position of someone learning music for the first time."So music's meanings, its motions and emotions, must necessarily be expressed through the devices of musical custom, and will be perceived only by those steeped in those customs."[29]

That said, there are different understandings of what music does, or means. Some believe that the meaning of a piece of music lies solely within the work itself, without reference to anything outside it. Others argue that music also conveys meanings that in some way refer to the nonmusical world of concepts, actions, and emotions. Some believe that the way meaning is perceived in a given piece of music is primarily intellectual, through understanding its musical patterns and relationships. More important, others claim, are the feelings and emotions that those musical relationships arouse in the listener.[30]

Nowadays, it is widely agreed that to set intellectual against emotional responses is a false opposition. Philosophically and psychologically, Leonard Meyer sees no gulf between affective and intellectual responses to music. Psychiatrist Anthony Storr agrees, arguing that anything that lessens our distress at being surrounded by chaos is bound to give us pleasure. Thus, *even the most abstract intellectual patterns engage our feelings.*"[31] Robert Jourdain finds that, in psychiatry and psychology, emotion is now seen as crucially important to

---

28. Meyer, *Meaning and Emotion in Music,* pp. 46 and 62.

29. Jourdain, *Music, the Brain, and Ecstasy,* p. 296.

30. Meyer categorizes these viewpoints as, respectively, absolutist, referentialist, formalist, and expressivist (*Meaning and Emotion in Music,* p. 103). See also Storr, *Music and the Mind,* pp. 77–78.

31. Storr, *Music and the Mind,* p. 177; emphasis his.

reasoning, planning, and decision making. To put it simply, we cannot pay attention to everything, so focus our reasoning, planning, and choosing on what most touches, concerns, and moves us.[32]

Moving Music

To say that music moves us can sometimes be literally true. Hospitalized in the 1970s after a skiing accident, neurosurgeon Oliver Sacks was for weeks bed-bound and partly paralyzed. He began to fear that he would never regain the ability to walk. Day by day he listened to a tape recording of a Mendelssohn violin concerto. Awakened by it one morning, he got up and walked across the room to turn off the tape, then realized two things: he had walked the length of the room, literally uplifted by the music; and the tape recorder wasn't playing. The music that had so literally *moved* him was playing only in his head.[33]

At Beth-Abraham hospital in the Bronx, Sacks saw how the melody, harmony, rhythms, and dynamics (loudness/softness) of music have a physiological impact and can trigger deep, nonverbal responses. "There were patients who couldn't speak, but who could sing. The power of music in these patients was instantaneous: from a frozen Parkinsonian state to a freely flowing, moving, speaking state."[34]

For people suffering from this particular type of Parkinson's disease, music proved to be a powerful but limited helper. The patient had to be musically sensitive, and in the right mood. The music had to suit the patient's taste. Sharp, percussive music was counterproductive: it caused the sufferer to jerk like a marionette. Moderately paced, shapely music, was best: music with a "beat," pronounced but embedded in rolling melody. Besides music, other kinds of flowing movement proved equally effective. One patient talked of how he would walk to town by "hitching a ride" on someone else's walk-rhythm.

Clearly, then, music was not for these patients a generic "medicine": one couldn't write a prescription saying, "Take two doses of Mozart after every meal."[35] Equally clearly, something about certain kinds of music, and certain movements, could give temporary relief from the disabling incoherence of the disease. The "incoherence" is apparently

---

32. Jourdain, *Music, the Brain, and Ecstasy*, p. 308.
33. Collins, "Doctor of the Soul."
34. Ibid.
35. Recent reports cast doubt on the belief that the music of Mozart has greater or more specific beneficial effects than other kinds of music.

a failure of neurons in the core of the brain, such that intentions no longer reliably translate into physical actions. Somehow, music and other flowing movement can, as it were, bypass the damaged connections and coordinate the brain's activities, creating "a stream of intention to which patients can momentarily entrain their actions."[36]

Pattern and Process

Both the above stories have to do with flowing, meaningful movement: musical, and also physical. Music, then, can be perceived by the brain as "movement," and can in turn enable movement. Thus, when scholars say that music often appeals to us because of its pattern,[37] or because the human mind looks for patterns or gestalts,[38] it may be more accurate to use a less static word or phrase, like "process" or "patterned progression."

When we listen to music and hear sequences, development, and patterned progression, our brain is doing what it always seeks to do— making connections. Chaos cannot be accurately recalled, and does not prompt any obvious action. Coherence is essential to action and recollection: "We are compelled to make coherent patterns out of our mental processes if we are to retain them in consciousness."[39]

Thus, when separate events closely follow each other, we have a strong tendency to link them together into a coherent sequence. "When we listen to music, what we perceive as a tune is simply a succession of separate tones; *it is we who make it into a continuous melody.*"[40] To hear the same set of tones as separate, we must either greatly lengthen the time intervals between each tone or make the frequencies of the tones radically different from each other. The brain's determination to perceive a progressive sequence is demonstrated by an experiment called "dichotic listening" or the "scale illusion." If two series of tones, each consisting of wide leaps, are presented simultaneously, one to each ear, through headphones, the brain irons out the intervals and hears the two sets of tones as one connected sequence.[41]

A melody, then, is a set of relationships between tones, perceived

---

36. For this quotation, and the preceding paragraph, see Jourdain, *Music, the Brain, and Ecstasy*, pp. 302–3.

37. Ibid., p. 314 , taking music of the baroque as an example.

38. Meyer, *Meaning and Emotion in Music*, pp. 83ff.

39. Storr, *Music and the Mind*, p. 175.

40. Ibid., p. 170, emphasis mine; see also p. 169.

41. Jourdain, *Music, the Brain, and Ecstasy*, p. 248; Storr, *Music and the Mind*, p. 171.

by the brain and held in memory. Once heard, "melody Z" remains "melody Z," whether it is sung, hummed, played on different instruments, varied, elaborated, or played in different keys. *"Through all these changes, it remains recognizably the same melody."*[42] As we listen to any kind of music, the scanning and sorting of melodic, harmonic, and rhythmic progressions proceed continuously. We mostly take it for granted and are hardly aware that it is happening. "But when we first discern an unexpected linkage, a new pattern, it brings us intense satisfaction."[43] The satisfaction is for some more "intellectual," for others more "emotional," but the difference is a matter of degree: both kinds of satisfaction are usually present.

Perhaps, then, music has "meaning" for us because it has flow as well as purpose. Most everyday movements are not a smooth, continuous flow. Driving a car, cooking a meal, tidying a room, and packing a suitcase are (hopefully!) purposeful activities. But they rarely flow smoothly. A driver must make sudden, unforeseen adjustments to brake, accelerator, and steering wheel in response to other traffic. The best-organized stir-fry cook must make rapid, disconnected movements as the meal progresses. Tidying a room and packing a suitcase typically involve darting to and fro, and making last-minute changes of plan or direction. By contrast:

> Well crafted music creates the very world it travels through, meeting every anticipation with a graceful resolution, and raising new anticipations at every turn.[44]

Or again:

> One of the reasons why music affects us deeply is its power to structure our auditory experience and thus to make sense out of it. . . .When we take part in music, or listen to an absorbing performance . . . we enter a special, secluded world in which order prevails and from which the incongruous is excluded.[45]

---

42. Storr, *Music and the Mind,* p. 172, emphasis his.

43. Ibid., p. 176. On the oft-touted connection between music and mathematics, Storr notes that music is less abstract than mathematics because it causes physiological arousal. The ordering process, and interest in "abstract" relationships, are similar, but because of its stronger, and measurable, physiological effects, "music is usually felt as more personally significant than mathematics, more immediately relevant to the ebb and flow of our subjective, sentient life" (p. 183).

44. Jourdain, *Music, the Brain, and Ecstasy,* pp. 302–3.

45. Storr, *Music and the Mind,* p. 105.

In other words, what music can do for Parkinson's patients, it can do less dramatically for all of us. "It lifts us from our frozen mental habits and makes our minds move in ways they ordinarily cannot."[46] Sometimes, as already demonstrated, music can also make our bodies move in ways they ordinarily cannot. Shortly before Pablo Casals's ninetieth birthday, Norman Cousins visited him at his Puerto Rico home. Afflicted by rheumatoid arthritis and emphysema, the great cellist had swollen hands and clenched fingers. Early in the morning, he walked slowly to his piano and slowly, painfully, sat down. As he placed his hands on the keys, his fingers unlocked, his back straightened, and he began the opening bars of Bach's *Well-Tempered Clavier.* Thereafter, he raced into a Brahms concerto, his fingers moving nimbly across the keyboard, his body freed from arthritic cramp. Finally, he stood up, stood erect, and walked smoothly into the adjoining room for breakfast, showing no trace of infirmity.[47]

Time Art

The reason why the sound of music can have such an immediate effect on the listener, Robert Jourdain suggests, is that musical sound unfolds across time, it moves—and movement is the nervous system's raison d'être. When we say that music "moves," or makes a "patterned progression," we are taking language about movement in space and using it to describe a time sequence. The connection is close, though not reciprocal: any spatial movement takes time, but a time sequence need not involve movement in space. Jourdain's comment suggests that our nervous system, being always concerned with activity and movement, makes the same response to musical time sequences as to spatial movement.

Music is time art. A sculpture, quilt, photograph, and flower arrangement exist in space. It takes time to create them and time to appreciate them, but once completed they remain unchanged over time, unless by damage and decay. A drama, movie, dance, TV program, and piece of music take time to unfold, time to be what they are. To say that music flows, or has patterned progressions, is another way of saying that music is "time art." Its patterned progressions cannot be exactly repeated: each hearing and performance are different,

---

46. Jourdain, *Music, the Brain, and Ecstasy,* p. 303.

47. Norman Cousins, "Anatomy of an Illness as Perceived by the Patient," in *Anatomy of an Illness* (New York: Norton, 1979), pp. 72–74, quoted in Campbell, *The Mozart Effect,* p. 61.

even when the same piece is played or the same song sung time after time.[48]

As we listen to music, our minds reach back and forth. Memory and anticipation work together. They "maintain a sort of map, partial and imperfect, of the composition passing before us."[49] Listening is led by anticipation, as our cerebral cortex draws on memory and searches for familiar patterns and devices. We anticipate what we already know, and in that sense "re-cognize" musical devices.[50] Using a variety of examples from Western music, Leonard Meyer analyzes some of the ways good music keeps our attention as it unfolds across time. They include anticipation (he calls it expectation); surprise and suspense ("What's going to happen? Where is this going? How will it 'resolve' itself and come to an end?"); repetition—which creates an expectation of eventual variation; and continuation—change within a continuous process. Listening is interactive. As we listen to music, "we are constantly revising our opinions of what has happened in the past in the light of present events . . . constantly altering our expectations." Our anticipations are not merely intellectual, but felt: an instinctive mental and motor response.[51]

We also anticipate, and hope for, completion and closure. Completion is not merely change or cessation. Music can change, or be stopped, without being completed. Completion arises from what has gone before, from relationships between antecedents and consequences. It is the musical equivalent of casting off knitting, coming home after a journey, or ending a story. "Completion is not simply cessation—silence. It involves conclusion."[52]

Given that most people can make melodies without musical training, it is not surprising that many can appreciate musical forms and structures without being able to express their appreciation in technical terms. The untrained listener is aware of repetition, dissonance resolving, key changes, and delays in resolution.[53] "The operation of

---

48. On music as time art, see Rock and Mealy, *Performer as Priest and Prophet*, pp. 9–17.

49. Jourdain, *Music, the Brain, and Ecstasy*, p. 137. Later, he uses similar spatial imagery, describing how a longer composition is perceived as having "slower-moving undercurrents of abstract relations, . . . which unfold as a sort of temporal landscape" (p. 139).

50. Ibid., p. 246.

51. Meyer, *Meaning and Emotion in Music*, pp. 49 and 61.

52. Ibid., pp. 129–30.

53. Storr, *Music and the Mind*, pp. 77–78.

intelligence in listening to music need never become self-conscious. We are continually behaving in an intelligent way, comprehending meaning and acting upon our perceptions, cognitions, evaluations without ever making the meanings themselves the object of our scrutiny."[54] A trained musician consciously waits for the expected resolution of a dominant seventh chord; the untrained, yet practiced, listener feels the delay without being able to verbalize it.[55] A contemporary's description of Sidney Bechet's jazz clarinet playing aptly shows how music works on the "untrained, yet practiced" ear:

> His most daring flights of improvisation may momentarily have made the listener a little nervous, a little doubtful of the outcome, but all were accomplished with confident ease.[56]

Music and Emotion

To say that Bechet's improvisations made listeners nervous, doubtful, then presumably relieved or delighted at their satisfactory outcome is to depict the emotional power of music. Here we move into the hazy landscape of imprecision. "Emotion" is hard to define, and there are many theories of what it is and how it works. Similar responses to a particular musical work are mostly culturally determined, and don't agree beyond generalities like "joyful," "lively," "tragic," and "sad."[57] Yet part of the "moving" power of music's temporal progressions is undoubtedly "emotional" rather than merely "intellectual."

To set the scene, an example may be helpful. In his comprehensive exploration, Robert Jourdain frequently visits a particular piece of music, Henry Mancini's theme for *The Pink Panther*. One of his visits ponders the relation between Mancini's theme and the movements and emotions associated with "stealth."

Mancini's theme was composed for the *Pink Panther* movies. Their title sequence shows a cartoon figure, the pink panther, creeping, stalking, jumping nervously, and leaping for cover. The character is

---

54. Meyer, *Meaning and Emotion in Music*, p. 38.
55. Ibid., p. 40.
56. Quoted in ibid., p. 208.
57. Storr, *Music and the Mind*, p. 70. For an intriguing theory of emotion that fits musical experience, see Jourdain, *Music, the Brain, and Ecstasy*, pp. 308ff.

ambiguous: panthers are tenacious, cunning, and dangerous, but this panther has a permanent blush of embarrassment and is skittish, unpredictable, and clumsy—much like the movies' central character, Peter Sellers's "Inspector Clouseau."

For anyone seeing the movie, Mancini's music aptly puts these visual elements in sonic form. Yet someone who hears the music, without seeing the movie, is unlikely to recognize it as, specifically, a nervous panther stalking its prey and diving for cover. At most, the first-time hearer, without the movie's visual cues, might say that the music "creeps along." How, then, does the music relate to stealthy movement? As Jourdain observes, stealthiness includes changes in the timing of body movements: restrained motion, sudden speed, stillness, more restrained motion, and so on—plus a low profile, so as not to be seen. Most of these changes are variations of timing. We feel such changes of timing in our bodies when we are being stealthy or when we see another human being, or another mammal, moving in the same way. In the *Pink Panther* theme, stealthy movement, and the comedic element of the panther's nervousness, are conveyed through the theme's rhythmic changes, harmony lurching into dissonance and quietness zooming into loudness. The *Pink Panther* theme does not *symbolize* stealth, in the precise, defined way that language can do. "This music *mimics* stealth: it doesn't *name* it."[58]

Perhaps, then, music evokes emotional responses because it mimics bodily movements and the ebb and flow of emotional states. The mimicry is eloquent, yet indirect. In one of Beethoven's piano sonatas (E-flat, Opus 31), the composer uses clearly recognizable motifs of question and answer. He does something similar in another piece, the finale of his last string quartet, of which Beethoven himself wrote, in a marginal note, "Must it be so? Yes, it must be so, it must be so!" (*"Muss es sein? Es muss sein! Es muss sein!"*). A question-and-answer pattern is imitated: we cannot, however, find words to show precisely what the question and answer are.[59]

When describing emotional states, words are in any case hard to find. Language can describe the outer world with some precision, but is less able to describe inner feelings, moods, emotions, and bodily sensations. When someone is embarrassed, sociable, or withdrawn, these emotional states are hard to verbalize, because emotional states

---

58. Jourdain, *Music, the Brain, and Ecstasy,* pp. 293–94 (quotation from p. 294).
59. Storr, *Music and the Mind,* p. 72.

and their visible results are a complex process, changing from moment to moment. Emotional states become easier to describe only at their extremes: rage, despair, exultation, perhaps. With those exceptions, the turbulent flow of emotions is as hard to describe in language as the turbulent flow of a stream. Music captures the turbulent flow that is hard to describe in language. With melody, harmonic progression, rhythm, and dynamics (movement between loudness and softness), music mimics emotional processes: "It carefully replicates the temporal patterns of interior feeling, surging in pitch and volume, as they surge, ebbing as they ebb. It leads opposing forces into battle and then to reconciliation. Or it just moves in interesting ways."[60]

One way in which music engages our emotional attention lies in its ability to set up tensions and then resolve them. Many psychologists now see emotion, not only at the extremes usually portrayed in common speech ("he was very emotional"), but as a general, less dramatic trigger of attentiveness.[61] On this view, "emotion" motivates not only plans needing effort, but ordinary, everyday actions. Emotion is also generated by the outcome of particular actions, especially when our expectation is exceeded or disappointed. When we touch the sixty-dollar key on an ATM, we expect sixty dollars to emerge from it. If sixty dollars emerges, we feel, at most, mild satisfaction, but more probably, nothing at all. Our anticipation has been met: nothing surprising about that; end of story. If, on the other hand, the ATM gives out five hundred dollars, or a message saying (against all our calculations) that our account is exhausted, we probably experience strong emotional reactions—positive, mixed, or negative.

Music mimics such experiences by setting up anticipations, then satisfying them, often after sufficient delay, surprise, or dissonance to keep our attention. As with movement, so with emotion: music organizes our responses. "Music idealizes emotions negative and positive alike. By so doing it momentarily perfects our individual emotional lives. . . . Music serves to perfect those responses, to make them beautiful. By so doing, music imparts dignity to experience that often is far from dignified. And by imparting pleasure even to negative emotions, music serves to justify sufferings large and small, assuring us that it has not all been for nothing."[62] By its suspenseful, surprising, and then

---

60. Jourdain, *Music, the Brain, and Ecstasy*, pp. 295–96, quotation from p. 296.

61. This section is drawn, in general, from ibid., pp. 310–22. The ATM example is mine.

62. Ibid., p. 322.

satisfying progressions, "music ensures that the emotions aroused by a particular event peak at the same moment." When a group is singing or listening to music, different individuals may have different emotional responses. But "what matters is the general state of arousal and its simultaneity. Because of its capacity to intensify crowd feeling, music has a power akin to that of the orator."[63]

Ambiguous Power

The ability of music to intensify crowd feelings may derive from the way it mimics emotional peaks and valleys but does not apply them to specific individuals or particular life stories. Because music's emotional movements are powerful, yet nonspecific, they can give the individual a sense of empathetic connection with other people's experience. "After playing Chopin," says Oscar Wilde, "I feel as if I had been weeping over sins I never committed, and mourning over tragedies that were not my own." For Wilde, music "creates for one a past of which one has been ignorant, and fills one with a sense of sorrows that have been hidden from one's tears." Similarly, philosopher Suzanne Langer says that music can "present emotions and moods we have not felt, passions we did not know before."[64]

Music's power to make empathetic connections and intensify crowd feelings is ethically ambiguous. In the movie *Leap of Faith*, Steve Martin plays a traveling evangelist who cons small-town America with tent-meeting spectaculars. Part of the magic is in the music: upbeat songs by a superb gospel choir. In another 1990s movie, *Bob Roberts*, a folk singer runs for senator, cynically manipulating the public. His persuasive power is enhanced by his folk songs, whose words and music turn the sounds of 1960s idealism into a 1980s message of racist, materialist greed. In the movie of the musical *Cabaret*, set in 1930s Germany, a lyrical song of hope, "Tomorrow belongs to me," is sung by a fresh-faced, blond-haired boy in the swastika-emblazoned uniform of the Hitler Youth; the juxtaposition of song and swastika hints at the persuasive power of music in Adolf Hitler's ideology, and the tragic, demonic outcome of that youth's "tomorrow." On a positive note, another movie, *Sister Act*, shows a community of nuns whose choir's upbeat singing draws in people from their

---

63. Storr, *Music and the Mind*, p. 30.
64. Oscar Wilde is quoted by Jourdain, *Music, the Brain, and Ecstasy*, p. 322. Suzanne Langer is quoted by Storr, *Music and the Mind*, p. 76.

inner-city neighborhood and helps revitalize their church's worship and mission.

Expected Surprises and Visceral Responses

If a particular song or instrumental work mimics emotional progressions in a satisfying way, we not only enjoy, but look forward to, hearing, playing, or singing it again. Theories that stress music's initial emotional delight or disappointment find it hard to account for this,[65] but it comes as no surprise to anyone who has followed the liturgical year, enjoyed a TV suspense series where the good characters always win, seen the same play, musical, or opera over and over again, or heard a child ask again and again to hear the same bedtime story. However we may account for it, looking forward to an expected surprise is a widespread, perhaps fundamental human experience, and familiar music is one of many ways of providing it. In different ways, and with different levels of complexity, musical forms often mimic narrative and story: symphonies, sonatas, and songs, for example.

Like mime, from which "mimic" and "mimicry" derive, the effect of music's emotional "mimicry" can be pleasing or irritating, uplifting or annoying, fulfilling or disturbing. If the purpose of emotion is to focus our attention on what most concerns us,[66] it is not surprising that a turbulent flow of emotion grabs our attention and can become so powerful as to be all-consuming. Because it mimics emotional flow, music too can arouse visceral emotional responses in individuals, crowds—and congregations. Such responses are particularly noticeable when they are negative. When people say, "I don't like that music,"[67] their tone is often emphatic, even hostile. Such emotional responses, deeply felt and hard to verbalize, make differences of musical taste hard to talk about, or to tolerate.

With a Smile and a Song

Returning to my initial question, it may now be possible to account, at least partially, for the appeal of the tunes people love to sing.

---

65. Meyer tries to explain it with the psychological mechanism of denial: we know what's coming but suspend disbelief (*Meaning and Emotion in Music*, p. 74). Yet listening to familiar music is surely not in the same category as grief's refusal to accept that a loved one has died.

66. Jourdain, *Music, the Brain, and Ecstasy*, p. 310.

67. To quote Robert Mitchell's apt book title: see Bibliography.

(Though I focus on congregational song, much of what follows applies to music, and church music, in general.) Like speech, the music of a congregational song is a highly organized stream of sound, experienced as conveying "meaning." Its progressions are perceived by the brain as "movement" and can themselves enable movement. On a small scale, the tunes people sing in worship mimic bodily movements and the ebb and flow of emotional states. They have the power—at least potentially—to give meaningful, flowing progression to life's chaos; to beautify and elevate our purposeful but uncoordinated activities; and to mimic the flow of emotion. On a small scale—and perhaps therefore more immediately than longer works of music—a tune can give both intellectual and emotional satisfaction, as singers intuitively chart its beginning, development, surprises (if any), and conclusion. It can momentarily perfect the emotional life of its singers, transmute ugliness into beauty, and impart dignity to undignified experience. Familiar and well-loved tunes give, in addition, the joy of the expected surprise and the assurance of a good story retold. Tunes sung together can intensify crowd feelings (for good and ill), arouse visceral emotional responses, and give a sense of empathetic connection with other people's experience.

Issue and Implications

It seems clear that part of the "meaning" of a congregational song lies in the appeal of its music. Evidently, the tune has its own work to do, not independently of its lyric, but autonomously in relation to it. "Autonomous" is an accurate word, in its original sense: "having laws of its own."

In principle, a good tune will have, say, meaningful progressions, suggesting that the singer's life story can be beautiful and meaningful and that the Christian story its lyric tells, responds to, or reflects on is rich and fulfilling. In practice, such qualities are difficult to pin down. Even music professionals find it hard to describe their nonverbal art form; analysis is skewed by the analyst's own emotional response; and technical descriptions demand either a training in music sufficient to understand them or a friendly professional with time to spare.

With or without musical analysis, word-centered worship traditions probably need to renegotiate the balance of power between tune and text. If "music embraces a new dimension of meaning" that can take worshipers "beyond the physical moment of a liturgical action, to another sphere of experience and understanding,"[68] it is inadequate to regard the tunes we sing merely as a means of vocalizing their lyrics.

Christian theologians have often focused on the importance of congregational lyrics, sometimes regarding their music with reserve or self-doubting enjoyment. Augustine of Hippo is a classic example. In his *Confessions*, written around 397 C.E., he wavers "between the danger that lies in gratifying the senses and the benefits which, as I know from experience, can accrue from singing." His knowledge of music is sophisticated; his attitude to music is, he admits, ambivalent: "I must allow it a position of some honor in my heart, and I find it difficult to assign it to its proper place." When they are sung, sacred words stir his mind to greater religious fervor "and kindle in me a more ardent flame of piety than they would if they were not sung." Music and song have particular modes, "corresponding to my various emotions and able to stimulate them because of the mysterious relationship between the two." In spite of this, the power of music makes him cautious, and his endorsement of music provisional: "When I find the singing itself more moving than the truth which it conveys, I confess that this is a grievous sin, and at those times I would prefer not to hear the singer."[69]

At the Reformation, both Calvin and Luther called music a gift from God, but with different emphases. While Luther celebrated music as God's own creation, Calvin regarded it as an indirect gift, given through fallible human invention. Both knew that the gift of music could be corrupted, but Calvin focused more on the risk of corruption, while Luther was more aware of music, especially song, as a medium through which the gospel can be preached and Christ's victory celebrated.[70]

Two centuries later, John Wesley echoed Augustine's mixture of enjoyment and ambivalence. Urging worshipers to "sing lustily, and with a good courage," he concludes his directions for singing thus: "Above all sing spiritually. Have an eye to God in every word you sing. Aim at pleasing God more than yourself, or any other creature. In order to do this, *attend strictly to the sense of what you sing, and see that your heart is not carried away with the sound, but offered to God continually.*"[71]

At the risk of scandalizing my Reformed heritage, I conclude that the "independent," meaning-making, and emotionally satisfying function of

---

68. Cole, "Hymns and Meaning."

69. For the full quotation, see Westermeyer, *Te Deum*, pp. 88–89.

70. Ibid., pp. 141–49 and 155–58.

71. Emphasis mine. For the full text of Wesley's "Directions for Singing," see the Appendix at the end of this book.

congregational song tunes calls for an attitude more Lutheran than Calvinist. And, while I need meaningful words to sing, prize well-crafted lyrics, and reject singing that is mindlessly enthusiastic, Wesley's final *Direction* needs qualification. Sometimes, our hearts surely ought to be carried away with the sound, as they are offered to God in song.

Managing Time

As a musical event unfolding through time, a congregational song can give an experience of meaningful progression and mimic the flow of emotion, as singers intuitively chart its beginning, development, and completion. It follows that congregational songs, and church music in general, should be chosen and used with regard to how they use the time allotted to them.

As time art, songs and instrumental music (like dance and drama) have the power to dramatize and unfold the Christian story, because music "spins itself out through time just like the story which the song recounts."[72] When music joins with words in a hymn, singing it becomes a minidrama of the gospel: "The words carry on, are linear; the tune is circular. The circles are repeated, but the words change: the direction of the hymn becomes clear, the structure unfolds, and then the last verse brings it to a conclusion."[73] Thus, when singing a hymn or any other congregational song combining textual development with musical repetition, we imitate the interplay between the cyclical rhythms of nature (days, months, seasons, years) and the unfolding story of God's purpose and love. To put it in verse,

> With music, moving on through time
> in sequences of sound,
> we show and tell God's story-line.
> of how the lost are found:
> the old, unfolding covenant
> of justice righting wrong,
> resounds through word and sacrament,
> and leads the people's song.

---

72. Westermeyer, *The Church Musician*, p. 35.
73. Watson, *The English Hymn*, p. 26.

It follows that when a hymn, a set of choruses, or an instrumental solo is played or sung, it should do more than fill in time or pass the time. When driving long solitary hours on an interstate highway, I tune the radio to low-volume country music, hearing some songs and ignoring others, to reduce tedium and preserve concentration. At home, I sometimes flake out and unwind by dozing through music of the baroque, or energize myself with rock music on the exercise bicycle. All such uses of music pass the time, but none is suitable for Christian worship. Because it is time art, worship music and congregational song should do something meaningful, something that makes a difference, something that moves us from one state of being to another. Whether classical or popular, congregational song and instrumental music should aim to be one or more of the following:

- *Formative*, shaping and modeling our faith as it tells a story within the whole story of God in Christ and draws us into the drama of God's saving love;
- *Transformative,* moving us from isolation to belonging, indifference to interest, interest to conviction, and conviction to commitment;
- *Cognitive,* giving us something to ponder and think about;
- *Educational,* teaching us something we didn't know about the Bible, the church, and Christian faith;
- *Inspirational,* lifting us out of ourselves into hope, joy, and peace.

In all traditions, music plays a key role in determining the flow and pace of the service. Again, this is not a question of playing any old music, or singing any old song, to pass the time. When music is used to manage transitions, as when an offering is collected, or a "contemporary" service moves from the opening number to the leader's welcome, the music should be suitable for the transition it is making, so that it can shape the transition and make it meaningful.

Emotional Flow

Several issues are raised by the ability of congregational song music to mimic the flow of emotion, momentarily perfect the emotional life of its singers, transmute ugliness into beauty, impart dignity to undignified experience, and arouse deep emotional responses. The music of our songs can both express our emotions and evoke them. "How greatly did I weep in thy hymns and canticles," says Augustine, "deeply moved by the voice of thy sweet-speaking Church." To this evocative power of song he expresses an emotional response, describing how "the agitation of my piety overflowed, and my tears ran over, and blessed was I therein."[74] Expression and evocation are two sides of the same coin. Emotions are felt and expressed by worshipers partly because music evokes them. It is helpful to distinguish between the two, though hard to pinpoint where one ends and the other begins.

Because a good tune can momentarily transmute ugliness into beauty and give emotional satisfaction, it is reasonable to expect, and welcome, what Charles Wesley called the "holy pleasure" of music and song. As Erik Routley says, in his hymn "For Musicians," "in praise of God meet duty and delight."[75] Within certain boundaries, giving delight is a proper aim of church music and congregational song. On a practical level, if worshipers find no enjoyment in the music, they will probably not be edified by either the music or the words.[76] Yet "delight" means more than entertainment, or the modern, self-gratifying sense of the word "pleasure." When choosing hymns, choruses, songs, anthems, and instrumental works for worship, it is not enough to ask, "Will it be enjoyed?" One must also ask, "In what context, to what end, and with what relevance to what precedes and follows it?" Congregational song gives holy delight only when it serves the prior claims of devotion to God, justice, and frugality.[77]

Sentimentality

Unfortunately, the delight engendered by music and song is sometimes mindless, either quite disconnected from the lyrics or exaggerated beyond their meaning—feeling for feeling's sake, as it were. Don Hustad calls this "sentimentality," and defines it as "superficial emotion, or emotion not based on full reality, association without communication." He recalls meeting someone who said that the nineteenth-century gospel song "In the Garden" was her favorite hymn, but didn't know and didn't care which garden it was. She was responding, not to Christ's resurrection encounter with Mary Magdalene, as versified in the lyric and

---

74. Quoted in Hustad, *Jubilate II*, p. 31.

75. First line of a hymn written in 1976 for the dedication of the organ in Westminster Presbyterian Church, Lincoln, Nebraska. © Hope Publishing Company. All rights reserved. Used by permission.

76. Hustad, *Jubilate II*, p. 29.

77. On this, see Chapter 5, below.

interpreted by the tune, but to something else, something less—nostalgia perhaps, or a pleasant tune known from childhood, or at best the experiential couplet, "And he walks with me, and he talks with me, and he tells me I am his own," where the "he" could be any desirable suitor rather than, specifically, Christ risen from the dead. Hustad describes his own, similar response when, as a child, he was moved by hearing his mother sing Norwegian Pietist hymns with guitar accompaniment, without understanding a word of the text.[78]

To sharpen our diagnostic skills, Don Hustad pinpoints symptoms of sentimentality in a church's music program.[79] One symptom is overuse of favorite music regardless of its liturgical significance. It is good to choose familiar and favorite hymns and anthems, but if they are placed anywhere, at random, just because we like them, we're falling into sentimentality.

Similarly, if the music bears little or no relationship to the rest of the service, it is being chosen for the wrong reasons. I vividly recall Sunday worship in a socially aware, spiritually alive Presbyterian church where the liturgical theme was the common virtues that God wishes to form in us, while the music was J. S. Bach superbly played on the organ and sung in German. Music and liturgy flowed through the service like two great rivers, Missouri and Mississippi—except that the rivers never met. Though this was high-quality art music, it was an example of aesthetic sentimentality. Other warning signs of sentimentality are a failure to sing up to the full theology and experience of the congregation and resistance to new musical selections and new forms of music.

Emotional Stage Management

When Oliver Sacks walked across a room to turn off a nonfunctioning tape recorder, he was experiencing the emotive power of music. But his experience was not stage-managed. Someone else had not chosen a Mendelssohn violin concerto in the hope that it would make him walk.

From ancient times, however, the emotional power of music has prompted attempts to use it deliberately to generate a particular response. The Hebrew Bible gives two classic examples. When the prophet Samuel anoints Saul as king of Israel, he tells him to go and meet a company of prophets. The prophets are playing music that has

---

78. Hustad, *Jubilate II,* pp. 32–33. I amplify and interpret Hustad's discussion.
79. Ibid., p. 33.

sent them into a frenzy. Saul will be similarly affected by the music, thrown into a prophetic frenzy with them, and "turned into a different person," divinely inspired (1 Samuel 10:5–7).

Music can also have a calming effect. Later in the narrative, Saul is subject to violent mood swings, as the Spirit of God leaves him and a destructive ("evil") spirit from God torments him. His servants suggest that he find someone skilled in playing the lyre, so that "when the evil spirit from God is upon you, he will play it, and you will feel better." David is chosen for the task, and his music therapy is so effective that he gets a permanent position. Thus, "whenever the evil spirit from God came upon Saul, David took the lyre and played it with his hand, and Saul would be relieved and feel better, and the evil spirit would depart from him" (1 Samuel 16:14–23).

Should we try to make the persuasive effect of particular styles of church music more predictable? Should we "muddle through," only half knowing what we're doing, or learn more, so that we can decide what not to do? The issues are not new, but modern knowledge, technology, and techniques make them more acute.

In the biblical narrative, Saul is advised to go into a music-induced trance, believing that God will use it to give him insight. In his culture, this was a believable, though unconventional move, and caused people to generate a short-lived catch-phrase, "Is Saul among the prophets?" (1 Samuel 10:9–12). Saul apparently trusted the One whose Spirit he believed was possessing him. Without trust and trustworthiness, persuasion becomes manipulation. Our culture makes us wary of manipulation, even as we are attracted by church marketing that appeals to our musical taste, income, and age bracket, or swayed by a barrage of thirty-second advertising spots whose blend of music, visual images, slogans, jingles, and dialogue approach the status of an art form. Because a Christian community is founded on God's trustworthy love, in which its members are called to live, move, and have their being, deception, deviousness, or covert action are inadmissible. As a stimulus to further work, here are four proposals:

1. *Be honest about the persuasive power of music, and pray that it may be wisely used.* Learn what you can about its evocative power, and pray your own prayer for the "true use of music."[80] Pray that music may inspire us, but not deceive us; that it may serve God's lov-

---

80. See Wesley's hymn, Chapter 1, and Appendix, at the end of this book.

ing purpose, not lesser human aims; and that it may move us, not merely to delight and enjoyment, but to experience God's love, joy, justice, and peace. The good news is that, though we may hope to evoke particular emotional responses, they cannot be guaranteed: in a socially diverse congregation, people react differently to different styles and to the same piece of music, according to their upbringing, gender, social class, and so on. Even in a congregation of upper-income, paleface, Midwestern American suburbanites presented with carefully chosen contemporary music, there will be a diversity of personal reactions.

2. *Recognize that, whatever music we choose for worship, and whatever else we hope it will do, we hope it will have some emotional impact.* Imagine being welcomed into worship with the announcement that "today's music includes an organ voluntary by Bach, inspirational choruses, favorite hymns, and contemporary music from our Praise Band. We hope it will leave you completely unmoved." Such a hope would be absurd and impractical: absurd, because pointless if achieved, and impractical, because almost all music is emotionally evocative. Certainly, there are effects we hope it *won't* have, such as, boredom, anger, distress, and despair.

3. *Choose music that aims to engage the mind as well as the emotions, and mimics meaningful progression as well as emotional flow.* Discussing the movie *Bob Roberts*, Linda Clark suggests that enthusiasm without discernment is mindless, leaving us open to manipulation. Discernment without enthusiasm is heartless, leaving us uninvolved, unable to give ourselves to God in our community of faith. Thus, "God's praise requires both enthusiasm and discernment. What better way to put them together than through singing, which requires both discernment (attending to what we sing) and commitment (surrender to God ineffable, God incarnate and God in our neighbor)?"[81]

4. *Let God be God.* Don't use music's evocative power crudely, as "a contrivance to get money,"[82] stampede people into a decision, or sway their emotions in times of vulnerability. (In a Pentecostal-type service I attended, the pastor's decision to cut out music during the healing time, so as not to sway our emotions, was refreshing, correct,

---

81. Clark, "From Inner, Material Necessity."
82. Thomas Symmes, of Bradford, Massachusetts, in 1712, quoted by Mitchell, *I Don't Like That Music*, p. 24.

and memorable.)[83] Make a space between evocative music and vulnerable moments, so that decisions are made, and trust bestowed, freely and responsibly. When music does accompany such moments, make it appropriate but nonintrusive. When music has moved a congregation, don't deflate enthusiasm or trample on silence by jumping in with commentary, announcements, or chat. Pause, wait, then say, "Thanks be to God" or "Amen."

Functional Art

The autonomous power of song tunes reminds us that congregational song, like church music in general, is a functional art, meaning that congregational songs are sung during the church's ordinary and festive activities, to add intensity to them and express their significance.[84] Not all music should be functional. Any culture, and all cultural levels, need music that challenges conventions and pushes the boundaries. To say that church music is a functional art does not mean that art music and popular music are superior or inferior to it. It means only that church music cannot be free art, an end in itself. "It is art brought to the cross, art which is dedicated to the service of God and the edifying of the church."[85]

"Functional" should not be reduced to mean simply "if it works," judged by whether the music is applauded, attracts more worshipers, gets media coverage, or multiplies financial pledges. To say that church music is a functional art means, on the contrary, that it is composed, played, and sung *to serve the purposes of God*, particularly in the church's expression of its worship, its fellowship, and its mission."[86] Accordingly, it should be judged by how well it fulfills those functions. "There is no point in comparing a worthy anthem or a historic hymn-and-tune with Mozart's opera, *Don Giovanni*, or even with his *Requiem*." Be it classical, folk, country, bluegrass, jazz, rock or, avant garde, "good church music glorifies God and edifies human beings in the context of the ministries of the church."[87]

---

83. New Life Christian Fellowship, Biddeford, Maine, May 1998.
84. Hustad, *Jubilate II*, p. 22.
85. Ibid., p. ix.
86. Ibid., p. 22; emphasis mine.
87. Ibid., pp. 23 and 24.

Tunes and Words

The autonomous power of music makes it necessary to examine the relationship between tunes and lyrics. A technical discussion is beyond my scope, and is best done with tune books in hand and a music professional at the keyboard. I can, however, suggest general principles and give one or two (I hope accessible) examples.

One approach is to ask if, and how, the music of a congregational song is meaningful and satisfying: In itself, irrespective of the words? In spite of the words? Especially with these words? Only with these words? Though it is impossible to be objective about tunes and texts already familiar, I surmise that Vaughan Williams's tune SINE NOMINE, customarily sung to "For All the Saints," is memorable in itself if we put the lyric aside and hear it simply as music. I have the same hunch about the soaring, falling, and "trembling" melody of WERE YOU THERE, the tune for "Were You There When They Crucified My Lord?" and CRUCIFER, Sydney Nicholson's tune customarily paired with Kitchin and Newbolt's lyric, "Lift High the Cross."

When considering the relationship between a particular text and tune, we can ask if it fits in any of the following categories, and if not, find a new one. Some of my categories can be investigated by singing different common-, long- or short-meter tunes to the same text, using the metrical index of a hymnal.[88]

- *Disconnection:* Text and tune are strangers or nodding acquaintances. Neither has much impact on the other.
- *Opposition:* Text and tune are at odds with each other. The most frequent North American choice for Edmund Sears's hymn "It Came Upon the Midnight Clear," is CAROL, a lullaby waltz that contradicts the lyric's original (and often eviscerated) protest against war and poverty.[89]
- *Compatibility:* Text and tune are hospitable to each other. Some tunes are "open" to a variety of lyrics. When searching for a public-domain tune to pair with a new lyric, I often find sixteenth-, seventeenth-, and eighteenth-century tunes more accommodating than their nineteenth-century successors. Examples include WIE LIEBLICH IST

---

88. On poetic meter, see Chapter 8, below. All three of these poetic meters have four-line stanzas. Long meter has four lines of eight syllables each; common meter has 8.6.8.6; short meter has 6.6.8.6.

89. For a full discussion of this hymn, see Chapter 9.

DER MAIEN, Johann Steurlein, 1575; DUNDEE, Scottish Psalter, 1615; WARUM SOLLT' ICH, Johann G. Ebeling, 1666; SALZBURG, Jacob Hintze, 1678; GRONINGEN (WUNDERBARER KÖNIG), Joachim Neander, 1680; and IN BABILONE, Anonymous, ca. 1710. To my ear, all are well crafted, with satisfying repetition, variation, development, and completion.[90]

- *Liftoff*: A pleasing tune "carries" an undistinguished, undesirable, or archaic lyric. The tune SPANISH HYMN (or MADRID), though repetitive, is to many ears not unpleasing, and in North America is usually paired with Christian Henry Bateman's "Come, Christians, Join to Sing," which has a series of predictable rhymes (sing/King; voice/rejoice/choice; high/sky; adore/evermore), no discernible direction, archaisms with nowadays weird or misleading meanings ("life shall not end the *strain*" and "to us he'll *condescend*"), clichés ("heaven's blissful shore"), gap-filling repetition ("praise *yet* the Lord *again*"), and the recurrent interruption of illogical "Amens."[91]

- *Unity*: when music is well matched to its text, "the music dramatizes, explains, underlines, 'breathes life' into the words, resulting in more meaning than the words themselves could express" and a more powerful effect than text or music alone.[92] Though it is hard to unravel the effect of

---

90. These tunes appear in a variety of recent hymnals. I have written new lyrics for them in my 1998 collection, *Visions and Revisions,* as follows: "Come, Let Us Praise What God Has Done" / DUNDEE, #5; "Joy Has Blossomed Out of Sadness" / IN BABILONE, #12; "Love Alone Unites Us" / GRONINGEN (WUNDERBARER KÖNIG), #39; "To Christ Our Hearts Now Given" / WIE LIEBLICH IST DER MAIEN, #25; "Stranger Christ, from Death Returning" / WARUM SOLLT' ICH, #33; and "Water, Splashing Hands and Face" / SALZBURG, #26.

91. Lyric and tune appear in many North American hymnals, sometimes slightly revised: for example, *Baptist,* #231; *Chalice,* #90; *Presbyterian,* #150; *Rejoice in the Lord,* #357; and *United Methodist,* #158. *Voices United* (#345) has an attractive remake, "Come, Children, Join to Sing," which drops the redundant "Amens." The United Methodist version reads: (1) "Come, Christians, join to sing: Alleluia! Amen! loud praise to Christ our King: Alleluia! Amen! Let all, with heart and voice, before his throne rejoice; praise is his gracious choice. Alleluia! Amen! (2) Come, lift your hearts on high: Alleluia! Amen! Let praises fill the sky: Alleluia! Amen! He is our guide and friend; to us he'll condescend; his love shall never end: Alleluia! Amen! (3) Praise yet the Lord again: Alleluia! Amen! Life shall not end the strain: Alleluia! Amen! On heaven's blissful shore his goodness we'll adore, singing forevermore: Alleluia! Amen!"

92. Hustad, *Jubilate II,* p. 31 and pp. 25–26.

familiarity, pairings like "Our God, Our Help in Ages Past" / ST. ANNE; "Amazing Grace" / AMAZING GRACE (NEW BRITAIN); and "Hark! the Herald Angels Sing" / MENDELSSOHN are nowadays widely experienced as "natural" or "inevitable."

Another approach, in counterpoint with the above, is to seek suitable metaphors for the relationship between tune and lyric. Does the lyric ride on the shoulders of the tune? Does the music color, illuminate, or overshadow the words? Does it marinate the lyric, embrace it, or undermine it?

The Matrix of Meaning

Finally, the meaning and significance of a congregational song depend on what Dwight Vogel calls their matrix of meaning,[93] namely, the interplay between the context in which the song is sung, the melody chosen, and its tempo, harmonization, and accompaniment style. The tune ORIENTIS PARTIBUS appears in many hymnals. It is a medieval French melody, in triple-time. In the *United Methodist Hymnal* (U.S.A., 1989) it is paired with two lyrics, my own "There's a Spirit in the Air" (in 6/4 time) and (with slight rhythmic variations, in 3/4 time) a Christmas carol entitled "The Friendly Beasts," whose opening stanza reads: "Jesus, our brother, strong and good, / was humbly born in a stable rude, / and the friendly beasts around him stood, / Jesus, our brother strong and good."

Many United Methodist churches use "The Friendly Beasts" as a processional hymn at Christmas services and pageants and are accustomed to playing and singing it sedately, as the procession slowly moves down the aisle. Sometimes, this performance practice spills over into a quite different context and affects the singing of "There's a Spirit in the Air," making it tediously slow. The error is easily avoided by reading the text, which invites joyful, energetic praise: "Lose your shyness, find your tongue; tell the world what God has done." When this is understood, it is clear that with my lyric, ORIENTIS PARTIBUS needs to move energetically, as a joyful dance. I conclude that one step toward the

---

93. Notes taken at a presentation by Dwight Vogel, Garrett-Evangelical Theological Seminary, Evanston, Illinois, July 1993. On "meaning" and "significance," see Chapter 5, "Assessing the Lyrics of Congregational Song."

most suitable matrix of meaning is to *read the lyric* of the hymn or song: the lyric will tell us how to sing it—and how not to sing it.[94]

One of my lyrics begins, "Christ is risen! Shout hosanna! / Celebrate this day of days. / Christ is risen! Hush in wonder; / all creation is amazed." In one hymnal it is paired with the tune HYMN TO JOY, simplified from the final movement of Beethoven's Ninth Symphony (the tune is more commonly sung with "Joyful, Joyful, We Adore Thee"). A moment's attention to the lyric, and minimal knowledge of German, will make it clear that this is a mismatch. Beethoven composed his theme for a German lyric; in German, no one syllable is stressed (spoken more loudly) than any other. In Beethoven's Ninth Symphony, the opening couplet of Goethe's poem reads: *"Freude schöne Götter-funken, tochter aus Elysium"* ("Joy, beautiful ray divine, daughter of Elysium"). Because each syllable is equally stressed, Beethoven's melody has a series of equal-value notes, with only one variant, so that the song is sung thus: "Freu-de-schö-ne-Göt-ter-fun-ken, toch-ter-aus-El-*y*-si-um." English, however, has a pattern of stressed and unstressed syllables; my lyric reads, *"Christ* is *ris-*en! *Shout* ho-san*-na! / Cel-e-brate* this *day* of *days!"* A good tune will match, at least partially, its lyric's stress pattern. To another hymnal committee I suggested a Polish carol tune, W ZLOBIE LEZY, widely sung with *"In*-fant *ho-*ly, *in-*fant *low*-ly, *in* his *bed,* a *cat*-tle *stall."* Moved from Christmas lullaby to Easter celebration, W ZLOBIE LEZY goes well with "Christ is risen! Shout hosanna!" provided it is sung and played brightly and with a quicker tempo. Here again, the lyric tells the careful listener what kind of tune best matches it, and how it should be sung.[95]

A good example of the matrix of meaning at work is Martin Rinkart's "Now Thank We All Our God." Rinkart (1586–1649) wrote the original German lyric in about the year 1633, as a table grace before meals. It is almost always paired with the tune NUN DANKET ALLE GOTT, composed for it by Johann Crüger (1598–1662) during or shortly before 1647. The "meaning" of this hymn will vary considerably according to when and why it is sung: at American Thanksgiving, for example, or at a funeral, after the birth of a child, at a wedding, in the aftermath of a

---

94. See *The United Methodist Hymnal,* #227 and #192. "There's a Spirit in the Air" is widely published elsewhere, most frequently (and most suitably) to John Wilson's tune, LAUDS.

95. *Presbyterian Hymnal,* #104, uses HYMN TO JOY (Ode to Joy). *United Methodist Hymnal,* #307, accepted W ZLOBIE LEZY at my suggestion; *Chalice Hymnal,* #222, followed suit.

natural disaster, or as invading troops approach a town. Its tempo, and (if played on an organ) registration will also alter its impact. Nowadays, the tune is mostly experienced through Fclix Mendelssohn's nineteenth-century harmonization, which in Erik Routley's view deformed it,[96] while the text reaches us through Catherine Winkworth's translation. These and other ingredients are part of the hymn's matrix of meaning. Our response to it may be altered, for example, when we hear that both tune and text were crafted in wartime. Crüger was twenty at the beginning of the Thirty Years War (1618–48) and fifty when it ended. The war preoccupied Rinkart from the time he was thirty-one until a year before his death at the age of sixty-three. War broke out the year after he was appointed archdeacon of Eilenburg in Saxony, and refugees flooded into the town, even though it was smitten by the plague. Eventually, Rinkart was the only pastor left alive in the city, and presided over five thousand funerals (including his wife's), sometimes numbering fifty to sixty per day. Against that background, he wrote his table prayer, based on Sirach 50:22–24:

> Now thank we all our God,
> with heart and hands and voices,
> who wondrous things has done,
> in whom this world rejoices;
> who from our mothers' arms
> has blessed us on our way
> with countless gifts of love,
> and still is ours today.
>
> O may this bounteous God
> through all our life be near us,
> with ever joyful hearts
> and blessed peace to cheer us;
> and keep us still in grace,
> and guide us when perplexed,
> and free us from all ills,
> in this world and the next.
>
> All praise and thanks to God
> the Father now be given;
> the Son, and him who reigns

---

96. See Young, *Companion to the United Methodist Hymnal*, p. 498.

with them in highest heaven;
the one eternal God,
whom heaven and earth adore,
for thus it was, is now,
and shall be evermore.[97]

Necessary Song

Because a good tune suggests bodily movement, moves musically in interesting ways, and mimics emotional flow, it is natural, even necessary, to put music into words and sing them. As Richard Watson observes, words sung together are no longer text on a screen or in a book, but language in action. "The writing comes off the page, back into the body, lungs, blood."[98] In other words, the physical activity of singing embodies, and matches, the way the song itself moves. Music that powerfully mimics meaningful progression almost cries out for words to match it. When text matches tune, the song moves, develops, and unfolds in an intensified way, because it incorporates the clearer, widely shared meanings that language provides.

Emotion, too, needs a singing voice. The expressive power of vocal sound has been understood from antiquity; the idea that musical instruments can express human emotion on their own is quite modern: Samuel Wesley (1766–1837) was surprised to find Haydn's instrumental music moved him, even though it was "performed by inarticulate instruments."[99] Because it needs no other instrument than the human voice, composer Alice Parker describes singing as the most human of the arts. "It needs no materials or tools, other than the ear and throat—along with mind and heart. When we sing alone, we are led out of ourselves into the world of the song. When we sing together, we create a community, a communion in sound. The group becomes more than the sum of its parts: It is creating beauty."[100]

Without a memorable and evocative melody, the best hymn, song lyric, or chorus is rarely sung and soon forgotten. Besides its autonomy as music, a tune also interprets the words that are sung, imposing pauses, fluidity, emphasis, and musical structure.[101] Yet,

---

97. Ibid., pp. 497–98, 737, 819.
98. Watson, *The English Hymn*, p. 24.
99. Storr, *Music and the Mind*, p. 66.
100. Parker, *Melodious Accord*, p. 115.
101. Watson, *The English Hymn*, p. 22.

though music has autonomous power, and though sung lyrics depend on their tune, there is a sense in which they take logical priority over it. Taizé choruses and Gregorian chant demonstrate the appeal of nonverbal, or uncomprehended, vocal sound. Nonetheless, congregational songs generally need sounds that make sense and say something.[102] To sing "doo doo dee dah dee dee dum doo" instead of "Our God, our help in ages past" has limited value and appeal. "Rhubarb and tulips sweetly grow, but we are singing rhubarb" would be a ludicrous lyric in worship, however appealing its music.

The words of a congregational song relate to its tune like passengers to an airplane. The words cannot be sung without the tune, just as passengers cannot fly without the plane. The tune can be played without the words, and a plane can fly without passengers. But no airline likes flying empty planes! The tune of a hymn, chorus, psalm response, or Sanctus makes limited sense on its own. If played without the words, it recalls them, if known to the hearer: one reason, perhaps, why hymn-tune organ arrangements get consistently good sales. When we hear such music, it is usually obvious that it's a hymn tune, whether or not we know the matching words. Even if you have scant recollection of Luther's "A Mighty Fortress Is Our God," hearing a chorale prelude on its tune (EIN FESTE BURG IST UNSER GOTT) may give you a quasi-Lutheran experience. To summarize, good music can make average words fly, or lift words better off grounded. It makes our best words soar, and stores them in memory. When emotion needs to be voiced, it expresses itself occasionally in wordless vocal sound. Usually, however, emotion needs words as well as music. As Paul Westermeyer puts it:

> Joy inevitably breaks into song. Speech alone cannot carry its hilarity. The physical equipment we use to laugh is the physical equipment we use to sing. From laughter to song is a small step. To praise God, the highest form of joy, is to make music . . . Sorrow also inevitably breaks into song. Speech alone cannot carry its moan. The physical equipment we use to cry is also the physical equipment we use to sing. From mourning to song is but a small step. To cry out to God in lament, the deepest form of sorrow, is to make music.[103]

---

102. On the appeal of nonverbal vocal sound, see Chapter 6, below.
103. Westermeyer, *Te Deum,* p. 28.

Hallmarks of Congregational Song

I have shown that congregational song tunes have musical autonomy, as they make meaningful progressions and give beauty to our emotional flow. Looking at the relationship between text and tune, I find that it is humanly natural, helpful, and sometimes necessary to break into song. This shows that congregational song is pragmatically important. I shall now try to show why it is indispensable.

Congregational song is by nature corporate, corporeal, and inclusive; at its best, it is creedal, ecclesial, inspirational, and evangelical. Each characteristic is theologically important.

Corporate

Congregational song is *corporate*. Singing together brings us together, whether we are a choir, a congregation, or a group of friends and relatives around a piano. On a practical level, musical melodies and rhythms make corporate speech more attractive and decisive. "Few congregations can speak well in unison, but many can sing very well together."[104]

More than that, as we sing together we belong to one another in the song. We agree, in effect, not to be soloists, self-absorbed meditators, or competitors, but to compromise with each other, join our voices as if joining hands, listen to each other, keep the same tempo, and thus love each other in the act of singing. For a congregation, its corporate song makes a theological statement: "We are the body of Christ." In the early church, the fact that the whole congregation sang together, in unison, was understood to be theologically important because it demonstrated the loving unity of all Christians. A first-century bishop, Ignatius of Antioch, said that the congregation was intended to be a united chorus,

> so that joined together in harmony [he means not musical harmony, but harmonious togetherness], and having received the godly strain in unison, you might sing in one voice through Christ to the Father, so that he might hear you and recognize you through your good deeds as members of his son.[105]

Today also, togetherness in song models togetherness in love, and reminds us that we are not a crowd, a mob, a swarm, or a flock, not a

---

104. Routley, *Hymns Today and Tomorrow*, p. 18.
105. Westermeyer, *Te Deum*, pp. 62–63.

chance agglomeration of individuals, but a unified, Christ-centered community. Though we do not submerge our identity in the crowd, singing together brings us together, demonstrating how we belong to one another in Christ.

Congregational song is corporate by choice, because individual persons decide to join with others. In John Wesley's *Directions for Singing,* the individual's response to God is the most important requirement. Yet the individual worshiper is not a soloist, but a member of the body of Christ. Because singing together is a powerful way of embodying our commitment to one another, Wesley insists that everyone join in everything ("Sing all"). Both he and his brother Charles were theologically trained clergy, well versed in music, who believed that the "holy pleasure" of congregational song was not merely enjoyable, but theological: so much so that when they met people who didn't like congregational singing, or said they couldn't sing, the Wesleys encouraged them to do so, saying, "Let not a slight degree of weakness or weariness hinder you. *If it is a cross to you, take it up, and you will find it a blessing"* (emphasis mine). John Wesley's "Directions" urges singers to listen to one another and keep time with everyone else, whether they like the tempo or not. They are to sing modestly, not bawl "so as to be heard above and distinct from the rest of the congregation." The point of these musical directions is theological: because their song is corporate, the singers should "strive to unite [their] voices together, so as to make one clear melodious sound."[106]

A member of a recent hymnal committee speaks in similar terms. Because God is the audience, it is clear that "the primary goal is not musical, but spiritual." The corporate nature of the song is signaled by the fact that no individual voice is heard, and no single participant receives recognition. When people give themselves to the song, "the congregation becomes a Spirit-filled organism which acts with one heart, mind and voice."[107]

Corporeal

Congregational song is *corporeal,* a body-experience. Music causes physiological arousal (using "arousal" in its psychological rather than narrowly sexual sense). It stimulates heightened alertness, awareness,

---

106. For the full text of these "Directions," see Appendix to this book.
107. William Lock, quoted by Hustad, *Jubilate II,* p. 448.

and excitement: "a generally enhanced state of being." Listening to music correlates with a marked increase in electrical activity of leg muscles, even when the subject is told to keep still.[108] When we listen to music, our brain apparently uses the body as a kind of storehouse or resonator. Though we can remember visual images, the brain has no built-in faculty for imaging, and remembering, time sequences. One solution is to use muscular movement: when we hear a phone number and have no immediate means of writing it down, we repeat it aloud over and over again in order to hold it temporarily in memory or memorize it. In effect, the brain is using the motor system of our throat, mouth, lips, and larynx to encode the information until we have it either memorized or otherwise recorded. Similarly, it seems that our brain remembers music partly by moving our bodies, even if the movement is so slight that it can be detected only experimentally. In this sense Nietzsche was right: we listen to our music through our muscles.[109] "When people insist that rhythm comes from the body, they are really talking about the pleasure they gain by representing rhythm in their motor systems."[110]

Conceivably, then, we use our muscle system to model the most important features of musical patterns. Though hard to prove, this certainly sounds plausible. Kinesthetic (bodily) motion lies deep in our existence. Hence, we can imagine the sequence of movements involved in opening the door of a car and easing into the driver's seat. We can feel the key as it slides into the ignition, coordinate gear lever, clutch, accelerator, and brake (or shift from park to drive), crane our neck as we back out of the driveway, steer the car, and drive off down the road—all without actually moving. Similarly, when we listen to music, "we use our bodies as resonators for auditory experience. The listener becomes the musical instrument, places himself [sic] in the hands of the music, allows himself [sic] to be played."[111]

Congregational singing is corporeal, also, in a more obvious sense: it is necessarily a physical, bodily activity. The Bible affirms that human flesh, and the human body, are part of the material universe that God creates and affirms as "very good" (Genesis 1:31: Paul's use of "flesh" in opposition to "spirit" describes, not the body as such, but

---

108. Storr, *Music and the Mind*, pp. 25–28.
109. As quoted by Oliver Sacks in Collins, "Doctor of the Soul."
110. Jourdain, *Music, the Brain, and Ecstasy*, pp. 148–49.
111. Ibid., pp. 325–26. Though his account is, he admits, speculative, it rings true.

human life in opposition to God[112]). Because "the Word became flesh and lived among us," revealing God's glory, full of grace and truth (John 1:14), we may logically affirm that "good is the flesh that the Word has become."[113]

By contrast, the early church acquired the increasingly powerful belief that the human body is shameful and distasteful, that sexual desire (seen as located in the body) is a temptation rather than a blessing, and that everything bodily is inferior to, and hostile to, our "spiritual" and "rational" nature. Though these beliefs and attitudes are fading, they cast a long shadow. Despite the growing use of dance, and a more informal atmosphere, many worship traditions still act as if the body were an embarrassment. We find it hard to talk or pray about bodily matters in worship. Our seating patterns minimize movement, and our movement vocabulary is limited. We stand, sit, crouch or kneel, pass the offering plate, and occasionally shake hands or hug each other as we pass the peace. At Communion, we take the tiniest portion of bread, wafer, juice, or wine, in the most disembodied manner possible, as if to say we're having a meal, but not really drinking and eating.

Yet God did not make us as brains walking on stilts, but as embodied beings. The Word became flesh, not disembodied intelligence, and our body life enhances or diminishes our spiritual life. Posture, eye contact, and body language help to shape our attitudes and relationships. When we sing from the heart, with full voice, some of us use our bodies more thoroughly, perhaps, than at any other time in worship. Our diaphragm expands to draw in air, which is expelled through the delicate muscles of the larynx, producing sound that resonates through the head, given meaning as tongue, teeth, jaw, and lips follow complex signals from the brain to form the words we sing. Persuade a congregation to sing the first stanza of "For All the Saints," giving it everything they've got so that the roof shakes, and you'll hear what a *bodily* experience congregational singing can be and rediscover how bodily commitment invites a commitment of spirit. Body and spirit are inseparable: when we sing with full voice our attitude changes. When body attitude combines with deepest beliefs, singers are taken out of themselves into a heightened awareness of God, beauty, faith, and one another.

---

112. Accordingly, the works of the "flesh" include strife, quarrels, dissension, and envy, as well as fornication and drunkenness (Galatians 5:19–20).

113. First line, and refrain of a hymn by Brian Wren, *Piece Together Praise*, #23.

Inclusive

Congregational song is *inclusive*. Almost everyone can sing, and everyone can make a joyful noise, whether or not it rates as tuneful. Male or female, old or young, few of us drone on one note. As already indicated, ordinary speech has frequent pitch changes, even within a single syllable. Only 5 percent of the population are "monotones" (or, more respectfully, "uncertain singers"), meaning they are unable to hear a half-step alteration in pitch.[114]

When we speak, most voices have varieties of pitch as well as rhythm. Singing organizes these variations. If you can imitate a fire siren, your voice can change pitch, and therefore, in principle, you can sing. Most people find it hard to speak for long in a monotone, even when trying to sound robotic. Whether child or adult, most North Americans who say "Uh-oh" are voicing a minor third. Though often untapped, musicality is inborn and flourishes when developed from an early age. "Original music arises naturally from minds exercised in it, not from some muse inhabiting a fortunate few."[115] Thus, when singing together is a priority people grow in confidence and enjoyment. In one congregation I visited, the choir director was offering adult classes, wittily called "Quavers," about the basics of music, chord structure, sight-reading, and other singing skills.[116]

Because congregational song is inclusive, "the crucial question is not, 'Do you have a voice?' but 'Do you have a song?' "[117]; not "Can you sing?" but "Will you make a joyful noise?" Unfortunately, not everyone feels able to make a joyful noise. "How can I keep from singing?" asks an old hymn. "With ease!" some will answer. "When I was seven years old I was told to stand in the back row, move my lips, and make no sound." (Sadly, when told they can't sing, most people are apt to believe it.)[118] Others say, "I can't carry a tune in a bucket," with a wry smile of sadness and relief, or "I'm embarrassed to hear my own voice"—perhaps because it can't compete with opera singers, paid soloists, and popular entertain-

---

114. Jourdain, *Music, the Brain, and Ecstasy*, pp. 112–13.

115. Ibid., pp. 186–87.

116. Dennis Deyo, at Greendale People's Church, Worcester, Massachusetts, in 1995.

117. Hustad, *Jubilate II*, p. 448.

118. Campbell, *The Mozart Effect*, p. 119, claims this as a research finding, adding that one high schooler who didn't believe it was Elvis Presley.

ers. Others say, "I'm a pastor, not a musician," as if that settled the matter, or more plausibly, "The tunes go so high I can't sing them."

This last is a common response from men. One source claims that the typical male voice has dropped a step or two in the past half-century, and that men, in general, do not like to sing.[119] As a man who has always enjoyed singing, I can't imagine why it should be thought "unmanly," but if the feeling is there, it should be addressed. Though "monotonism" probably runs in families, and is mostly a male phenomenon,[120] most men (like most women) have a God-given, though often undeveloped, ability to sing. Congregational song was never meant to be professional; it can and should be confident and worshipful.

Inclusivity in song is a theological value, a corollary of unity. A congregation cannot demonstrate its unity in Christ if people are shut out from its song. In the early church, as Paul Westermeyer shows, "everyone was included in the song—not only men, but women, children, the baptized past and present, everyone." Before women were subordinated and silenced, and long before the laity became spectators at the Mass, the whole congregation sang together, with one voice. "The song took incarnational shape as the participation of the whole body was welcomed. Nobody was excluded."[121]

It follows that the unity of singers is more important than the quality of their song. When congregations learn how to sing more tunefully, they generally sing more joyfully. Nevertheless, it is more important to be joyful than tuneful. Not long ago, I had supper with one of the leading New Testament scholars in North America. He, his spouse, and I had just been to a Taizé-style vesper service in an Episcopal church. The conversation turned to hymns and congregational singing. "I need to sing," he said, "even though I don't know when I'm on key." I knew this was true, because we had sat next to each other in worship. "But singing is important to me. When I'm in a crowd with others, I can sing from my heart, and not worry about how it sounds."

How refreshing, today, to meet someone who knows this truth about congregational song! Years ago, when I first went to church, I joined in the singing because everyone else did. It would not have occurred to anyone to worry about how their voices sounded. Time and time again, in succeeding years, I have been in congregations

---

119. Wright, *A Community of Joy*, p. 33.
120. Jourdain, *Music, the Brain, and Ecstasy*, pp. 112–13.
121. Westermeyer, *Te Deum*, p. 64.

where people sing for the joy of it, smiling affectionately at the man who bawls off-key, or the woman whose voice cuts through concrete. Congregational song is healthy when people know they are accepted as they are, want to express their faith, and feel sufficiently convinced about it to make a joyful noise together, knowing they are not performing to one another, but offering themselves to God.

Creedal

Congregational song is *creedal.* Though ancient and modern creeds can certainly be sung, I am using "creedal" in a wider sense, meaning that congregational song helps us express a believing response in a self-committing way. Thus, "creedal" includes praise, thanksgiving, lament, trust, and commitment as well as statements of belief.

The creedal power of congregational song is rooted in our nervous system. In most people, the brain's left hemisphere prioritizes language skills, while the right hemisphere deals with musicality and the musical aspects of language. When severe left-brain injury damages or wipes out language skills, many can still sing the words to songs they know well, even though they can no longer speak them.[122]

Words-with-music, then, are memorized together, in a seamless unity of lyric and tune. When a tune is consistently sung with a given text, it gains mnemonic power. In other words, the music revives memories associated with its previous hearing, and brings to consciousness words repeatedly sung with it. Most listeners cannot recall melodies without at the same time remembering their lyrics.[123] At workshops and conferences, I often ask people to imagine being trapped in our meeting place by some natural disaster; we have food and water, but no hymnals, Bibles, or other worship aids. I suggest that in such a situation someone would eventually start to sing. To find out what might happen, I begin singing a hymn, inviting people to join me if they can. After the opening lines, I hold back, throwing the group on its communal memory. In North America, I use "Amazing Grace"; in Britain, "O God, Our Help in Ages Past." In almost every setting, Protestant, Catholic, or ecumenical, the group reconstructs the entire hymn, as people sing what they remember, tail off, then pick up again from cues given by others. If I ask audience members individually to

---

122. Jourdain, *Music, the Brian, and Ecstasy,* p. 274.
123. Ibid., p. 256. Most people, however, readily recognize lyrics apart from their melodies.

try to recall the words of a well-known hymn, many people instinctively hum or sing the tune, because the tune helps them recall the words. That is why, as Paul Westermeyer observes, "a group who sings together becomes one and remembers its story, and therefore who it is, in a particularly potent way."[124]

Congregational song is creedal, then, because the words of familiar songs help shape a congregation's theology, and music summons them in time of need. From a survey of congregational song, Linda Clark reports on the importance of familiarity. "People remarked over and over again on the importance to them of the *Gloria Patri* and the *Doxology*. Indeed, one research team reported that the only time there was any visible sign of life in their congregation occurred at the singing of the *Doxology* that accompanied the Offertory procession. With familiar music, people put down their books and sing their hearts out."[125]

Thomas Day tells a similar story. Visiting a thriving suburban congregation, he was not surprised to find, yet again, the "struggling-invalid singing so common in Catholic parishes." In the responsorial psalm, however, "the whole church seemed to light up with singing, and the booming sound of the congregation was astonishing."

Afterward, the organist revealed the secret of her success. She had taken a simple melodic formula that she thought was Anglican plainsong, and used it almost year-round as the congregation's refrain to the psalm. The words changed weekly, but the congregation heard the same melodic idea. They joined in because the familiar music evoked a sense of pride in ownership. Their singing had an effortless quality, and was part of the ritual, "not something irrelevant added to keep everyone busy." There was no coercion; the melodies sounded important, as if they had existed forever; and the tune was familiar and memorized.[126]

When a familiar song is sung, the meaning of the words is sometimes unimportant compared with the enjoyment of the tune. Yet, because music holds the words in memory, they can break into consciousness and surprise the singer. As Linda Clark observes, "The images of a particular hymn, both poetic and musical, initially draw the worshipper into the world of a hymn." When the hymn (or other song)

---

124. Westermeyer, *The Church Musician*, p. 34.
125. Clark, *Music in Churches*, p. 28.
126. Day, *Why Catholics Can't Sing*, pp. 86–87.

is familiar, its images "accompany the singers throughout their lives and surface in ordinary places, often without bidding, to reinterpret experience."[127]

By way of example, Tom Hunter recalls being in a congregation singing "The Church's One Foundation," a hymn his father described as an old chestnut, roasted through many singings. Unsure about whether he approved of all the metaphors (a female church as Christ's bride, for example), he nonetheless sang on: "I suppose it's sometimes best just to sing and not think about it. Besides, there's a pretty good tenor part in this one." His enjoyment of singing grew stronger, and he was drawn more by the music than the lyric. Then, in the second line of the fifth stanza, *an image pounced:* the 'mystic, sweet communion [with] those whose rest is won.' " Immediately he thought of his nineteen-year-old brother who had died, his nine-day-old niece, his wife's parents, the struggles of a dying father. "It's amazing how many people can flash through your mind in a span of six words. Suddenly the pain was so real I don't remember singing the last lines. I do remember wiping tears off the hymnal. What a relief for those people to win a little rest."

As the service continued the image spread, as he thought of others who need rest here and now. Sermon, prayers, Communion all contributed to this process. The final hymn was "Spirit of the Living God, Fall Afresh on Me." "It had," says Hunter. "It fell from an image in an old familiar hymn which is not even one of my favorites."[128]

The creedal power of congregational song has pastoral implications, because people made speechless or speech-impaired through illness or injury are often still able to sing. When Sarah Miller's mother-in-law was eighty-one, she had a stroke that made her unable to walk, speak, or care for herself. For five years she lived in a Minneapolis nursing home, giving her relatives the occasional alert look, but mostly with no sign that she knew them.

One New Year's Eve, Hugh and Sarah Miller went to see her. She sat in the lounge, in a wheelchair, held in her seat by a cloth strap, making no response. On New Year's Day her relatives gathered for dinner—sixteen adults and two babes in arms. They played games and watched TV till someone said, "Let's sing round the piano like we used to." They gathered and sang, enjoying the experience. Someone said,

---

127. Clark, *Music in Churches,* p. 6.
128. Hunter, "Thoughts While Singing: During the Hymn."

"Let's go get Mom." Three of the men drove off to bring her back from the nursing home. They wheeled her to the piano, and one of her sons stood beside her, his arm around her shoulders. They sang from an old book of hymns, and when they came to "Silent Night" they could hardly believe their ears. "Mom was singing too. Her voice was soft, but she was on key and she knew the words." Amazed, they kept on singing.

"They smiled at her and she nodded. They sang other carols and then went on to some of Mom's favorite hymns—'Amazing Grace,' 'What a Friend We Have in Jesus,' 'Holy, Holy, Holy.' She sang them all. It was a moment of incredible warmth and joy, blessing and almost magical beauty. Even when she couldn't recognize the faces of her own children, even when she seemed incapable of laughter or tears, the songs of faith were still alive. Deep within her spirit, below the frost line of illness and death, the hymns survived."[129]

Ecclesial

I have already noted that when a congregation sings together, its song is an acted parable of community. In the act of singing, the members not only support one another, but proclaim a community of faith reaching beyond the congregation that sings. Thus, the corporate inclusiveness of congregational song is *ecclesial*: it declares what the church aims and hopes to be, and reminds the singers of their common faith and hope. Discussing the slave song "Were You There When They Crucified My Lord?" Linda Clark notes that its question retrieves, not the event of the crucifixion, but its meaning for the singers, including the promise of resurrection. To this promise worshipers bring their own, present suffering, and the communal song brings hope to birth in the soul of the singers. "Even standing mute, letting the community take over when one's voice fails, an individual can have suffering transformed through the hope being proclaimed by others."[130]

Congregational song is ecclesial when we know that the community sings for us, even when we cannot join in, and that the song joins us with other singers, local and distant, past and present. When we sing a hymn by Isaac Watts, an African American slave

---

129. Miller, "Below the Frost Line."
130. Clark, *Music in Churches,* p. 7.

song, a translation of a third-century Latin hymn, or a South African freedom song, the song can take us, in imagination, beyond the place where we are singing, into the past and into other parts of today's world. Sometimes a brief introductory word can highlight, and dramatize, the spatiotemporal transcendence of congregational song.

An example may be helpful. Dietrich Bonhoeffer was a Lutheran pastor put to death for his opposition to Adolf Hitler in Nazi Germany. From childhood, Dietrich was surrounded by hymn singing, and drew particular strength and inspiration from the hymns of Paul Gerhardt. Arrested and imprisoned because of his connections with plans to overthrow Hitler's government, Bonhoeffer wrote that "Paul Gerhardt has been an unexpectedly helpful standby." In a letter to his parents he said, "It is good to read Paul Gerhardt's hymns and learn them by heart, as I am doing now."

Bonhoeffer was upheld by Gerhardt's hymns not because they appealed to him simply as poetry, or as songs of personal devotion. For him, their inspirational power was inseparable from their function as congregational songs. He recited them, or hummed them to himself in his prison cell, because they were songs he had sung in company with other Christians. In a book written before his imprisonment, he writes: "It is the voice of the Church that is heard in singing together. It is not you that sings, it is the Church that is singing, and you, as a member of the Church, may share in its song."[131] As Gerhardt inspired Bonhoeffer, so Bonhoeffer inspires others. People who sing Fred Pratt Green's translation of Bonhoeffer's prison poem, "By gracious powers so wonderfully sheltered,"[132] continue the chain of hymnodic inspiration.

---

131. Sydnor, "Dietrich Bonhoeffer and Hymns," p. 20.

132. See, for example, *A New Hymnal for Colleges and Schools,* #467 (with the heading, "Dietrich Bonhoeffer, 1944: a New Year's Eve poem from prison, translated by Fred Pratt Green, 1972"); *Hymnal 21* (United Church of Christ in Japan), #469 (in Japanese, translated from Bonhoeffer's German text, "Von guten Mächten treu und still umgeben"); *New Century Hymnal,* #413 (with the footnote, "Dietrich Bonhoeffer, theologian, professor, and leader of the German Opposition, composed the poem on which this hymn is based, 'New Year 1945,' while imprisoned by the Gestapo in Berlin. Four months later, Bonhoeffer was executed by special order of Himmler"); *Presbyterian Hymnal,* #342; *Rejoice in the Lord,* #55; *Rejoice and Sing,* #486 (with the footnote, "Written in prison, for the New Year 1945, a few months before his execution"); *Together in Song,* #617; and *United Methodist Hymnal,* #517. The date of Bonhoeffer's poem is poignantly significant: the war in Europe ended in May 1945, a matter of weeks after his death in the Tegel Prison, Berlin.

Inspirational

Because congregational song includes everyone, enabling a Christian community to express its faith in a unifying, self-involving way, it is also *inspirational*, lifting us out of the mundane and the ordinary. Singing puts the words of the song in motion, so that they are no longer "static sets of words on a page but shapes of sound that exist in time, beginning at one moment, traveling towards a point, and then drawing to a close and stopping at another moment." Because our lives also exist in time, and move through time with beginnings, developments, and endings, the music of a congregational song is "an aural image of the shape of feeling alive. When a congregation sings together, the words of the hymn come alive to them and mean more than just a statement of fact."[133] When words come alive in this way, through self-involving community song, worshipers experience the presence of God. William Cowper put this experience into words when he wrote, "Sometimes a light surprises / the Christian *while [s]he sings* / It is the Lord who rises / with healing in his wings." Isaac Watts did likewise: "Let those refuse to sing / *who never knew our God*; / But children of the heavenly King / May speak their joys abroad."[134] In the words of theologian Karl Barth, "The praise of God which constitutes the [Christian] community and its assemblies seeks to bind and commit and therefore to be expressed, to well up and be sung in concert. The Christian community sings. It's not a choral society. Its singing is not a concert. But from inner, material necessity it sings."[135]

Congregational song can elevate and heal the individual singer. In the fall of 1983, Oliver Sacks met Martin, then aged sixty-one. Suffering from Parkinson's disease, he had been admitted to a care facility, unable any longer to look after himself. Meningitis in infancy had left him mentally and physically impaired and subject to seizures. His schooling was as limited as his IQ, but he had a remarkable knowledge of music, derived from his father, a renowned opera singer. Though unable to read music, Martin had memorized over two thousand operas, was able to retain operas and oratorios after a single hearing, and could detail their singers, scenery, costumes, and staging. His singing voice was gruff and unstable, but he could sing in a choir, which was his greatest joy. For fifty years he had sung in churches and

---

133. Clark, *Music in Churches*, p. 6.

134. Leaver, "Hymnody and the Reality of God." (Emphasis mine.)

135. Karl Barth, *Church Dogmatics*, IV/3, 2, trans. G. W. Bromiley (Edinburgh: T. & T. Clark, 1962), pp. 866–67.

cathedrals, and in the large choruses of Wagner and Verdi at the old New York Met and later at Lincoln Center.

In January of the following year, Sacks saw Martin again. He was distressed, in pain both physical and spiritual. Asked what was wrong, he replied, "I've got to sing. I can't live without it. I've got to go [to church]. It'll kill me if I don't."

Not far away was a church. Transport was provided, and Martin was again able to sing. His encyclopedic knowledge of Johann Sebastian Bach made him a valuable resource at this, the only church in the diocese with an orchestra and choir, where Bach was regularly played and sung. Martin's knowledge, Sacks realized, was more than a body of facts. "For all his intellectual limitations, Martin's musical intelligence was fully up to appreciating much of the technical complexity of Bach." Central to Martin, as to his father, was the spirit of music, and the human voice "as the divine instrument made and ordained to sing, to raise itself in jubilation and praise." When Martin returned to singing, and to church, he recovered himself, "recollected himself, became real again."

> But the marvel, the real marvel, was to see Martin when he was actually singing, or in communion with music. . . . All that was defective or pathological fell away, and one saw only absorption and animation, wholeness and health. . . . As he soared up into the music Martin forgot that he was "retarded," forgot all the sadness and badness of his life, sensed a great spaciousness enfold him, felt himself both a true man and a true child of God.[136]

Evangelical

Finally, congregational song is *evangelical.* In today's culture, perhaps more than previously, "unbelievers come to church, not primarily to investigate the claims of Christ, but to investigate the Christ in us."[137] When congregational song is in good health, says Don Hustad, "it demonstrates the love relationship of the children of God and tends to reach out with 'arms of melody' to include those who are not already a part of the church," so that uncommitted people can sense "the reality of the Christian life in the voices and faces of the community of faith surrounding them."[138]

---

136. Sacks, *The Man Who Mistook His Wife for a Hat,* pp. 186–92.
137. Sally Morgenthaler, quoted in Hustad, *Jubilate II,* p. 310.
138. Hustad, *Jubilate II,* pp. 383 and 389.

Besides congregational song, other worship activities can—and should—be corporate, corporeal, inclusive, creedal, ecclesial, inspirational, and evangelical. But because congregational song is all these things in ways often powerful and at times unique, it is an indispensable component of Christian public worship. And because the church's beliefs, inclusiveness, corporate worship, communal nature, universality, and evangelical outreach are theologically important, congregational song is the proper concern of all its members, especially its music leaders, worship leaders, and pastors.

A parent's heart will feel the hurt
    each time a child is bruised,
and God was weeping like a child
    when Jesus was abused.

Which one of us would give a child
    a stone in place of bread?
What kind of God would be content
    as Jesus cried and bled?

The will of God is just and good
    but human choice can kill;
rejected love endured the cross
    and earth and heaven kept still.

We meet our Maker at the wound
    exchanging broken bread;
we share our grief with one who knows
    the pain when blood flows red.

Although we miss God's first design
    as Jesus dies alone,
God's final will cannot be lost;
    love rolls away the stone.

Daniel Charles Damon

Chapter Three

"A More Profound Alleluia": Encouraging the People's Song

How often, making music, we have found
a new dimension in the world of sound
as music moved us to a more profound
Alleluia!

To stop a door hinge's squeaking, it is essential to oil it; applying lubricant is neither an option nor an experiment, but a necessity. If congregational song is indispensable to Christian public worship, what are the essential procedures for strengthening it? Some guidelines have already emerged. This chapter will outline others, then summarize them all.

To encourage good congregational singing, we need to know what a particular congregational song can or cannot do in worship. For this purpose, let us look at two overlapping classifications: functional, and relative. Other purposes make other distinctions: between, for example, metrical psalm tunes and chorales; gospel hymns and social gospel hymns; the congregational song of Shakers, Mennonites, and Moravians;[1] and more recently between African American gospel music,

---

1. See, for example: on White gospel, Wilhoit, "The Music of Urban Revivalism" and " 'Sing Me a Sankey' "; and on social gospel hymns, Spencer, "Hymns of the Social Awakening." A helpful comparison between gospel and social gospel hymns is in Young, *My Great Redeemer's Praise*, pp. 92–104. On African American congregational song, see foreword and research notes in Farley Smith, *Songs of Deliverance;*

contemporary Christian sound, and Roman Catholic pop.[2] I shall step around such differences and focus on what congregational songs can or cannot do, and why.

Functional Genres

By "functional" I mean what one genre of congregational song necessarily does, or is able to do, that distinguishes it from other genres.[3] For a full appreciation of different genres we have to sing them, because they are differentiated by musical idiom as much as by their lyrics. Yet verbal discussion can give sufficient clarification.

Hymns are one important genre of congregational song. Dan Damon's hymn "A Parent's Heart Will Feel the Hurt" (p. 98) is an example. In form, it is a poem, designed for group singing, and written as a sequence of identical units, called stanzas. Each stanza has the same line length, rhythms, and rhyme scheme (if the hymn uses rhyme) as its predecessor, so that the hymn can be sung, stanza by stanza, to the same tune (I shall discuss the poetic structure of hymns in Chapter 8). Though I use the word "hymn" mostly in this functional sense, it is often used to describe the unity of text and tune ("We sang a hymn"), or more loosely ("hymn number 319"), to indicate items in a hymnal that may belong to this or other genres of congregational song.

Like other recent definitions of "hymn," mine is narrower than Saint Augustine's, who described a hymn as "a song embodying the praise of God." Though Augustine aptly describes the relationship between words and music,[4] his use of "hymn" is too broad for today's

---

Walker, *"Somebody's Calling My Name"*; Spencer, *Protest and Praise;* and Reagon, ed., *We'll Understand It Better By and By.* On Moravians and Shakers, see Teuscher, " 'Jesus, Still Lead On' "; and Christenson, "A History of the Early Shakers and Their Music."

2. Price, "The Impact of Popular Culture on Congregational Song."

3. Hustad lists the following types of congregational music in American churches: chant, chorales, metrical psalms, standard hymns, spirituals (white/black), gospel songs,"Southern" gospel songs (from the 1930s, associated with the Stamps-Baxter quartet), historic folk hymns, contemporary popular hymns (gospel, folk, country, rock, "soul," ballads), ethnic hymnody, and praise and worship music (*Jubilate II*, pp. 52–53). Though suitable for his purposes, Hustad's classification separates some types with similar functions (such as chorales, metrical psalms, and standard hymns), and leaves out others (such as rounds and canons, refrains, and service music).

4. "A hymn is a song embodying the praise of God. If there is merely praise, but not praise of God, it is not a hymn. If there be praise, and praise of God, but not a song, it is not a hymn. For it to be a hymn, it is needful, therefore, for it to have three things— praise, praise of God, and these sung." Young, *My Great Redeemer's Praise,* p. 14. Recent writers cited by Young use "hymn" in the narrower sense I am following.

varied genres, and his focus on praise excludes other responses such as lament, confession of sin, and telling the Christian story.

Because it consists of a sequence of stanzas, a hymn can develop a theme and reach a conclusion. It can expound a doctrine or viewpoint, paraphrase an extended passage of scripture, or tell a story (functionally, then, my definition of "hymn" includes chorales and metrical psalms).

Dan Damon's hymn makes the most of these possibilities. Like all hymns, it arises from the author's viewpoint and invites singers to journey through it, saying yes or no to its theme. It begins with a comparison. As (good) parents feel pain when their children suffer, so God suffers when Jesus is crucified. The second stanza grounds this understanding of God in one of the "How much more?" comparisons of Jesus: "Is there anyone among you who, if your child asks for bread, will give a stone? Or if the child asks for a fish, will give a snake?" Because the only possible answer, from any normal parent, is "of course not," and because God is immeasurably more generous than we are, it follows that "If you then, who are evil, know how to give good gifts to your children, how much more will your Father give good things to those who ask him!" (Matthew 7:9–11).

By extension, a loving God could not possibly be glad when Jesus suffers on the cross, because "the will of God is just and good." Though divine wisdom no doubt foresaw rejection and crucifixion as a likely, or probable, outcome, it is not something God hoped would happen: it was human decisions that killed Jesus. At Communion, remembering Jesus' sacrifice, we meet our Maker, strengthened and comforted by the knowledge that God, also, "knows the pain when blood flows red." The final stanza draws a conclusion and adds an affirmation of faith. The crucifixion is neither God's "first design," nor humanity's last word. Because God's final will is life, not death, "love rolls away the stone," a line that concludes the hymn, ends the earthly story of Jesus, and opens the new story of the risen Christ.

The *chorus* is another genre of congregational song. Its lyric is a short statement, often but not always in verse. When sung, it is typically repeated, or "chained" with other choruses. It states its theme without developing it. Designed for easy singing, it aims to foster a mood of unity and "uplift" by soothing or energizing its singers. Examples include Karen Lafferty's "Seek Ye First the Kingdom of God"; Laurie Klein's "I Love You, Lord"; Les Garrett's "This Is the Day"; Jacques Berthier's "Jesus, Remember Me When You Come into Your Kingdom" and "Eat This Bread, Drink This Cup"; and Bob McGee's "Emmanuel."

It may seem strange to put Karen Lafferty, Bob McGee, Laurie Klein, and Les Garrett in the same bracket as Jacques Berthier, whose music from the Taizé monastery in France is a continent away from songs associated with evangelical-charismatic renewal. Yet, though different in theology and musical style, "Taizé" and "evangelical"[5] choruses are functionally more similar than different. Both have short, simple lyrics, with simple and, at best, memorable melodies. Both rely on repetition and lose much of their power without it. Only the most stubbornly intellectual congregation will sing a chorus only once. In "charismatic," "Taizé," and "contemporary" worship, repetition lasts for as long as it carries conviction. "The effect may vary from boredom—where a piece may actually stall after a while—to elevation, in which a piece may seem to take on a life of its own and one may be transported beyond the music and the text into a state of heightened awareness of some deep, unarticulated mystery."[6]

One difference between "Taizé" and "evangelical" choruses is that in the former the singing is typically quiet and meditative, with little or no accompaniment, while the latter is often loud and boisterous, with a powerful instrumental sound.[7] "Taizé" lyrics span a range of themes, usually related to historic liturgy and the church year, while "evangelical" choruses focus more on "me and Jesus." I shall discuss both forms of chorus in more detail in Chapter 6, below.

Despite their functional differences, the boundary between chorus and hymn is flexible. Some congregational songs combine a chorus-refrain with a degree of thematic development in the stanzas, as in Al Carmines's "Many Gifts, One Spirit" and Donald Fishel's "Alleluia, Alleluia, Give Thanks to the Risen Lord."

Rounds are a third distinct genre of congregational song. In traditional rounds like "Three Blind Mice" and "Frère Jacques," or congregational rounds like Jacques Berthier's "Gloria, Gloria, in Excelsis Deo" and Natalie Sleeth's "Go Now in Peace," each singer or group of singers sings the same melody, starting at defined intervals after each other, then returns to the beginning, continuing until group feeling or

---

5. It is hard to find an apt label for choruses of this type. "Charismatic chorus" is ecclesiastically inaccurate: noncharismatic Baptists also sing them. "Praise chorus" is descriptively inadequate: not all such utterances are praise. For want of a better word, I use "evangelical," to locate this type of chorus in the mainstream of North American revivalism.

6. Tamblyn, "Has the Hymn Had Its Day?"

7. Hustad, *Jubilate II*, pp. 46ff.

leader's signal ends the singing. A round resembles a chorus in its simplicity, and, of course, a chorus can be composed as a round. In a round, however, congregational unity is enhanced by the "to and fro" effect whereby one section of the melody resounds pleasingly against another, and the congregation can enjoy the effects of part-song without having to learn different voice parts.

Technically, a round is a type of canon, where a musical theme, or "subject," is begun by instrument(s) or human voice(s), then copied ("imitated") at a specified short interval by other instrument(s) or voice(s).[8] The imitation can be an exact copy, or the subject can be sung or played backward, upside down, at a different tempo, or in other modified ways. The precise term for my phrase, "exact copy," is "canon at the unison." A number of hymn melodies can be treated as canons at the unison, with the congregation divided into two or more voice parts, or with voice parts and handbells. Examples include "For the Beauty of the Earth" (tune: DIX), "Many and Great" (LACQUIPARLE), "Amazing Grace" (AMAZING GRACE / NEW BRITAIN), "O Little Town of Bethlehem" (FOREST GREEN), "Be Thou My Vision" (SLANE), and of course the tune TALLIS' CANON, to "All Praise to Thee, My God, This Night" or "Praise God, from Whom All Blessings Flow."[9]

The difference between rounds and other canons is in their ending. In a "finite canon," the leading instrument or singer (the *dux*—Latin for "leader") has to add notes, or a short coda, to make up the time lag between it and the following parts. The *dux* cannot begin the melody again until everyone else has, as it were, caught up. In a round, however, each instrument or singer can go straight back to the beginning, start over, and keep going indefinitely, or until an agreed signal prompts everyone to stop. Thus, the relationship between "round" and "canon" is that all rounds are canons, but not all canons can be treated as rounds.

Many songs, hymns, and gospel songs have *refrains*, in which one or more lines of lyric are repeated at the end of succeeding stanzas. Though lines can of course be repeated *within* stanzas, I focus on end-of-stanza refrains because they are the type most easily separated out for congregational singing.[10]

---

8. For a more precise account, see the *New Harvard Dictionary of Music*, s.v. "Canon," and "Round."

9. Examples from Hopson, *The Creative Use of Handbells in Worship*, pp. 31–32.

10. Lorenz, "Chorus, Refrain, Burden," discusses different types of repetition in congregational song.

Refrains, then, are a fourth functional genre of congregational song. In both "classic" and "contemporary" worship, a refrain can summarize the essential message of a congregational song or provide a memorable moment of participation in a song otherwise inappropriate, or too difficult, for the congregation to sing.

The American "gospel song" or "gospel hymn" has become a classic example of the first type of refrain. Though typically nowadays sung congregationally, gospel songs like "Wonderful Words of Life" (P. P. Bliss) or "Standing on the Promises" (R. Kelso Carter) were created for mass evangelism in an era when many members of the target audience were either illiterate or could not read well. The stanzas carried the message of the song, while the refrain provided the punch line, designed to be sung, and remembered, by the audience. Like music-hall songs of the same period, the refrain was what the audience wanted to sing, preferably several times over. As with advertisements then and now, the refrain provided the slogan designed to make the "product" memorable and appealing. Now, as then, such refrains are "inclusive": when well known they have wide appeal and enable everyone, including prereading children, partially literate adults, and sight-impaired seniors, to join in the song.

In the second type, a song is sung *to* the congregation or audience, to which its refrain makes a simple, unified, congregational response. Such refrains have a long tradition, with many variants. As Bill Tamblyn observes, "the shantyman helped coordinate the activities of sailors by using call-response forms"; music-hall and pub singers used refrains to help the audience "own" the song; solo songs with congregational refrains occur in evangelical outreach past and present; and the call-response method is a consistent, original feature of African, and African American, worship.[11]

Today, as in the past, the song sung to a congregation can be of several types, such as a praise-band rock number presenting today's

---

11. Tamblyn, "Has the Hymn Had Its Day?" Examples of call-response form include the African American slave songs "Come Out the Wilderness" (e.g., *United Methodist Hymnal*, # 416); "He Never Said a Mumbalin' Word" (e.g., *Chalice Hymnal*, #208, *Presbyterian Hymnal*, #95, *United Methodist Hymnal*, #291); and "Standin' in the Need of Prayer" (e.g., *Chalice Hymnal*, #579, *New Century Hymnal*, #519, *United Methodist Hymnal*, #352). A more recent African example is "Thuma Mina" ["Send Me, Jesus"], (e.g., *Chalice Hymnal,* #447, *New Century Hymnal,* #360, *Together in Song,* #249, and *Voices United,* #572).

theme to an audience of seekers; a psalm chanted by a cantor; or a song from a solo guitarist in folk, folk-rock, soft-rock, country, or other popular style. In both "contemporary" and "traditional" worship, the call-response or stanza-refrain has many possibilities. "The soloist can bring the psalm to life, can help focus the meditation, [and] can teach the people their part as a structural feature of the music in 'responsorial' settings where soloist and assembly mirror one another."[12] If the gathering enjoys singing, the refrain is an anticipated time of participation; if unused to corporate song, the refrain gives an opportunity to grow into it and rediscover its "holy pleasure." Congregational refrains free the song writer and singer to express their message in the stanzas without being limited by the claims of communal utterance. A refrain responding to the presumed voice of God (presented by choir or soloist) also frees the congregation from the illogicality, not to mention arrogance, of singing as if it were, itself, God.

Three other functionally distinct genres must be mentioned. By *chant*, I mean any music, in whatever style, that makes it possible for text not written in English verse (such as psalms and canticles) to be sung by a congregation. This is a loose definition, putting Gregorian, Anglican, Byzantine, Gelineau, and other subgenres under one roof, but it suits my particular and limited purpose.[13] During the 1970s, a British choral group, the King's Singers, demonstrated the versatility of the genre by rendering the Highway Code (Driving Manual), with solemn humor, in Anglican chant.

Ritual song (a more accurate term than "service music"[14]) describes short, congregational utterances that move the action of worship. Examples in the Roman Catholic Mass and Protestant Word and Table liturgies include the Sanctus ("Holy, holy, holy") and Agnus Dei ("Lamb of God, who takes away the sin of the world"), which have prescribed places in the action, as the congregation responds to what the worship leader has said or sung. In other traditions, these and other pieces are used more freely, though

---

12. Tamblyn, "Has the Hymn Had Its Day?"

13. *The New Harvard Dictionary of Music*, s.v. "Chant," "Plainsong," "Gregorian Chant," "Byzantine Chant," and "Anglican Chant." Though these types differ, they share the capability of making unmetered verse, or prose, congregationally singable.

14. I owe this insight to Don Saliers. The utterance is a song, not merely "music," and it moves the ritual, meaning the action of the worship service.

usually predictably, as with the widespread American use of "Praise
God, from Whom All Blessings Flow" to the tune, OLD HUNDREDTH
(quaintly known as "*The* Doxology"), at the presentation of the offering,[15] or a particular sung "Amen" at the end of the service.

Last but not least, from Pentecostal traditions comes *spirit singing*,
an informal, improvised congregational utterance. Individual worshipers sing in tongues, or sing phrases like "Thank you, Jesus," "Praise
you, Lord," "Hallelujah," or "Praise the name of Jesus." They sing
simultaneously, with varied tempos, rhythms, and pitches. According
to Calvin Johansson, most utterances are sung on one pitch, chanted
freely, or in a monotone, with an overall effect not unlike chant. Melis-
mata (more than one note to a syllable) are often used: the singer uses
any syllable of any word to sing several notes in a continuous string.
Normally only one chord, the tonic, forms the harmonic basis of the
song, with individuals singing the root, third, and fifth, with passing
notes, neighbor tones, and other embellishments. There are no set
beginnings or endings. When a congregation worships in this fashion,
each person singing individually without regard to coordinating with
another's song, "the whole effect is similar to the gentle strumming of
a harp."[16]

Don Hustad uses a similar comparison when describing how, at one
service he attended, the pastor invited the congregation to "let the
Holy Spirit have its way in prayer." The organ struck a chord in F, and
everybody began to improvise Spirit singing. "The effect was that of a
sustained F major chord, with auxiliary and passing tones, as if it were
produced by wind blowing through the strings of an Aeolian harp."
After a while, the pastor led out in a refrain of "Great Is Thy Faithfulness," which produced the best singing of the evening.[17]

---

15. In Britain, singing this doxology at the presentation of the offering used to be
(and perhaps still is) the preserve of Presbyterians. In the U.S.A., other doxologies are
sometimes sung at this point, as a variant or substitute.

16. Johansson, *Music and Ministry*, p. 141.

17. Hustad, *Jubilate II*, pp. 284–85. See his articles, "Let's Not Just Praise the
Lord" and "The Historical Roots of Music in the Pentecostal and Neo-Pentecostal
Movements." See also Duncan, "Music among Early Pentecostals"; Larson, "We
Have Come a Long Way"; Wohlgemuth, "Praise Singing"; Harvey, "An Active Process
of Responding to God"; and Johansson, "Singing in the Spirit."

Relative Classifications

Congregational songs can also be classified in terms of how they relate to a particular worship tradition. In any tradition or congregation, it can be helpful to distinguish between "our songs" (well known, often sung, probably from "our" culture and history) and "other people's songs" (familiar or unfamiliar, but from a different culture, language, and experience). If the distinction is made provisionally, reverently, and inclusively, it opens us to the diversity of Christian experience, and takes us beyond our own horizons, thus dramatizing the ecclesial aspect of congregational song (see pp. 93–94). In a paleface, middle-class congregation, for example, slave songs, black gospel songs, Hispanic, Native People's, and "global" songs can be sung in two ways: without comment or introduction, if familiar, as songs that express the congregation's own faith; or with brief background, as songs that also express the joy, sorrow, faith, and struggle of other members of the body of Christ.

In categorizing the genres of congregational song in functional and relative terms, I aim to be practical. My list of functional categories may be incomplete, and the boundaries between them are flexible. If you accept my analysis, it follows that a *"good congregational song" is one that is excellent and has integrity in terms of its own genre,* in its words, music, and interaction between them. It makes no sense to compare hymns, choruses, rounds and refrains and declare that one genre is superior or inferior to another. It also follows that a single genre can include varying musical styles, as with "Taizé" and "evangelical" choruses.

Acoustics, Architecture, and Seating

In a book on contemporary worship, Timothy Wright says that "people enjoy the comfort of their home, and they look for that same homey feeling in church." Fair enough, but not if we follow his advice and install too much in the way of "comfortable padded pews" and "appropriate drapery."[18] When considering the acoustics of their

---

18. Wright, *A Community of Joy,* p. 49. British English would replace "homey" with "homely," which to Americans means plain and unattractive.

worship space, congregations often move from good intentions to disastrous conclusions. Yes, it should be as welcoming as a good home. No, it shouldn't be filled with soft fabrics. However "homey" we want it to be, a church sanctuary is a public space, not a private space; a meeting room, not a living room. In that space, people should be able to hear one another when they sing, so that they can be brought together in a community of song.

Acoustically, a worship space must reconcile different, sometimes conflicting, claims. For worship leaders' speech, the sound of musical instruments, and the singing of choirs, vocal ensembles, and soloists, a worship space can be compared to a concert hall or lecture room. By contrast, congregational singing asks that the whole room be treated as a sound source. This is an important distinction, and not all architects and acousticians are aware of it.[19]

For effective congregational singing, the acoustic environment must provide support and encouragement for the ordinary voice, enriching and enhancing it, "so that the singer feels encouraged to sing out, to participate in the communal act of lifting the voice in praise." When we sing together, the acoustic response of the worship space should give each individual a sense of being part of the assembly, "an assurance that one is not alone nor unduly exposed," and that "as small as one's contribution may seem, it is a meaningful part of the whole."[20]

Some surfaces absorb sound; others reflect it. If the sound source is at a distance from the sound absorber, the sound will blossom and fill the space before absorption begins to dampen it. In congregational singing, however, the sound producer is also a sound absorber. From an ordinary, untrained voice, the greatest concentration of sound energy usually projects forward and down at a slight angle—into the back of the person in front, who provides as much sound absorption as four to six square feet of conventional acoustical ceiling tile.[21]

It follows that a singing congregation needs acoustically reflective surfaces as near as possible to all the singers. Though walls can assist the speech, song, and instrumental music of worship leaders, they are too far away to help most singers in the congregation. Ceilings have some value, provided they are sloped or undulating; a flat ceiling reflects the singers' own voices at first rebound, and singers don't hear

---

19. Sövik, "Architecture for Hymn Singing," p. 14.
20. Fleisher, "Acoustics for Congregational Singing" (in *Acoustics of Liturgy*).
21. Ibid.

other people as well as they ought.[22] Crucially important, therefore, are pews, chairs, and floor.

Pew and chair cushions absorb sound and cover up the sound-reflecting quality of their surface. When comfort requires cushioning, it should be kept to a minimum, and made with a vinyl covering or from fabrics with a latex or vinyl backing, which provide less sound absorption than more common fabric upholstery.[23]

Carpets absorb sound and negate the sound-reflective quality of the floor. Where essential for public safety, or to minimize the sound of footfalls, they should be of the thinnest material possible over the minimum area necessary.[24] Otherwise, carpets should be banished from church sanctuaries in favor of attractive, sound-reflective alternatives like quarry tile and wood parquet.

Seating patterns affect congregational singing. The more we can see other singers in the congregation, the more we are likely to hear each other, as other voices reach us before being absorbed, and visibility enhances our sense of singing together. Architect Edward Sövik notes that "if you ask a group of people, young or old, to sing together in a free space without an audience, they will almost inevitably gather in a circle."[25] Without verbalizing it, they are shaping themselves as a community. Because a congregation is not a theater audience, an army parading before its officers, a class of medical students watching an operation, or a workforce being motivated by its CEO, its seating pattern should not follow such secular models.

Thus, the appropriate configuration for congregational song is not the arrangement dictated by what goes on in cinemas, parade grounds, classrooms, and lecture theaters, but something more like a circle, square, or rectangle. In such a setting, people are more aware of one another and have a stronger sense that they are a single body whose parts belong together.[26]

---

22. Sövik, "Architecture for Hymn Singing."

23. Fleisher, "Acoustics for Congregational Singing."

24. Ibid., pp. 9–10.

25. Sövik, "Architecture for Hymn Singing."

26. Ibid. Sövik says that a fan shape may seem appropriate, but isn't. Its concentric arcs focus on a center point, "and though the comparison to a bull ring or arena may be exaggerated, it is not inapt; in the arena, architecture 'instructs' people that they should pay attention, not to each other, but only to the thing or event at the center." He recommends "a geometry that is not as static as a fan or circle and does not so clearly imply an audience / performer division" (p. 11).

The space may be properly configured, but if people sit too far apart, their singing fades away. Congregational singing requires proximity. "If I am more than three feet away from you, I don't sing, because you might hear me. If I am less than three feet away, I do sing, because I can hear you."[27] When the space is too large for the congregation, worshipers instinctively scatter, like sheep seeking pasture. Once they understand the importance of "togetherness," people are more likely to accept roping off unused space, or making physical alterations.

Finally, the worship space must be as free as possible from external and internal background noise, be it traffic in the street, or the air conditioner, ventilator, or heating system inside the building.

Respect the Familiar—Repeat the New

Don Saliers asked a group of older adults which hymns meant most to them, and why. One factor was body memory: people remembered when they first sang the song, and memories of sight, hearing, smell, and touch associated with it. The songs that meant most had been learned in happy social situations and reinforced by being sung on different occasions, in different types of gathering.[28]

Congregational songs have formative and inspirational power only when repeated, repeated, repeated, and repeated until familiar. When the song is familiar and beloved, people sing their hearts out. Yet new songs need to be learned, as old ones lose their relevance and appeal.

It follows that pastors, musicians, and educators should develop strategies for teaching songs and repeating them, till they become part of a congregation's repertoire. When membership turnover is rapid, frequent repetition becomes more important, since newcomers need to learn songs already familiar to others. For new songs to be learned, and old ones coherently repeated, it is essential to cooperate and plan ahead. Following are some principles and suggestions.

1. *Find out and use people's favorite hymns and songs:* whether liturgically (coherently in the flow of worship) or informally, as in an opening sequence where one song is chosen by a member of the con-

---

27. Not an exact quotation, but taken from notes on an address by John Bell to the Hymn Society in the U.S.A. and Canada, San Diego, July 1995.

28. From notes taken at a workshop led by Don Saliers, April 1998.

gregation. If we respect what people know, and honor it by using it appropriately, they are more likely to trust us when we offer something new.

2. *Think generationally, but not stereotypically.* In an all-age congregation, the heart-songs in people's memory banks may range from late nineteenth-century parlor music to the latest hits in popular music subcultures. Some of the young, however, like old songs, and the young in heart like new ones. Make occasions for people from different age groups to choose, and have played or sung a song they cherish, and say why. Story sharing opens windows of understanding and reduces conflict over musical styles.

3. *Respect the contract of enjoyment.* If segments of the congregation have a repertoire of familiar songs, the contract of enjoyment is engraved on their hearts. Unwritten and unsigned, it is as real as a salary agreement. The positive version reads, "If you choose three songs we know, we'll gladly try one we don't." In the negative version, "grudgingly" replaces "gladly."

4. *Look over the lectionary wall.* If you follow a lectionary, you probably have booklets suggesting five hymns and three choruses to fit next Sunday's scripture readings. Choose from that selection only, and you'll have liturgically appropriate songs and no congregational repertoire. One or two lectionary-minded songs are enough.

5. *When introducing a new song, begin with the words* (particularly important for hymns and choruses). Read them aloud. Read them to the congregation. They are not text on a screen, or syllables under musical notes, but language in action. Are these words worth singing? Do we believe what they say? Let people dwell on their meaning as spoken and experience their power.

6. *Unless the tune is instantly accessible, have the congregation hear it several times before singing it.* Plan three or four Sundays ahead, so that the organist or pianist can work the music of the song into a variety of liturgical situations several weeks before it will be congregationally sung. Use all or part of the song as a choir introit, instrumental solo, vocal solo, youth choir anthem, and so on. By this method, an unusual tune starts sounding familiar. People may even say, "Why can't *we* sing this?"—a much better response than, "Why did you dump that new hymn on us this morning?"

7. *Teach new songs in happy social situations.* If your church doesn't have any, you have deeper problems than languishing congregational song.

8. *Repeat a new song two or three times within the first six months after it is introduced.* Learning to sing a song is like learning to drive a car: theory is insufficient—mind and body need to practice what is being learned. Thus, worshipers need repetition if they are to remember and enjoy the song.

9. *Sing short congregational songs on every possible occasion:* at potlucks, committee meetings, prayer meetings, retreats, and Sunday school classes. They can be rounds, choruses, hymn stanzas. Build a repertoire, and keep using it, so that newcomers learn the songs.

10. *Connect the song repertoires of Sunday school, vacation Bible school, church camp, and worshiping congregation.* Not every song crosses all the boundaries; be sure some do.

11. *Don't teach anything that must be denied in order to grow.* Southern Baptist friends tell me of a song they loved to sing in childhood Sunday school. It was a favorite because of its catchy tune and enjoyable rhymes. Sadly, the day came when its theology condemned it to extinction. They let it go, but with a sense of loss. The lyric ran: "The bells of hell go ting-a-ling-ling / for you, but not for me. / The blessed angels sing-a-ling-a-ling / through all eternity. / O death, where is thy sting- a-ling-a-ling, / O grave, thy victory? / No ting-a-ling-a-ling, no sting-a-ling-a-ling, / but sing-a-ling-a-ling for me."[29]

12. *Keep records of what is sung.* One day you will leave, and another Sunday school superintendent, organist, choir director, or pastor will take your place. They need to know, accurately, what this congregation has previously sung.

Choosing What to Sing

Asked to explain their hymn choices during the previous month, a pastors' workshop brainstormed more than thirty reasons. Some reflected personal agendas: "It was my Mom's favorite"; "It was sung at my wedding, and I want to sing it again"; "I like it, and I want the congregation to learn it so they can sing it at my funeral." Others had a whiff of congregational politics: "To honor a choir member"; "The

---

29. Price, "The Impact of Popular Culture on Congregational Song," pp. 11–19, quotes the lyric from Henry Wilder Foote, saying that Foote records it as having been sung during the nineteenth century. I have met people who remember it from the 1940s and '50s.

organist likes it"; "The organist dislikes it." Most reasons were liturgical: "To fit the season of the liturgical year"; "To prepare for or respond
to prayer / scripture / the sermon / Communion," and so on. Some
responded to the needs and perceptions of the congregation: "It is
familiar, and builds community"; "To respect our congregation's tradition, while hoping to expand it"; "To recognize its value to the people who requested it."

Whatever the reasons for choosing a song, it will be sung with
energy only when it makes sense to the singers. Yet worshipers and
worship leaders may have different perceptions of the kind of sense it
should make. In her congregational survey, Linda Clark found that
"those in a position to choose hymns for worship pick out those that
follow principles of good worship design; congregations like to sing
hymns they are familiar with."[30] Clergy and musicians typically seek
theological and liturgical coherence (response to a scripture reading,
appropriateness for the liturgical season, preparation for Communion,
and the like). The congregation is more interested in experiential
coherence, whereby the song coheres with people's lives. As people
bring their life experience, and previous religious experience, into the
sanctuary, their "old hymns" function as musical and verbal icons, able
to reconnect them with previous experience and transform that experience in light of the present day. Liturgical coherence relates to the
ordering of the worship event. Experiential coherence relates the worship event to the life of the congregation and the lives of individual
worshipers.

Both views believe the shape of worship is important: that, for
example, an opening hymn should bring people together and help
them "cohere." From both viewpoints, a familiar opening song is
essential so that, "through exuberant singing, the worries of the week
and the hassle of getting the kids out of the house that morning are put
aside."[31] When people say they like or dislike particular hymns or
songs, what they often mean is that "the music of worship needs to
provide a voice for my faith."[32] If worshipers are to find a singing voice
for their faith, worship leaders must choose congregational songs that
are experientially, as well as liturgically, coherent.

---

30. Clark, *Music in Churches*, p. 30.
31. This and the preceding quotation are from Clark, *Music in Churches*, p. 31.
32. Ibid., p. 71.

Finding or Becoming a Song Leader

When I first visited the United States I was convinced that people could sing together only with piano or organ accompaniment, and that I could not possibly lead them in song. I had sung in church choirs, enjoyed singing, but had no special training. In America, age forty-seven, my sense of vocal incompetence was reinforced. I kept meeting people who amazed me by the fact that they had studied voice, and who sang superbly: rich baritones, electrifying altos, soaring sopranos, arresting tenors. I couldn't do what they could do: how could I possibly stand up in front of an audience or congregation and teach them a new song?

Gradually, both preconceptions were overturned. I learned that some songs go as well or better without accompaniment, and that I, even I, can lead a group of people in song. I can't conduct, and I'm limited to hymns, choruses, and other songs I know well. But for the purposes of congregational singing, I've learned to be an amateur song leader.

If I can do it, you probably can! If you like singing, can carry a tune, and believe in the song you're singing, you can learn how to lead a congregation in song. In saying this, I intend no disparagement of professional music training. Professional training is important if not essential for instrumental leadership in worship, choral conducting, high quality singing, and teaching others to understand and appreciate music. Many musicians are skilled in encouraging congregations to sing and leading them in song. Most of what I have learned about song leadership I've picked up from watching them and reading what they write. All I mean to suggest is that song leadership can be learned, to a greater or lesser extent, by the interested amateur. In some situations, the interested amateur is the only person available.

Here, then, are some principles and suggestions. If you're already a song leader, you probably know most of them. If you're not, I encourage you to start.

1. *Why we need a song leader:* A human being with an ordinary voice is in almost all circumstances the best teacher, because human beings with ordinary voices will be singing the song. Playing a hymn through on organ or piano is much less effective. Having a choir sing it is less effective, though feasible. But a group of singers does not provide the best model for one voice; a piano produces sound by tapping

strings; and an organ uses or digitally imitates the sound of pipes. Neither organ nor piano can do what voices do, nor can they model the lines and phrases of a song. "And no instrument can cope with words— a prime responsibility of the model."[33]

People learn best not only from hearing another voice but also from seeing the song leader. When musical notes are signed in the air (an age-old practice known as chironomy[34]), sighted singers pick up their pitch and rhythm much more easily than when they are merely sung.[35] In large gatherings, sound travels slowly, but the speed of light is practically instantaneous. When the song leader moves arm and hand, everyone can respond at once. Hearing a cue from an organ is different. The sound takes so long to travel that by the time those at the back of a large room hear it, the organ has moved to the next note.[36]

A song leader humanizes the song and makes learning a memorable experience. "A loved face is inextricably bound up with the song in memory, as it should be. Song comes from human beings to human beings, and the best teaching comes from someone who loves to sing, who loves the song and the assembly and can bring them together."[37]

2. *Qualifications, partly psychological:* A song leader must be able to sing in tune, with "a true voice, but not necessarily a trained one."[38] Too "professional" a voice can inhibit, rather than encourage, ordinary singers. I know an outstanding song leader with a thin, reedy voice— in tune, but not vocally pleasing. When she sings, you sometimes wonder if she can finish the line. She always does, and the congregation always sings back confidently. Her musical skill, confidence in the song, and willingness to let us hear her less-than-wonderful voice give encouragement and inspiration.

---

33. Parker, *Melodious Accord,* pp. 78 and 83.

34. *New Harvard Dictionary of Music,* s.v. "Chironomy." The use of hand movements to indicate approximate pitch and duration is widely attested: in ancient Egypt, Israel, and Greece, Byzantine cultures from about the 8th century C.E., in India, and in Coptic and Jewish communities of the Near and Middle East to the present day, especially in cultures without musical notation. See also Foley, *Foundations of Christian Music,* p. 65.

35. Bell and Maule, "Ten Golden Rules for enabling the least confident of people to teach new songs to the most cynical of congregations," *Heaven Shall Not Wait,* pp. 140–41.

36. Parker, *Melodious Accord,* p. 81.

37. Ibid.

38. Ibid., p. 82.

If you can learn, over time, to show the length and pitch of notes with your hands, that's helpful, but not essential. If you do, make gestures simple, clear, and unobtrusively welcoming, "helping each individual focus on the song."[39]

Beyond that, believe in your own voice as a teaching instrument: "It is the voice of an apprentice angel."[40] Believe that others can enjoy singing as much as you do, and show that you believe in them. "Years of being told, and telling themselves, that they cannot sing can be redeemed by the confidence you show in others' abilities."[41] Show your confidence verbally, in the way you introduce a song, and nonverbally: through face and body language, show contact with and sympathy for each individual in the group.[42]

3. *When to teach a song:* In worship, the best time to teach a song is before the service begins. If I am a worshiper and you are my song leader, don't ask me to learn a song in the middle of worship—I will be annoyed and distracted because suddenly, instead of worshiping God, I have to worry about following your directions. At committees, potlucks, and hymn-sings the atmosphere is more informal, but it is still often helpful to teach the song at the beginning, so that it can be enjoyed and entered into later.

4. *How to teach a song:* Begin by learning it yourself. Learn the melody by ear, and by heart, so that you know the song and don't have to worry about notes on a page. If, like me, you can't always sight-read the melody or pick it out on a piano, find someone who can play it and have you sing it back, phrase by phrase, until you know it. Sing it in the shower and in your car. Sing it to your children or to the cat. Sing it, enjoy it, and believe in it: "If you are uncertain about a song, that will be the first thing your 'trainees' detect."[43]

As you learn the song, analyze it as best you can. How does the complete melody break into shorter phrases? Where will ordinary singers need to take a breath? When teaching it, take a breath there yourself, to model the most natural phrasing—but rarely, if ever, tell a congregation when to breathe: it's one directive too many. Does the song have a chorus, a melodic phrase repeated exactly, or the same melodic

---

39. Ibid.
40. Bell and Maule, "Ten Golden Rules."
41. Ibid.
42. Parker, *Melodious Accord*, p. 82.
43. Bell and Maule, "Ten Golden Rules."

idea a step higher? What are its ups and downs, its peaks and valleys? Congregations intuitively recognize some of these features: bringing them to conscious awareness makes a song more manageable.

Plan how you will teach the song and what to say about its structure, so that you can teach the melody in recognizable sections. If it has a chorus, say so and teach it first; then sing the first two stanzas yourself; have everyone join in the chorus then pick up the tune of the remaining stanzas as you go along.[44]

"Introduce a new song with enthusiasm; never with an apology."[45] Don't kill a song by saying, mournfully, "Well, we've got a new hymn this morning; the organist chose it. You won't know it, but maybe you'll pick it up as we go. So the organist will play it, and the choir will render it, and then we'll see what we can do."

Teach by having people hear you sing the melody, not see you look at music. In the United States, one reason why people don't sing is their belief that singing means reading music. This perception stems, paradoxically, from nineteenth-century attempts to improve congregational song by printing words "interlined" with music, and teaching people how to "read" it (sing it at sight) off the printed page. Though much good came of these developments, they left the abiding impression that the reading of music precedes the singing of music. "The obvious corollary has been drawn by those who were not good readers or singers: they could not and should not sing in church with their congregations."[46] Some do read music; it is nice if you can; and many people are helped by seeing the visual shape of a melody on a page. But mostly, in most parts of the world, people learn a new tune by hearing it and joining in. So do that. Have people put away songbooks and hymnals and learn the melody by ear. Strange though it may seem, "it is easier to teach an unfamiliar song. People will echo back what they have just heard rather than what they remember or what they see on the page."[47] They will also mimic your mistakes, unless you disarmingly correct yourself.

Work in musical phrases: "A phrase is a 'memorable unit'—anything longer is too much to remember."[48] "Teach a breath or two lines

44. Ibid.

45. Ibid.

46. Westermeyer, discussing the influence of composer and teacher Lowell Mason, *Te Deum,* p. 289.

47. Parker, *Melodious Accord,* p. 79.

48. Ibid., p. 83.

at a time, whichever is shorter," and "Don't teach a new phrase until the present one is recognizable."[49] Hearing and singing back the melody a phrase or line at a time (lining out) is an efficient way to learn a new song, provided it isn't dragged on through several stanzas. This old method still works well, because "one voice is providing the model for each individual listening, teaching the whole (pitch, rhythm, text, mood, dynamics, affect) without extraneous material (harmony or accompaniment) to confuse the listener."[50] If the melody is too long or too difficult to put words with it first time round, teach and have it sung to "la."[51] Sometimes the last line should be taught first, so that the singers reach it with a feeling of coming home, not getting lost. Sometimes the rhythm of a line or chorus is best taught first, by hand clapping, before the notes are sung.

Use your most natural, expressive voice, and show that you love the song and want to share it. You are a worshiper to be copied, not a performer to be admired. Have the members of the group listen to one another as they sing, and "require the group to sing lightly. I call this 'listening singing' and it's the opposite of the football cheer."[52]

In general, teach without accompaniment. As the song becomes known piano, organ, and other instruments can enrich and support the singing. But, as indicated above, an unaccompanied voice is often the best teacher. "Accompaniment does not help the congregation sing better. Sometimes it gives them a convenient excuse: The music will continue whether we sing or not."[53]

If you have conducting skills, attend closely to the congregation and don't go through the motions of directing a symphony chorus. I vividly remember chapel worship at a Southern Baptist seminary. As preacher for the day, I faced a large congregation, filling the chapel. In front of me was a song leader, who also faced the congregation and conducted all the hymns. There he stood, stanza by stanza, moving his arms like a spider spinning a web, following a ritual once meaningful, now pointless—because out of three hundred worshipers, no one was watching him. Be sure, therefore, to keep eye contact with the group.

---

49. Bell and Maule, "Ten Golden Rules."
50. Parker, *Melodious Accord,* p. 83.
51. Bell and Maule, "Ten Golden Rules."
52. Parker, *Melodious Accord,* p. 87.
53. Ibid., p. 83.

"By your attitude, keep inviting everyone in the room to participate, from young to old, from accomplished musicians to beginners."[54]

5. *How to sing a song:* For a chorus, round, or other short song have everyone sing everything. In a longer song newly learned, have soloist(s) sing the first couple of stanzas, refreshing everyone's memory, then invite people to join in as the song proceeds. For variation, and because "people enjoy a [longer] song much more when they don't have to sing all of it,"[55] try alternating stanzas between different sections of the group. Beware of stereotyping. When alternating women and men, for example, don't assume that women should sing, "Dear mother earth, who day by day / unfoldest blessings on our way," and men respond with, "Thou rushing wind that art so strong."[56]

A Singer-Friendly Range

In previous generations, congregational hymns were often sung in harmony. Sopranos on the melody line could comfortably reach notes (E and F), too high for other singers, who sang harmony lines in the range most comfortable to them. Thus, the melody range could be greater than that of a song sung today in unison, by everyone in the congregation. Today, in settings where people rarely sing communally, and have fewer opportunities to exercise and extend their vocal range, it is important to choose tunes within a range that both low and high voices can sing.

Like other muscles, vocal cords warm up and become more flexible with use: most people can reach higher notes in the evening than in the morning. It follows that morning worship should usually begin with songs of medium pitch that everyone can sing.

Choirs typically enjoy singing in harmony, but many people in today's congregations do not. As one observer comments, "Most Americans do not have the skill to sing confidently in harmony and often stop singing if those around them do."[57] Though the speaker probably means "paleface Americans," he has a point. Thus, unless your congregation has a tradition of singing in four-part harmony,

---

54. Ibid., p. 87.
55. Bell and Maule, "Ten Golden Rules."
56. From the hymn "All Creatures of Our God and King."
57. Collins and Weidler, *Sound Decisions,* p. 9.

passed on invitingly to children and newcomers, strong unison singing should be the norm, aided by strong unison singing from the choir, at least during the opening stanzas of a hymn or verses of a song. When a four-part-harmony hymn has several stanzas, let the choir sing one, unaccompanied, in harmony. This highlights the words being sung, allows the choir to offer its skills, and gives the congregation opportunity to hear the hymn in a different way. If some worshipers like singing in harmony, invite four-part harmony in a specific stanza, supported by the choir.

Unaccompanied Song

Congregations sing well once they discover their own voice, which happens most easily when they sing familiar songs without accompaniment. This is not to deny the value of choirs and musical instruments. A good organ is a fine resource. It can call us to worship, move us to tears, and support a congregation that has found its voice and loves to sing. But it can't teach people to sing, because its sound is produced differently from that of the human voice and its volume can prevent you from hearing your own voice or the voices of others.

A good band, and good vocalists, are a fine resource. But if their volume overwhelms the congregation, or the vocalists are performers unable to encourage the people's song, band and vocalists become a liability. A choir is a wonderful resource, but if it siphons off the best singers, performs when it should be leading, or becomes a church's chief musical focus, it disempowers the congregation.

Because a congregation most easily finds its own voice through unaccompanied singing, a distinguished choral composer recommends singing at least one unaccompanied song per Sunday. "What we are after," she says, "is not 'art' as an unapproachable ideal, but the building of community through song." She has never found a group that couldn't sing. "But I have found that I must take away the helps: no accompaniment, no soloists, or choirs. Let the ministers and choir physically join the congregation, and allow people to focus on meaningful sound rather than on reading music." Once a congregational voice has been established, the organ and choir can enhance the musical experience. "But they can never be an adequate replacement for the song of the people."[58]

---

58. Parker, "How Can We Sing without the Organ?"

Questions for Music Leaders

Because congregational song is indispensable and needs to be fostered, it follows that the most important role of music leaders is to enable and empower the people's song. Once a year, pastors, worship committees, choir directors, choir members, organists, band members, and vocalists should get together and question assumptions. If we were starting a choir from scratch, with this group of volunteer voices, how could they best be used to help this particular congregation sing? Is it a priority, for that purpose, to have a new anthem every week? Is our band too focused on performance? Do its vocalists know how to teach our people to sing, and bring them in on a song refrain? Do choir and organist practice hymns and other congregational songs with the energy and commitment they give to voluntaries and anthems?

Whether they are leading the people's song or inviting a congregation to worship by hearing a musical offering, church music leaders should consider three questions. One is, "Can you be heard?" All too frequently, I visit churches where it seems that a generation has passed since the organist, choir director, or choir members sat in the back row and listened to organ music, vocal soloists, and choral works sung from "up front." Organs are rarely inaudible—but choirs often are. Choral anthems that resound across the chancel and bounce up and down from the ceiling, often sound thin or muffled at the back of the church. The words, too, get lost. The solution is simple, though often resisted: when a choir sings, whether it is offering an anthem or leading a congregational song, it should face the congregation and sing out, with clear enunciation, so that every word is heard.

When vocal and instrumental leaders face the congregation, they answer "Yes" to the second question: "Can you be seen?" In the age of radio, invisible choirs were culture-friendly. Today, our visual culture needs visible leaders. We need to see who's talking, singing, and playing and meet them, as far as possible, on our level. In our culture, "putting the choir up front augments the presentation rather than detracting from it. The joyful facial expressions and enthusiasm of the choir members add to the spiritual experience," and touch more of our God-given senses.[59]

The third question is: "Can you hear the congregation?" In her

---

59. Wright, *A Community of Joy,* p. 48.

survey of congregational song, Linda Clark found that "leaders of worship were not good judges of the quality of congregational singing. In many instances they considered the congregational singing to be better than the team reported it to be. Thus, the problem of the congregation's participation was often not even noticed."[60] The most likely explanation is that the music leaders in question were not able to hear the congregation's song because their own singing, or instrumental accompaniment, was too loud.

Be it organ, piano, synthesizer, or band, the instrumental accompaniment of congregational song is a fine art. It must be loud enough to lead, yet modest enough to support, the people's song. When it goes off track, it usually veers toward loudness. Today, high volume is a stylistic feature of live popular music, and over the years there have been frequent conversations about whether the organ was "too loud." But just because bands and organs can shake the walls, it does not mean that they have to. In their discussion of contemporary worship music in Lutheran churches, Dori Collins and Scott Weidler argue that "in worship, volume is not a question of instrumentation, it is a question of power. The power of sheer volume must be harnessed into a role of support rather than domination."[61] The key question is, can the congregation be heard over the instrument(s) and choir or vocal team? Their answer: "If you lead worship with an organ, guitars and piano, or an ensemble with electric instruments, this is a good rule of thumb: *if you can't hear the congregation, you are probably too loud.* It takes great care to be sure that you are not overpowering your congregation, and you need to find a way to welcome feedback on the subject." Because high-volume leadership smothers congregational singing, we should "challenge ourselves with the lowest possible level of amplification," recognizing that amplification may not be needed if the worship space is sufficiently resonant.[62]

Live Music, Low Amplification

Finally, congregational song is healthiest when live musicians lead it. If worship is an encounter with the living God, order must dance with spontaneity. A backing tape of organ music for hymns or a con-

---

60. Clark, *Music in Churches,* p. 43.
61. Collins and Weidler, *Sound Decisions,* p. 25.
62. Ibid., emphasis mine.

temporary Christian song solo has the order of law, untouched by the freedom of the gospel. Soloist or congregation is, in effect, singing someone else's song, and someone else's theology, from someone else's situation.

Live musicians—organist, pianist, guitarist, or band—can be sensitive to the mood of the congregation, the needs of the local community, and the flow of this week's worship, and can respond with "a new tempo, an emphasis on this or that phrase or word, holding such and such a note a bit longer than usual, or singing with slightly different mood and pacing."[63]

Summary

Here are some guidelines for encouraging congregational song. The first five are from Chapter 2. For the others, see above.

1. Choose songs to engage the mind as well as the emotions.
2. Avoid sentimentality, whether classical or popular.
3. Choose transitional music suitable for the transition it is making.
4. Don't use songs to fill in time or pass the time.
5. Recognize the persuasive power of music and use it reverently; don't use evocative music to sway people's decisions.
6. Know the functional genres of congregational song, including:
   Hymn: A sequence of stanzas, able to develop a theme and reach a conclusion.
   Chorus: A short song that states a theme without developing it—for easy singing, repetition, and "uplift."
   Round: A type of chorus, giving the effects of part-song.
   Refrain: An end-of-stanza chorus summarizing the message of a congregational song or giving a moment of participation in a song sung to the congregation.
   Chant: Music permitting a text not written in verse to be sung by a congregation.
   Ritual song: A short, congregational utterance that moves the action of worship.
   Spirit singing: Improvised congregational singing, usually based on a major chord.

---

63. Johansson, *Music and Ministry,* p. 148.

7. Distinguish between "our songs" and "other people's songs," and allow the latter to speak about the faith, hope, and struggle of other Christians.
8. Be sure the worship space has acoustics helping congregational singers hear one another: pews, chairs, and floor are crucially important.
9. Have people sit so that they can see as well as hear others: circle, square, or rectangle are the best configurations.
10. Be sure that people sit close enough together to hear one another sing.
11. Discover, respect, and repeat the familiar.
12. Strategize how to teach and repeat new songs.
13. Find out and use people's favorite hymns and songs.
14. Think generationally, but not stereotypically.
15. Respect the contract of enjoyment.
16. Look over the lectionary wall.
17. When introducing a song, read the words aloud, and speak them to the congregation.
18. Unless a tune is instantly accessible, have the congregation hear it several times before singing it.
19. Teach new songs in happy social situations.
20. Sing short congregational songs on every possible occasion.
21. Connect the song repertoires of Sunday school, vacation Bible school, church camp, and worshiping congregation.
22. Don't teach anything that must be denied in order to grow.
23. Keep records of what is sung.
24. Choose congregational songs that are experientially, as well as liturgically, coherent.
25. Find or become a song leader: a visible human being is the best teacher.
26. Believe in your own voice as a teaching instrument.
27. Believe that others can enjoy singing as much as you do, and show that you believe in them.
28. Teach new songs before the service begins, not during worship.
29. Introduce a new song with enthusiasm; never with an apology.
30. Before teaching a new song, learn the melody by ear, and by heart.
31. Teach a new melody in recognizable sections.

32. Teach by having people hear you sing the melody, not see you look at music.
33. Use your natural voice, and show that you love the song and want to share it.
34. Teach new songs without accompaniment.
35. Choose tunes within a range both low and high voices can sing.
36. Begin worship with songs of medium pitch.
37. Encourage strong, unison singing as the norm.
38. Have at least one unaccompanied congregational song per Sunday.
39. Remember the two most important questions for music leaders: "Can you be heard?" and "Can you hear the congregation?"
40. Use the lowest possible level of amplification.
41. Use live musicians, not backing tapes.

Chapter Four

—————

"Some Demand a Driving Beat":
Contemporary Worship Music

Pastor, lead our circle dance
  which the Spirit has begun.
Help us hand in hand advance,
  show us how to move as one.
Some demand a driving beat,
  others ask to slow the pace.
Teach us how to bend and meet
  our conflicted needs with grace

First stanza of hymn by Thomas H. Troeger (born 1945), from *Borrowed Light*. © 1994 Oxford
University Press, Inc. Used by permission. All rights reserved.

No discussion of congregational song can ignore the phenomenon
of "contemporary" worship music. In this chapter I shall ask what
it is, why it is hard to discuss, and how it relates to the emergence of
electronic culture. I shall argue that evangelical necessity summons
liberal churches (and of course others) to give a critical (repeat, critical) welcome to contemporary worship music.

Snapshots

Not long ago my marriage-partner pastor had a short leave of absence
from parish work. We took the opportunity to visit churches in driving
distance advertising some form of "contemporary worship." For us,
driving distance meant northern New England. This is what we found:
  Caribou, northern Maine: Gray Memorial United Methodist Church.
Sixty people at a 9 A.M. service in the fellowship hall (11 A.M. traditional

service in sanctuary); chairs in shallow semicircles; two acoustic guitars, tambourine, maracas, small drum; folk-style music; good congregational singing;[1] all-age congregation, many young families, friendly to visitors; portable screen at front for song lyrics and a color-slide meditation; thirty-minute service; short message based on scripture reading, spoken without notes by pastor at floor level.

Portland, southern Maine: Charismatic Episcopal Church of the Holy Spirit.[2] Fifty people at their mid-morning Sunday service, held in the chapel of a Catholic high school; Episcopal liturgy of Word and Table; older congregation, some under thirty, most over fifty, friendly to visitors; guitar, violin, and keyboard; good congregational singing; renewal songs with a " '70s" feel plus one hymn, from a booklet incorporating the liturgy; ninety-minute service; robed pastor with engaging message, spoken at floor level, without visible notes.

Biddeford, southern Maine: New Life Christian Fellowship.[3] Two hundred people at the 9:00 A.M. Sunday service in a purpose-built worship space; all-age, mostly under forty, very welcoming to visitors; chairs in shallow semicircles; two built-in rear projection screens, visible but unobtrusive; five singers and a guitarist (the full band was on a mission trip) on a platform, at the front but off-center; exuberant soft rock music; hand-clapping congregational singing; songs with easy refrains; three-hour service including Communion and healing; biblical message given at floor level, without visible notes.

Holden, near Boston, Massachusetts: St. Francis Episcopal Church. Ninety people at a 5 P.M. Saturday service in a modern-Gothic, fixed-pew sanctuary (traditional worship services are on Sunday); all-age, including children (church school concurrent with the service), friendly to visitors; Episcopal liturgy of Word and Table; five-piece well-rehearsed band of church members; keyboard, drum set, bass guitar, lead guitar, vocalist; good congregational singing; sixty-minute service; robed pastor, biblically based message.

Somerville, near Boston, Massachusetts: College Avenue United Methodist Church. Twenty-five people at the 9:30 A.M. "folk rock ser-

---

1. The congregations in our sample had a high degree of congregational participation in song. Our experience may not be universal.

2. A new denomination, "Charismatic Episcopal." We were told it includes Pentecostal congregations wanting to connect with the Episcopal tradition, and Episcopal congregations who have rejected the perceived "liberalism" of their former connection.

3. An Advent Christian church with Pentecostal style worship.

vice," in the fellowship hall (traditional service at 11 A.M. in sanctuary); mostly young adults, children, friendly to visitors; five-piece well-rehearsed band of church members, including pastor, some doubling as vocalists; keyboard, electric bass guitar, acoustic amped guitar (guitarist also played harmonica and banjo), vocalist, second acoustic amped guitar, drum set; folk-rock songs, many composed by the pastor, engaging, and with strong social awareness; good congregational singing; child-friendly worship, including junior choir (two boys and a girl) attentively heard by the congregation; forty-five-minute service; congregational discussion after scripture reading and pastor's brief introduction.

In addition to these worship services, we took in a weekday evening concert by a contemporary Christian praise band, fresh from an international tour. There was a crowded, rock-concert atmosphere, with high amplification, flashing lights, and driving rhythm. The youngish audience wasn't sitting back and listening: teens danced in the aisle and up front, while adults stood, swayed, and hand-clapped to the beat. Trying to identify what made the experience so attractive to so many people, I surmise that it was partly the message—sincere, caring, theologically conservative, and with touches of insight; partly the sound, lights, band singers' star-shed glamour, and the excitement of being in a crowd; and the compelling rhythms of the music, whose lyrics and melodies surged and ebbed like the tide, yet left few ripples on the sands of memory. What we remembered was the beat.

The "beat" was what the worship services, too, had in common. Different in theology, from "me and Jesus" to "the Spirit among us" to "love God and do justice"; different in musical dialect, from folk and folk rock to renewal music and soft rock; what they shared was the insistent rhythms of popular music in our culture.

Feeling the Beat

Let me try to define "beat" more precisely. An evenly ticking clock, or a metronome, has what Leonard Meyer calls a pulse: each "tick" is the same as any other, and there is no pattern of louder and softer "ticks." I suggest, however, that the ear resists such sameness, and tends to perceive, say, "tick" as louder than "tock." This moves us to what Meyer calls "meter," in which there is a regular recurrence of accented and unaccented beats, but as yet no sense of their being grouped in any way, as (perhaps) in "*ya*-da-*ya*-da-*ya*-da-*ya*-da-*ya*" (and so on, indefinitely). A further step (which Meyer calls "rhythm") is to group one or more unaccented beats in relation to an accented beat, as in "*tick*-tock, *tick*-tock," or "lickety-*split*, lickety-*split*."[4]

Robert Jourdain makes a simpler, practical distinction between the rhythms of organic movement and accentuated beats.[5] The rhythms of organic movement are exemplified by a human runner, cascading water, and speech, and are sometimes called "phrasing" or "vocal rhythm," of which plainsong is a classic example. The rhythms of marked or accentuated beats have regular recurrences, and are sometimes called "instrumental rhythm":

> Phrasing is "vocal" because it naturally arises from song, and thus from speech. [Musical] meter is "instrumental" in that it derives from the way we play musical instruments, which generally permit greater speed than the voice and finer temporal accuracy. One is the rhythm of the throat, the other the rhythm of the hands.[6]

Instrumental rhythms travel through solid structures and can be experienced as a physical "thumping" or vibration. Helen Keller apparently learned to hear through her hands, by feeling sound waves as vibrations. The great Scots percussionist, Evelyn Glennie, is deaf. She tunes timpani by feeling their vibrations with her face and feet. It is said that she learned to recognize low and high notes by placing her hands on the wall outside her high school music room. Some notes made her fingers tingle, others vibrated in her wrist.[7] At the other extreme, high-decibel sound and accentuated beats can permanently damage the delicate mechanisms of the ear. "Rock concerts are among the worst threats, which is why, unbeknownst to fans, most rock musicians wear earplugs when they perform." Even classical vocalists can, it seems, be at risk from their own voices, which can reach 110, 120, even 140 decibels.[8]

When people talk about "music with a beat," then, what they prob-

---

4. Meyer, *Meaning and Emotion in Music*, pp. 102–3. I may, or may not, have accurately captured his distinction between "meter" and "rhythm."

5. Like Meyer he defines "pulse" as the "unceasing clock-beat that rhythmic patterns overlay." Jourdain, *Music, the Brain, and Ecstasy*, p. 123.

6. Ibid.

7. Campbell, *The Mozart Effect*, p. 40.

8. Ibid., pp. 37–38.

ably have in mind are the strongly accentuated instrumental rhythms of most current popular music, delivered at high enough amplification to "thump" through flesh, bone, and concrete. Though "contemporary worship music" has many variants, almost all of it " is written with a backbeat and inner pop rhythmic structures in mind. This is true for music of any tempo, as even the slowest pieces have a percussive element."[9]

"Contemporary" and Other Definitions

When I talk about "contemporary worship music,"[10] therefore, I mean music with a beat, as defined above. I shall not waste time bewailing the fact that an honorable word like "contemporary" has been demoted to label a particular type of music. My concern is to be understood, not patrol the dictionary. Since "contemporary" has been enlisted to describe music with a beat, we need terms to fill the space it used to occupy. By "recent," I mean anything said, written, composed, or done within, say, the past five, ten, twenty, or fifty years. The time span varies according to the context and to the speaker's age-group and viewpoint. "Recent" is, therefore, a chronological indication. By "topical" I mean lyrics or music designed for the present time, using metaphors, slogans, and allusions current at the time of writing, or melodies and musical idioms current at the time of composition. By "timely" I mean lyrics or music in touch with our times, and in tune with God's timing. Obviously, what counts as timely varies from theology to theology. I shall elaborate my own understanding of timeliness later in this book.

As even our limited experiences show, "contemporary worship music" has a variety of meanings and styles. Though boundaries are fluid, and categories subject to change, Richard Webb's classification is a useful starting point.[11] He speaks from North America, but much

---

9. Collins and Weidler, *Sound Decisions*, p. 5.

10. Yee ("Shared Meaning and Significance") distinguishes between "contemporary Christian music" (album oriented, professionally performed folk/rock) and "praise music" (folk/rock suitable for congregational singing). I choose "contemporary worship music" because "praise" is not the only kind of song that is, or can be, sung to music with a beat.

11. Webb, "Contemporary." Quotations in following paragraphs are from this source.

of his analysis probably applies more widely. He finds six major categories: Country, jazz and blues, rock 'n' roll, contemporary liturgical, praise and worship, and alternative.

The first three types are currently less widespread than the last three. In cities as well as rural areas, sacred country music is increasingly diverse. Though the country music found in most congregations is based mostly on its earlier manifestations (bluegrass and Southern gospel), mainstream country styles are finding their way into congregational singing. Jazz and blues, widespread in congregational worship during the '60s and '70s, are nowadays less popular, though some forms are making their way back into "congregations that minister within the postmodern community." Rock 'n' roll, less common in mainstream contemporary worship, "has been kept alive by youth ministry leaders within Lutheran and many other denominational traditions." It typically relies heavily on blues chord progressions and driving rhythms.

Contemporary liturgical music is widely influential. Largely created by composers and lyricists within the Roman Catholic tradition, it began in the 1960s, after the Second Vatican Council approved translation of the Latin Mass (Communion) into today's languages. Though it has produced many fine hymns and other congregational songs, its central task has been to provide musical settings for invariable parts of the Mass. Contemporary liturgical music therefore rapidly found its way into Episcopal, Lutheran, and other traditions celebrating weekly Communion in a Word and Table liturgy. Influenced by Gregorian chant, American folk music, and multicultural music, it makes less use of pop/rock rhythms than "praise and worship" and "alternative" styles. "Also, while this style shares many elements essential to contemporary music—strongly accented rhythm, orally conceived melodies, and guitar-based harmonies—there is more reliance on harmonies found in European art music." Instrumental ensembles use a wide variety of instruments, including synthesizer, piano, pipe organ, dulcimer, recorder, and electric guitar. The "average" ensemble has two or three acoustic guitars, a synthesizer, perhaps a drum set, one or more song leaders, and any available melody-line instruments.

Praise and worship is the largest subgroup within contemporary music, partly because it appeals especially to one of the largest segments of the population. To be specific, it appeals particularly to "suburban baby boomers of northern European background, born between 1940 and 1960." With roots in charismatic and Pentecostal renewal, it draws mainly from gospel, country, folk, and pop music. "Its melodies can sound like Broadway tunes, country ballads, smooth jazz, and pop jingles, or even simple Taizé-like mantras." Ensembles typically include two or more acoustic or electric guitars, an electric bass, keyboard, drums and other percussion, solo instruments, and vocalists.

Alternative music is the most recent type of contemporary worship music. Appealing mainly to young adults born since the early 1960s, it has a different sound from the praise and worship music of its immediate "seniors." It rarely uses keyboards, and usually relies on two or three guitars (electric or acoustic), a drum set, electric bass, Latin hand percussion, and vocal ensemble—plus any available solo instruments. In many ways a reaction against "the highly styled and layered sound of praise music," alternative music is very simple, "making use of extremely long melodic lines and sparse diatonic harmonies." Composed for local worship settings as opposed to the mass market, alternative music is mostly available locally, rather than through publishing houses. This may change, of course, as it grows in popularity.

Prickles on the Pathway

Contemporary worship music is a tricky issue to discuss. Mention it, and a peaceful picnic bristles with partisans; trenches are dug, and battle engaged.

One obstacle to conversation is that contemporary worship music arouses strong emotional responses. Discussion easily gets switched onto the wrong track, or derailed, by the likes and dislikes of the protagonists.

Negative responses are not new. Popular music has often been ridiculed by the older generation of the day and by church authorities. In 1805 the waltz was popular, yet derided by cultured despisers. In 1899 a pundit raged against ragtime: "A wave of vulgar, filthy and suggestive music has inundated the land. . . . It is artistically and morally depressing, and should be suppressed by press and pulpit." In 1914 the archbishop of Paris lambasted the tango, "which by its lascivious nature offends morality." In the late 1920s, a pastor, Dr. A. W. Beaven, called jazz "a combination of nervousness, lawlessness, primitive and savage animalism and lasciviousness." Ten years later, the culprit was swing, described by Archbishop Francis Beckman as "a degenerating and demoralizing musical system. . . turned loose to gnaw away at the moral fiber of young people."[12]

When rock emerged in the 1950s, the chorus of condemnation revived. There is a continued widespread dislike of popular music among pundits, pastors, and church musicians. Marva Dawn, more open-minded musically than some, nonetheless declares that we shouldn't make changes "for the sake of *the masses*" (a class-laden, disparaging term for ordinary people). Comparing some kinds of worship to candy, she declares that "candy is very popular with children, but we wouldn't feed them only candy if we want them to grow strong and healthy." The comparison is not inapt, but the implication is patronizing: people who perhaps sway with the beat, raise their hands while singing, cherish disposable lyrics, and respond emotionally to rhythm, are being compared to children by someone who, by implication more adult, knows what is good for them.[13]

Musical Taste

Because it is beyond my competence to disentangle the historical roots of negative responses to popular music, I offer three hunches for consideration. Some of the negativity is, I suspect, class-based: middle-class eyebrows raised against lowbrow music (on this, see below). Part of it is probably generational. Musical taste is formed by notions of music's function and role.[14] We like music that puts us in a good mood or has "meaning" for us. If we enjoy dancing or drama, we like music that supports dramatic flow or gets us moving. More important, however, are the subcultures and groups we identify with, socially and economically. Though there are many individual exceptions, research shows that most people make personal musical choices for reasons neither personal nor musical. "Rather, they listen to conform, taking on music as an emblem of social solidarity with their peers, each generation adopting its own conspicuously different styles."[15] Art music will appeal partly if one aspires to be in the class of people who like it and produce it. Popular music has more appeal for people of any age (but

---

12. Mitchell, *I Don't Like That Music,* pp. 56–69.
13. Dawn, *Reaching Out without Dumbing Down,* p. 167, emphasis mine.
14. For what follows, see Jourdain, *Music, the Brain, and Ecstasy,* pp. 260–63.
15. Ibid., p. 263.

especially youth) whose ethos is antihierarchical, egalitarian, and/or anti-intellectual. Though people are apt to prefer greater complexity in their music of choice as they grow older, musical taste, once formed, is long-lasting. "Most people acquire their musical taste during adolescence among friends of the same age, and they carry early preferences right through to the grave. This powerful force overrides considerations of individual neurology and personality."[16] If we have internalized one kind of taste in music, it is hard to respond sympathetically to music that is radically different.

In today's Western culture, rapid change affects musical taste as it does everything else: trends come and go more rapidly, as longer life spans increase the number of different generations. Thus, our society probably has seven or more strata of generational memory banks, and a sharper divide between old and young. As Robert Jourdain observes, rock is "the first important genre of music in history to be composed and performed largely by young people for an audience of young people."[17]

A further complication is that some people are, by training or natural endowment, more sonically sensitive than others. These differences show up in our response to melody, harmony, rhythm, and musical phrasing. The average listener is attuned to melody.[18] Melodic contour is our first musical competence. Melody is the one musical device that nearly everyone can make sense of, remember, and reproduce. Research shows that most people like melodies slightly challenging to the ear, that go "just beyond the expectations we have been taught by prior musical experience."[19] Professional musicians, however, hear and analyze melody differently from nonprofessionals. For most people, melody cannot be stretched much longer than the average three-minute length of a popular song. With training, musicians acquire the ability to break the melody into a sequence of fragments held together by abstract relations. In neurological terms, their left hemisphere becomes dominant, whereas the right hemisphere remains dominant in untrained listeners.

As with melody, so with harmony. Studies consistently show that perceptiveness for complex harmony is the rarest of listening skills,

---

16. Ibid.
17. Ibid., p. 262.
18. For this, and what follows, see ibid., pp. 265, 259, and 84.
19. Ibid., p. 259.

with wide disparities between professional musicians and others. In fact, many people are essentially deaf to complex harmony, and hear only a spattering of tones.[20] "Harmony is inherently complex, inherently intellectual, inherently difficult. . . . It is the last aspect of musicality to mature in the young, and tests show that many people never achieve harmonic sophistication."[21] Similarly, complex musical phrasing is observable only by a mind steeped in its techniques and conventions. For someone who can follow complex soundscapes of infinite variation and surprise, popular music is tedious.[22] It may be for this reason, at least in part, that for one open-minded and exceptionally gifted church musician, Don Hustad, "rock music is the most primitive popular music form to appear in modern Western culture." Significantly, he opines that a major symptom of "primitiveness" [= tediousness?] is that "it possesses little significant melody and shows no harmonic development."[23]

Popular Music Skills

Perhaps partly because of such differences in musical taste and appreciation, professional church music training is not geared to the acquisition of popular music skills and performance practices. Suppose your congregation has, or had, an organist and/or choir director. Loving music, and loving the church, this individual trained over many years, with much labor, and at considerable personal expense. Until the mid-1980s, the skills thus developed were valued and applauded. Then, out of the blue, people started agitating for "contemporary worship." Since the organist/choir director was the music professional, it was his or her job to create it. But this is easier said than done. Playing contemporary worship music means moving from classical hymnody, typically unsyncopated and with one chord per word, to syncopated music with two chords per line and a greater use of what classical music counts as discords. Your colleague's training didn't necessarily teach how to do this.

More than that, classical music training probably inculcated the

---

20. Ibid., pp. 257 and 112.
21. Ibid., p. 118.
22. Ibid., p. 130.
23. Hustad, *True Worship,* p. 174, emphasis his.

conviction that such popular music styles are unmusical. Chords with more than four notes are rare in most early classical music. "The one significant exception to this rule is J. S. Bach, who regularly used chords of which any contemporary jazz player would be proud."[24] However, the rise of jazz and blues allowed musicians to experiment with extra notes that did not really belong in the chords, "but which in their own way added atmosphere and, yes, beauty to more traditional chord structures." Just as impressionist paintings were frowned on for flouting accepted views of good painting, so contemporary music chords are frowned on because they break classical rules. "Many of their harmonic components are simply not in the vocabulary of some classically trained church musicians, who might regard them as simply 'wrong' in the same way that Botticelli might have regarded Turner's painting as 'messy.'"

The rhythms of modern popular music, and the role of improvisation, are also unfamiliar territory to many church musicians. "A good renewal repertoire might contain everything from hard rock to bossa nova, from swing to jazz waltz, and even Latin and reggae beats. Increasingly, there is experimentation with the latest dance, rave and rap rhythms." Improvisation is required, not only between songs, but within them. Songbooks provide written arrangements, but they are not intended to be followed slavishly. Improvisation means taking a new approach, which cannot be learned from the notes on the page.

Not surprisingly, contemporary worship seems more threat than promise to many church musicians. "Today, numbers of musicians are finding their life's work dismissed out-of-hand by their congregations. They experience it as not only a portent of economic hardship but also a threat to their very existence because their system of meaning is lost."[25]

Unworthy?

A related problem is that institutions training church musicians classify popular music as unworthy of church worship, with techniques to be avoided, not acquired.

---

24. This and following quotations are from Leach, *Hymns and Spiritual Song*, pp. 8 and 9.

25. Clark, *Music in Churches*, p. 76.

Though Western culture has long lived in a creative tension between "art music" and popular music, the present gulf between them is recent. In the Middle Ages, there was frequent interaction between "serious" music and popular folk song, whose melodies were sometimes used as themes in a mass or motet.[26]

At the Reformation, Martin Luther's commitment to popular church music went hand in hand with a desire for more challenging forms. Though he did not borrow tunes from the local tavern, as many erroneously suppose,[27] Luther composed hymn tunes for congregational use and encouraged the composition and use of complex polyphonic music by great composers with trained choirs. For the singing of metrical psalms in Geneva, Louis Bourgeois adapted some tunes from French and German secular songs, and some from Gregorian chant. He composed others in similar style (see Chapter 1, above). His metrical psalm tunes were radically different from traditional liturgical music. Because of their dance rhythms, Queen Elizabeth I of England referred to them derisively as "Geneva jigs," and Shakespeare satirized the Genevan practice of "singing songs to hornpipes."[28]

In later times, Handel frequently used the same music for his religious and "profane" texts; Mozart composed operas (*Singspiele*) for both the nobility and the common people (the *Magic Flute* was composed for a popular audience); Brahms wrote beer-drinking songs as well as sophisticated symphonic works; and Verdi constructed his *Requiem* from the same music materials as his operas.[29]

From the middle of the nineteenth century, however, Western art music began to grow away from the average ear. Harmonic innovation was reaching its limits. "By 1850, composers had tried out seemingly every combination of chords."[30] Using remote chromatic tones, or wandering among foreign keys, demanded more of the listener, and

---

26. Hustad, *Jubilate II,* p. 7.

27. Music, "Getting Luther out of the Barroom," *New Harvard Dictionary of Music,* s.v. "Bar form," and Westermeyer, *Te Deum,* p. 148. "Bar form" does not mean "bar" as in "tavern," but a lyric/music structure, common in German songs of the time, whereby two identical phrases are followed by a third, contrasting phrase. In German, this AAB sequence is called *Barform,* and the Meistersinger, from whom the term is borrowed, called a complete song of this type a *Bar.*

28. Mitchell, *I Don't Like That Music,* p. 26.

29. Ibid., p. 62.

30. Jourdain, *Music, the Brain, and Ecstasy,* p. 97.

many listeners were unable to follow the wandering. Harmonic elongation, and experiments with symphonic timbre (the interplay of orchestral instrumental sound) were also pushed to their limits. In the early twentieth century, some composers modified the classical system, and others abandoned it. The net result of a complex process was that art music became harder and harder to appreciate, because "while music had changed, brain structure had not."[31] One consequence was that popular music took its own direction. Its creative movements came not from schools of music but from the streets, in ragtime, Dixieland, and other early forms of jazz.[32]

Class factors were at work here. Paleface urban middle-class people, aspiring socially upward, perceived working class and African American music as beneath them (though sometimes their younger generations embraced it as exotic). Church music institutions, being themselves paleface, urban, and middle class, followed suit. From the late nineteenth century to the mid-twentieth century, urban Protestant church life reflected middle-class musical and literary standards. Worship moved away from revivalist preaching (seen as suitable only for the unsophisticated) toward middle-class views of what was fitting and beautiful. In some churches worship also became part of social gospel outreach.

From these developments sprang a new-style church musician "who, like his or her counterpart in Anglican and Roman contexts, incorporated the skills of the orchestral director, instrumental or keyboard artist, music teacher, private voice teacher, and composer."[33] Popular music styles, both secular and sacred (the gospel song, for example), were rejected as bad music. Church musicians were schooled to disdain African American styles of music and their by-products, such as jazz, blues, and gospel. Schools and colleges of sacred music entrenched such viewpoints, "by deeming particular sounds and performance styles aesthetically unworthy as a sacrificial offering to God." Their students "received the commission to go into the world of church music and displace bad music with offerings of good music."

In liberal Protestant churches, these developments created a

---

31. Ibid., p. 98. I have abridged his helpful discussion (pp. 96–100).

32. See Webb, "Contemporary," p. 83.

33. This and immediately following quotations are from Young, *My Great Redeemer's Praise: An Introduction to Christian Hymns*, pp. 2, 5, and 6.

contradiction that still bedevils us. Theologically, we preach acceptance and inclusiveness. Musically, we proclaim rejection and exclusion, on the culturally conditioned belief that "good taste is more pleasing to God than bad taste."

For more than a decade, traveling throughout the United States, I have visited half a dozen schools of church music and hundreds of churches of all denominations. I stand in awe of the performance skills of singers, organists, choir directors, and composers. Their skill, dedication to God, and love of music are an inspiration. Having known job insecurity myself, I feel for professional musicians whose livelihood is put in question by the rising demand for contemporary worship music. However, whenever I ask a group of church musicians, "Were you trained in the skills of popular music?" they invariably answer, "No." If I then ask whether the above analysis of institutional attitudes is correct, they almost invariably answer, "Yes."

It is fair to conclude that most of today's church musicians were trained in institutions teaching (or assuming) negative views of popular music as a vehicle for worship. It is hard for professional musicians to take a sympathetic approach to music they have been schooled to regard as unworthy and inferior. In the unlikely event of my ever being invited to give a graduation speech at a school of sacred music, my message can be summarized thus: "For Christ's sake (I speak with all seriousness), send your students on placements where they can learn the skills of popular music performance practice, so that they can move confidently from organ console to electronic keyboard, from guitar to Gregorian chant, and from Purcell to praise band."

Clergy and Musicians

A final obstacle to constructive discussion of contemporary worship music is that relationships between clergy and musicians are not always marked by understanding and respect. Some pastors are skilled in music, reflecting the fact that many more professionally trained musicians become clergy than vice versa. Others, perhaps a minority, regard themselves as unmusical. Because they don't know how to talk about church music, or ask intelligent questions, they relate uneasily to professional music colleagues. Few clergy, and few seminarians, have wandered through the halls of a conservatory of music and listened to the cacophony of sound from practice rooms and cubicles: a soprano here, a pianist there; here a trombonist, there a cellist; threads of music soaring high, then breaking off in mid-flight, as a phrase is repeated, repeated, and repeated—repeated until it comes right. Without such knowledge it is hard to appreciate the rigor of professional music training and of the musicians' working life:

> Through years of training they accrue
> the skills of mind and hand,
> which hours of practice must renew,
> enliven, and expand.

Brian Wren, "Give Thanks for Music-Making Art," copyright © 1993 by Hope Publishing Company for the U.S.A., Canada, Australia, and New Zealand, and by Stainer & Bell Ltd., London, England, for all other territories. All rights reserved. Used by permission.

Unsure about music, and unaware of its disciplines, some clergy claim power without knowledge. Some musicians similarly defend their turf, perceiving their clergy counterparts as arrogant and unmusical.

Even when clergy-musician relationships are healthy and respectful, there are differences of view. One survey asked whether a committee of staff and lay leaders should exercise direction of the church's music program. Of the clergy sampled, 56 percent agreed (8 percent strongly). By contrast, 61 percent of the musicians disagreed (50 percent strongly). Asked whether the music director should choose the hymns, there was a similar difference of opinion: 58 percent of the musicians said yes; 75 percent of the clergy said no. Another question was, "What is the most meaningful musical activity in worship?" "Anthems," said 41 percent of the musicians (but only 7 percent of the clergy). "Hymns," said 79 percent of the clergy (but only 38 percent of the musicians).[34]

Perennial Objections

To summarize, discussions of contemporary worship music easily get blown apart by a combustible mix of professional anxiety, economic insecurity, interprofessional antipathy, generational differences, class disdain, and the different choices and capacities of musical taste. This potent mixture ignites unconvincing objections to popular music, catalogued by Robert Mitchell. "It's secular, not sacred." But the Bible doesn't make such distinctions, and "secular" music dialects

---

34. Clark, *Music in Churches,* pp. 56–57.

have often migrated into worship. "It's undignified." Perception of what constitutes "dignity" is culturally relative. For example, six-teenth- and seventeenth-century opera-going was probably more akin to the circus atmosphere of today's popular music concerts than to the reverent silence of symphony concert halls.[35] "It's too loud." Often true. Overamplification does indeed cause hearing loss. That said, per-ceptions of loudness are partially a matter of preference, in any kind of music. Visiting a church one Sunday, Mitchell and spouse were excited by the pipe organ prelude played at full volume. Another cou-ple found it painfully loud. As Mitchell puts it, "All 'pop' music is not loud, and all loud music is not 'pop.' "[36]

Another frequent objection is, "I can't understand the words." Again, often true, but as true, equally often, of choir anthems and solos. To be consistent, the objector must reject every item in classic choral literature where different words are sung at the same time. Mitchell's conclusion is: "Be critical, but use the same criteria to eval-uate all music, not just that which you dislike."[37]

Summarizing his discussion of musical imports into worship, Mitchell finds a repeated pattern. Time after time, church music becomes "classic," specialized, and "sacred." Time after time, a new idiom is then brought into worship from the "secular" world and is greeted by widespread scorn and rejection. Yet time after time, the "new" idiom soon becomes "part of the distinctive cultic musical expression of the church."[38] Were I able to revisit earth in a hundred years time, I would not be surprised to find elderly worshipers lament-ing the demise of classic liturgical rap.

Calvin Johansson

To dig deeper into the roots of dislike, I shall look more closely at one classically trained critic of popular music, Calvin Johansson, who helpfully notes that the issue is not simplicity versus complexity. Pop-ular music often exhibits simplicity, yet great music can also be sim-ple.[39] Elsewhere, Johansson shows a keen dislike of popular music,

---

35. Jourdain, *Music, the Brain, and Ecstasy,* p. 242.
36. Mitchell, *I Don't Like That Music,* p. 62.
37. Ibid., p. 63.
38. Ibid., p. 28.
39. Johansson, *Music and Ministry,* p. 54.

saying that mass production molds and markets music into patterns of banality. It lowers artistic standards, encourages "musical tasteless-ness," and promotes artistic inertia.[40] Entertainment music is "pur-posely immature," so cannot convey a gospel that calls us to maturity.[41]

Johansson sets out biblical principles for music ministry, then pre-sents a list of values drawn from the gospel, contrasted with the char-acteristics he perceives in popular music:

Gospel characteristics	Pop-music characteristics
Individuality	Quantity
Nonmaterialism	Material profit
Principles above success	Success first of all
Creativity	Novelty
Sacrifice	Immediate gratification
Joy	Entertainment
High standards	Lowest common denominator
Encouragement of the best	Mediocrity
Reality	Romanticism
Meekness	Sensationalism
Permanence	Transience

Unsurprisingly, these contrasts convince Johansson that gospel values are incompatible with popular music. Since he has already argued that music is not a neutral medium, but affects the words it voices, he con-cludes that "there is no possibility whatsoever of successfully match-ing the two in a pop song. . . . To use pop music as a medium for the gospel message is wrong."[42]

One weakness in Johansson's analysis is that he takes a variety of musical dialects and lumps them all together as "pop." His dislike of popular music is so all-embracing that, unlike Richard Webb (see above) he sees no distinctions within it. In this respect, Johannson joins company with many others. Whenever I hear a classically trained musician talking disparagingly about "rock" or "pop," I invariably find that, unlike the *New Harvard Dictionary of Music,* for example, the speaker sees no difference between rock 'n' roll and rock, or between

40. Ibid., p. 48.
41. Johansson, *Discipling Music Ministry,* p. 53.
42. Johansson, *Music and Ministry,* p. 55.

disco music, folk rock, heavy metal, new wave, punk rock, motown, rhythm and blues, and soul.[43]

Crucially, Johansson overlooks the fact that he, and the music of which he approves, are as much part of the market economy as the music he criticizes. The gospel, he argues, promotes the value of individuality, whereas popular music elevates quantity. Yet mass production is characteristic not merely of popular music, but of our society as a whole. Johansson probably buys mass-produced goods, and his books are certainly mass-produced and marketed. So, also, is classical music.

Similar considerations apply to Johansson's contrasts between "Nonmaterialism" and "Material profit," and between "Principles above success" and "Success first of all." Profit is not synonymous with profiteering. Publishers of the classical music Johansson prefers must make a profit or go out of business. The drive for material success is indeed one of our society's idols: *in everything, not merely popular music*. Music publishers, "classical" church musicians, popular music composers, contemporary worship leaders, clergy, worshipers, and lay leaders are all in the same boat: we either worship these idols or resist them.

Again, Johansson argues that the composer of popular music barters "his" [*sic*] artistic integrity in exchange for general acceptance from the masses. "The composer is no longer his own man [*sic*], for every creative impulse must be checked by, 'What will they think?' 'Will they like it?' and 'Will it sell?' "[44] To the extent that this is true, it applies to everyone who composes. Church music publishers and composers of my acquaintance are all obliged to ask not only, "Is this good theology, in fresh, creative music? "but, "Is there a market for this piece? Is it playable and singable in that market?" and, yes, "What will they think? Will they like it?" and "Will it sell?"

In Johansson's view, the gospel is characterized by permanence and creativity, while popular music falls captive to novelty and transience. Gospel permanence versus pop-music transience is another false opposition. Granted that God's love is unchanging, transience

---

43. *New Harvard Dictionary of Music*, s.v. "Rock," "Rock 'n' Roll," "Disco music," "Folk Rock," "Heavy Metal," "New Wave," "Punk Rock," "Motown," "Rhythm and Blues," and "Soul."

44. Johansson, *Music and Ministry*, p. 54.

and impermanence apply to all human life, not merely popular music.

Of popular music, Johansson observes that "durability and depth are not characteristics of its products. Wearing out soon, they must be quickly replaced."[45] True, but some popular music has a longer shelf life, and most medium-size cities have radio stations playing and replaying "classic" hits of the previous five decades. Seeking to respond to the perceived needs of its customers, church music itself follows fashion and bows down to another of Johansson's bogeys, "ease of consumption." Bach, Handel, and Vivaldi are published, sometimes unchanged but more often rearranged, simplified, and repackaged as products for today's handbell ringers, semiprofessional choral groups, low-voice vocal soloists, and two-part choirs in small churches. And why not? Moreover, as anyone who enjoys a good meal knows, transience does not equate with unworthiness: good food is by definition transient. If church music is suitable for its purpose and topical, it matters not whether it proves transient or long-lasting.

Johansson's critique also ignores the probability that a considerable portion of music now heard attentively as "classical" was itself originally intended for ease of consumption, as background music for the leisure pursuits of aristocratic society. Whether or not King George II of Britain rose from his seat in honor of Handel's "Hallelujah Chorus," he is unlikely to have said, of the same composer, "Stop the fireworks. I want to hear the music."[46]

Finally, I question Johansson's contrast between the gospel's "High standards" and "Encouragement of the best," and popular music's emphasis on "Mediocrity" and the "Lowest common denominator." The implication seems to be that the music Johansson prefers has creativity and high standards, while popular music does not. Because Johansson dislikes all "commercial" popular music, he judges it in terms of the genres he values, and finds it wanting. Such judgments are elitist and mistaken. In terms of its own genres and possibilities, popular music allows plenty of room for creativity and for debate about aesthetic and moral standards. Moreover, large chunks of

---

45. Ibid., p. 51.

46. The king is said to have made his dramatic gesture at a London performance of *Messiah* in 1743, obliging the audience to follow protocol and stand with him, and initiating a British tradition whenever *Messiah* is performed. Handel's *Music for the Royal Fireworks* was first performed in 1749.

today's "classical" church music can undoubtedly be classified as mediocre.

Bending the Gifted Ear

I have outlined some of the difficulties in discussing contemporary worship music, and looked more closely at a critic of popular music styles. One issue needs further comment. It seems clear that by training, natural endowment, or both, a minority of people are able to appreciate complex harmony, extended melody, and the wider horizons of phrasing and timbre. When people thus gifted regard popular music as tedious or unsatisfying, it is not primarily (I suggest) because they have weighed evidence and reached a reasoned conclusion. *It is because they unavoidably hear it that way.* Reasoning and weighing evidence are involved, but beneath them lie an immediate, compelling, "self-evident" perception to which it seems incontestably obvious, say, that Beethoven is immeasurably more enriching than the Beach Boys. "*Es muss sein!* How can anyone not hear it?" is the puzzled response. Such puzzlement can prompt either a journey into enlightenment or a leap into premature conclusions: that those who don't hear it are not trying hard enough, perhaps, or that they perversely refuse to try. Thus does pride lurk in the shadow of giftedness.

Let me offer a parallel, by way of illustration. I am unable to detect the difference between certain shades of red and green and a group of other tints which keener eyes easily distinguish. Though more gifted color-perceivers sometimes act as if "color-blindness" means that I view the world in monochrome, they are wrong. Like them, I find New England fall colors visually breathtaking. They do (presumably!) see more subtleties than I do. Yet this in no way means that I am morally inferior, or that my color-gifted friends have the right to pity my "infirmity," tell me what to see and what not to see, or look down on my less-nuanced appreciation.

As with color, so with music. If we are blessed with the capacity (learned or inherited) to be moved and enlightened by harmony, melody, and phrasing inaudible to the average ear, this should be, simply, an occasion for joy, thanksgiving, and humility. It is illogical, and unethical, to assume that it confers superiority over the average ear, or what the average ear enjoys hearing.

Musical Wiring

Because likes and dislikes sway arguments about music, I had better state my own. In my youth I imbibed, with many others, the assumption that popular music was inferior to classical. This was a prejudice, often unstated, never explained. Sustainable against the popular music of the '50s, it was vaporized by the Beatles, with their memorable melodies and indelible lyrics.

Today, I love and enjoy hymns, and my music of choice remains classical: Bach, Britten, Elgar, Ives, Vaughan Williams, Beethoven, Brahms, Stravinsky, and Birtwhistle challenge, feed, and move me. When not singing congregationally, I love the nonverbal element in music: most of what stirs me from the above composers is instrumental, including organ music, Bach and Messiaen for example.

My first experience of church (age fourteen) was a little chapel whose congregation sang choruses from a booklet with tiny print. I found the music boring, and the lyrics uninspired. Today, I appreciate what choruses can do, and enjoy and appreciate some of them. Because I have come to enjoy soft rock, folk rock, and some current popular bands, I can worship through some styles of contemporary worship music, provided the words are worth singing. I am momentarily excited by driving rhythms, but the effect soon wears off unless the lyrics, too, are memorable. Though I have seen many people touched and moved merely, it seems, by "the beat," I am not one of them. Whatever the musical dialect, I need lyrics, whether simple or complex, that feed the mind and stir the imagination.

The way I respond to music and words is not easily changed. It is, as it were, part my mental wiring. Over the years, some circuits have gone out of use, and fresh connections have been made. Even so, the way I dance (if I do!) is determined by the music I danced to as a youth and young adult, and the music that moves me is the music I came to love in those formative years. "Mental wiring" is an important metaphor, and I shall return to it.

Electronic Culture

Up to this point, I have described some of the most common types of contemporary worship music, shown why it often proves hard to discuss, and argued that the intense dislike shown by some critics is unreasonable. I shall now make a case for giving it a critical welcome.

Whether classical or contemporary, church music and congregational song do not exist on their own, but in, with, or against their culture. It is widely agreed that "Western" cultures (and perhaps others) are in the midst of a revolution in communication comparable to the introduction of printing at the time of the Reformation. Almost every recent study of Christian worship tries to describe this revolution and respond to it. Techno-optimists embrace its changes.[47] Techno-pessimists speak against them.[48] Moderates analyze them and suggest varied responses.[49]

Common ground for most commentators is that our consumerized culture, and worship within it, are subject to particular temptations. One is the lure of *pragmatism* (whatever gets results and draws crowds must be OK). Another is our culture's *narcissism* (focusing on my own feelings and emotions, instead of on God). Third, worship all too easily gets confused with *entertainment* (thirsting for whatever pleases and distracts us, instead of giving God our whole heart). Some advocates of contemporary worship music are aware of these issues. Emphasizing that a contemporary worship band's central function is to lead the congregation's song, a Lutheran commentator argues that traditional worship also needs such reminders. "For the entertainment mindset knows no limits, and can pervade the finest liturgical choir as well as a vocal team of six people."[50] As Donald Hustad also observes, all "modern church music is subject to the temptation of aestheticism (in worshiping high art) or of hedonism (in preoccupation with entertainment music in church); actually, *both result from excessive emphasis on the 'pleasure meaning' in music.*"[51]

Most commentators note that our culture accustoms us to fast-moving, nonlinear images and shortens our attention spans. Others note the importance of "music with a beat" to generations born since

---

47. See, for example, Kallestad, *Entertainment Evangelism,* and the host of books on church marketing and church growth.

48. Most notably, and powerfully, Marva J. Dawn, *Reaching Out without Dumbing Down.*

49. For example, Benedict and Miller, *Contemporary Worship for the 21st Century;* Doran and Troeger, *Trouble at the Table;* Jensen, *Thinking in Story;* Roof, *A Generation of Seekers;* and White, *Christian Worship and Technological Change.*

50. Collins and Weidler, *Sound Decisions,* p. 25.

51. Hustad, *Jubilate II,* p. 58, emphasis mine.

the Second World War. Recently, Tex Sample has connected the two.[52] Neither optimist nor pessimist, Sample wishes to understand our culture from within. From that understanding, he finds elements in electronic culture able to critique it, and himself offers a powerful critique of the economic order that sustains it. He argues against tendencies to idealize print culture and demonize electronic, on the ground that the demonic is not limited to one cultural formation.[53]

Sound, Light, and Wiring

In common with others, Sample notes that generations born since the Second World War have developed a new relation to sound, affected by technological developments in music and the practices associated with them. Rock 'n' roll and its varied successors captivated their ears and bodies. Amplification in performance made the beat more insistent and, if you dislike it, more intrusive. Magnetic tape and its digital successors allowed sophisticated intervention between first take and finished product. Transistorization, then miniaturization, made audio devices cheaper and more easily transportable.[54] Music with a beat, of one kind or another, became the "heart music" of post–Second World War generations, a familiar and indelible part of their culture. Even Calvin Johansson recognizes that "the music of our culture which has most influenced late twentieth-century church music is rock music. It is unquestionably the most popular form of music in the world." He recalls how social scientists at Temple University decided to study rock music, but had to abandon the project "because no control group could be found among the student body who fulfilled the criteria of disliking it!"[55] Because musical taste, once formed, lasts a lifetime (see above), it is overwhelmingly probable that people steeped in rhythm-driven popular music "will not develop a craving for classical music as they age, nor will they mature into it. They will rock and roll to their graves."[56]

Our culture has certainly become more visual. TVs, VCRs, and their updated equivalents are ubiquitous, and we watch them. When we do,

52. Sample, *The Spectacle of Worship*.
53. Ibid., p. 24.
54. Ibid., p. 47.
55. Johansson, *Discipling Music Ministry*, p. 24.
56. Wright, *A Community of Joy*, p. 33.

our eye-brain system absorbs visual images a billion times faster than print.[57] Fewer young adults read books, while older adults read as much as they used to. On the other hand, more young adults now visit art museums and galleries. Among eighteen- to twenty-four-year-olds, 29 percent reported visits to art museums or galleries in 1992 compared to 23 percent in 1982. This increase is all the more interesting since formal arts education in school markedly declined during the same period.[58]

In electronic culture, sound and vision are increasingly integrated. When a ten-year-old girl gets off a New York subway train and asks her friend, "Have you *seen* the latest Michael Jackson *song?*"[59] she testifies to that integration: she has seen the video and heard the song, as one integrated experience. What people used to hear, on vinyl records then compact discs, they now see and hear on video. Tex Sample shows that though music with a beat is centrally important to electronic culture, it is a mistake to equate it with sound alone. In musical performances, sound and light are integrated and imitate each other. "Music in electronic spectacles now uses not only polyrhythmic beat, but light in similar multirhythmic and layering ways. Pulsing illumination employed in this layering fashion sweeps an audience." Though sound "enters" our bodies physically in a way that visual images cannot, "the percussive character of light now accompanying sound takes on a role and importance it has not had before," so much so that "light has come to take on something like the character of sound."[60]

The power of visual images, sound as beat, and their integration create a sharp culture gap between those who grew up with it, enjoy it, and live in it and those who didn't grow up with it, feel estranged from it, and dislike it. For both extremes, and the many in between, the way we hear, see, and feel is not a universal constant, but socially and culturally conditioned. What could be more universal (for the sighted) than sight? Sighted people have more or less the same ocular and neural equipment. Yet seeing is not as straightforward as it sounds. People born without sight who later gain the power to see do not immediately open their eyes and see a chair, a window, and clouds in the sky. Instead, "the patient is immediately confronted with a wall

57. Sample, *The Spectacle of Worship*, p. 30.
58. Ibid., pp. 47–48.
59. Ibid., p. 47.
60. Ibid., p. 64.

of brightness containing color patches that blend indistinguishably into one another." Shapes previously known by touch, such as triangles and squares, cannot at first be visually recognized, and the newly sighted person has no sense of size and distance. Learning to see requires training and mental effort, and our naming and interpretation of what we see are shaped by the culture and generation in which we live.[61]

Our senses, then, are historically and socially organized.[62] Discussing "soul music," meaning whatever music appeals deeply to a particular generation or subculture, Tex Sample shows how one's soul music is both chosen and formative. "Soul music is as deep as muscle and bone, as intimate as feeling, and as close cognitively as the way we know the world around us. The word *soul*, then, is a good one because music of this kind is profoundly bound up with one's very being."[63] For some people, hymns are soul music: learned in childhood and stored in memory, so that hearing them evokes memory, words, and music. Dance routines learned as a teenager become, as it were, encoded in our mind-body system. Familiar dance music gets us moving without thinking. Unfamiliar rhythms leave us stranded, and we move awkwardly or clap on the wrong beat. The metaphor of "mental wiring" helps us understand what is going on. Tex Sample puts it thus:

> Our senses, our feelings, our bodies, and our ways of engaging life are culturally and historically structured. . . . I really am "wired differently" from my children and grandchildren. What speaks to me does not speak to them. What moves me, entertains me, touches me is not what does so to them. *People of my age will not engage younger generations until we recognize this otherness and concede that along with images, sound and especially sound as beat are crucial to that recognition.*[64]

Why Bother?

Tex Sample's conclusion raises serious questions. If we do not feel at home in the emerging culture he describes, why should we bother with sound as beat, visualization, and their integration? Why not stay

---

61. Ibid., p. 25. The quotation is from research by Marius Von Senden.
62. Research by Walter Ong, quoted by Tex Sample, ibid., p. 16.
63. Ibid., p. 66.
64. Ibid., p. 42, emphasis mine.

within the boundaries of our own cultural preference and musical taste? Those who share our preference will come and worship with us (perhaps). Those who don't, or won't, can go elsewhere.

Such gut feelings do not, I think, take us very far. Few of us stand apart from the culture we live in. We could try to live like the Amish, but mostly we don't. Gladly or grudgingly, we migrate from fountain pen to typewriter, to word processor, to computer, to e-mail, and eventually to Web site. In church, we may balk at rear-projection screens, yet love banners and drama, and feel shortchanged if the pastor reverts to yesteryear's wordy worship. More profoundly, most of us believe we have something worth sharing, and some desire to communicate it.

Perhaps contemporary worship is like a foreign language, which we, as liturgical missionaries, need to learn. When the Holy Spirit came at Pentecost, people heard the good news of Jesus Christ, not in what was for most of them a foreign language, Judean Aramaic, nor in what was for many of them a fluent second language, common Greek, but directly, in their native tongue (Acts 2:11). Their response suggests both surprise and delight. They were "amazed and astonished" because *"in our own languages"* they heard the news of Jesus Christ. That is why the message touched them to the heart. If contemporary worship music is, for many, their "native" musical idiom, it is bound to touch them more directly than "foreign" music can do.

The language model is appealing, but limited. If I, as a Bach-lover, pass your church door and hear music which appeals to me, it is unlikely to be a heavy metal number played in the style of a Bach fugue. As indicated above (p. 56), music does not readily translate from one style into another. Moreover, learning a new musical idiom is not as radical as learning a new language. It takes years for an English-speaker to become fluent in Hindi and articulate a Christian message in terms meaningful to Hindu culture. By contrast, English-speaking worship traditionalists migrating to contemporary worship music are more likely, at most, to learn English idioms previously unknown to them.

Perhaps, then, we should think of contemporary worship music as a means to attract the attention of people steeped in popular musical idioms and make them feel at home. In the movie *Sister Act*, people cross the street and enter the church because they hear lively, rhythmic singing from the convent choir within. Recently, I played a recording of an energetic rock number during a church service while dancers imitated Saul and the prophets going into a music-induced frenzy (1 Samuel 10:5–13, see Chapter 2, above). The children were on their way out to Sunday school, but as soon as the music started they rushed back into the gallery to see what was going on.

Suppose, however, that people do indeed come, drawn by the sound or promise of music that makes them feel at home. What do we do then? Roll up the screen, cover the drum set, unlock the organ, and pass out hymnals? Presumably not. To use contemporary worship music, of whatever kind, entails an ongoing process and the possibility that "their" taste, and culture, will interact with and influence ours.

"Inculturation"

This suggests that music with a beat is not a "language" we need to learn, but (as integrated with visualization) a cultural form, in which we need to work, and with which we wish to converse, in open yet critical dialogue. A helpful word for such a process is "inculturation," meaning "the ongoing dialogue between faith and culture or cultures" or "the creative and dynamic relationship between the Christian message and a culture or cultures."[65] Though "inculturation" can be understood in different ways,[66] I am using it to suggest a two-way process, whereby Christians reach out to a culture different from their own, respect it, enter it, and interact with it, neither losing their identity nor remaining unchanged.

From this perspective, one purpose in using contemporary worship music is to invite people into the drama of Christian worship, and win a hearing for a Christian message, by using culturally familiar forms: visual, dramatic, and musical. Paul's letter to the Corinthians encapsulates the problems and possibilities of this approach:

> To the Jews I became as a Jew, in order to win Jews. To those
> under the law I became as one under the law (though I myself
> am not under the law) so that I might win those under the law.
> To those outside the law [Gentiles] I became as one outside the
> law (though I am not free from God's law but am under Christ's

---

65. Shorter, *Toward a Theology of Inculturation*, p. 11. Shorter distinguishes "inculturation" from "enculturation," a sociological term for the cultural learning process by which an individual is socialized, and from "acculturation," the encounter between one culture and another (ibid., pp. 5, 7). Anscar Chupungco follows Shorter, and shows the inadequacy of terms like "indigenization," "incarnation," and "contextualization" (*Liturgical Inculturation*, pp. 16–19).

66. For example, Chupungco limits it to ways of grafting unchangeable Roman Catholic liturgical texts into the cultural patterns of a local church (ibid., p. 37).

law) so that I might win those outside the law. . . . I have become
all things to all people, that I might by all means save some. I do
it all for the sake of the gospel, so that I may share in its blessings.
(1 Corinthians 9:20–23)

Does Paul mean that he pretended to be what he was not, and wore
any disguise, tried any trick, and used any form of persuasion that
would convince his hearers he was one of them? Though the phrase,
"all things to all people" has come to have that meaning, it is unlikely
that this is what Paul meant by it. Paul did not need to pretend to be
Jewish: he *was* a Jew, and never ceased to be one. Though church and
synagogue eventually separated, in Paul's lifetime his Jewishness was
never in doubt. Though he regarded himself, in Christ, as free from
the law of Moses, he did not see himself as above it. He respected it,
and believed that by God's grace he could honor its best intention.

Gentiles knew that Paul was a Jew. There is no evidence that he hid
his Jewish origins and identity; in his letters he is repeatedly vocal
about it. But he didn't require male Gentile Christians to be circumcised,[67] and kept table fellowship with them—scandalous to many
other Jews, no doubt, but not an abrogation of Jewishness. If we give
Paul a sympathetic reading, his remarks suggest he was able to be
alongside others in ways they found hospitable and respectful, *because
he knew who he was—or rather "whose" he was—and acted from the
security of that grace-founded Christian identity.*

Knowing Whose We Are

The example suggests that those who offer contemporary worship
need to know who, and whose, they are. Many exponents of contemporary worship know whose they are with strident conviction, and use
music to wrap a package of simple certainties, authoritatively presented and by many gratefully accepted.[68] Not surprisingly, more

---

67. His reported decision to have Timothy circumcised was an exception, out of
consideration for local Jewish scruples (Acts 16:1–3).

68. In times of rapid change, and cultural or social uncertainty, "fundamentalism
appeals to original sources and originating experiences in an oversimplified and literal
way. It commands allegiance by its deceptive simplicity. As a result, it encourages religious and cultural incapsulation and often a fanatical opposition towards other religious and cultural systems." Shorter, *Toward a Theology of Inculturation,* p. 41.

moderate churches shy away from such music, and equate "contemporary" with "conservative" or "fundamentalist."

It need not be so. I believe that if "moderate" and "liberal" churches embrace contemporary worship, "contemporary" songs will emerge to express a more open, and more open-minded theology. In my tradition, faith is centered on the person of Jesus Christ, not a package of doctrinal certainties, and "evangelism" springs from an experience of God that we believe is worth sharing. To be an evangelist it is not necessary to believe that other faiths are godless, that unbelievers go to hell, or that the world will end tomorrow. Because Jesus reveals God to us, because his story is life-changing, because the Spirit of Christ can give hope and liberation, and because a Christian worldview makes sense of the cosmos, history, and our lives, we have a treasure to be shared.

As I am using the term, inculturation is the process of sharing that treasure. It means offering a Christian message, centered on the person of Jesus Christ, in the language of today's cultures and subcultures, using their familiar musical forms. Thus understood, liturgical inculturation has many precedents. Wishing to be topical and timely, writers and composers have often imported "secular" musical idioms, and whole melodies, into congregational song. The now-classic, deeply sorrowful tune for "O Sacred Head Sore Wounded" was borrowed from a love song, titled (in translation) "My Heart Was Wounded for the Love of a Fair Maiden."[69] In the eighteenth century, the tune associated with Samuel Stennett's "On Jordan's Stormy Banks I Stand" strongly resembles one associated with "I'll Go and Enlist for a Sailor" in Sharp's *Morris Dances.*[70]

In Protestant history, worthy lyrics have often been seen as sanctifying a secular melody. Watts and Wesley both argue on these lines, as did the German Reformers. A Frankfurt title page from 1571 offers *"geistige, güte, nütze Texte und Worte"* (spiritual, pure, and useful lyrics) for the *"böse und ärgerliche Wese, unnütze und schampere Liedlin"* (evil and irritating style of the useless and shameful ditties) in popular use.[71]

---

69. Mitchell, *I Don't Like That Music*, p. 26.
70. Hustad, *Jubilate II*, p. 225.
71. Ibid., p. 211.

Lyricists have perennially tried to be topical. Isaac Watts drew upon the commonplace scientific knowledge of his day. He speaks of the earth as a sphere,[72] and explicitly describes the circulation of the blood:

> He [God] spoke, and strait our Hearts and Brains
>   In all their Motions rose;
> Let Blood, said he, flow round the Veins,
>   And round the Veins it flows.
>
> While we have Breath or use our Tongues
>   our Maker we'll adore;
> His Spirit moves our heaving Lungs
>   or they would breathe no more.[73]

Similarly, Charles Wesley's "The True Use of Music" was a Christian lyric written specifically for a popular song, with topical allusions designed to appeal to the sailors he invited to sing it.[74] In American revivalism, the best "witness songs" have always been couched in topical language. In the mid–nineteenth century, P. P. Bliss wrote gospel songs based on topical events, such as "Hold the Fort, for I Am Coming" (see Chapter 1, above).

As indicated above, the interplay between the faith of a "liturgical missionary" and the idioms of contemporary music is best understood as a dialogue. The "missionary's" faith, however, is already culturally shaped: by middle-class values, for example. Thus, "when we describe inculturation as a dialogue between faith and culture, we are really speaking of a dialogue between a culture and the faith in cultural form."[75] If mainstream middle-class churches begin to offer forms of

---

72. "Then am I dead to all the *globe*, / and all the *globe* is dead to me" in "When I Survey the Wondrous Cross."

73. Watts, *Hymns and Spiritual Songs,* Book II, no. 19, stanzas 5 and 6 (Selma Bishop, p. 175), in an amplification of the Creation narrative in Genesis 1—2. William Harvey (1578–1657) published his epoch-making book, *An Anatomical Treatise on the Motion of the Heart and Blood in Animals,* in 1628, some seventy years before Watts's hymn.

74. See above, Chapter 1.

75. Shorter, *Toward a Theology of Inculturation,* p. 12.

contemporary worship, they may find their own cultural values challenged and modified. Conversely, they may hope to modify electronic culture from within. For, "if it is correctly carried out, evangelization should help people, not to despise their own culture, but to reappraise it in the light of Gospel values."[76]

There is, of course, a risk that the culture being encountered and evangelized will distort or domesticate Christian faith. "It is dangerous to assume," says Peter Moger, "that 'secular' music automatically sheds its connotations when transferred to a new context. Music is not sonically neutral and does not exist only as an available medium for a message."[77] Given the autonomous power of music (see chapter 2), this is certainly plausible. The problem is that there is rarely consensus as to what constitutes the "connotations" of a given piece of music. In its own, "secular," context, some popular music admittedly has unchristian or anti-Christian associations. But if psalm tunes can be modeled on secular dance, a love song reborn as a Good Friday chorale, and a tavern tune transmuted into a Methodist hymn, it is hard to argue that, even in an apparently extreme case, secular associations cannot be changed.

To put the matter theologically, the Spirit of Christ is no stranger to today's emerging electronic culture and its "music with a beat." Because Christ is risen and alive in the world, it follows that:

> Wherever we may venture
>   to witness, heal and care,
> the Spirit of our Savior
>   has long been lodging there.

Hopefully, then, as (we) "missionaries become culturally educated, and strive to present the person of Christ and his teaching in terms of the new culture, [we] should begin to perceive new insights into [our] Christian faith." The clumsy translations and fumbling of our first attempts at contemporary worship will be replaced by new connections and new ideas:[78]

---

76. Ibid., p. 27.
77. Moger, *Music and Worship*, p. 16.
78. Shorter, *Toward a Theology of Inculturation*, p. 63.

Then let us give with gladness,
    not claiming to deserve
the wisdom, strength and kindness
    of those we kneel to serve.

Cultural Familiarity

I have argued that, for great numbers of people in our culture, especially those born since the late 1940s, music with a beat, and the integration of music, visual images, and dance, are so deeply embedded in consciousness that they constitute the only cultural format in which they are likely to hear, see, and experience the good news of Jesus Christ. Thus understood, using contemporary worship music is both evangelical opportunity and evangelical obligation.

When cultural familiarity is absent or withheld, fewer people stay and listen to the "foreign" music being offered. Tex Sample tells how a Midwestern shopping mall was thronged with adults, who shopped, and teenagers, who had little money to spend and came along to hang out with their friends. The teens hung out in such numbers that the shoppers were discouraged from shopping. The merchants pondered what to do. They didn't want to tell the teens to leave and so alienate future customers. Their solution was to play "easy listening" music over the loudspeakers in the mall. In no time the teens quietly disappeared: the music was too foreign to them. As Sample says, "Sound can bring the spirit or it can drive the spirit away."[79]

Conversely, if their preferred music is respected and accepted, people without a church background are more likely to feel at home in church. One reason for the popularity of music with a beat is that, once public schools began to drop music from their curriculum, people found it more and more difficult to access styles of music removed from everyday experience. So they began to ask for worship music that sounded more like what they heard on their radios, televisions, and stereos.[80] Like it or not, in the United States the megachurch move-

---

79. Sample, *The Spectacle of Worship*, p. 35.
80. Webb, "Contemporary," p. 84.

ment has changed the way many people think about church music. Nowadays, "thousands of North American Christians simply assume that music in worship is properly rendered by a guitar-led praise band, not an organ; and that the basic genre of liturgical music is not hymnody, but choruses and ballads."[81]

In worship, for people formed by electronic culture, music with a beat will not stand on its own but go hand in hand with visual images, artwork, video, drama, movement, and (from time to time) "spectacles" as powerful as rock concerts but filled with the glory of the gospel.[82] Though I have no space to develop this theme, it is fundamentally important for future developments of congregational song. Hymn-singing traditions, too, will need to make hymns more visual, by capitalizing on the visual element in many hymn lyrics.

The power of contemporary music can be overstated. That "the generations born after 1946 *have forever changed the course of music*" is a claim that risks looking silly in fifty years time.[83] Simply because only 2 percent of the population buy recordings of classical music,[84] it does not follow that the other 98 percent hate singing hymns. Hymnody and classical music are two different entities.[85] Nor does it mean that "contemporary" worshipers will never appreciate hymnody. With these provisos, pastors, musicians, and worshipers in hymn-singing traditions should give a critical welcome to contemporary worship music in congregational song.

Performance Practice

Before underlining the word "critically," I shall look briefly at performance practice in contemporary music, the choice between "blended" and "alternative" worship, the issue of "durable versus disposable," and the need to make contemporary music congregational.

To simplify (drastically, but I hope not misleadingly), music has three main elements: melody, harmony, and rhythm. In Western music, melody was dominant during the era of plainsong. Later, harmony came to prominence. In contemporary music, rhythm takes

---

81. Witvliet, "The Blessing and Bane of the North American Megachurch," p. 8.
82. On spectacle, see the closing chapters of Sample, *The Spectacle of Worship*.
83. Wright, *A Community of Joy*, p. 33.
84. Ibid.
85. Dawn, *Reaching Out without Dumbing Down*, p. 180.

center stage. "The tunes may be fatuous and the harmony may consist of one chord change per line up to a maximum of about three, but the rhythm drives the song and makes it a memorable and exciting experience for the worshipers."[86]

In worship music, as elsewhere, different dialects need different instruments. For melody, a solo violin or flute is excellent but can add little to harmony on its own, even when racing up and down in arpeggios. A well-played drum set gives good rhythms, but does almost nothing for melody. A pipe organ is fine for melody and harmony, but hard to play very rhythmically, "not least because of the time-lag between hitting the key and hearing the sound." Thus, in contemporary worship instrumentation moves away from the organ "onto the guitar (which can provide rhythm and harmony) and piano (which is pretty good for all three)."[87] Because such instrumental changes necessarily accompany changes in musical dialect, they are not in themselves a rebuke to organists, flutists, and violinists, but simply a matter of "horses for courses."

Powerful rhythms are not new in church music. Bach's preludes and fugues, some choruses from Handel's *Messiah*, and tub-thumping gospel songs like "Standing on the Promises" and "Leaning on the Everlasting Arms" have strong rhythmic elements.[88] Yet when intense rhythms are amplified, relentlessly pursued, or both, they become compulsive. Though the compulsive element in music is not restricted to any one idiom, nor absent from traditional church music, the rhythmic power of contemporary music makes compulsiveness a particular temptation. The power of rhythm must be recognized, and "its intentional use for the purpose of compelling a desired response must be renounced."[89]

That said, strong rhythms have positive possibilities. Timothy Wright aptly describes the post-1946 and post-1964 generations when he says that "people value experience-oriented services. They want to know that God is present."[90] Played with love and conviction, rhyth-

---

86. Leach, *Hymns and Spiritual Songs*, p. 7.

87. Ibid.

88. Bach's preludes and fugues and Handel's *Messiah* did not originate as music for liturgical use; they have, however, often been enacted or performed in church worship.

89. Mitchell, *I Don't Like That Music*, p. 61.

90. Wright, *A Community of Joy*, p. 42.

mic music, in a variety of musical dialects, can bring people together, get worship moving, and proclaim that God is here and greatly to be praised. When strong rhythms are neither incessant nor over-amplified, music with a beat can energize us, promoting joy, hope, unity, and delight.

Partly because rhythm is central, contemporary worship songs need new approaches and performance practices. Their styles and origins call for an ensemble sound. "To lead them with an ensemble is to treat them with the greatest musical integrity." An organ achieves texture and expression with different registrations. "An ensemble does so in the differentiation between instruments,"[91] and gives worship songs more freshness because over time it can replay them with varied emphasis and expression.

When building an ensemble, a piano or keyboard is a good begin-ning. Bass guitar and drum set come next, to give tonal and rhythmic support and the most suitable instrumentation. Acoustic and electric guitars can follow, then a synthesizer, to add musical colorations. Thereafter, any available melody instruments can add texture and expression and help the congregation learn new melodies.[92]

In contemporary worship music, performance practices are learned more from people than from the printed page. "As in an oral tradition, the knowledge of contemporary worship music is passed from person to person."[93] A synthesizer's capabilities are best learned by hearing other people play it, live or recorded. Doing this, one can learn how to use the synthesizer as an instrument in its own right, not as a sub-stitute for others. Aural signals are learned by example. "The piano and drums are primary instruments for giving aural signals to the con-gregation. These signals are called 'fills' and function in various ways, depending on the song. When done properly, fills aurally signal a con-gregation (so that it knows when to begin, resume and end singing)."[94]

Listening becomes more important than looking. Most musicians have been taught to see music, read it, then play it. Contemporary music often means hearing, then playing—a scary prospect if you have been taught to rely on looking at the printed page. Scary or not, "since modern church music is much more based around improvisation and

---

91. Collins and Weidler, *Sound Decisions,* p. 23.
92. Ibid.
93. Ibid.
94. Ibid., p. 25.

playing by ear, it is important to make the switch from visual to aural learning." A good first step is to listen analytically to recordings, noting what chords sound like in relation to one another and trying to anticipate likely sequences and memorize them. Finding a keyboard in a deserted place, in a soundproof room, or in the home of tolerant friends, the aspiring improviser can then practice, experiment, and cultivate rhythmic playing.[95]

Contemporary worship songs are designed to be repeated, in whole and in part. "A single line may be repeated several times with a progressively different feel, getting louder and more triumphant, or dying away to a whisper. A chorus may be sung unaccompanied or with drums only, and so on. Flexibility is the watchword."[96]

Finally, contemporary worship music puts a high priority on improvisation. "Improvisation is something to be used not just after the song, but during it as well." Again, this is an approach best learned by listening to other musicians, and working with them.[97]

Blended or Alternative?

If your congregation introduces contemporary worship music, will it have one blended service, or two or more different services?[98] Size may determine the answer: a fifty-person congregation may be too small to float two services. Of the five congregations we visited, two—one large and one small—worship only in contemporary style. Either they began that way or they had radically changed their worship. Different services would not be an option, because neither would want a hymn-based alternative.

Three congregations, each with a "traditional" (hymn- and organ-based) service, had started a contemporary service at a different time. St. Francis Episcopal "contemporized" the music of its Word and Table liturgy and worshiped in the sanctuary. The United Methodist churches used a different, informal space and had short, informal worship.

For a Word and Table tradition, it makes good sense to blend contemporary music with the familiar order culminating in Communion.

---

95. Leach, *Hymns and Spiritual Songs,* pp. 19–20.

96. Ibid., p. 11.

97. Ibid., p. 9.

98. For a full discussion and advocacy of "blended worship," from a liturgical-evangelical perspective, see Webber, *Blended Worship, Planning Blended Worship,* and *Renew.*

For others, it makes equal sense to try something shorter, informal, and different—either from scratch or by weighing what others have done.[99]

Both United Methodist services began with a "set" of worship songs inviting congregational participation; both had music and song throughout; and both had short prayers, a Bible reading, and a message (or congregational discussion) based on the reading. To us, as visitors, the informal style and informal space made a positive difference. Informality—prepared and practiced informality, not ramshackle casualness—is a keynote of contemporary worship, and worship blossoms when worship space matches worship style.

If existing worship is hymn- and organ-based, a blended service may be sustainable provided congregational subcultures are willing to compromise. Asked what kind of music is appropriate for worship, a quarter of Linda Clark's sample (24 percent) replied that "since music in worship is an offering to God, only the best is appropriate." Three-quarters of this group were age fifty-one or older. Encouragingly, nearly half the sample (47 percent) believed that "any kind of music is appropriate as long as the congregation can use it to praise God." Three-fifths of that group were age fifty-one or younger.[100] A single, blended service could thrive only if such differences were discovered and negotiated. Even then, it might not be practical.

Does having two or more different services prove divisive? Theologically, Christian churches are by definition inclusive communities, where people of varied age, gender, class, culture, orientation, ethnicity, and theological conviction are baptized into Christ and meet around Christ's table. In practice, such differences so divide us that few congregations live up to the ideal. The alleged divisiveness of differently styled worship services is a real problem, but no less real than our other divisions. Some argue that a church with six or seven different styles of worship services becomes the equivalent of a liturgical cafeteria, where people eat and run but hardly meet. Equally plausibly, such a church can be a hospitality center, housing a network of face-to-face ecclesial communities.

A powerful argument for musical diversity is that "one size doesn't fit all." As Richard Webb observes, worship planners often mistakenly

---

99. For a variety of formats, see Wright, *A Community of Joy*, Appendix A, pp. 131–37.

100. Clark, *Music in Churches*, pp. 31–32.

assume that "contemporary music generally sounds all the same and reaches the same kinds of people." It doesn't. To take one example, urban and suburban people born since the 1960s are apt to find baby-boomer praise music just as foreign as traditional hymns. Conversely, their music is apt to be perceived by their boomer elders as "depressing, aggressive, and 'whiny.' "[101]

On similar lines, Kathy and Tim Carson write that when considering contemporary worship, preliminary questions include: "What musical cultures will we be tapping?" "To which musical cultures are we hoping to appeal?" "What is our social location?" and "From what generation(s) do we come?" From the answers, a congregation should decide how many services to hold and what kind of "contemporary" music they should offer. "In our congregation," they write, "we have answered that question with multiple services. Our traditional service is a 'high-culture' service that most often includes music from the broad classic repertoire. Our contemporary service is a 'popular culture' service that is driven by an eclectic collection of music in the jazz, rock, folk, and world music idioms."[102]

If we opt for liturgical diversity, we face the same questions as before: How can people of different culture, age, gender, ethnicity, and orientation meet each other in Jesus Christ? How can people who worship differently converse, pray, and sing together—in small groups, Bible study, social events, committees, and retreats, for example? It is, surely, no harder to live with that question when the people in question worship under one roof, than when they worship separately in suburbia and downtown.

Durable or Disposable?

Should contemporary congregational songs be throwaway music, sung for a month then forgotten? From the past, according to Robert Mitchell, "the Church has a history of using, losing, and regaining the concept of 'disposable music.' " Many of Charles Wesley's hymns (he wrote more than six thousand) fall into that category.[103] Today, argues John Leach, songs designed to work on the emotional level are neces-

---

101. Webb, "Contemporary," p. 84.
102. Tim and Kathy Carson, *So You're Thinking about Contemporary Worship*, p. 68.
103. Mitchell, *I Don't Like That Music,* p. 67.

sarily short-lived. Designed as a response to what God is doing now, in the midst of worship, they have "no logical or theological content able to stand the test of time and outlive the emotional moment."[104]

There is nothing wrong with topical, disposable songs. Many hymns are also topical and short-lived. Yet Leach is overenthusiastic about topicality. If all our songs are ephemeral, we shall widen, not bridge, the communication gap between generations. When a song has no logical or theological content, repetition diminishes its emotional impact, for without content feelings fade more rapidly than a thermal fax in sunlight. A related problem is that "subjectivities cannot be shared; telling you about my feelings will not bring about the same feelings in you. Only if I tell you what aroused my feelings can you respond to the same stimulus with subjective reactions of your own."[105]

Whether we sing hymns or contemporary songs, we need some songs that travel beyond the moment, because faith needs to tell "the old, old story." From Baptist to Catholic, Presbyterian to Pentecostal, we worship God who became known in history and who weaves the whole human story, past as well as present. We belong in that story, supremely in the story of Jesus Christ. If we tell that story topically and faithfully, the Spirit will move us, so that we respond with feeling. Without logic and theology, songs cannot connect us to the story. Telling the story also gives us a sense of history. Jesus did not speak the words of scripture yesterday in our town, or last night in our ears. They were spoken and recorded centuries ago, and by the grace of God the Spirit brings them alive for us now. Finally, we need songs that transcend the moment because we belong to a global faith community whose songs enrich our own, and to the company of believers, future, past, and present.

Becoming Congregational

A song written for soloist or ensemble probably won't work for a congregation. A composer-performer can sometimes present such a song so winningly that people join in. But for congregational music, in any idiom, the test of a song is whether an instrumentalist can play it, and a congregation sing it, when the composer is silent or absent.

---

104. Leach, *Hymns and Spiritual Songs*, p. 12.
105. Dawn, *Reaching Out without Dumbing Down*, p. 175.

Because congregational song is indispensable, any style of contemporary music needs to be, or become, congregational. Composing congregational song is a fine art, a miniature rather than a landscape. In contemporary music, as elsewhere, a stepwise movement (one note up or down at a time) is generally more singable. Singability depends on careful design of steps, leaps, and also syncopation, which is singable when artfully sequenced and predictable, but not when random or unpredictable. As previously mentioned, the tune must lie within a range that both low and high voices can sing. Memorable without being dominant, its mood and emphases should support and match its text. It should usually have repetition and, almost invariably, a refrain vividly presenting its message, which the congregation can sing easily and confidently.[106]

Conclusion

I have argued that evangelical necessity calls us to give a critical welcome to contemporary worship music in congregational song. By a critical approach, I mean that our contemporary music must be thoroughly congregational, not soloistic and performance driven. It will be energetic, but not compulsive; meaningful, not merely emotional; topical, yet able to connect us to the whole Christian story.

As I have already suggested, the biggest problem with contemporary worship music is not the music, but the lyrics that come with it. Because most of it has emerged from churches historically revivalist and theologically conservative, its lyrics typically emphasize personal devotion, subjective feelings, and personal conversion, with little room for service and social justice. The lyrics are also saturated with male-dominance God-language.

It follows that we should give careful scrutiny to the lyrics, as well as the music, of contemporary worship music. In welcoming its musical idioms, we will seek, and write, lyrics more centered on God and our relationship with God than on the worshiper's feelings, and more open to the social dimension of the gospel. In the next and succeeding chapters I shall look more closely at the lyrics of congregational song.

---

106. Ideas partly from Collins and Weidler, *Sound Decisions,* p. 9.

Chapter Five

"And Speak Some Boundless Thing": Assessing the Lyrics of Congregational Song

Begin, my tongue, some heavenly theme
and speak some boundless thing:
the mighty works, and mightier name
of our eternal King.

—Isaac Watts

New hymnals often spark controversy, but rarely in the pages of *Newsweek*. When the United Church of Christ (U.S.A.) published *The New Century Hymnal* in 1995, hostile coverage was guaranteed by wholesale changes in hymn lyrics and critics crying "Heresy!"[1] The Hymnal Committee wanted to provide "varied metaphors for singing about God, and language to sing about people that excludes no one—words that all people can sing."[2] Critics lambasted many changes as inelegant, and argued that the omission of "Father," "Son," and "Lord" obscured or distorted crucial elements of Christian faith.[3]

Though sharply divided, supporters and critics of *The New Century Hymnal* were at opposite ends of common ground. Their controversy was impassioned (though usually civil) *because they agreed that words matter;* that the language of worship partially shapes the beliefs and

---

1. Woodward, "Hymns, Hers, and Theirs."
2. James W. Crawford, *The New Century Hymnal*, p. ix.
3. For a full presentation, see Christensen, ed., *How Shall We Sing the Lord's Song?*

attitudes of the worshiper; and that music gives particular power to the lyrics of congregational song.

Because the music of a song has its own autonomous meaning and emotional impact, it can override the lyrics, or make them seem unimportant. When people listen to songs, they don't always worry about what the words say. Tex Sample recalls a conversation with his fourteen-year-old granddaughter. They talked about a song by the rock group she particularly likes and likes to dance to. Because he couldn't understand the words as sung on the video, he bought the sheet music, studied the lyrics, and found them unpleasant and misogynistic. When he asked what the group were saying in the song, his granddaughter replied, "I don't know, Grandpa, I never listen to the words . . . I hear them, but I just don't pay attention to them." He was responding to the text, to "its discourse and the woman-hating character of its lyrics." She was responding to the percussive sound of the beat and the way the group moved and danced. Though she did not in the least appreciate negative views of women, her focus was not on the words, but on the sound and images in the video.[4]

On the other hand, lyrics become more prominent when someone, or something, prompts us to take notice of them. One of Tex Sample's students, Annalise Fonza, loves rap music, but was troubled by the misogynist lyrics of some songs. She gathered a group of African American teenage girls and asked them why they liked the songs. Like Sample's granddaughter, they liked the percussive character of the beat, and did not pay attention to the lyrics. Annalise Fonza got the lyrics of the songs and asked the group to listen, watch, and pay attention to what the words said. "How are you honored in the song?" she asked. After the videos had been played, she asked the group to draw pictures showing how they were honored in the song. Then they talked about the pictures they had made. "In discussing their images, they all noted that the singers of the songs did not honor them at all, but were seeking their own gratification without any evident concern for women."[5]

Clearly, words matter when we pay attention to them. When we listen to a song, we may miss or ignore what the words say. When we sing the song ourselves, and take the words on our lips, it is harder to ignore them. The muscular actions involved in articulating the lyric make it

---

4. Sample, *The Spectacle of Worship,* p. 29.
5. Ibid., p. 99.

more likely to be remembered. Even if we take little notice of them, the words are being stored in memory, inextricably linked to their music (see above, Chapter 2). For these reasons it is a reasonable assumption that we pay more attention to lyrics we sing than to lyrics we hear and that, accordingly, it matters what lyrics we sing.

Sometimes, of course, we tolerate words that are inadequate. When worship language goes against our beliefs, we can, to some extent, ignore it, say a mental "No!" or inwardly translate it into more acceptable forms. But eventually, the tension must be resolved: we either accept the language or go elsewhere.

Similarly, when Christians draw together against opposition, it is not always essential to "get the words right." In September 1988 I visited Pitt Street Uniting Church, Sydney, Australia, a congregation receiving abuse and intimidation because of its openness to gays and lesbians and its advocacy of aboriginal land rights. When the backlash began, old hymns proved unifying, despite their archaic and often irrelevant language. As time went on, however, they found or wrote songs better able to express their beliefs and commitment.

In the long run, then, words matter. Congregational song lyrics deserve careful attention, because they help to shape and express our faith. To save space, I shall use "lyric" to mean the words of a Christian congregational song.

Meaning

The "meaning" of words said or sung is a complex matter. Applied to a piece of speech or writing, the phrase "what it means" itself has many different meanings, and postmodern views are pessimistic about finding shared meaning in a given text. I shall sketch some approaches, sufficient, I hope, to know what meanings we are talking about and how far they can be shared when a congregational song is sung.

"What did you mean by that?" people sometimes ask, pointing to a word or phrase in a hymn of mine. "I'll gladly say what I think I intended to convey," I reply, "provided you first tell me what it conveys to you. Because that's what's really important." In a congregational lyric, the author's intention is interesting perhaps, but secondary. A living author is usually absent when the song is sung, and a dead author is absent by definition. Once the lyric is published, it has a life of its own. Whoever owns the copyright, the congregation "owns" the text. Congregation and author may coincide, more or less, in their understanding of what a lyric means—though we can rarely know this. Experts may help us interpret a lyric's word meanings, metaphors, and theological concepts—but their influence is modest and indirect. What counts is not expert advice or author's intent, but how wor-shipers understand the words they are singing.

Take, for example, these lines from Edmund Sears's hymn "It Came Upon the Midnight Clear":

> And ye, beneath life's crushing load,
>   whose forms are bending low,
> who toil along the climbing way
>   with painful steps and slow,
> look now! for glad and golden hours
>   come swiftly on the wing.
> O rest beside the weary road,
>   and hear the angels sing.[6]

It is conceivable that when Sears wrote this stanza he had in mind the suffering of New England mill workers: overworked, exploited, underpaid. What the text presents, however, is an image of people trekking up a steep path or road, bent double by the cruel loads they must carry. Few, if any, congregations would connect this metaphor with textile mills. Its evocative power is general, not specific. If Sears wanted us to make the specific connection, he did not succeed. If, on the other hand, he coined the metaphor hoping it would evoke more varied experiences of painful steps and crushing loads, he was more successful. Whatever his intent, this metaphor "means" what a con-gregation sees in it.

Thus, though one of the earliest meanings of a lyric is what the author intends to communicate, it is more important to ask what it means to the people who first sang it, and what it means today. Then or now, "what it means" to a given congregation includes the general sense of the lyric as a whole; the way it interacts with the tune to which it is sung; the customary sense (dictionary meaning) of particular words and phrases; their secondary associations (connotations); and the most common interpretation of metaphors, similes, and other fig-ures of speech.

In principle, we could test particular lyrics by conducting a survey

---

6. See further below, Chapter 9.

to find out what people understand and how much is clear or unclear to them. Because this is beyond my capabilities, I shall rely on dictionary meanings and the analysis of metaphor, simile, and syntax, inviting you to check your interpretation against my own.

People probably understand a lyric with different degrees of precision. When a congregation sings, "Hark! the herald angels sing, 'Glory to the newborn King,'" it doesn't matter if only a minority know what a "herald" is and only one singer in a hundred knows the exact meaning of "Hark." If they have in mind angels praising baby Jesus, their understanding, though incomplete, is enough to constitute a shared meaning. They are essentially singing about the same thing.

Similar considerations apply to metaphor, even though metaphors allow a wider range of interpretation than words like "angels," "newborn," and "sing." The first stanza of my hymn "When Love Is Found" reads:

> When love is found
>   and hope comes home,
> sing and be glad
>   that two are one.
> When love explodes
>   and fills the sky,
> praise God, and share
>   our Maker's joy.[7]

For most people, "When love explodes and fills the sky" evokes (I hope) the joyful surprise of love discovered, the wonder of saying, "I love you!" and being loved in return, and the all-pervading power of mutual attraction. The image is hinted, not fully stated: a fireworks display, perhaps.

Call that range of possibilities the metaphor's circle of coherence. By this I mean the range of interpretations likely to be made by most singers and similar enough to constitute a shared meaning when people sing these words together. If one singer sees, not fireworks but a spectacular sunrise, that interpretation stays within the circle, because the joy and wonder of love's beginning are still in view. If someone else imagines an erupting volcano, that too is within the circle of coherence: volcanoes too can be said to explode and fill the sky. Nevertheless, the

---

7. Wren, "When Love Is Found," *Piece Together Praise,* #146.

volcano image might have different associations (usually called connotations) for different people: positive, perhaps, for a volcanologist, negative for someone who barely survived an eruption.

Suppose, however, that another singer takes "explodes" to mean "blown apart so that it [love] ceases to exist." This interpretation falls outside the circle of coherence, because it disregards the immediate context (from "When *love is found*" to "*share our Maker's joy*"), which makes it clear (I hope) that "explodes" means "expand suddenly" not "blow apart and be destroyed."

For nonmetaphorical statements, the circle of coherence is smaller. The third stanza of "When Love Is Found" reads:

> When love is tried
> *as loved ones change,*
> hold still to hope
> though all seems strange,
> till ease returns
> and love grows wise
> through listening ears
> and opened eyes.

Because the hymn is about two people committing themselves to each other, the phrase "as loved ones change" most coherently refers to the two people in question, as they develop, have different experiences, and sometimes, perhaps, grow apart. I once met someone who read "loved ones" as meaning "a succession of partners," and thought that "change" meant exchanging one partner for another. If I have correctly described the hymn's circle of coherence, this is a misreading, and few would make it.

Writers cannot prevent individual misreadings and negative connotations. Should a negative connotation or misreading become widespread, however, a lyric risks losing coherence and appeal. When this happens, an editor, copyright owner, or writer (if living) will sometimes amend it, hoping to preserve its value and coherence. If by the year 2050 "loved ones" has indeed come to mean "partners," my publishers or executors will, I hope, amend the stanza or omit it.

I shall discuss language-change issues later, in Chapter 9. For the moment, I argue that, when a congregation says or sings a song lyric, "what it means" is what the singers understand themselves to be expressing. I hypothesize that, despite individual misreadings, stray connotations, and different degrees of precision, there can be—and usually is— enough agreement to constitute a shared meaning. My hypothesis could be tested, and congregational understandings of particular lyrics quantified, by anyone with time, money, and expertise. I shall assume that, pending such investigation, the shared meaning of a text can be plausibly hypothesized by analyzing its "dictionary meanings," metaphors, syntax, and so on.

Significance

Russell Yee helpfully distinguishes between the meaning of a lyric and its significance. Meaning is what the lyric intends, or is understood to intend, as defined above. Significance is what the lyric's meaning suggests, evokes, and conveys to individuals in a particular time and place (see also the discussion of a song's matrix of meaning, in Chapter 2, above).[8] Despite variations in the way it is understood, the meaning of a lyric does not change wildly from one moment to the next. John Oxenham's "In Christ There Is No East or West" does not suddenly mean "The Spirit came at Pentecost." By contrast, a lyric's significance varies from person to person, and from day to day. I have sung "In Christ There Is No East or West" in response to scripture readings, at mission conferences, and in ecumenical services; I sang it with congregations in apartheid South Africa, and heard it sung at the funeral of Dr. Martin Luther King, Jr. Its meaning did not change, but its significance was different on each occasion.

Though significance is more personal than communal, it can sometimes be shared. If an inner-city congregation is struggling against drug-related crime, to sing "A Mighty Fortress Is Our God" may signify, for many, their hope and faith in that struggle[9]—especially if a prayer on this theme has just been offered.

When a congregation sings a song, the music affects the significance of the words, even though it does not alter their meaning. A dreary tune can drain the joy out of thanksgiving; a lullaby can tame the passion of a prophet.

---

8. Yee, "Shared Meaning and Significance."
9. Example developed from Yee, "Shared Meaning and Significance."

Sometimes the autonomous meanings of the music override the lyric, and we become "perfectly capable of singing just because we like the music, or to go along with the crowd, or to feel pious, or out of sheer habit."[10] Pious unreality is a perennial temptation. In late-nineteenth-century England, John Ruskin described the hymns of his day as "half paralytic, half profane . . . consisting partly of the expression of what the singers never in their lives felt, or attempted to feel, and partly in the address of prayers to God, which nothing could more disagreeably astonish them than [God's] attending to." As an example, he cited a hymn recently sung with fervor, in which the congregation expressed its wish to die and be immediately with God. Yet if the smallest piece of plaster had fallen from the ceiling, he opined, the whole congregation, fearful of its prayers being answered by a collapsing roof, would have dropped their hymnals and scuttled unceremoniously out of the sanctuary.[11]

Sometimes we know what the words mean, yet struggle with their significance. If I sing, "Take my silver and my gold, / not a mite would I withhold,"[12] the meaning is clear, and I want to intend it. But as I sing, I struggle with what it signifies, or might signify for me. For many who lead worship, argues Russell Yee, "it is easier for us to worry about the significance of the singing than its significance as an act of worship. . . . Only when other issues press us to pay attention, say, inclusive language or inculturation concerns, do we stop to ask whether we intend what we are singing."[13]

As a writer of words for worship, I have no influence on what their meaning may signify for worshipers. As a worship leader, my influence is slight: occasionally I can highlight the possible shared significance in a lyric or a prayer. What I can most usefully do, as worship leader or writer, is investigate the likely meanings of a lyric and assess its value for Christian worship.

When we ask, "What makes a good lyric for congregational song?" our answers are shaped by factors such as gender, life experience, and theology. Supporters and critics of language changes in the *New Century Hymnal* appealed to different views of their denomination's tradition. A Lutheran source asks general Christian questions like, "Does

---

10. Ibid., p. 8.
11. John Ruskin, cited in Watson, "The Victorian Hymn."
12. Frances Ridley Havergal, "Take My Life, and Let It Be."
13. Yee, "Shared Meaning and Significance," p. 8.

the text speak the gospel clearly, pointing to the crucified and risen Christ?" and "Which persons of the Trinity are active or referred to?" along with questions more characteristically Lutheran, such as, "Is there a balance or creative tension between Law and Gospel?"[14]

My own tradition is "Reformed": an amalgam of English Congregational and Presbyterian; not rigorously Calvinist, but cherishing John Calvin as mentor; less beholden to historic creeds and confessions than some of its cousins; and historically one of the homelands of hymn singing. My first three guidelines connect the inclusiveness, ecclesial nature, evangelical potential, and "creedal" power of congregational song with what Calvin saw as essential marks of the Christian life.[15] Other guidelines are more closely related to the necessary corporateness, and inspirational possibilities, of words sung together in worship.

Devout

A lyric should be devout. By "devout" I intend the plain meaning of the word, "devoted to divine worship or service," not the negative overtones that sometimes go with being "pious" and "religious."[16] Thus, from my perspective, "devout" means God-centered, focused on serving God alone, and on praising, glorifying, and delighting in the Name Unnamed, creator of the universe, embracing all things, incarnate in Jesus Christ, present as Holy Spirit. In my usage, words like "God," "the divine," "the Living One," or "the Name" are shorthand for this more complete understanding. If your faith is not Trinitarian, you will need to reshape my discussion; if you are not deistic,[17] "devout" may be an inappropriate concept.

Trinitarian faith shares the conviction of Israel's psalmists that God is not a nameless, impersonal mystery, but "a known, named, identifiable

---

14. Collins and Weidler, *Sound Decisions*. The questions mentioned are paraphrased, not directly quoted.

15. Rice, *Reformed Spirituality*, says Calvin saw the Christian life as having three essential qualities: Righteousness, Frugality, and Holiness (= sanctification, growing in grace). I have rearranged and altered Calvin's terminology, preferring "devout(ness)" as clearer than "holiness" and "just(ice)" as more accurate than "righteousness."

16. *Random House Webster's College Dictionary*, updated 2d ed., 1997, 1998, s.v. "devout."

17. For example, Unitarians who do not believe in a "personal God."

Thou." In Israel's faith, God is "known by the story that always comes with the name": in historical interventions making Israel God's covenant people; in creating and governing the world; and in actions bringing life out of chaos, light out of darkness, and food in the face of hunger.[18] Though a theology of God's universal love and current knowledge of the universe make it hard to believe that God directly intervenes on behalf of some and against others, Christian worship still focuses on "the story that comes with the name": the tale, and promise, of what God has done, does, and will do—in us, in the past, and in earth's societies and civilizations.

In our conception and imaging of the divine, devout lyrics balance intimacy with awe, so that God is neither remote and distant, nor reduced to human dimensions. Taken as a whole, they will bring many names and titles to celebrate the One in Three, reverently aware that God is not limited by titles, pinned down by labels, nor summoned by names. Without ignoring our moral failure and need for new life, devout lyrics express "dependence without cringing," praise without groveling, and thanksgiving without wheedling.[19]

In our portrayal of God in relationship with human beings, devout lyrics balance companionship with reverence. God is Immanuel, God with us, God alongside us, for us, traveling with us. Yet our companion is also our Creator, whose purpose ranges far beyond our sight. Devout lyrics unite the two great commandments: love the Living One, your God, with all your heart and soul and mind and strength, and your neighbor as yourself. The first commandment has logical priority, but cannot be understood or obeyed apart from the second.

In our portrayal of God and the world, our lyrics will make space for both celebration and lament. The universe, the earth, life, and human life are marvelous and wonderful, themes for unclouded praise, thanksgiving, and delight. It is right, and always right, to praise God everywhere and always. Yet because our world also knows suffering, tragedy, and unspeakable evil, we cannot hide behind happy hallelujahs in a garden of parochial praise. Devout lyrics grieve over the pain of people and nations, and keep covenant with God without pretense or naïveté, preferring doubt and lament to denial and despair.

A devout lyric speaks honestly about life and experience, putting

---

18. Brueggemann, "The Psalms as Prayer."
19. Idle, "The Language of Hymnody."

aside pretense and pomposity. Because God knows and loves the world, devout lyrics avoid "spurious emotions for spurious characters,"[20] and speak about people as they are and the world as it is. A good lyric will rarely reveal the author's state of mind, but will speak truthfully only if the author has gone outside the walls of conventional wisdom and stood barefoot on the concrete of human experience, in rain, snow, and sunshine.

Devout lyrics come in different forms. For example, a lyric may speak to God, speak about God, or focus on the worshiping community. Whatever its grammatical form, it will not trivialize or take God lightly. To put it negatively, nothing in it will hinder or contradict the devoutness of the worship in which it is used.

Though not all lyrics are addressed to God, a lyric has particular power when it joins direct speech with a recital of what God has done. Consider this lyric by Shirley Murray:

> Because you came and sat beside us,
> because you came and heard us speak,
> and we ignored you and we refused you,
>   we ask forgiveness, Lord Jesus Christ.
>
> Because you laughed and loved the child-like,
> because you lived from day to day,
> and we love status and steady money,
>   we ask forgiveness, Lord Jesus Christ.
>
> Because our peace was your agenda,
> because you wept to see us war,
> and we love power, and winning battles,
>   we ask forgiveness, Lord Jesus Christ.
>
> Because your Cross compels an answer,
> because your love absorbs our sin
> and we are wounded because we wound you,
>   we ask forgiveness, Lord Jesus Christ.
>
> Because you came on Easter morning,
> because you come at Pentecost,

---

20. "Most bad writing is the result of ignoring one's own experiences and contriving spurious emotions for spurious characters": Oscar Hammerstein, quoted in Davis, *Successful Lyric Writing*, p. 86.

and in the Spirit, we are forgiven,
we live to praise you, Lord Jesus Christ!

When we say or sing these words, we speak directly to Jesus Christ. The ancient title, "Kyrios," translated customarily as "Lord," is interpreted in stanzas 1–4 by memories of Christ's earthly life, each beginning with "Because." In plain, contemporary English these clauses do what New Testament authors classically did: redefine "lordship" away from dominance into a supremely appealing, yet uncoercive, way of leadership. This is the "Lord" who sits beside us, listens, laughs and loves, seeks peace, weeps at war, conquers death, and absorbs our sin. The "and" clauses are the second half of a three-part argument ("Because X, and [because] Y, therefore we do Z"). They confess our distance from Christ, implicitly express contrition, and lead into the last line of stanzas 1–4, which asks forgiveness.

Though it gives snapshots of the Jesus story, rather than narratives, Murray's lyric meets the living Christ directly, through and in that story. Such lyrics have three considerable advantages. They guard against spiritual vagueness: we are meeting Jesus Christ, not a fuzzy feel-good phenomenon. They remind us of key events in the story— ever more important as the story becomes less and less well known. And by focusing our attention on Christ, they lift us out of preoccupation with "myself," "my feelings," and "my own state of mind." In Shirley Murray's lyric, we, the worshipers, are not silent or absent. We are present—very much so, because we are confessing our need for forgiveness. But we are present not as self-absorbed, feeling-centered, experience-hungry individuals (though we may, indeed, be so), but as a community of disciples, worshiping together, and focusing on the One who has called us.[21]

Because of the Bible's central place in Christianity, a good lyric will usually be, in some sense, "biblical." In the strict sense of the word a "biblical" lyric directly responds to a biblical text, for example, by quotation, allusion, or paraphrase. It respects the text, without misrepresenting it, misquoting it, or filling its silences with unwarranted

---

21. Brueggemann shows how the psalms deliver Israel from spiritual vagueness, because the story always comes with the Name; and from subjectivism (the self as the source of our being), because they meet God as the source of all life. See "The Psalms as Prayer."

speculation. More broadly, a lyric is biblical when its writer takes the Bible as the primary, indispensable record of the Judeo-Christian encounter with God and the classic documentation of Christian faith, and, as in our example above, brings her understanding of the Bible into conversation with her knowledge, experience, and understanding of today's world. As my hymnological mentor, Erik Routley, once said to me, "the great glory of God and the contemporary needs of humanity must be made to collide in modern verse."

Just

To love our neighbors includes treating them justly and fairly, in action, speech, and song. Because a congregational song is sung by a faith community, it will speak fairly and justly about the members of that community and about their global neighbors. Because God loves every human being and creates humankind in the divine image (Genesis 1:27), a just lyric reflects God's valuation of the potential and dignity of human beings, and is not marred by language that wounds, stereotypes, degrades, and excludes. Recognizing such language is a lifelong journey, because from childhood we absorb, not only the grammar and syntax of our native tongue, but countless assumptions, stereotypes, and beliefs, all enshrined in the word choices of our forebears. Some are questionable, once we begin to question them, and many are changeable, once we accept the need for change. Everything I learn about justice in language comes from others who correct me.

For example, though darkness and light are natural opposites, darkness can mean mystery as well as disorientation, hiddenness as well as danger. Yet few lyrics explore these positive themes. Centuries-old associations of darkness with blackness, and blackness with evil, have become the witting or unwitting tools of white racism. A just lyric avoids such associations and the assumptions they convey.

Similarly, a just lyric will nowadays step around the habit of thought by which blindness is so often a metaphor for "stubbornness," as in John Newton's hymn "Amazing Grace" ("I once was lost, but now am found, was blind, but now I see"). Though the metaphor has biblical roots,[22] it is unfair to unsighted persons if their condition is recognized in worship only in this negative fashion. Tom Troeger shows a better way when he imagines Thomas as an unsighted man whose sense of

---

22. See, for example, Isaiah 6:10 and John 9:35–41.

touch is so acute that his fingers touch the risen Christ and read "like Braille/the markings of the spear and nail" (see below, p. 370).

A just lyric will not reinforce cultural stereotypes of age and gender. If we routinely portray youth as energetic and impassioned and old age as weary and hidebound, we are neither doing justice, nor telling the truth. Similar problems apply to the assumption, in most classic liturgies and prayers, that the typical, universal sin is pride, by which human beings rebel against God and reject God's authority. Because most of these "classical" authors were men, feminist scholars suggest that pride is seen as the besetting sin because male experience is being projected universally. Just lyrics will recognize the equally damaging distortions—experienced by many women, and also some men—of socialized subordination, learned passivity, losing ourselves in taking care of others, and that first symptom of estrangement recorded in the Bible, namely, hiding ourselves from God (Genesis 3:8).[23]

Frugal

Frugality means the practice of economy, a down-to-earth simplicity acknowledging our dependence on God's goodness. The opposite of extravagance, frugality means being content with less than abundance. A classic expression of frugality comes from seventeenth-century England. In Part II of John Bunyan's *Pilgrim's Progress*, Mr. Greatheart and the other pilgrims meet a shepherd boy, who sings:

> I am content with what I have,
>   little be it or much;
> and, Lord, contentment still I crave,
>   because thou savest such.
>
> Fullness to such a burden is
>   that go on pilgrimage*;
> here little, and hereafter bliss,
>   is best from age to age.[24]

*Material wealth (fullness) is an impediment (burden) to those who follow Christ ("such . . . that go on pilgrimage").

---

23. See Grey, *Feminist Redemption and the Christian Tradition;* Dunfee, *Beyond Servanthood;* and Saiving, "The Human Situation: A Feminine View."

24. From "He that is down needs fear no fall," Hymn 676 in *Hymns and Psalms.* For a background note, see *Companion to "Hymns and Psalms,"* p. 384.

In worship, we practice frugality by avoiding speech and actions that are showy and extravagant—sound and beauty signifying nothing. In congregational song lyrics, frugality manifests itself as clarity, simplicity, and brevity. Clarity gives allusion without confusion,[25] in a lyric whose meaning can be grasped at first sight. Though we may not fully comprehend it, we sufficiently grasp its meaning to make a yes-or-no response to it as we sing. To put it negatively, nothing in the lyric will make us say, "Eh? What?"

Congregational song lyrics should be simple because, in the words of nineteenth-century hymn writer John Ellerton (speaking about hymns), they "are not for the few, but for the many . . . they should be easy to understand; the language plain, the thoughts not too far-fetched." Brevity makes simplicity memorable. Without it, says Ellerton, a hymn "flows on till it has outgrown its strength."[26] In the words of the old English proverb, a good lyric practices frugality because enough is as good as a feast.

Beautiful

Beauty in song lyrics is marked by words and phrases memorable enough to withstand repetition, whose hallmarks include metaphor, smile, epigram, and economy, cast in pleasing sounds and rhythms. A lyric has beauty when we smile at the pleasure of an arresting phrase, an exact choice of words, or a vivid metaphor. In its absence we groan inwardly at words and phrases that are trite, unsurprising, and uninspired. When phrases recur, as in a refrain or repeated chorus, there are, I suggest, two kinds of expectation. When the recurring words are apt, fresh, and exact, with pleasing sounds and rhythms, they are gladly anticipated; when flat and banal, their recurrence is disappointing or depressing.

Such judgments are partly a matter of taste—but not entirely. Eugene Nida, a linguist and Bible translator, uses the word "information" to mean data with an impact, words and phrases that register at a deep, motivating level. "If we can predict the occurrence of a particular word or expression," says Nida, "then that word carries very little 'information' or impact." When we sing a lyric whose rhymes, phrases, and word choices are so obvious that we can see· them

---

25. Idle, "The Language of Hymnody."
26. "John Ellerton on Good Hymnody."

coming, they have little power to inspire and motivate us (unless, perhaps, the music is independently memorable). Applying Nida's insight to words and music in worship, Robert Mitchell concludes that "the more predictable it is, the less impact it will have on our consciousness."[27]

In worship lyrics, as in worship, beauty is not an end in itself. If not devout, pleasing sounds are hollow and empty. Without frugality, beauty becomes extravagant, as when an artist's self-expression upstages the worship of God and the needs of the worshiping community. When prayer and praise are escapist and uncaring, when language excludes or makes people invisible, or when pleasing sounds convey or hide oppressive meanings, worship lyrics (and worship itself) though beautiful, can be unjust.

Take, for example, *The Book of Common Prayer,* which originated in sixteenth-century England and was not revised until the early years of the twentieth century. In many cases, its now archaic language is still fresh, truthful, and appealing, as in the Collect for Purity:

> Almighty God,
> unto whom all hearts be open,
> all desires known,
> and from whom no secrets are hid;
> Cleanse the thoughts of our hearts
> by the inspiration of thy Holy Spirit
> that we may perfectly love thee,
> and worthily magnify thy holy Name;
> through Christ our Lord.

Sometimes, however, the language is more questionable. The compilers of *The Book of Common Prayer* lived in an age of absolute monarchy. From Henry VIII to Elizabeth I, Tudor monarchs ruled with an iron hand. To defend their thrones against internal dissidents and external enemies, they used bribery, threats, spies, imprisonment, torture, show trials, and the executioner's block. Not surprisingly, the compilers of *The Book of Common Prayer* sometimes see God as a Tudorized monarch: unpredictable, suspicious, and dangerous; a power to be feared and placated, a terrifying authority requiring submission and tribute, as in the following prayer:

---

27. Mitchell, *I Don't Like That Music,* p. 29.

> We acknowledge and *bewail* our *manifold* sins and *wickedness*,
> which we from time to time *most grievously* have committed,
> by thought, word, and deed, *against thy divine Majesty*,
> *provoking* most justly thy *wrath and indignation* against us.
> We do *earnestly* repent,
> and are *heartily* sorry for these our misdoings;
> *The remembrance of them is grievous unto us*,
> *the burden of them is intolerable.* [Emphases mine.]

Say this prayer aloud, and you will, I think, hear pleasing sounds, rhythms that make for easy congregational reading, a coherent structure, and neat rhetorical devices like the balancing phrases at the end of the quotation (remembrance—grievous / burden—intolerable). However, because God is viewed through the distorting lens of Tudor monarchy, divine holiness mutates into ferocity, and human contrition degenerates into groveling. Therefore, to put my argument in verse:

> We cannot be beguiled by pleasant sounds.
> The cadences of Cranmer and King James
> caress the palate, smooth as ancient wine,
> yet clothe the humble power of love divine
> in Tudor pomp, and Absolutist claims,
> while soaring plainsong from a thousand tongues
> sent Inquisition victims to the flames.
> We cannot be beguiled by pleasant sounds.[28]

To put the point I'm arguing another way, liturgical beauty does not stand alone, but is a desirable quality of devoutness, justice, and frugality. In congregational song lyrics, we hope to find, not "beauty" for its own sake, but language that is beautifully just, beautifully frugal, and beautifully devout. When these conditions are met, we legitimately delight in the sound and rhythm of well-chosen words, the clarity, brevity, and simplicity of phrases, the satisfaction of a surprising and appropriate rhyme, the intellectual and emotive power of well-crafted, well-ordered similes and metaphors, and the conceptual, syntactical, phonetic, and semantic architecture of the whole.

---

28. Wren, "We cannot be beguiled by pleasant sounds" (*Piece Together Praise*, #201). The first line is from Jennings: "Why are you walking away?"

When beauty combines with devoutness, justice and frugality, the result, in any kind of lyric, is what hymn writer John Ellerton called "vigor . . . the most important intellectual characteristic of a hymn." A vigorous lyric, says Ellerton, is "animated; not too reflective and diffuse; speaking in words which, though calm, are forcible." It has no "tame and spiritless imitation," no "weak dilution" of a mentor's work. Reviewing great hymns of the past, he concludes that some are long, some short, and all differ widely in merit: "but they have one thing in common—vigor—and therefore they live and speak on to human hearts."[29]

Communal

Congregational song is by definition communal. Though its lyrics come from individual authors, their primary purpose is not to express an individual viewpoint and display the author's personality, but to give "shared expression to shared experience."[30] They are community speech, sung (or spoken) by a congregation.

Because it is communal, a congregational lyric should be clear in meaning and open to multiple significance. Using the Latin translation of Luke 2:14, Jacques Berthier fashions the angel song, "Glory to God in the highest," into a well-known congregational round:

> Gloria, gloria, in excelsis Deo!
> Gloria, gloria! Alleluia! Alleluia!
>
> Words: Public domain. The music to this chorus is © 1979 Les Presses de Taizé, France. Used by permission of G.I.A. Publications, Inc.

The meaning is clear and simple: an outpouring of praise, unrestricted and unqualified, so that the singers can bring to it their own particular reasons for praising God. The lyric can signify any number of reasons for giving praise, and a wide range of feelings and attitudes: calm, exuberance, relief, penitence, wonder, and commitment, for example.

Some lyrics continue to be sung because their meanings remain timely, and so open to new significance. In the summer of 1930, Harry Emerson Fosdick wrote a processional hymn, "God of Grace and God of Glory," for the opening service of the new Riverside Church in New

---

29. "John Ellerton on Good Hymnody."
30. Idle, "The Language of Hymnody."

York City in October of that year. Today, when its singers ask God to give wisdom and courage for "the facing of this hour" and "the living of these days," the words specify the present time, and are always meaningful, because the present time, whenever it is, is when the words are being sung. More remarkably, though our culture has radically changed since 1930, Fosdick's language still delineates not only the "warring madness" of our world, but the "selfish gladness" of a mass-consumption society, "rich in things and poor in soul."[31]

Because congregational song is communal, one test of a lyric is: Can people of different gender, generations, cultures, and circumstances find themselves in these words? Can they be sung "by a family that has just visited its high-schooler in a psychiatric ward and by newlyweds home from their honeymoon"? Can they help "the wanderer on an agonizing spiritual journey and an old-timer secure in faith before death"?[32]

Many congregational songs use the first-person singular, but this does not necessarily prevent them from being communal. A statement of deep devotion or commitment to God may require us all to say "I" as we sing it together, because "we" is less intense and commits the individual singer less strongly. A lyric saying "I" can be a communal utterance if it focuses the singer on God and is implicitly or explicitly aware of the community in which each individual sings.

The meaning of "I" in worship has changed over time. In the eighteenth century, the "I" in Isaac Watts's hymn "When I Survey the Wondrous Cross" meant the model believer with whom the singers were expected to identify, thus hopefully growing in faith. "When I survey" meant "I, in common with everyone else in this congregation."

Nowadays, "I" more likely means, "I, as distinct from you and everyone else." Each singer is believed to be an autonomous individual who makes "free" (though mostly market-driven) choices and has distinctive personal experiences (as when Lanny Wolfe says, "*I can feel* his [God's] mighty power"[33]). In our individualistic culture, the "I" in a good congregational song should take special pains to be devout, focusing mainly on God and minimally on itself.

It ought to go without saying that the "I" in congregational song is

---

31. See Young, *Companion to the United Methodist Hymnal*, p. 266. Fosdick's hymn appears in most modern hymnals.

32. Ramshaw, "Words Worth Singing."

33. See p. 210.

a human voice, not the voice of God, except in brief biblical quotations, peripheral to the theme, where a divine voice is heard. This cannot go without saying, however, because of the popularity of "I am God" songs in today's worship. However appealing their music, it is illogical and presumptuous for us to take upon ourselves the voice of God. Though God is closer than breathing, we are not divine, and should avoid the temptation to play God, and put ourselves in the place of God. For this reason I minimize the use of such songs; prefer the third-person adaptation of Michael Joncas's "On Eagle's Wings" ("And God will raise you / us up . . ."—originally "I [God] will raise you up"); and usually ask soloists or choir to sing the stanzas of Dan Schutte's dramatization of Isaiah 6:8 ("I, the Lord of Sea and Sky"), with the congregation joining in the refrain ("Here I am, Lord. . . . I have heard you calling in the night").[34]

Because hymns express communal viewpoints, it is important to ask whom they include and exclude. When a congregation sings the first-person plural, it may intend only to affirm its own identity; yet each time it sings "we" it defines who it is in relation—or opposition—to someone else, and sends a message about itself to anyone who may be listening. Sometimes the message is explicit, as in the favorite hymn of a strict Calvinist sect which in former times allegedly held open-air worship in London's Hyde Park:

> We are the Savior's Chosen few.
>   The rest of You Be Damned.
> There's Room enough in Hell for You.
>   We can't have Heaven Crammed.

Thus, it is important to ask, "Who are 'we' in a given song, prayer, or other piece of liturgy?" Does it mean "we palefaces"? How might it sound to Native Americans and African Americans? "we Americans"? How might it sound to Mexicans, Iranians, and Filipinos? "we English"? How might it sound to other Europeans, and to Scots, Irish, and Welsh? "we suburbanites"? How might it sound to a downtown congregation? "we men"? How might it sound to women and children? "we middle-aged"? How might it sound to young adults and teenagers, whose formative experiences are different?

Every lyric presents a viewpoint. Some appeal widely. Others get

---

34. See the *United Methodist Hymnal*, #143 and #593.

limited use, because their viewpoint is less widely acceptable. Because a song cannot usually argue its viewpoint, but must state or assume it, a critic who dissents from its viewpoint may dismiss it as "preachy." The label is not justified, however, simply because you disagree with what the lyric says. If a congregation accepts its viewpoint and sings the song, it may simply be that you belong in a different congregation. "Preachiness" is a label best reserved for cases where the writer has placed him/herself outside the presumed congregation and is talking at it, rather than speaking for it from within. One of my early hymns, which I'd prefer not to perpetuate, began as follows:

> Half the world is hungry, Lord.
>   Christian people, sleekly fed,
> Christian comforts can afford:
>   worship, faith, and daily bread.
> Others crave for earthly food,
>   starving, have no strength to pray.
>   [Glib, we sing how God is good—
> we] shall eat and drink today.[35]

Though I apparently included myself in the congregation by using the first-person plural ("We shall eat and drink today"), other word choices betray me: I was the one who was "glib," in not seriously regarding myself as one of the "Christian people" I hoped would be converted by singing the hymn. The result is a tone accurately described as preachy—even if some congregations still choose to sing it!

Finally, because the lyrics of congregational song are intended for communal use, a faith community may, in principle, amend them to meet changes in language, convictions, and needs. I shall discuss this issue when looking at hymn lyrics (Chapter 8, below), though it applies, in principle, to any form of congregational song.

Purposeful

A good song lyric is purposeful; it fulfills the potential of its genre and does more than simply pass the time. For example: a purposeful chorus memorably states its theme; a purposeful refrain vividly

---

35. Wren, *Piece Together Praise*, #189.

responds to the message of its song; and a purposeful hymn develops its theme and comes to a satisfying conclusion. I shall look at purposefulness again in the next and succeeding chapters.

Musical

Finally, a good lyric is musical, meaning that it is fit to be set to music and composer-friendly. Composer Sue Mitchell-Wallace affirms that "good writing helps good composing. Graphic images, metaphors, drama, action words coupled with disciplined, consistent meter and rhythm stimulate a composer's imagination and creativity."[36] Hymn writer John Ellerton writes in similar vein, arguing that "the meter . . . ought not to be too complex, or greatly varied. The rhythm ought not to be rugged, nor the diction bald and prosaic."[37] Sue Mitchell-Wallace adds that polysyllabic words are hard to set and tedious to sing. Rhythm is the most important link in congregational song, and, unless chosen carefully and sparingly, three- and four-syllable words break up the word rhythm and flow. Consistency of form is important. If the song is longer than a chorus, the pattern of emphasis must be consistent between like-numbered lines of each succeeding stanza. If line two of stanza one goes, "DA-de-DA-de-DA-de-DA," and line two of stanza two goes, "DA-de-de-DA-de-de-DA," most tunes will stumble awkwardly at the inconsistency. A composer-friendly lyric will often have patterns of repetition (a refrain, a phrase, or a word), so that "a composer can give that word or phrase similar or sequential melodic and/or rhythmic treatment." A "musical" text is economical in its subject matter; if there are too many topics, the music cannot do justice to the content. "It is easier to work with a few central ideas so that the music complements the text."[38]

Conclusion

Analyzing the lyrics of congregational song, I have argued that shared meaning is possible, even when a song lyric is understood with varying degrees of precision; metaphors receive a range of interpretations; words, phrases, and metaphors are misread and misunderstood;

---

36. Mitchell-Wallace, "The Composer's Connection."
37. "John Ellerton on Good Hymnody."
38. Mitchell-Wallace, "The Composer's Connection."

and individual connotations skew individual interpretations. By contrast with a lyric's meaning, its "significance" (what its meaning suggests, evokes, and conveys to individuals) varies from time to time and from place to place. Though significance is more personal than communal, it can sometimes be shared. When a congregation sings a song, the music affects the significance of the words, but does not alter their meaning.

From my perspective in a "Reformed" tradition, I have argued that a good congregational song lyric is devout, just, frugal, beautiful, communal, purposeful, and musical. In succeeding chapters I shall apply these principles to the lyrics of the genres identified in Chapter 3, beginning with rounds, refrains, and choruses.

Chapter Six

"Sing Them Over Again to Me": Refrains, Choruses, and Other People's Songs

Sing them over again to me,
Wonderful words of life.
        —P. P. Bliss, 1874

Earlier, I argued that congregational song lyrics deserve critical attention. As works of popular theology, memorized if repeatedly sung, they influence and express our beliefs. I proposed two overlapping types of classification, relative and functional, and found seven functionally different genres: hymns, choruses, rounds, refrains, chant, ritual song, and spirit singing. In the preceding chapter, I argued that congregational song lyrics are necessarily communal, and should also be devout, just, frugal, beautiful, purposeful, and musical. In this and following chapters I shall examine the lyrics of particular genres (see Chapter 3, above).

Some genres need only brief comment. Like choruses, *rounds* are typically short and designed for repeated singing. The main difference is musical: a round's repetition gives the effect of part song. In terms of their lyrics, rounds have the same characteristics as choruses. When a congregation *sings in the Spirit,* little can usefully be said about lyrics, if any, because they are individual choices, made spontaneously. It would be interesting to compare spirit-singing congregations to see if individual word choices fall into patterns influenced by social, theological, and other factors; this may have been done, but I have no data.

Other genres need more discussion. In this chapter, I look briefly at a relative category, "other people's songs," then consider refrains and choruses, whose lyrics are typically short and designed for easy repetition.

"Other People's Songs"

Relatively speaking, some songs are "our songs" (familiar to our congregation, probably from our own culture and tradition). Others, in relation to "us," are "other people's songs" (familiar or unfamiliar, but from a different culture and experience). A familiar song can, of course, be sung without comment. If so, we need ask only how well the lyric fulfills the function of the song's particular genre: as hymn, chorus, or ritual song, for example. For we are assuming, whether we realize it or not, that the lyric speaks for "us," expressing our faith, hopes, and worldview.

By definition, "other people's songs" also express the wisdom, faith, sorrow, struggle, and hope of other members of the body of Christ. To sing them as such, we need information. Most recent hymnals have companion volumes about their music and lyrics, and "global" song collections usually describe their origins.[1] When a song is "other" to us, its origin is important, as also the meaning: why it says what it says. The music may also "sound different," but the whys and wherefores of different musics are beyond my scope.

The best way to experience a song's "otherness" is to teach the tune, if necessary (see Chapter 3 above), briefly describe the original context, and read or quote from the lyric. If the song is new to "us," it is helpful to hear the words before singing them; if familiar, quotation jogs our memory.

Sometimes, as with one widely known Native American hymn, we need to do little more than mention its origin and history (in giving examples I speak, as always, from my own cultural perspective). "Wakantanka taku nitawa" was written in the Dakota language for a traditional Dakota tune, sometime between 1835 and 1842, by Joseph Renville, a Dakota-French fur trader and Bible translator, at the Lac qui Parle ("Talking Lake") Indian mission, in what is now western Minnesota. From a words-only hymnal for Dakota congregations in

---

1. A comprehensive list of sources can be obtained from the Book Service, Hymn Society in the U.S.A. and Canada, Boston University School of Theology, 745 Commonwealth Ave., Boston, MA 02215-1401.

Nebraska, the Dakotas, and Montana, it began appearing in camp songbooks throughout the United States. Young paleface Americans loved it for its tune, even without knowing the meaning of the words.[2]

In 1929, Philip Frazier, a Native American Congregational minister, rendered the hymn into English. In 1995, the *New Century Hymnal* published both Frazier's version and a more complete translation by Sidney Bird, a Dakota Presbyterian pastor in Santa Fe.[3] Both versions have the traditional Dakota melody, identified by the old mission name, LACQUIPARLE. Frazier's version reads:

> Many and great, O God, are your works,
>   Maker of earth and sky;
> your hands have set the heavens with stars,
> your fingers spread the mountains and plains.
> Lo, at your word the waters were formed;
>   deep seas obey your voice.
>
> Grant unto us communion with you,
>   O star-abiding One;
> come unto us and dwell with us:
> with you are found the gifts of life.
> Bless us with life that has no end,
>   eternal life with you.

The historical note, above, gives important information about the origin of the song—for example, that Joseph Renville was not a French missionary, as his name might suggest, but bilingual (French-Dakotan), writing in one of his own languages. As such, and as a Bible translator, his lyric builds a bridge between Christian faith and Dakota traditions. According to one account, "The Dakotas had always believed in a Power greater than themselves, manifesting itself in the universe. They referred to it as Wakan, sought to understand it, and worshipped it through its various revelations," whether beneficent (such as rivers, the warm sun, and growing plants) or terrifying (thunder, for example).[4]

Another historical note is more poignant, and more troubling.

---

2. Young, *Companion to the United Methodist Hymnal*, p. 480 ("Many and Great").

3. *The New Century Hymnal*, #3 and #341.

4. Young, *Companion to the United Methodist Hymnal*, p. 480 ("Many and Great"), quoting from *Lift Every Voice*, a Methodist Church publication from 1953.

Recalling accounts told by his grandfather and others, Sidney Bird tells how "this hymn was sung by thirty-eight Dakota Indian prisoners of war as they went to the gallows at Mankato, Minnesota, on December 26, 1862, in the largest mass execution in American history."[5] Did watching American soldiers know, I wonder, that Christians were singing in the face of death?

Sometimes the lyrics of "someone else's song" can tell us more than we might previously have suspected. "O Mary, Don't You Weep, Don't You Mourn" is one of the African American songs commonly known as "spirituals." More accurately, William Farley Smith calls them "slave songs,"[6] a label that describes their origin among the enslaved and recalls the suffering and resistance to which they bear witness. I follow Farley Smith's suggestion, noting that because they have proved capable of inspiring other struggles for freedom, a slave song is also a freedom song.[7] The lyric reads:

REFRAIN:
O Mary, don't you weep, don't you mourn,
O Mary, don't you weep, don't you mourn;
Pharaoh's army got drownded,
O Mary, don't you weep.
    One of these mornings bright and fair,
    goin'a take my wings and cleave the air;
    Pharaoh's army got drownded,
    O Mary, don't you weep.
(Refrain)
    When I get to heaven goin'a sing and shout,
    ain't nobody there goin'a turn me out;
    Pharaoh's army got drownded,
    O Mary, don't you weep.
(Refrain)
    When I get to heaven goin'a put on my shoes,
    goin'a run about and spread the news;
    Pharaoh's army got drownded,
    O Mary, don't you weep.
(Refrain)[8]

---

5. Footnote beneath "Great Spirit God," Sidney H. Bird's translation of this hymn, *The New Century Hymnal*, #341.

6. Smith, *Songs of Deliverance*, p. 9 and throughout.

7. I owe this insight to a workshop participant at Associated Mennonite Biblical Seminary, Elkhart, Indiana, in February 1997.

8. The lyric has several minor variants. This version is from the *United Methodist Hymnal*, #134, emphasis mine.

Like many other slave songs, "O Mary, Don't You Weep, Don't You Mourn" has coded messages of hope and resistance.[9] Whether the Mary in question is the mother of Jesus standing by the cross or Mary Magdalene weeping by the tomb, the interjection, "Pharaoh's army got drownded," has a double meaning. It reminds us that God, who saved Israel in the exodus, can overturn the death sentence on Jesus Christ. And it affirms that today's pharaohs will be overthrown and their slaves set free. On one level, the singer looks forward to going to heaven, an otherworldly hope unlikely to disturb slave owners who might have chanced to hear it. Dig deeper, and we hear the enslaved congregation singing about a place, and a time, when no one will be excluded ("ain't nobody there goin'a turn me out") and the singers have both the footwear and freedom of movement denied them as slaves.

Refrains

Besides asking whether a refrain is communal, devout, just, frugal, beautiful, and musical, it should be assessed in terms of its purpose: to summarize the message of a congregational song, or to give a moment of participation in a song sung to the congregation. In today's culture, a refrain should generally be short and to the point. As punch line and sound bite, a good refrain is remembered long after the rest of the song is forgotten. From the nineteenth century, memorable refrains include "Wonderful words of life" (P. P. Bliss), "Standing on the promises" (R. Kelso Carter), and "This is my story, this is my song" (Fanny J. Crosby). By contrast, Louisa Stead's "Trust in Jesus" has less impact.

> Jesus, Jesus, how I trust him!
> How I've proved him o'er and o'er!
> Jesus, Jesus, precious Jesus!
> O for grace to trust him more!

Its sequence of devotional acclamations has minimal originality, focuses heavily in the singer, and responds to a verse lyric itself full of clichés, some still in use ("'Tis so sweet," "O how sweet," "Yes, 'tis sweet," "take him at his word," "just to trust," and "trust his cleansing blood"). A good refrain is more than a bunch of catchphrases tacked

---

9. The coded messages in slave songs are well documented. See Smith, *Songs of Deliverance*, and Walker, *"Somebody's Calling My Name."*

onto a song. As slogan and punch line, it should summarize or answer the verses to which it responds. A skilled writer can lead up to the refrain in such a way that something new is said each time the expected words arrive, as Fred Pratt Green does here, with the single word, "Alleluia!":

> When in our music God is glorified,
> and adoration leaves no room for pride,
> it is as though the whole creation cried: Alleluia!
>
> How often, making music, we have found
> a new dimension in the world of sound,
> as worship moved us to a more profound Alleluia.
>
> So has the church, in liturgy and song,
> in faith and love, through centuries of wrong,
> borne witness to the truth in every tongue: Alleluia!

In the first stanza, "Alleluia!" is creation's response to God, and the object of the verb "cried." In the second, as a noun qualified by "more profound," it is our response to God, prompted by music. In the third, it stands grammatically alone, as an exclamation celebrating the church's witness to God's truth.

In form, a refrain should exactly repeat itself, so that singers of all ages can learn it, know what is coming, and sing it with confidence. I have heard contemporary songs whose refrain varies from verse to verse, with the aim, perhaps, of adding interest or meaning. Though I have done this myself, I now regard it as mistaken. Take, for example, this extract from a hymn of mine based on the *New English Bible* translation of Romans 12:9–17:

> We want to love
> antagonists and enemies,
> giving blessings,
> meaning what we say:
> > *Deep, cool, well of peace,*
> > *wine of mercy at the feast,*
> > *Holy Spirit, come!*
>
> We want to serve
> with confident humility,

facing trouble,
never losing heart:
> *Green, strong, living oak,*
> *seed and root and flower of hope,*
> *Holy Spirit, come!*

Though the emphasized lines are formatted as a refrain, they have too much variation to function effectively as such, and are best understood as part of the hymn.

Choruses—Taizé

Earlier, I defined a chorus as a short congregational song that states its theme without developing it, in words and music designed for easy singing, repetition, and "uplift." Thus defined, the genre includes both "Taizé" and "evangelical" choruses, despite their liturgical and musical differences.[10]

The Taizé community was founded in 1949, in Burgundy, France. Though originally a Protestant initiative, it is ecumenical in character and keeps close informal contacts with the Roman Catholic Church. With a spirituality that combines personal discipleship and social awareness, it has become an international center. People—especially youth—come to Taizé from all over Europe and from throughout the world.

The music of Taizé is thoroughly congregational. Its flexibility "has brought it into use in all sorts of circumstances, from a small gathering with a guitar or keyboard to a large assembly accompanied by an orchestra."[11] It loses its power if used for performance or entertainment, because by design it is intended for prayer, especially communal prayer. Because Taizé choruses have a wide musical appeal and are typically given repeated singing, they can enter a singer's memory bank and become part of one's prayer life, as people "become aware of a certain melody running through their heads, or find themselves humming a tune: an expression of joy or confidence in God that is not

---

10. See pp. 101–2. I focus on single-verse choruses, leaving aside longer songs that straddle the boundary between "chorus" and "hymn."
11. Wilson-Dickson, *The Story of Christian Music*, p. 227.

always fully conscious."[12] The goal of Taizé-style worship is a particular kind of celebration characterized by an all-inclusive welcome, promoting "a spirit of recollection and an atmosphere of silence."[13]

In the 1970s, the growing international and youth appeal of Taizé led the community to change its song. Musically, what was sung had to appeal across different cultures and be easily learned (there being little time for rehearsal), so that singers could worship through the songs, not struggle with them. Jacques Berthier, a musician friend of Taizé, tried a number of different approaches, and found a solution in the use of "repetitive structures, namely, short musical phrases with singable melodic units that could be readily memorized by everybody," and which used "simple [musical] elements . . . of real musical quality so that genuine prayer could be expressed through them." Building on these elements, other parts could be, and were, included (such as a cantor, choir, and instruments), and "a tonal or modal musical language was expressly chosen to be within the reach of all."

Initially, the community tried having everyone sing in one of the languages represented by participants. This method proved unsatisfactory. In any international gathering, the choice of one language as the medium of communication doubly disadvantages those for whom it is not their first tongue. While they hesitate and stumble, native speakers fluently flow. In discussion, native speakers tend to dominate. At international church conferences, I have heard French participants speak witheringly, with good reason, about "the imperialism of English." Thus, though people gather at Taizé for worship, not debate, it was soon apparent "that some people were being favored while others, for whom that language was 'foreign,' stumbled over the pitfalls of pronunciation." In such circumstances, the song, however beautiful, devout, frugal, communal, purposeful, and musical, could not be described as just.

The solution was to use Latin. A decade earlier, Latin would have been a nonstarter. Until the mid-1960s, it was for most European Protestants negatively associated with exams, elitism, archaism, and Catholicism. Once the Roman Mass had been rendered into people's own languages and Latin ceased to be a university-entrance require-

---

12. Brother Robert, "Foreword" and "Performance Notes" to Berthier, *Music from Taizé: Responses, Litanies, Acclamations, Canons*, pp. vii–viii.

13. These and following quotations before the next footnote are from Brother Robert, "Foreword" and "Performance Notes," pp. vii–viii, x.

ment, these negative associations faded. When the Taizé community began using simple Latin as lyrics for its songs, it was well received. As a dead language, it is roughly equidistant from everyone—I say "roughly" because it may appear less remote to speakers of modern languages (Italian, French, Spanish, Portuguese, and Romanian) directly derived from it. Because it is "foreign" to everyone, it was experienced as neutral: "Everyone is on an equal footing with a language that does not belong to a particular group." It is not hard to pronounce, and variations in pronunciation are unproblematic.

The Sound of What Is Sung

Nowadays, few people speak Latin well enough to think in the language.[14] Though it is an open question whether Latin syllables have uniquely musical qualities[15] (as compared, say, with Japanese, Tamil, Zulu, and Russian), their sound becomes more prominent in Taizé choruses. Frequent repetition highlights the sound of what is repeated. Its meaning, though perhaps intellectually understood, is linguistically "foreign" and "other" to most singers. Like German and French, church Latin has pure vowels, which sound pleasing when elongated in song (aaah, eeeee, etc.), unlike the frequent diphthongs in English (such as—in U.K. standard English—"I" [aa-ee], "out" [aa-oo-t] and "oil" [aw-ee-l]). Finally, the music is crafted to express these particular sounds, so that "the link between the gentle stresses of the Latin and the rhythmic patterns of the music is very close."[16]

The Taizé phenomenon highlights the importance of the sound of what is sung. Grafted as I am into a Reformed tradition, which emphasizes the divine Word and the importance of word meanings, it is important to consider the sonority of simple words sung repeatedly and of vocal sound without verbal meaning.

Shrieks, yells, wails, lullabies, moans, and keening are examples of vocal sound whose semantic content, if any, is secondary to their visceral impact. Variant forms of yodeling, from the European Alps, the

---

14. The few include some professors of ancient languages and members of the Roman *curia*.

15. "There is no doubting the musical sound qualities of Latin syllables," Brother Robert, "Foreword" and "Performance Notes."

16. Wilson-Dickson, *The Story of Christian Music*, p. 227. Brother Robert speaks similarly of "the close link which binds the music to the word-sounds which inspired the music" (See "Foreword" and "Performance Notes").

mountains of China and Kentucky, Pygmy-inhabited African forests, and the Australian outback, all originate as a method of vocal, nonverbal communication across a distance, in areas where visual contact is difficult.[17] In folk songs, children's songs, and recurrently in pop songs, nonsense syllables have perennial appeal. In English, they include true non-sense ("hey, nonny, nonny," "with a too-re-lye-addy-ai-addy-ai-ay," and "de-do-ron-ron-ron, de-do-ron-ron"); words meaningful in other contexts, but semantically displaced and used only for sound ("*hickory*-dickory-*dock*"), and trivial phrases used for vocal effect (in a 1940s popular song, the catchiness of "Mairzy-doats-and-doazy-doats-and-little-lambsy-tivy" lay in its sound, the semantic content being unimportant and probably inaccurate—unless little lambs can indeed eat ivy).

In Western classical music, instances of textless vocal sound range from the sixteenth century to the twentieth, where concert examples include Host's *The Planets* and Debussy's *Nocturnes.*[18] In recent years, thousands of people have bought CDs of Gregorian chant, and hundreds flock to choral vesper services sung in Latin; in both cases, the main attraction is not the meaning of what is sung, but the evocative power of its sound. "New age" and other postmodern music demonstrate the revived appeal of nonverbal vocalization. A striking example, in between art music and pop, is a 1995 compact sound disc, *Adiemus: Songs of Sanctuary,* "an extended choral type work based on the European classical tradition, but where the vocal sound is more akin to 'ethnic' or 'world' music." Musically, it uses classical forms such as the rondo and da capo aria. But the text is written phonetically "with the words viewed as instrumental sound, the idea being to maximize the melisma (an expressive vocal phrase) by removing the distraction, if one can call it that, of words." The choruses are intended to sound "tribal," while the solo parts are intoned in a "sometimes ecclesiastical, sometimes celtic manner."[19] Track titles include Latin or Latin-sounding words, such as *Tintinnabulum, Cantus Inequalis,* and *Cantus Insolitus,* along with non-European sounds (*Amaté Adea,*

---

17. *Grolier Multimedia Encyclopedia,* 1997, s.v. "Yodel."

18. *The New Harvard Dictionary of Music,* s.v. "Vocalise," cites examples in 16th- and 17th-century instrumental works known as "ricercars," as well as the concert works mentioned. The word *"vocalise"* is a French noun meaning "a composition for voice without text." Its counterpart, the verb "to vocalize," means the production of textless sound, mostly done to warm up vocal muscles in readiness for singing.

19. Jenkins, Cover Notes to *Adiemus.*

Kayama) and the English word *Hymn*. The title track, "Adiemus," is an exhilarating vocal flight, heard by millions as the soundtrack to a Delta Airlines TV commercial.[20]

It seems clear that vocal sound has wide appeal, and that the music of Taizé has grown in popularity in an era when textless song has become more widely acceptable. Taizé choruses do, of course, have lyrics conveying meaning. The importance of their vocal sound, however, combined with the customary use of extended repetition, has led some observers to describe them as "mantras," giving the word a negative or positive spin according to the observer's viewpoint and theology. In Hinduism and Buddhism, a *mantra* is "a mystical syllable or phrase used (repeatedly) in ritual and meditation." It has meaning, and repeated singing is believed to link the singer to the divine beings, or spiritual forces, to which it points. By contrast, *Bija-mantras*, or "seed-sounds," have no semantic value; their sound alone is believed to be spiritually efficacious. In the West, the best known *Bija-mantra* is the repeated chant, "Om" (with a long "o," as in "own").[21]

If there are Christian equivalents of *Bija-mantras*, they are outside the mainstream of Christian faith. For most Christian worshipers, the evocative power of vocal sound is inextricably linked with the word meanings it conveys. Clearly, Taizé choruses are not *Bija-mantras*. Their words have meaning and are mostly from the Bible or early Christian tradition. When given extended repetition, however, they can accurately be described as *Christian mantras*, sung in the belief that devout repetition "can promote a kind of inner unity of the person allowing the spirit to be more open and more attentive to what is essential."[22] Such extended repetition links them to other traditions of Christian prayer, such as the Jesus prayer in the early Greek Church and the rosary in the Western Church.

My own tradition comes to Taizé worship with a long-standing suspicion of the nonverbal and nonrational, still only gradually and patchily diminishing. As late as the early 1980s, I recall my then home church, in Oxford, England, being asked to sing a Taizé "Alleluia" three times through, as an acclamation. We sang it once, then coughed

---

20. The Taizé community is well aware of the appeal of nonverbal vocals. Speaking about the musical sound qualities of Latin syllables, Brother Robert adds that, "in this respect, the 'invented languages' found in some contemporary compositions come to mind" ("Foreword" and "Performance Notes").

21. *Grolier Multimedia Encyclopedia*, 1997, s.v. "Mantra."

22. Brother Robert, "Foreword" and "Performance Notes."

and shuffled in embarrassment; it went against the grain to repeat it.
If asked for a rationale, we might have appealed to Matthew 6:7,
ingrained in Presbyterian and Congregationalist memories in its King
James Version ("but when ye pray, use not *vain repetitions,* as the heathen do" [emphasis mine]), which in more disputatious times had
been our body armor against Catholic and Anglican liturgy. A recent
translation reads:

> When you are praying, do not heap up empty phrases as the Gen-
> tiles do; for they think that they will be heard because of their
> many words. Do not be like them, for your Father knows what
> you need before you ask him. (Matthew 6:7–8; the Prayer of Jesus
> [Our Father] follows)[23]

Though repetition can perhaps be described as "heaping up," this
passage cannot validly be used against the songs of Taizé. Whether it
condemns the invocation of many gods, the repetition of prayer formulas, or empty and insincere talk, it is opposing the belief that "one
must impress or gain the attention of the deity or use the correct formula" if the prayer is to be effective. It reminds us that Christian prayer
is not "a manipulative function for the self-interest of the one praying,"
but "an expression of trust in a God who knows our needs before we
ask."[24] In line with this understanding of prayer, Taizé choruses aim to
open the worshiper to God, not bend God in favor of the worshiper.
Nor can repetition of Taizé lyrics be described as "heaping up empty
phrases." Though simple, they are neither empty nor trivial, but classic
expressions of wonder, love, thanksgiving, lament, penitence, longing,
and praise. The sound of the words is important: repetition can enable
us to let go of left-brain constraints and become more open to wonder,
mystery, and transcendence. The sound of the words is important; but
even when sung in Latin, their meaning resonates through their
sounds. Thus, "we receive a bonus, for these sound units compose
words filled with meaning, one which is easily explained and already
'translated' into music by the musician's art and sensitivity."[25]

---

23. NRSV. Compare Sirach 7:14: "Do not babble in the assembly of the elders, and
do not repeat yourself when you pray."

24. M. Eugene Boring, "Matthew," NIB, vol. 7 (1995), ad loc.

25. Brother Robert, "Foreword" and "Performance Notes."

Taizé Lyrics

Taizé chorus lyrics use titles and metaphors drawn from the dominant story line of biblical language and classic Christian creeds. Though they tell the full story only in two settings of the Apostles' Creed, the word choices of other Taizé choruses presuppose it—though some aspects of the story are deemphasized. To summarize the story line, God is portrayed as the monarch of all creation, imaged in male terms and addressed accordingly, as "King" or "Lord." God's son, the crown prince, gives up his place at his father's side, becomes human in Jesus, suffers, dies, is raised from death, and ascends to sit again in glory, able now to give the Holy Spirit, the agent of his (and the father's) living presence, to all who believe.[26] In Taizé lyrics, Father/Son language is not prominent, and "king" is used only rarely, and with reference to Jesus. Divine pronouns are rare, but invariably masculine ("him," "he"). The Holy Spirit is mostly ungendered, but occasionally given the ancient title "father of the poor." The most common title, for God and for Jesus Christ, is "Lord" (or, in Latin, *Dominus*). God is sometimes addressed simply as *Deus* (or the English equivalent, "God"). Though most often called *Dominus* (or, in English, "Lord") Jesus Christ is also frequently addressed directly, or in terms such as "Christ," or simply, "Jesus." Other choruses pray directly to the Holy Spirit, or use an unspecified second-person form of address ("you" or its Latin equivalent). Some say, simply, "Alleluia!" with no specified title for the divine.[27] These variations allow users of Taizé music to fashion worship that follows traditional God-language or avoids it. Though I believe that

---

26. For a full discussion, see my book *What Language Shall I Borrow?*

27. The first two volumes of Taizé music published in North America list a total of 110 items (67 in vol. 1, 43 in vol. 2). Adding variant settings of Alleluias, the Kyrie, Dominus Miserere, Amen, and Tu Solus Sanctus, plus a Cantate Domino with three additional lyrics to the same tune (vol. 1, p. 89) brings the total to approximately 132 items. Of these, 24 speak of God as Dominus (or Lord); 7 use Deus (or God), and 4 use both. In approximately 7 instances, it is unclear whether Dominus (or Lord), means God, Jesus Christ, or both. Seventeen items use Dominus (or Lord) for Jesus Christ, while 14 others say "Jesus," "Jesus Christ," "Lamb," and "Salvator [Savior]." Approximately 6 items use variants of Father/Son/Spirit language. Five items invoke the Holy Spirit; 5 others use various forms of second-person address. There are 10 Alleluias whose divine referent is unspecified. Eight items show God, or Jesus, speaking to us. "King" is used once or twice, with reference to Jesus, and "kingdom of God/kingdom of heaven" occurs from time to time in quotations from the Gospels. See Berthier, *Music from Taizé*, vol. 2.

"LORD" for God is problematic (see below, pp. 243–52), it is arguably less obtrusive in Taizé lyrics than elsewhere. Frequent use of Latin puts some titles for God at one remove from the singer's native language, while lyrics and music alike emphasize reverence, joy, and mystery. Overall, there is a notable focus on Jesus, his teaching, death, resurrection, and life-giving blessings.[28]

The power of meaning, music, and vocal sound in Taizé-style worship can be experienced not only in Latin, but in the worshiper's own tongue. Not long ago I worshiped at an Episcopal cathedral in a vesper-cum-Communion service built musically with Taizé songs. As hundreds filed forward to receive Communion, we sang, and sang, and sang:

> Eat this bread, drink this cup.
> Come to me, and never be hungry.
> Eat this bread, drink this cup.
> Trust in me, and you will not thirst.[29]

> © 1984 Les Presses de Taizé, France. Used by permission of G.I.A. Publications, Inc.

The whole congregation sang, with individual voices now loud, now soft, now in unison, now in harmony, some off-key but vocally embraced by the majority. I lost count of the number of repetitions as I, also, was embraced by the sound. Yet for all the beauty of the music and the sonority of the words, I never found myself distant from their meaning, and never felt tired or bored. On the contrary, the repetition of these deep, yet simple, phrases brought a profound sense of wonder. joy, gratitude, and peace, focused on the Table, the bread, and the wine. Interest and vocal color were added by melody-based instruments and by the verses, sung by the cantor, weaving over and under our own unbroken song.

"Evangelical" Choruses

There are thousands of evangelical choruses in circulation. For theological reasons, or because they are ephemeral, many are unlikely to be considered by mainline churches. Because of this, and because I can't cover all the material, I shall take examples from the *Abingdon*

---

28. Extended verses for the cantor include the Beatitudes (Matthew 5:1–12), narrative of the foot washing (based on John 13:1–17), and the complete story of Jesus' life, death, and resurrection (*Music from Taizé*, vol. 1, pp. 4, 14, and 63).

29. Berthier, *Music from Taizé,* vol. 2, pp. 30–31.

Chorus Book 1, a compilation specifically aiming to be a "worship resource for 'mainline' or 'traditional' churches."[30] More varied theologically than most such collections,[31] it has eighty-eight choruses and similar items, arranged to facilitate their inclusion in "traditional" liturgies throughout the church year. These choruses are culturally, and probably generationally, specific. I suspect that they appeal mainly to particular socioeconomic subgroups of the "boomer" generation (born 1946–64),[32] in paleface congregations. I hope that some of the issues they raise will also apply to "alternative" congregational songs (as defined above, p. 133), but don't have enough access to this music to discuss it. I shall look at the theology of individual lyrics, at choruses sung in sequence, and at broader language issues raised by these and similar examples of the genre.

However one views their theology, these songs are deeply devout, in both lyrics and music. The linguistic world of the evangelical chorus places the singer in a direct, personal, loving relationship with God, or Jesus—sometimes it is unclear whether we are addressing both or one or the other. "I love you, Lord," we sing. "All I need is Jesus"; "We bring the sacrifice of praise, we worship and adore you"; "Your loving-kindness is better than life"; "Blessed be the name of the Lord." These and similar statements occur frequently, reinforced by repetition.

The lyrics are usually clear in meaning. Whether they are open to varied significance[33] depends partly on the lyric itself and partly on the worshiper's response to its theology. A chorus reiterating the word "Alleluia!" is open to multiple significance, as are the psalmic penitential phrase "Create in me a clean heart, O God" and the repeated exclamation, "Thank you, Lord!"—provided we are at home with its "Lord" language and the clichéd "I *just* want to thank you, Lord" that concludes it (on "LORD," see below, pp. 243–52).[34] By contrast, our

---

30. See Bibliography at Bryan et al.

31. The eighty-eight items in *Abingdon Chorus Book 1* include two slave songs, at least three "black gospel" songs, three Taizé choruses, a Jewish folk song, and songs or choruses from Mexico (1), Spain (3), Ghana (1), Zimbabwe (1), and Pakistan (1). Marvin Frey's camp song, "Kum by Yah" (originally, "Come by Here") is wrongly identified as African American. See VanDyke, "Closing the Case on 'Kum ba Yah.'"

32. See Roof, *A Generation of Seekers.*

33. See above, p. 173.

34. See the first stanza of "Alleluia!" by Jerry Sinclair, "Create in me a clean heart, O God" (Psalm 51:10), and the traditional, "Thank you, Lord," nos. 8, 50, and 77 in *Abingdon Chorus Book 1.*

theological viewpoint will determine the openness and acceptability, or otherwise, of being "cleansed by the blood of the Lamb."[35]

Earlier, I suggested that a devout lyric for congregational song will usually be "biblical," in a broader or stricter sense. In the broader sense, it will take the Bible as the primary, indispensable record of the Judeo-Christian encounter with God, and bring it into conversation with the lyricist's knowledge, experience, and understanding of today's world. Or, in the stricter sense, it will respond directly to a biblical text, without misrepresenting it, misquoting it, or filling its silences with unwarranted speculation.

In common with kindred compilations, the *Abingdon Chorus Book 1* claims to follow the stricter sense of "biblical." It presents its material as "rooted in scripture and tradition" and "returning to scripture itself as the source of the lyrics."[36] Both claims are partly right, and partly wrong. An overgenerous index of scripture references blurs important differences in the way scripture sources are used, and half of them are merely passages that one could profitably link with a chorus, not sources having a direct verbal connection to it. Analyzing the lyrics, I find four distinguishable relationships with biblical material, on a spectrum where some categories shade into others.

At one end of the spectrum is direct quotation: a lyric quotes one or more scripture passages, without addition or alteration, except occasional minor changes of syntax. Thus, Gary Alan Smith takes Isaiah 60:1 and sets it to music: "Arise, shine; for your light has come, and the glory of the LORD has risen upon you."[37] A step away from this is partial quotation with interpretation. In Philippians 2:9–11, Paul writes:

> Therefore God also highly exalted him
>   and gave him the name
>   that is above every name,
> so that at the name of Jesus
>   every knee should bend, . . .
> and every tongue . . . confess
>   that Jesus Christ is Lord,
>   to the glory of God the Father.

---

35. Gerrit Gustafson, "Only by Grace," no. 50 in *Abingdon Chorus Book 1*.
36. *Abingdon Chorus Book 1*, p. iii.
37. Ibid., #2.

In response, Naida Hearns adds other acclamations, in her lyric:

> Jesus, Name above all names, beautiful Savior, glorious Lord.
> Emmanuel, God is with us, blessed Redeemer, living Word.[38]

Another example is the following lyric by David Haas:

> Do not be afraid, I am with you.
> I have called you by name.
> Come and follow me. I will bring you home.
> I love you and you are mine.[39]

The author here quotes and reinterprets Isaiah 43:1:

> But now thus says the LORD,
>   he who created you, O Jacob,
>   he who formed you, O Israel:
> Do not fear, for I have redeemed you;
>   I have called you by name, you are mine.

More remote are choruses whose generic phrases have no obvious roots in any one passage, as in this traditional song:

> We worship and adore you, bowing down before you, songs of
>   praises singing, hallelujahs ringing. Hallelujah, hallelujah,
>   hallelujah, hallelujah, Amen.[40]

Finally, a substantial number of lyrics are free composition, using scriptural motifs instead of direct quotation, as in this lyric by Henry Smith:

> Give thanks with a grateful heart; give thanks to the Holy One;
> give thanks because he's given Jesus Christ his Son. [Repeat]
> And now let the weak say, "I am strong,"

---

38. *Abingdon Chorus Book 1*, #33. Three additional, anonymous stanzas add other titles of Christ, including "Light of the Gentiles," "Son of David," "Rose of Sharon," "Bread of Life," and "Living Water."

39. Ibid., # 54.

40. Ibid., #6.

let the poor say, "I am rich,"
because of what the Lord has done for us. [Repeat]
Give thanks, give thanks, give thanks![41]

When we read or sing a freely composed lyric, its theological stance is usually obvious, even if its scriptural roots are generic or remote. A lyric that quotes from the Bible also expresses its own theological viewpoint. Even a direct quotation inevitably interprets what is quoted. *There is no such thing as "simply singing scripture."*

Suppose, for example, that we sing Gary Alan Smith's quotation from Isaiah 60:1;

> Arise, shine; for your light has come,
>   and the glory of the LORD has risen upon you.

The music, in 6/8 time, is aptly described as "dance-like,"[42] and the lyric is cast in a call-response pattern between song leader and congregation: "Arise, shine!"—"*Arise, shine!*"—"for your light has come,"—"*for your light has come,*" and so on. In context, the present-day congregation is being called to "rise and shine" because God's glory has risen upon them. The song is a wake-up call to "us," whoever and wherever we are. Well and good—provided we recognize that we are at some distance from the original. Isaiah 60 comes from a time not long after the people of Israel had returned—some of them at least—from exile in Babylon. In an era of hardship, yet hope, an unknown prophet in the Isaiah tradition gives a wake-up call, *not to a church congregation, but to the whole nation,* and reiterates God's promise of historical deliverance:

> Arise, shine; for your light has come,
>   and the glory of the LORD has risen upon you.
> . . . .
> Nations shall come to your light,
>   and kings to the brightness of your dawn.
> . . . .
> your sons shall come from far away,
>   and your daughters shall be carried on their nurses' arms.
> . . . .
> the wealth of the nations shall come to you.
>
>   (Isaiah. 60:1–5)

---

41. Ibid., #62. Among several possible, but distantly related, passages are 1 Samuel 2:4–8; Luke 1:51–53; 2 Corinthians 9:15; and Colossians 3:15–17.

42. Ibid., #2, rubric next to the key signature.

By quoting the first verse of the prophecy, and casting it as a call-response song for a Christian congregation, the song writer is interpreting it, and following a long tradition which applies this verse of scripture to the birth of Jesus Christ.

Like many hymn writers, chorus writers often quote from the Bible as they develop their own vision and viewpoint. Matthew 1:23 is a quotation from the Greek translation of Isaiah 7:14, and reads,

> "Look, the virgin shall conceive and bear a son,
>   and they shall name him Emmanuel,"
> which means, "God is with us."

Bob McGee takes the last phrase and writes:

> Emmanuel, Emmanuel,
> his name is called Emmanuel.
> God with us, revealed in us,
> his name is called Emmanuel.[43]

The lyric is simple, yet well constructed. The repeated "Emmanuel, Emmanuel" emphasizes the importance of the name. Because it is the first thing said and sung, it suggests not only naming the name, but calling it, as a form of address: "Emmanuel!" The quotation from Matthew 1:23 is followed by a double interpretation. "God with us," itself a quotation from the source, is the literal meaning of the name. The added interpretation, "revealed in us," affirms that God is with us, not only historically in Jesus of Nazareth, but as Christ's living presence in ourselves and other members of the gathered faith community. The final "his name is called Emmanuel" adds both emphasis and meaning. Having sung the preceding line, we now know what, and who, we are talking about. The lyricist stays with the biblical text, and interprets it. Additional interpretation comes from the music, which in this case suggests that "God (is) with us" in a manner not challenging or disturbing, but friendly and comforting. Thus,

---

43. "Emmanuel," *Abingdon Chorus Book 1*, #29. The Hebrew of Isaiah 7:14 reads, "Therefore *Adonai* himself will give you a sign. Look, the young woman is with child and shall bear a son, and shall name him Immanuel." In the Greek (Septuagint) translation, the Hebrew word for "young woman" was rendered as *parthenos*, "virgin."

Matthew's meaning-laden *narrative* ("X will happen and it means Z") is transformed into a devotional *meditation*.

Sometimes a quotation becomes a springboard to images and ideas only slenderly connected with its original context. In Genesis 28: 10–17, Jacob has camped overnight in "a certain place," using a stone as his pillow. He dreams of a ladder (perhaps more accurately a ramp or stairway), between earth and heaven, with God's angelic messengers going up and down on it. Then God stands beside him in his dream, identified as "the God of Abraham your father and the God of Isaac." The Abrahamic promise is reiterated. The land where Jacob is sleeping will be given to him, "and all the families of the earth shall be blessed in you and in your offspring." God promises to be with Jacob, keep him safe, and bring him back to the land through which he now wanders, "for I will not leave you until I have done what I have promised you." When Jacob wakes, he says, "Surely the LORD is in this place —*and I did not know it!* . . . How awesome is this place! This is none other than the house of God, and this is the gate of heaven."

By contrast, Lanny Wolfe quotes Genesis 28:16 and writes:

> Surely the presence of the Lord is in this place.
> *I can feel his mighty power and his grace.*
> I can hear the brush of angels' wings,
> I see glory on each face.
> Surely the presence of the Lord is in this place.[44]

"Surely the Presence of the Lord is in this place," words and music by Lanny Wolfe. Copyright © 1997 Lanny Wolfe Music ASCAP. All rights controlled by Gaither Copyright Management. Used by permission.

In Lanny Wolfe's chorus, "this place" is the place where today's congregation is meeting. God's presence is felt and known immediately, not recognized after the event. With three sense-perception verbs (feel, hear, see), the lyric moves from the singer's experience to a recognition of God's (or is it Christ's?) glory in the faces of other worshipers. The secondary source—recognized by the author or not—is 2 Corinthians 3:18: "And all of us, with unveiled faces, seeing the glory of the Lord as though reflected in a mirror, are being transformed into the same image from one degree of glory to another; for this comes from the Lord, the Spirit."[45]

---

44. Ibid., #1, emphasis mine here and in the scripture quotation above.
45. Not referenced by *Abingdon Chorus Book 1*. Compare 2 Corinthians 4:6.

Thus, in contrast to Bob McGee's "Emmanuel," which stays in close orbit around its scripture source, Lanny Wolfe lifts his quotation from Genesis, treats it as a freestanding motif, and applies it to Christian experience. Both methods of interpretation have precedents. From the seventeenth century, Isaac Watts looms over Lanny Wolfe with his Christianized versions of the psalms.[46] From the eighteenth century, Charles Wesley antedates Bob McGee with an exegetical poem where the believer wrestles, Jacob-like, with God.[47]

Of the two ways of dealing with the Bible, the "motif" method is risky, unless the motif is used in a manner parallel to, or at least not at variance with, its original meaning. In this respect, Lanny Wolfe's lyric is open to question. As a freely composed lyric hailing Christ's presence in the congregation, it is, I think, sound and singable. To tag it with the reference to Genesis 28:16, however, is misleading, because the lyric is extracting a scriptural phrase, not following its meaning. The words are lifted from the Jacob story, which no longer influences or informs their interpretation. In the process, the quotation reverses its meaning, from "God was here and I didn't realize it," to "God is here and I feel it." In hymnody, a classic example of meaning-reversal is Love Maria Willis's "Father, Hear the Prayer We Offer," which quotes Psalm 23, but briskly sets the psalmist straight:

> Not for ever in green pastures
>   do we ask our way to be [!]:
> but the steep and rugged pathway
>   may we tread rejoicingly.
>
> Not for ever by still waters
>   would we idly rest and stay [!]:
> but would smite the living fountains
>   from the rocks along our way.[48]

Sometimes the ancient context is arguably too remote to be relevant. Michael O'Shields makes a lively chorus from the King James

---

46. A classic example is Watts's version of Psalm 72, part 2, "Jesus shall reign where'er the sun / doth his successive journeys run; / His kingdom stretch from shore to shore / till moons shall wax and wane no more," etc.

47. "Come, O Thou Traveler Unknown," *United Methodist Hymnal*, #387.

48. Love Maria Willis, revised by Samuel Longfellow and others. See *Congregational Praise*, #523, and *Hymns and Psalms*, #436. For a background note, see *Companion to "Hymns and Psalms*," #436, p. 266.

Version of two verses in Psalm 18: "I will call upon the LORD, who is worthy to be praised, so shall I be saved from my enemies. . . . The LORD liveth, and blessed be the rock, and let the God of my salvation be exalted."[49] The mood of the chorus is consistent with that of the psalm, and some of the psalm would, if quoted, be open to contemporary significance. Many worshipers could tell how "the cords of death encompassed me; the torrents of perdition assailed me; in my distress I called upon the LORD; to my God I cried for help." Few, however, would perceive God as immediately present in a thunderstorm, "his canopy dark clouds thick with water," as the earth is devastated "by the blast of the breath of your nostrils." And only in the presence of demonic evil, or deep confusion between Christ and Caesar, could Christian worshipers rejoice that "you made my enemies turn their backs to me, and those who hated me I destroyed. . . . People whom I had not known served me. As soon as they heard of me they obeyed me; foreigners came cringing to me. Foreigners lost heart, and came trembling out of their strongholds," *and this is how we know that* "The LORD lives! Blessed be my rock, and exalted be the God of my salvation!"

Yet some scriptural themes are, surely, perennial. In Israel's psalms, God is praised, adored, and thanked—without reservation, but never without reason. A constant reason for praising God is God's faithfulness, shown by God's mighty deeds in setting Israel free from slavery in Egypt, settling them in the "promised land," and establishing a treaty-covenant with the whole nation, in which Israel is called to live up to God's passion for right living, including social justice. Because Israel's society is so often unjust, God takes special care of the poor and economically marginal members of society. These themes well up again and again in the psalms. Analyzing the psalms as prayer, Walter Brueggemann finds that "Israel's prayer life, in lament as in doxology, is saturated with the issue of justice. Indeed, Israel has no other issue to bring before God."[50]

Our society and global economy are deeply unjust. Yet few choruses touch these themes. Here is an anonymous chorus quoting Psalm 113:3, "From the rising of the sun to its setting / the name of the LORD is to be praised." Interpreted by calm, gentle music, the lyric is devout,

---

49. Psalm 18:3 and 46 (a variant of this psalm occurs in 2 Samuel 22, where David thanks God for deliverance from his enemies). See, "I will call upon the Lord," *Abingdon Chorus Book 1*, #9.

50. Brueggemann, "The Psalms as Prayer."

clear in meaning—and innocuous. By contrast, the psalmist follows the call to praise with specific motivators for universal praise, all of which have to do with God's impassioned action on behalf of people who are vulnerable and downtrodden:

> Who is like the LORD our God,
>   who is seated on high,
> who looks far down
>   on the heavens and the earth?
> *He raises the poor from the dust,*
>   *and lifts the needy from the ash heap,*
> *to make them sit with princes,*
>   *with the princes of his people.*
> *He gives the barren woman a home,*
>   *making her the joyous mother of children.*[51]

Another example comes from Rich Mullins:

> Our God is an awesome God;
>   he reigns from heaven above
>   with wisdom, power and love.
> Our God is an awesome God.[52]
>
> © 1988 BMG Songs, Inc. (ASCAP). All rights reserved. Used by permission.

The lyric partially quotes Deuteronomy 10:17–18, with echoes of Matthew's description of Jesus as having wisdom and doing deeds of power (Matthew 13:54). Though the lyric expresses adoration, "wisdom, power and love" do not convey the Deuteronomist's specific, historical reasons why God is "awesome":

> For the LORD your God is God of gods and Lord of lords, the great God, mighty and awesome, *who is not partial and takes no bribe, who executes justice for the orphan and the widow, and who loves the strangers, providing them food and clothing.* [Emphasis mine]

I have shown, I hope, that to quote from the Bible, or describe a chorus as a "scripture song," does not necessarily mean that the biblical context, and major biblical themes, are being heard and respected.

---

51. Psalm 113:5–9, emphasis mine. See "From the Rising of the Sun," *Abingdon Chorus Book 1,* #9. There is a secondary reference to Malachi 1:11, where the wording and context are different.

52. *Abingdon Chorus Book 1,* #15.

In other words, not all "scripture songs" are "biblical." On the other hand, because scripture is being quoted, a chorus can often be reinterpreted and reinforced by putting it back in its biblical context. For example, Rich Mullins's chorus can be powerfully recontexted if its biblical source is spoken (over instrumental improvisation) between its first and second singing. An anonymous chorus quoting Psalm 103:1 could be given similar treatment, its repeated singing interspersed by additional quotations from the psalm, spoken over instrumental continuo:

Sung: "Bless the LORD, O my soul, and all that is within me, bless his holy name."[53]
      Spoken: "Who forgives all your iniquity, who heals all your diseases, who redeems your life from the Pit, who crowns you with steadfast love and mercy, who satisfies you with good as long as you live so that your youth is renewed like the eagle's."

Sung: "Bless the LORD, O my soul, and all that is within me, bless his holy name."
      Spoken: "The LORD works vindication and justice for all who are oppressed."

Sung: "Bless the LORD, O my soul, and all that is within me, bless his holy name."
      Spoken: "The LORD is merciful and gracious, slow to anger and abounding in steadfast love. . . . For as the heavens are high above the earth, so great is his steadfast love toward those who fear him; as far as the east is from the west, so far he removes our transgressions from us."

Sung: "Bless the LORD, O my soul, and all that is within me, bless his holy name."
      Spoken: "The steadfast love of the LORD is from everlasting to everlasting on those who [revere] him, and his righteousness to children's children."

Sung: "Bless the LORD, O my soul, and all that is within me, bless his holy name."

As an Easter celebration, Les Garrett's "This Is the Day" could be treated similarly, prefaced by Easter acclamations drawn from

---

53. Ibid., #25.

1 Corinthians 15 and 1 Peter 1, then sung three to five times, interspersed with other quotations from Psalm 118, such as:

> The LORD is my strength and my might;
> he has become my salvation.
> There are glad songs of victory in the tents of the righteous
> . . . .
> I shall not die, but I shall live,
>   and recount the deeds of the LORD.
> . . . .
> Open to me the gates of righteousness,
>   that I may enter through them
>   and give thanks to the LORD.
> . . . .
> The stone that the builders rejected
>   has become the chief cornerstone.
> This is the LORD's doing;
>   it is marvelous in our eyes.

From ancient times, Psalm 118 has been sung as a celebration of Christ's victory over death. Recontexting Garrett's chorus would deepen its meaning for singers and align them with early Christian tradition.

Another biblical text whose context is usually ignored is Lamentations 3:22–23:

> The steadfast love of the LORD never ceases,
>   his mercies never come to an end;
> they are new every morning;
>   great is your faithfulness.

In this respect, Edith McNeill's serene chorus[54] is no different from countless anthems, prayers, and sermons on this text. Yet the quoted affirmation derives part of its power and poignancy from its context. It is a daring leap of faith and hope in the face of terrible suffering, at a time when Judah has been invaded, Jerusalem destroyed, thousands deported, thousands slaughtered, and survivors are starving. In times of war, genocide, and "ethnic cleansing," the biblical counterpoint of lament and hope could be powerfully evoked by singing McNeill's chorus against a background of lament at the evils of war and prayers

---

54. Ibid., #26, "The steadfast love of the Lord."

for peace, over a background of suitable music, and drawing on some of the haunting description of its context, Lamentations 2:20–26; 3:19, 21. For example:

Chorus: "The steadfast love of the Lord . . ."
Lament: "Look, O LORD, and consider! . . . Should women eat their offspring, the children they have borne? . . . The young and the old are lying on the ground in the streets; my young women and my young men have fallen by the sword."

Prayer for the victims of war, and for allies, enemies, reconciliation, and peace.

Affirmation: "The thought of my affliction and my homelessness is bitter. . . . But this I call to mind, and therefore I have hope:
Chorus: "The steadfast love of the Lord . . ."
Lament: "You invited my enemies from all around as if for a day of festival; . . . no one escaped or survived; those whom I bore and reared my enemy has destroyed."

Prayer for the victims of war, and for allies, enemies, reconciliation, and peace.

Affirmation: "The thought of my affliction and my homelessness is bitter. . .But this I call to mind, and therefore I have hope:
Chorus: "The steadfast love of the Lord . . ."
Lament: "You have made my teeth grind on gravel, and made me cower in ashes; my soul is bereft of peace; I have forgotten what happiness is."
Prayer, Affirmation, Chorus: "The steadfast love of the Lord . . ."

Chorus Chains

Evangelical choruses are not usually sung in isolation, but joined with other choruses in a chain or set, in which successive choruses are usually linked with verbal commentary and sometimes interspersed with scripture quotations and prayer. As far as their lyrics are concerned, "the intended meanings of these various elements combine like the several stanzas of a hymn. And these meanings can be shared by the congregation as it worships."[55] The main difference is that while a hymn develops its theme over several stanzas using the same tune, a set of choruses develops its theme (if there is one) using tunes and lyrics that are different. Thus, my criteria for assessing lyrics apply not only to individual choruses, but to a given set: taken as a whole, are the lyrics devout, musical, communal, beautiful, frugal, just, and purposeful?

Though chorus sets vary widely, many churches use them at the beginning of worship, to start with a bang and establish an upbeat mood. If they begin with choruses of exuberant praise and thanksgiving inviting congregational hand-clapping and body movement, move on to devotional songs dwelling on God's glory, beauty, and majesty, and end with quiet songs invoking God's immediate presence, they are borrowing a Pentecostal-based theology which may, or may not, be at home in their worship tradition.

What is being borrowed, consciously or not, is a notion of approaching God supposedly based on ancient Hebrew practice,[56] whereby the worshipers move in procession from the gate of the Temple, through the outer courts, and into the Holy Place, or Holy of Holies. A text sometimes quoted as backing is Psalm 100:4: "Enter his *gates* with *thanksgiving*, and his *courts* with *praise*" (emphasis mine), interpreted, not as parallel ideas in Hebrew poetry, but as a literal sequence. The procession begins at the gate, where *thanksgiving* inspires physical acts: singing, clapping, and dancing. As it moves into the outer courts, thanksgiving becomes *praise:* songs of devotion, not tied to particular thanksgivings, but focusing on God's being. Finally, in the Holy Place, or Holy of Holies, comes *worship*, meaning not the service as a whole, but an experience of the immediate presence of God, invoked and dramatized by songs of awe and wonder, often accompanied by individual "prophecies" and speaking in tongues.[57]

In assessing this use of congregational song I have in mind, not congregations who reject it because it goes against liturgical tradition, but those who borrow its methods because they want to enliven their

---

55. Yee, "Shared Meaning and Significance," p. 10.

56. The connections are, I think, tenuous, but the matter is too large to consider here.

57. For this description, and much of what follows, see Hustad, *Jubilate II*, pp. 279–97, and *True Worship*, pp. 120–22.

worship and reach a wider constituency. From this perspective, the "temple procession" practices, and others like them, spring from convictions that include the following:

- God, beyond and within us, is present in worship, and wishes to encounter us at every level of our being: body, mind, and spirit.
- Worship should involve the whole person, be eagerly anticipated, joyfully enacted, and go beyond the rational and the didactic.
- Worship is the work of the people, not merely of worship leaders, soloists, preachers, and choirs.
- Worship should minister to a widely felt cultural longing for *"the tangible experience of a direct relationship with God."*[58]
- Because genuine, heartfelt praise opens us to the wonder and mystery of God, it is a more effective *beginning* for the spiritual life than penitence; penitence comes later, as a response to the worshiper's encounter with God.
- Congregational praise is sacramental; it enables God to do things that God cannot do otherwise.

Some of these beliefs seem unquestionably valid, and all are worthy of consideration. But these convictions, and their theological underpinnings, do not fully explain why congregations so enthusiastically stand, clap, move, sing, and pray in a chain of choruses lasting from thirty to forty minutes. How can the "temple procession" concept be so attractive when there is, in fact, no procession? The congregation does not move from one room to another, or from outside the building to within. Fronds are not usually waved, nor banners carried. Gates are not unlocked, the ark of the covenant is not paraded, no bulls bellow before being sacrificed, and no lambs have their blood drained out at the altar.

What is going on is music, specifically the music of congregational song. "In this pattern music . . . is sacramental. *Music functions . . . to generate a palpable experience that is interpreted to be an encounter with God."*[59] And this is as problematic as it is powerful. As I have

---

58. Witvliet, "The Blessing and Bane of the North American Megachurch." (Emphasis mine.)

59. Ibid., emphasis mine.

already shown (see pp. 66–67), the power of music and song is ambiguous. My feelings alone, stirred by music, song, and bodily participation, do not guarantee that I am meeting the living God revealed in Jesus Christ. Community spirit can give a sense of safety and belonging, and the spirit of music can take us out of ourselves, but one of the earliest Christian writings cautions us to "test the spirits, to see whether they are from God" (1 John 4:1). So we must test the spirit of the temple-procession pattern. To what action does it lead? Does it move us to love one another, welcome strangers, love our enemies, treat family members with care and respect, stand with the downtrodden and dispossessed, and spread the good news of Jesus Christ? Though these questions are by no means unasked, I emphasize them because some practitioners give the impression that a certain type of contemporary music, performed in a certain way, will guarantee an experience of God's presence,[60] and that the music alone, and our feelings alone, are sufficient evidence that we are truly meeting God.

The music of the temple-procession pattern is persuasive because it forms the script of a psychodrama. Though there is no literal procession, the *notion* of a procession into God's temple is attractive. It appeals to the imagination, interprets the feelings generated by the music (of, say, warmth, belonging, excitement, wonder, and joy), and validates them theologically. In other words, the temple-procession metaphor functions as a *myth*, not in the old-fashioned sense of "falsehood," but in the widely accepted sense of myth as a compelling story that points to "the inner meaning of the universe and of human life."[61] Like other myths, the temple procession is a powerful image, easy to identify with. It draws the worshiper into its "world," and shapes awareness and action. Like all myths, it is "received as in some way true."[62]

As a mythic psychodrama, recognized as such, the temple-procession pattern can be as uplifting as, say, a Palm Sunday procession, Maundy Thursday supper, Christmas nativity pageant, or Good Friday passion play. One difference is that these other examples are central to the Christian story. By contrast, the temple-procession pattern

---

60. From notes taken from "Praise Singing," an address by Donald P. Hustad at the Hymn Society in the U.S.A. and Canada's annual conference, July 1994, Knoxville, Tenn.

61. Alan Watt, quoted in Ramshaw, *God beyond Gender*, p. 60.

62. Ramshaw, *God beyond Gender*, ibid.

relies, not on the Christian story and insights directly derived from it, but on a particular interpretation of ancient Hebrew worship. Its mythic appeal submerges the questions that early Christian scripture might lead one to ask. The apostle Paul, for example, is no stranger to the power of the nonverbal in worship. Writing to the Corinthian church about speaking in tongues, he accepts the phenomenon as valid and claims to have experienced it. On balance, however, he cautions against relying on such nonverbal and nonrational experiences, and prefers the clarity of prophecy to the language of ecstasy (1 Corinthians 14). Though worship should move us beyond and beneath what is rational and didactic, it should not bypass it.

Another set of cautionary notes about the temple-procession psychodrama applies more widely. Ancient Israel's Temple worship was saturated with praise, but also with thanksgiving and lament. It was subject to critique and disturbance from prophets like Amos of Tekoa and Isaiah of Jerusalem—so much so that the prophetic critique was eventually incorporated into some of the psalms themselves. Few North American churches, of whatever theological stripe, know how to lament with, and before, God or are willing to venture a prophetic critique of our foundational economic systems and institutions. Nowadays, thanksgiving tends to be individualistic and generic, rather than historical. Moreover, in his discussion of the temple-procession motif, Donald Hustad observes that the thanksgiving part of the sequence is often omitted, and that songs of thanksgiving are rarely, if ever, featured on promotional tapes and included in published praise and worship music.[63]

Thanksgiving differs from praise. In Christian theology, as in everyday life, praising and giving thanks are interpersonal actions, overlapping but distinct. Thanksgiving is the acknowledgment of something given, said, or done by another that benefits the recipient. Praise affirms and delights in another, whether or not we have cause to thank the one praised.

In Jewish and Christian traditions, thanksgiving is centrally important. Thanks are due, and given, for what God is doing and has done. In the worship of ancient Israel, the primary focus is historical. Israel thanks God for deliverance from slavery and for the love-gift of law, covenant, and living space, all of which happen in history and form a narrative, a story, which Israel recites. Such thanksgiving springs from

---

63. Hustad, *Jubilate II*, p. 288.

and is nourished by memory: the story of God's gracious actions is told and retold, and worshipers are called upon to remember it. Christian faith and worship inherit thanksgiving as a recital of what God does and has done, in the telling of its own remembered story and crucial actions, such as, "Do this in remembrance of me."

In all Christian traditions there is a crisis of thanksgiving. The breathtaking discoveries of cosmology, physics, and biology make it hard to know how we might credibly thank God for modifying the ongoing universe. Genocide, war, and systemic injustice undermine the belief that a loving God is effectively active in history. As the world becomes more integrated, and peoples formerly silenced raise their voices, we find that, over and over again, one group's narrative of salvation is another group's narrative of dispossession, enslavement, and genocide. Faced with such obstacles, cosmic and historical thanksgivings get muted, generalized, or abandoned; and thanksgiving is either replaced with "pure praise" or restricted to God's general creativity, self-disclosure in Jesus, and action in the believer's personal life.

As scholars wrestle with these issues, we catch occasional glimmers of possibility. Perhaps the universe is more open to divine action than we have thought; perhaps we can plausibly speak of the divine Spirit working to humanize and question our endeavors; perhaps we can give more bearable accounts of God's active love amid and against radical human evil.[64] Though scholarly work is indispensable, liturgy cannot wait for "perhaps" to become "possibility." We need to reestablish the cosmic and historical dimensions of thanksgiving in worship, giving specific thanks where we can and longing and lament where we cannot.

The Great Journey

In place of a temple procession, Christian tradition offers another journey with a compelling narrative, leading not to a temple, but to a table. It is a journey through space and time, drawn from the prayer before Communion, the Great Thanksgiving. I am speaking here not of the often formal and archaic wording of this prayer, but of its general framework. Imagine, then, a service of worship, framed as a journey through space and time, a great journey of thanksgiving, with

---

64. I am not qualified to give a bibliography. On the dialogue between theology and science see, for example, *Theology Today* 54/1 (April 1997) and 55/3 (October 1998). On God's humanizing action in history, see Kaufman, *Theology for a Nuclear Age*. On suffering and radical evil, see, for example, Johnson, *She Who Is*, chap. 12.

opportunity for prayer, lament, Bible reading, and preaching on its themes. It is a multimedia event, with music, congregational songs in classical and/or contemporary style, color photographs, video clips, banners, drama, gesture, and movement. The Great Journey celebrates where human beings come from (God in creation and earth's evolution); how we have journeyed (God in human history, and human spirituality); God's particular journey with us (God in ancient Israel, Jewish faith today, and Christian history); God's coming among us in person (God in Jesus Christ); where we are today (Christ's invitation to the universal Table, where all are welcomed and fed); and how we travel on (the Spirit of God/Spirit of Jesus, who is with us always).

This framework offers a rich variety of thanksgivings, with opportunities also for prayer and lament. Here is an extended "map" of the journey, from which a given act of worship would select and highlight particular themes:

1. *Gather* with praise to God, within us, beyond us, and beside us.
2. *Creation;* thanksgiving to God, who:
   • conceived and gave birth to this universe of space/time, and whose Spirit inhabits all things;
   • designed this wondrous universe, with conditions in which life could begin and sufficient time for life to grow and flourish (here, and possibly/probably elsewhere);
   • nurtured planet earth, through its formation and development;
   • cherishes the web of living things, in all its interdependent variety;
   • brought the human race into being, through aeons of evolution, shaping us in the divine image and likeness.
3. *Human history, and spirituality;* thanksgiving to God, whose Spirit:
   • moves among us throughout the human story;
   • is present in every people's hopes for freedom, justice, love, and peace;
   • cherishes the human spirit in its search for spiritual meaning, in all worldviews and faiths.
4. *The story of ancient Israel, and Jewish faith today;* thanksgiving to God, whose Spirit:
   • gave us, through Israel's story, knowledge that God has

a purpose, life has meaning, and history has hope and direction;

- showed us the divine longing to love us, to be known by us, and to be in relationship (covenant) with us;
- allows and encourages us, as partners with God, to open our hearts in prayer, praise, thanksgiving, pain, anger, doubt, and lament;
- reveals God's passion for truth, social justice, and peace (*shalom*) on earth.
- nourishes Jewish and Christian faith, as cousins on different paths, traveling with the one God.

5. *God in Jesus of Nazareth:* thanksgiving for Jesus, who:
   - revealed the living God in a human life, through everything he did and said;
   - announced and demonstrated God's universal commonwealth of love, by teaching, healing, practicing peace, confronting evil with good, befriending outcasts, and bringing good news to the poor;
   - did not work alone, but called people to join with him, established a pattern of equitable community, and sent them out to tell the good news;
   - followed God's way completely, through betrayal, capture, and crucifixion, and trusted in God, even when God's presence was withdrawn.

6. *God in Jesus Christ, risen and alive,* who:
   - overcame evil and death forever, and for everyone;
   - lives always among us, and in the heart of God;
   - calls us to be a loving community of faith, open to all;
   - invites us to gather round the universal Table, where all are welcomed, all are honored, all are fed and nourished, no one goes hungry, no one is despised, no one is turned away.

At this point, if possible, the congregation gathers physically around the Table, in a large circle or series of circles, and offers songs of praise celebrating Christ's universal welcome. Physical movement is important; more than a visual aid, it enacts the people's gathering. Greetings of peace, love, and forgiveness and reconciliation are exchanged, and prayers offered, including prayer for members of the community, but always reaching out to the wider world. In a congregation where Communion is infrequent, the table gathering is an anticipation of Communion. Where there is a weekly Communion, it happens there and then.

The table gathering concludes with *thanksgiving for the Spirit of God/Spirit of Jesus,* who:

- travels with us as we depart;
- promises to be with us always;
- will meet us tomorrow, through relatives, strangers, friends, and enemies;
- waits to bring us home, to the universal feast in God's new creation.

A number of Taizé and evangelical choruses, and hymns, would fit this framework; others would have to be composed and written.

Me and Jesus

Following the long tradition of American revivalism, the devotional accent of many evangelical choruses and chorus sets is subjective. "I love you," "I praise your name," and "I worship and adore you" are typical formulations. Insofar as repetition of such sentiments is spiritually formative, they can deepen the singer's faith commitment, provided that the textual and musical emphasis is more on the verb (love, praise, thank, adore) or the object of praise (Jesus, God, the Holy Spirit), than on the subject, the "I" who praises. To evaluate these devotional utterances, we must, therefore, ask where, on balance, is the emphasis? Is it on the One to whom we speak, or on the singer's feelings and state of mind? The *Abingdon Chorus Book 1* excludes extremes of subjectivity, but other sources are less scrupulous. Frederick "Whitfield's nineteenth-century gospel song, still in print today, begins by declaring "There is a name I love to hear, / I love to sing its worth, / it sounds as music in my ear, / the sweetest name on earth," followed by the refrain, *"Oh, how I love Jesus, / Oh, how I love Jesus, / Oh, how I love Jesus, / because he first loved me."* The repeated focus on what the singer is feeling about herself/himself is only partially mitigated by the concluding phrase ("because he first loved me"), and by the remaining verses, where the name of Jesus tells of the "Savior's love, who died to set me free," the assurance of God's providence, and of "One whose loving heart can feel my deepest woe."[65] Some modern choruses come quite close to the following, which is, I hasten to add, a parody, hopefully never used seriously in worship:

---

65. For the full text, with music, see *The Baptist Hymnal,* #218.

Oh, I'm thinking of me praising Jesus,
and loving the feeling I feel.
When I think of his touch
I am feeling so much
that tomorrow I'll praise him for real.

"It Takes Away the Stress"

One Friday evening in Georgia, my marriage-partner and I were preparing to lead a parish retreat for an Episcopal congregation. The evening began with a long set of devotional, but to me trite and sentimental, choruses. To counter the turnoff effect, and hoping to come to terms with my prejudice, I turned to her and whispered, "What do you think is the attraction of these songs?" "I think that if you've had a hard week and a long day," she replied, "this kind of easy music takes away the stress, and puts you at ease." "Hmph," I muttered, unwilling to be convinced. Moments later, asked why this music was so important to her, one of the singers said, almost word for word, "Well, when I've had a hard day, and life gets on top of me, I come and sing these songs and the stress and strain of life just ebbs away."

As the Beatles said about something else, "Well, you know that can't be bad." The musical style of some choruses performs a similar function to the music of Taizé, but for a different constituency. In both cases, sung repetition brings people from stress to calm, and from worry to well-being, so that they can focus on Jesus Christ. In evangelical choruses, the lyrics match the music, in words carrying the assurance that Christ knows, loves, and accepts us; and that God (or Jesus, or the Holy Spirit) is not remote and uncaring, but lovingly present. This is good news, but its scope is restricted. The evangelical chorus's subjective focus on "me and Jesus" tames the gospel by keeping it inside the small, safe world of the believer's personal life and state of mind. Unless the scope of the message is widened, we are in danger of meeting Christ the Soother, not Christ the Savior.

Me and My King

I have noted that the lyrics of many evangelical choruses are deeply devout, but have questioned the extent of their subjectivity, the validity of the temple-procession myth, and the way some lyrics make use of the Bible. I shall conclude this discussion by comparing their image of God's action with their portrayal of God's being.

On the one hand, the choruses in my sample speak movingly and consistently of divine acts of gentleness, love, and faithfulness. Jesus Christ says, "Come and follow me, I will bring you home, I love you and you are mine." Singers tell themselves and each other that "God cares for me, he's so good to me"; "Jesus is the beautiful Savior"; "O how he loves you and me"; "his name is like fragrance after the rain." "Through it all," we affirm, "I've learned to trust in Jesus, to give him all sadness and pain," because "the one who knows me best loves me most and he has made something beautiful of my life." In response, we say, "Take our hearts, we love you, we are yours; your loving-kindness is better than life; you are more beautiful than diamonds; all I need is you, Jesus. You are faithful and loving to me."

On the other hand, some of the most common titles for God, and for Jesus Christ, are at odds with this intimate picture. In common with Taizé choruses, evangelical choruses draw from the ancient story line of God as ruling King, and Jesus as the crown prince (or king) at his side. By contrast with Taizé, evangelical choruses are saturated with King-Almighty-Lord-Father language.[66] God (occasionally called Jehovah) reigns in majesty, reigns in heaven above. He is King, the King of kings, exalted on high, an awesome God, the source of all authority. In response, we, his subjects, bow before the throne and worship his majesty, crying: "We worship and adore you, we bow down before you, we gaze on your kingly brightness." Jesus Christ also is the mighty King, the master of everything. To him we cry, "All hail, King Jesus." As "children of the King," our status is secure. Soon and very soon we're going to see the King; then, and now, we cry, "Glory to the King of kings; our God reigns, our God reigns."

The idea of divine kingship goes back three thousand years, to the city-states of the ancient Near East: Sumer, Egypt, Assyria, and Babylon.[67] As settled societies developed an excess of food and goods, better transportation and communication, and a sophisticated division of labor, their social order changed and took the form of a pyramid. At

---

66. The *Abingdon Chorus Book 1* casts its net more widely than most such compilations, and has one or two examples of more varied imagery. Additional titles for "Jesus, Name above All Names" (#34) include El Shaddai, Shepherd of Souls, Lily of the Valley, Rose of Sharon, Bread of Life, and Living Water. Another chorus praises God as "the Breath in me," "the Sun," "the Mystery," and "the One, the One who made me" ("You are the wind that dances through the heavens," #21).

67. For much of what follows I am indebted to Ramshaw, "The Myth of the Crown," chap. 6 in *God beyond Gender.*

the top was the monarch, almost invariably male, ruling from the central city. Power and authority devolved downward through the ranks of the social pyramid, from the one at the top to the many at the bottom. Society was perceived as a unit; the notion of individual rights was centuries in the future. Stepping outside one's place endangered the community. Society's offenders were exiled, forced outside the pyramid, and sent beyond the walls of the city (or the borders of the state) to die in the unsettled wilderness.

Like all social orders (including democracies), the royal pyramid needed stories to explain how it arose, why it was legitimate, and how it allegedly sustained every level of society, thus deserving allegiance. In a time when religion, politics, family, and the individual life were inseparable, the pyramid's explanatory story was inevitably about a god, or gods, and their relationship with the ruler of the city-state. The stories varied in detail but had a common pattern. In its original state, the world (meaning both the whole earth as far as it was known and the "world" of the particular city-state) had been chaos, filled with disaster and uncertainty. The chaos was both cosmological and social. A deity, usually a god, had brought order out of chaos, often by slaying the chaos-monster in battle. To keep chaos from returning, and to guarantee everything from civil peace to good harvests, the deity established the city-state's monarchy. The original king, and each successor, was designated as the "son" of the city-state's god. As the god's representative, he made laws, upheld justice, ensured the fertility of land and people, and personified the power of divine good over the disorder and evil lurking on the edges of the community. Though several such kingdoms could exist during the same epoch, most people (especially those at the bottom of the pyramid) knew only their own; for them, there was no other "world."

This notion, or rather narrative, was—and is—a powerful myth. It gave meaning to the universe, society, religion, the family, and individual human life. It was—and in its modern variants still is— persuasive, pervasive, and perceived as true. Gail Ramshaw calls it "the myth of the crown." It applies to any society, with or without kings and queens, where *the chain of downward supervision and upward obedience holds together natural, social, and religious life,* and is touted and perceived as the source of security, salvation, and happiness.[68] Its benefits include order, security, food, shelter, protection, and

---

68. Ibid., p. 60.

community organization. Its costs include abuse of the weaker by the stronger; the diminished humanity inherent in master-servant and master-slave relationships; and the recurrent threat of corruption, abuse of power, and—at worst—totalitarianism.

In ancient Israel, the kingship myth was adopted, somewhat modified by the developing belief that the God of Abraham, Isaac, Moses, and David is the only true God, God of gods and Lord of lords. Several psalms speak of the earthly king as God's "son," appointed to rule in Zion, and commanded to rule justly by defending the cause of the poor and needy.[69] Israel's worship praises God as king, ruling the whole earth, and its psalms are a major source of the kingship language in evangelical choruses. When the nation ceased to have kings, kingship was projected forward in the messianic hope: one day God would anoint another kingly figure, who would finally "save" Israel and establish divine peace, justice, and well-being through Israel over all nations.

In early Christianity, Jesus Christ was acclaimed as "king,"[70] but in the most contradictory way possible. The "King of the Jews" was not victorious in battle, but asphyxiated on a cross; not acclaimed at a coronation, but killed naked, his head bleeding from the piercing sarcasm of a "coronet" of thorns. I emphasize the contradiction because it is so often, and so easily, glossed over and forgotten. Gail Ramshaw puts it well: "Despite Jesus' revolutionary witness against the status quo, the myth of the crown, so powerful in imagination and pervasive in speech, shaped the proclamation of the gospel with its ancient values, its pyramidal assumptions, and its triumphalist tone."[71]

Thus, in Christian history, the contradictory nature of Jesus' "kingship" has almost invariably been overwhelmed by the fundamental, built-in, earthly meanings of the myth of the crown: *authority, command, the glamour of power, control, submission, and obedience.* To see God as the *liberating* sovereign was a radical departure, an infusion of opposite meanings not easily absorbed. In its original context,

---

69. See Psalms 2; 47; 73; and 89.

70. Ramshaw cites Acts 4:25–26 and Acts 13:33–34 (*Gender and the Name of God,* p. 64).

71. Ibid. Tracing a variety of verbal and visual images of Jesus down the centuries, Jaroslav Pelikan underlines the importance, for good and ill, of the "kingship" of Jesus. Its historical development and interaction with other political symbols helps us to understand "a large part of what is noble and a large part of what is demonic in the political history of the West" (*The Illustrated Jesus through the Centuries,* p. 49).

the metaphor of the "crucified king" had the shock of the unexpected. A crucified Messiah was a stumbling block to Jews and an absurdity to Greeks, which is why Paul talks about the foolishness of the cross and contrasts human wisdom and power with God's wise folly and empowering powerlessness (1 Corinthians 1).

Again and again, when the shock wore off, the "earthly" meaning of kingship reasserted itself. When Christianity won the Roman emperor's recognition, its kingship vocabulary smoothly served imperial interests. As God was to the universe, so the emperor was to the empire. Emperor worship was refocused on Christ, who crowned the emperor as his earthly deputy and validated his rule. Paintings of Christ in majesty show him sitting on a jewel-encrusted throne, with all the marks of Roman imperial rank: rich robes, purple cushions, and the royal halo, surrounded by a heavenly council of palace officials:[72] a world away from the torture of Golgotha.

Later centuries saw a long tussle between pre-Christian and post-resurrection interpretations of divine kingship. The pre-Christian argument was that if God is the King of kings, God rules (yet also appoints) the earthly monarch, and our role is to be that monarch's submissively obedient subjects. Thus, for King James I of England (James VI of Scotland), "Kings are justly called gods, for they exercise a manner or resemblance of divine power on earth." Against this ran the postresurrection argument, more in tune with Christ's "kingship": if God is the only king, earthly society should be a kingless republic. Thus, for Quakers like James Parnel, a contemporary of James I, "amongst us there are no superiors after the flesh, but Christ is the head. . . . Here God alone is the king and he alone is honored, exalted and worshipped."

In the end, the egalitarian interpretation won the day, however imperfectly realized in today's democracies. In the American colonies, the British king's disobedient subjects learned that abuse of executive power is best prevented by a republic with built-in checks and balances, where sovereignty resides not in a person, but in the people. Today's constitutional monarchs have lost their political power and most of their residual glamour. Societies with despotic leaders are seen as aberrations. The perennial attractiveness of the "strong leader" in times of crisis is viewed as unfortunate, a temporary necessity.

---

72. On this, and what follows, see my book *What Language Shall I Borrow?* pp. 127–28.

Societies that still have ruling monarchs are anachronisms, not models for imitation.

The myth of the crown has shaped Christian theology's description of God. It pervades the language of doctrine, liturgical language, and congregational song. Great, classic hymns have thoroughly explored it. Modern lyrics reiterate their themes, but rarely add anything fresh: the old mine is worked out and only glimmers of gold can be panned from the streambed. Yet, because God-as-King language occurs frequently in some parts of the Bible, it still seems, to many, the "obvious," "scriptural" language of congregational song. Indeed, for many who write and compose evangelical choruses, the language of God as King-Lord-Almighty-Father-Protector is not *one* way of knowing and praising God, but the ruling way, the only way.

Language Limitations

Though this choice of language springs from personal piety, and respect for the Bible, it has grave limitations. When first used, the language of God as ruling king was in harmony with commonsense observation of the universe. Earth was flat, the dead were in the land of shades below it, and God was enthroned in heaven, high above. Nowadays, we live in a vast, expanding universe, a seamless web of space/time, paradoxically described as "finite, yet unbounded" (Stephen Hawking). Because there is nowhere for a king to sit, we struggle to describe how God can credibly be active in the universe's development (see p. 221). The language of God-as-King-of-the-Universe has become an increasingly tenuous metaphor. It is colorful, yet uninformative.

When first coined, the language of divine kingship explained how human societies ought to work, and how people should behave within them. As long as monarchy was the norm, the images of God-as-King and Christ-the-King gave guidelines for public life. Though royalists and republicans drew opposite conclusions, divine kingship was for both a living, meaningful symbol, with clear and direct application in society. In today's democracies, divine kingship no longer gives meaning and direction to public life. To call God "King" gives no clues or pointers about how to vote, what causes to support, and how to live as citizens in a republic whose powerful institutions, political and economic, crave power and need to be held accountable. Because divine kingship language has no meaning for public life, it puts us at a distance from our society. Personal, family, and church life become the only sphere where God can still be worshiped as king. Thus, emphatic use of kingship symbolism is "a symptom of religion's deprivation of an appropriate public role in our world."[73] It feeds nostalgia, but gives no direction to discipleship.

Though God-as-King language has narrowed in scope and declined in value, it retains its ambiguity. To use it emphatically is dangerous. If we bow before God in unquestioning submission, we are more likely to submit uncritically to God's human servants. For, despite their disadvantages, social pyramids are stable structures. In times of change and uncertainty, churches, movements, and societies all too easily fall sway to domineering, charismatic leaders, as "people willingly take their ancient place at the base of the pyramid and let the crown take over."[74] One danger signal is that, though the best human speech about God is always, in some respects, untrue, Christianity tends to emphasize only the "true" side of the myth of the crown. When we sing, "God, you are my rock," we are usually quite willing to add, "but of course God is not literally a rock." But when we sing, "My God, my King," the image is so attractive, so compelling, so hallowed by repeated use, that we rarely go on to say, "but of course God is not literally a king."[75] Such uncritical use of God-as-King language also perpetuates the mistaken idea that God is male, or more male than female.

To summarize, though God-as-King language is drawn from the Bible, it cannot now do what it once did. It yields no meaningful way of depicting God's activity in the universe and no clue as to how to live in a democratic society. It perpetuates a male image of God, and is perennially susceptible to misuse. Used occasionally, it might be illuminating; used persistently and emphatically, it narrows the worshiper's focus, and God's authority, to the world of personal and family life.

Ways Forward

What, then, can we suggest to lyricists who love God and respect the Bible? Some ideas and images are best avoided. Songs, pictures,

---

73. Everett, *God's Federal Republic*, p. 17.
74. Ramshaw, *God beyond Gender*, pp. 66–67.
75. Ibid., p. 68.

and stained-glass windows should not represent God as a crowned and bearded male monarch. Crosses, song lyrics, and other media should not portray Jesus Christ as a robed and crowned figure, because *"Christ is [not] a king who was crucified in a golden robe and a bejeweled diadem. . . . Rather . . . kingship itself was crucified."*[76] Hundreds of hymns and choruses have royal court language of bowing, kneeling, petitioning, and beseeching: there is no need to write more. Festivals celebrating "the reign of Christ," or "Christ the King," should be celebrated, if at all, with an emphasis on Christ crucified, and the recollection that Jesus refused kingship and its corollaries: battle, war, and conquest. Lyric writers and liturgists could draw inspiration from G. A. Studdert-Kennedy, who heard "God, the Almighty King" invoked by opposing armies in the First World War, and saw Christ crucified in the hell of trench warfare. He argues that God-as-King could be enlisted by armies of opposed "Christian" nations only because people had become ashamed of the cross, and could not see it as God's real throne. So they invented the glorified Christ:

> White-robed angels stand about Him bowing to his least command, shouts of triumph greet His entrance, the mighty gates lift up their heads and the King of glory enters in. All the pageantry of earthly power, all the pomp of courts and kings *which He on earth refused*, are used to make him beautiful. . . . This glorified Christ in regal robes is a degraded Christ bereft of real majesty; these baubles are not worthy of the King.

In other words, the regal Christ sitting in triumph with God the Almighty King is an idol, not the one, loving and living God:

> We may still worship idols, but in our hearts we despise them, and despise ourselves for worshipping them. The only thing we can respect and remain self-respecting, is loving service. . . . *So, at last, the great suffering, striving God of service and of love is coming into his own, and as he comes into his own, so the High and Mighty Potentate, King of kings and Lord of lords, Almighty God, powerful, passionless, and serene, is being deposed from his throne* . . . , and in his place there standeth one amongst us whom we knew not, with bloody brow and pierced hands, majestic in his nakedness, superb in his simplicity, the King whose crown is a crown of thorns. He is God.[77]

---

76. Ibid., p. 61, emphasis mine.
77. Studdert-Kennedy, *The Hardest Part*, pp. 72–73, emphasis mine.

Another way forward is to speak of God's "sovereignty" without using the language of kingship. We need to speak of God's liberating sovereignty to counter the empty belief that we are self-sufficient, accountable to no one, and sovereign over ourselves. Arguing this point, Gail Ramshaw suggests "sovereign" as a translation of biblical God-titles usually rendered as "king."[78] Other possibilities include using verbs ("God reigns"), and replacing "kingdom of God" with "rule," "domain," "realm," or "commonwealth."[79] Though "sovereignty" may be viable ("for the sovereignty, the power, and the glory are yours"), I am less convinced about "Sovereign." As a form of address, "O God our sovereign" has no parallel in human greetings, and sounds almost as unnatural as "Hello, Parent." The word is more appropriate when used as an adjective: for example, "sovereign Love" and "sovereign Creator."

In general, the relationship between God, as sovereign, and the universe, including human beings, is best expressed in terms of the relationship between Creator and created. Besides being biblically familiar, "Creator" locates us as created beings, accountable to the One who brought us into being. More than that, as sentient creatures, the Creator-created relationship makes us responsible for the way we treat other creatures and our planetary home. Our Creator is immeasurably greater than ourselves, but greatness does not necessarily mean dominance. Applied to human beings, "greatness" sometimes includes autocratic behavior and sometimes not. When greatness is not domineering, it may evoke admiration, wonder, and awe, or envy, hatred, and rejection. In neither case does it evoke submission. Though our culture loves to debunk sainthood, Mahatma Gandhi is, I think, an example of "greatness" so understood.

How can we praise and thank God in language that maps appropriate behavior for citizens in a democracy? Perhaps God can be understood as presiding over human societies, or moderating and arbitrating our competing claims. Perhaps the doctrine of God as Trinity implies

---

78. Ramshaw, *God beyond Gender*, p. 70, with reference to Hebrew *melek* and Greek *basileus*. "With effort and artistry, royal psalms can present a gender-neutral image of the sovereign, at least denying the assumption that the mighty one on top must be male. . . . The word, while not commonplace, is not archaic." Ramshaw notes that not every occurrence of "king" in the Bible should be translated "sovereign": the ancient Hebrews wanted a king, not a queen, for example, and Herod was a king.

79. Ibid., p. 71. "Domain" is my suggestion. As Ramshaw notes, "rule" is perhaps too legal in tone.

a social order based not on monarchy but on mutuality. Or perhaps God is the liberating, lawgiving, and death-defeating Economist, whose biblical trajectory leaves warnings and encouragements for social action and economic organization.[80] These and other explorations stimulate thought, but have not yet generated titles and metaphors suitable for worship. For the present, I suggest that the person and work of Jesus Christ give the most helpful pointers to public action.

A good starting point for lyricists is Paul's strategy on his first visit to Corinth, "not to know any thing among you, save Jesus Christ, *and him crucified*" (emphasis mine)—or, as a modern translation has it, "I resolved that while I was with you I would not claim to know anything but Jesus Christ—Christ nailed to the cross" (1 Corinthians 2:2, KJV and REB). Even in a democracy, Christian citizens never forget that Jesus was crucified by the governing powers. Though our social, political, and economic institutions are far removed from imperial Rome, they are equally unable to hear the good news of God's sovereignty through Jesus Christ. They too are judged, disarmed, and put in their proper place by the resurrection. The risen Christ punctures their pretensions, demagnetizes their glamour, and makes their claims provisional and negotiable. In Christ all things cohere (Colossians 1:17–20 and 2: 14–15). As followers of Christ, we are on a journey. Alive among us, Christ leads and accompanies us, in public as well as private life. Though the record of Christ's earthly life provides no political program, it is the best reference point for our social, political, and economic priorities. As we journey on, Christ meets us through strangers, neighbors, enemies, and outcasts. The Spirit of Christ breathes through every hope and struggle for peace and social justice, whether or not it is consciously Christian. In the church, Christ presides at a table where all are fed, all are welcome, all are honored, and no one is turned away. Christ also presides over the church as a commonwealth community, where the Spirit is given through all and for all.

When the church follows Christ as One crucified by our governing powers yet risen over them, the language of kingship and coronation is bestowed, not on God, nor on Jesus Christ, but on ordinary people. Toppled from its imperial pedestal, it comes into its own as it cherishes and dignifies the poor and oppressed. In nineteenth-century

---

80. See, respectively, Everett, *God's Federal Republic;* LaCugna, *God for Us;* and Meeks, *God the Economist.*

England, the Oxford Movement created worship full of ceremony and ornamentation. At worst escapist, it was at best prophetic and inspirational. In one parish, a visitor reports how an impoverished woman and her two children came for baptism. They came in rags, but were treated as royalty. Wearing their robes, clergy and choir honored the baptismal party by coming in procession to stand around the font:

> We could not have done more honor to the Queen's children and their sponsors, but we did not put to shame the tattered rags and mean appearance of these poor people. . . . I never witnessed one of the powers of the church more forcibly—that of raising up the poor. And by inference I felt another of the powers—that of pulling down the rich.[81]

Here indeed, and perhaps only here, is Christ truly crowned.

---

81. James Davies, quoted in Ramshaw, *God beyond Gender*, p. 70.

Chapter Seven

"Captured by Gender":
Chant and Ritual Song

How shall we find you,
God who is Holy,
captured by gender, color and code?
how shall we worship,
God of the Presence,
action and essence, meaning and mode?
—Shirley Erena Murray, 1995

I shall now take a look at two genres, whose function is different but whose lyrics raise similar questions about the repetition of divine names and titles in worship.

Ritual Song

In ritual song (short, sung utterances that move the action of worship), the lyric's importance lies not in its brevity, but in the fact that it is so frequently repeated: an asset if you agree with its theology, a liability if not. Consider the following phrases, from classic ritual songs:

> O Lord God, heavenly King, God the Father Almighty. . . .
> O Lord, the only begotten Son, Jesus Christ: . . .
> Thou that sittest at the right hand of God the Father, . . .
> [T]hou only, O Christ,

with the Holy Ghost,
art most high in the glory of God the Father.
("The Greater Doxology," 3d–4th century C.E.)[1]

Glory be to the Father and to the Son and to the Holy Ghost;
as it was in the beginning, is now, and ever shall be,
world without end. Amen.
                    (the "Lesser Doxology," 3d–4th century C.E.)[2]

Praise God, from whom all blessings flow;
praise Him, all creatures here below;
praise Him above, ye heavenly host;
praise Father, Son, and Holy Ghost.
                              Thomas Ken, 1674

The "Greater" (longer) and "Lesser" (shorter) doxologies, imitated by Thomas Ken, attempt to express the complex yet fundamental Christian doctrine of the Trinity. They were originally intended to give believers a formative worship language, theologically accurate and clearly understood. Nowadays, there are disagreements about their accuracy, adequacy, and clarity. If, like some, you regard their formulations as theologically accurate, unlikely to confuse or mislead today's worshipers, and completely adequate for the praise and worship of God, you will rightly refuse to change them. If, like me, you find them classic but questionable, they pose several problems for congregational song. If some are so familiar that worshipers get a rare opportunity to raise the roof with wholehearted singing, is it fair to throw them out? Is it fair to alter them so radically that they are, in effect, new songs? If we should, to use a business euphemism, "let them go," how shall we replace them?

It is not hard to show that classic Trinitarian songs have become problematic. The apparently simple phrase "Father, Son, and Holy Spirit," abridges the complex result of a long process. In that process, guided by the biblical story of God, Jesus Christ, and the Holy Spirit, Christian thinkers broke away from monarchical conceptions of divinity.[3] Though there is but one God, and God is one, the doctrine of the Trinity presents, as Gail Ramshaw puts it, "the model of interrelated-

1. *Book of Common Prayer* translation. For information, see *Companion to the United Methodist Hymnal*, pp. 253–54.

2. For information, see *Companion to the United Methodist Hymnal*, p. 355.

3. See my book *What Language Shall I Borrow?* esp. chap. 7.

ness, the image of order without subordination, the God both beyond and within."[4]

If "Father, Son, and Holy Spirit" adequately translated the doctrine, singing would immediately evoke it. The words would need no explanation: we would recognize, and encounter, God as relatedness, not monarchical apartness; God as order without hierarchy; God transcending maleness and femaleness; God whose divinity is not apart from, but forever joined to, our humanity. For most worshipers today, I submit that this simply does not happen. On the contrary, "these . . . . astounding assertions about the Christian God [are] all too often obscured by the church"[5]—and by the very language chosen to formulate them.

With Gail Ramshaw's help,[6] let me show how, in worship, Trinitarian formulas came unglued from Trinitarian doctrine. The "Father-Son" language of classic Trinitarianism is rooted in patriarchal civilization. In ancient Israel, the king was the "son" of God. By patriarchal logic, God (though neither human nor male) was therefore the "father" of the king, and by extension of the people. At first used quite rarely, God as "father" had become more common in the time of Jesus. Pious Jews called God "father," in protest against the emperor Augustus, one of whose self-designations, *Pater patriae* (father of the fatherland), was an implicit claim to divinity. The Gospel record shows Jesus calling God "Abba, Father," in ways contradicting the mini-monarchy of household fathers.[7] Later, however, Christian understandings of "God the Father" took shape in "the crowded field of Greco-Roman religious, political, social and linguistic fathers."[8] Ancient misunderstandings of human procreation played a key role. Aristotle's theory, universally accepted, was that "the entire substance of the human infant resided in the father's sperm."[9] The mother's womb was merely the seedbed. Grounded in inaccurate biology, father terminology

---

4. Ramshaw, *God beyond Gender*, p. 84.

5. Ibid., p. 86.

6. Ramshaw, *God beyond Gender*. Unless otherwise referenced, my examples are drawn from pp. 76–81 of her book.

7. See, for example, my book *What Language Shall I Borrow?* chap. 8. When I say that the Gospel record shows this, I am being precise; scholars differ, however, as to whether "Abba" was in fact centrally important to Jesus. See *God beyond Gender*, pp. 78–79.

8. Ramshaw, *God beyond Gender*, p. 78.

9. Ibid., p. 79.

flourished theologically. Just as fathers were believed to solely originate their children, so God was the origin, and "father," of all.

Early Trinitarian theologians distanced themselves from such ideas, regarding "Father," "Son," and "Holy Spirit" as labels rather than images, and claiming that "God comes with the biblical name Father . . . not that God acts like a father."[10] Their successors used father-language differently. One example is Martin Luther, who wrote that God the Father is the model of all father figures. Though "Father, Son, and Holy Spirit" was theologically correct, its intended meanings were thoroughly subverted by preachers, teachers, and artists. Repeated pictures of the Trinity as "an old man, a young man, and a third thing"[11] filled the worshiping imagination with indelible misconceptions: that "God the Father" is like an old man; that the man Jesus embodies a male (or male-like) divinity; and that the technical phrase "three Persons" implies that God is three separate, male beings.

As Ramshaw shows, classic Trinitarian doctrine is magnificent, but male-centered. Developed within the thought forms of patriarchal cultures, it transcended them—*at a technical, abstract level.* But the doctrine was often understood in male-centered ways, and its abstractions were never successfully expressed in liturgical art and language.[12] In worship, "*Father* came to mean not Abba, not resistance to emperor worship, not the philosophical Unoriginate Origin, not the key to Christology, but a personalized masculine authority figure."[13]

I conclude that, in the sea of patriarchal culture, classic Trinitarianism is a humpback whale. It emerges for air, but spends most of its time underwater. Streamlined to swim against the current, it mostly goes with the flow. Though air gives it life, it can never leave its ocean. I therefore endorse Gail Ramshaw's conclusion. In ritual song, as elsewhere, "the church cannot continue to repeat classical Christian language, whether of father or of person, claim that the words do not mean what people think they mean, and ignore the resulting confusion."[14]

---

10. Ibid., p. 80.

11. Ibid., p. 77.

12. For what follows, except where otherwise referenced, see Ramshaw, *God beyond Gender,* pp. 77–81.

13. Ibid., p. 81.

14. Ibid., p. 87. For a recent discussion of Trinitarian doctrine in liturgy, see Duck and Wilson-Kastner, *Praising God.*

To return to my initial questions, Is it fair to throw out ritual songs so familiar? Previous guidelines give mixed signals. Misleading or confusing lyrics should be abandoned, because singing them is creedally malformative. Yet congregations typically include diverse theologies: what I find unbearably misleading, you may find inspirationally accurate, and we should both be treated justly. In their liturgical context, boosted by familiar music, invalid lyrics may have valid personal significance. Justice requires that change be consensual, not imposed. In many congregations the best way forward may be to retain some familiar, "classic" ritual songs and complement them with new songs in more varied Trinitarian language.

Is it fair to alter classic Trinitarian songs so radically that they are, in effect, new songs? Fair or unfair, major alterations may prove infeasible. Words and phrases in classic doxologies are not a "Trinity kit," easily interchangeable with other words and phrases from a set of universal religious building blocks. Like the parts of a specialized construction set, they interlock with each other in a unique linguistic and theological system. Each classic Trinitarian formulation is like a vertical radio mast, bolted and welded from straight steel bars, and anchored by strong steel cables. Suppose some of the bars show metal fatigue, and we try replacing them with curves and spirals. Even if the parts can be made to fit together, the mast will look peculiar and may prove unsafe in a storm.

Thus, because classic Trinitarian words and phrases interlock systematically, radical alterations are unlikely to be viable. Minor changes may be feasible, and others tolerable as a stopgap. New Trinitarian songs winning widespread acceptance cannot be created, however, by smoothing and sanding the old ones or adding kinder, gentler parts. New Trinitarian songs will come only from new, fundamental, theological and poetic work. To my third question, What new, singable, theologically appropriate songs can replace the classic ritual songs? I must therefore reply, "We don't have them yet." At the more cautious end of the spectrum, a sung doxology could be developed from the baptismal formula of the Riverside Church in New York City, whose final phrase is dissonant enough, perhaps, to dislocate "Father-Son" from a one-parent-family interpretation:

> Glory and praise to the Trinity,
> who was, and is, and will always be

Father, Son, and Holy Spirit,
One God, Mother of us all.[15]

Adaptation © Brian Wren, 1998.

My own attempts are inadequate, but may encourage others to go farther. Here is a doxology developing Saint Augustine's metaphor of the Trinity as One who loves, One who is loved, and the Bond of love between them:

Praise the Lover of Creation,
Praise the Spirit, Friend of Friends,
Praise the true Beloved, our Savior,
Praise the God who makes and mends,
   strong, surrendered, many-splendored,
   Three whose Oneness never ends.

Meter: 8.7.8.7.8.7. To be sung to the tune REGENT SQUARE. Brian Wren, copyright © 1989 by Hope Publishing Company for the U.S.A., Canada, Australia, and New Zealand, and by Stainer & Bell Ltd., London, England, for all other territories. All rights reserved. Used by permission.

For comparison, here are three "Trinitarian blessings," singable together or on their own:

May the Sending One sing in you,
May the Seeking One walk with you,
May the Greeting One stand by you,
   in your gladness and in your grieving.

May the Gifted One relieve you,
May the Given One retrieve you,
May the Giving One receive you,
   in your falling and your restoring.

May the Binding One unite you,
May the One Belov'd invite you,
May the Loving One delight you,
   Three-in-One, joy in life unending.

Brian Wren, copyright © 1989 by Hope Publishing Company for the U.S.A., Canada, Australia, and New Zealand, and by Stainer & Bell Ltd., London, England, for all other territories. All rights reserved. Used by permission.

---

15. The original formula reads, "I baptize you in the name of the Father, the Son, and the Holy Spirit, one God, Mother of us all." See Duck, *Gender and the Name of God,* pp. 163–66.

Finally, a reminder. Not all ritual songs are printed in service books. The first stanza of Jeremiah Rankin's "God Be with You Till We Meet Again" is a ritual song when sung invariably as, or after, the benediction.[16] I know congregations whose ritual songs include "Happy Birthday to You," sung to the child or adult whose birthday it is, and Christianized by singing, "Happy birthday, *God bless you*," in place of their name(s).

Chant

By "chant" I mean a song whose music makes it possible for texts not written in English verse to be sung by a congregation.[17] Translations of Hebrew psalms are frequently sung (or read aloud) in English-language worship, and customarily render the Hebrew name of God as "LORD" or "the LORD." Because repeated words are formative, especially when sung, this title, perhaps more than any other, has for generations shaped our images and concepts of God. To test its adequacy, I must first tell its story.

In English versions of the Bible, "Lord" renders meanings from two sources, sometimes signified by different typographies. In Christian scripture (the New, or Second Testament), "Lord" and "the Lord" (lowercase with capital L) is a title given sometimes to God (see below), and more often to Jesus Christ. It translates the Greek word *kyrios*, whose meanings range, roughly, from "mister" to "master," with a specifically male reference. Sometimes it is a polite greeting to a man (not a woman) whom one respects but does not know well. More frequently, it acclaims the risen Christ as alive forever, victor over death and sin, next to God in heaven, and the only One, anywhere, who deserves and claims our worship. To say *Kyrios Yesous!* ("Jesus is Lord!" 1 Corinthians 12:3) meant that Jesus Christ had our complete loyalty, in direct contrast with everyone else who claimed the title, including the emperor of Rome. Thus, *Kyrios Yesous!* or *Kyrios Yesous Christos!* ("Jesus Christ is Lord," Philippians 2:11) had a wider, politically riskier meaning than the personal, private "I love you, Lord" in today's hymns and choruses.

In English versions of Hebrew scripture (the "Old" or First Testament of the Christian Bible), the story is longer and the issues more

---

16. See, for example, *United Methodist Hymnal,* #672 and #673.

17. See above, p. 105.

complex. Sometimes "Lord" translates Hebrew *Adonai,* a plural form used to intensify the rank of an individual. Its meanings (all male) include "master," "proprietor," "governor," "husband," "prince" (or chieftain), and "king."[18]

Far more frequently, however, the word "Lord" is set in capital and small captial letters ("[the] LORD"). Though it also refers to God, the circumstances are different, because *Adonai* (which it translates) is not the word written in the Hebrew text. The Hebrew has a different word, which we may render as "yhwh," or (with spaces for vowel sounds) *Y~hw~h.* It is God's mysterious name, probably pronounced "Yahweh." Ancient Hebrew did not have written vowels, but speakers knew which vowels were meant (as we would if confronted with, "W gthr t wrshp gd, nd prs gd's hly nm"). The rendering, *Y~hw~h* transliterates the Hebrew consonants into their rough English equivalents, and leaves space for the vowels that English could supply if we knew for certain what they were.

The divine name *Y~hw~h* was in use before 1300 B.C.E., by tribal peoples of the eastern Sinai.[19] It is the name given to Moses when he encounters the divine presence in the burning bush (Exodus 3). In that meeting, which grounds and characterizes Israel's faith, there are critically important themes. Unlike "God," "Creator," "Savior," and "Lord," *Y~hw~h* is a name as well as a title.[20] Just as your own name, when spoken, identifies you and usually gets your attention, this name could be, and initially was, spoken directly to the Holy One of Israel.

Because God is God, *Y~hw~h* is not a name Moses guesses, invents, or discovers, but what God discloses after Moses asks, "What is your name?" In the burning bush narrative, *Y~hw~h* is, as it were, God's "given" and "proper" name.

Though there is no certainty as to what *Y~hw~h* originally meant, the burning bush narrative connects it with the verb "to be." The name is not announced directly, however. When Moses asks God's name, the reply is not "My name is *Y~hw~h,*" but two statements, positive yet enigmatic. The second is usually translated as, "Thus you shall say to the Israelites, 'I AM has sent me to you,'" but the Hebrew could also be

18. Brown, Driver, Briggs, *Hebrew and English Lexicon of the Old Testament* (Oxford: Clarendon Press, 1907).

19. Ramshaw, *God beyond Gender,* p. 48.

20. See Exodus 3:15: "This is my name forever, and this my title for all generations."

translated as "I WILL BE." For the first, and longer statement, there is no single, exact translation. English verbs come with tenses, identifying an action as past, present, or future,[21] and the customary English rendering is the present tense, "I am what [or "who"] I am" (often reverentially capitalized as I AM WHAT I AM). Hebrew verbs, however, do not by themselves mark past, present, or future; other parts of speech, and the context, give those indications. What the Hebrew here designates is an incomplete action, without clear time reference. "I am what I am" is one possibility. Equally possible is the NRSV's marginal note, "I will be what I will be." More intriguingly, and just as accurately, it could be translated, "I am what I will be," or, "I will be what I am."

The name $Y\sim hw\sim h$ appears beforehand in the narrative ("$Y\sim h\sim w\sim h$ saw," "$Y\sim h\sim w\sim h$ said"), and afterward, when God says, "Go and assemble the elders of Israel, and say to them, $Y\sim hw\sim h$, the God of your ancestors, the God of Abraham, of Isaac, and of Jacob, has appeared to me, saying: I have given heed to you and to what has been done to you in Egypt" (Exodus 3:16).

Thus, the name $Y\sim h\sim w\sim h$ connects the Israelites with their ancestors and summarizes the promise contained in the various renderings of "I am what I will be": God was alive and purposefully active in the past, is alive and liberatingly active now; and will be alive and providentially active in the future.

To summarize, $Y\sim hw\sim h$ is not a title, but a "personal" name. Disclosed by God, it reminds the Israelites that God is enigmatic and elusive, yet knowable and trustworthy. Israel's psalmists celebrate "the story that comes with the name."[22] This is the Name that comes with the story, in which $Y\sim hw\sim h$ chooses, loves, guides, liberates, and forgives the people of Israel.

At first, the Name was spoken freely. When the people sang psalms, they cried, "$Y\sim hw\sim h$!" or described the great deeds of $Y\sim hw\sim h$. Later, by the third or fourth century B.C.E.,[23] the Name began to be avoided. One plausible explanation is that, in the ancient world, saying someone's name was believed to give the power of summoning them, and the Living God can never be commanded to appear. In its place, people said or sang *Adonai*. First-century Aramaic-speaking

---

21. With, of course, many possible subcategories: conditional, future conditional, perfect, imperfect, future perfect, historic present, and so on.

22. See above, p. 176.

23. Duck, *What to Do about "Lord,"* p. 5, citing Phyllis Bird.

Samaritans said *shema* ("the name"). Some Orthodox Jews today say *hashshem* (Hebrew: "the name"). In the early years of the twentieth century, the *American Standard Version* of the Bible used the hybrid construction "Jehovah," which combines the vowels of Adonai with the consonants YHWH ("y-*e*-h-*o*-w-*a*-h").[24] Some contemporary Reformed Jews say "the Eternal" or "Eternal One," either to be gender-inclusive or to avoid association with "Lord" as a title for Jesus.[25]

By the time of Jesus, thousands of Jews lived outside Judea, all over the known world. Because many no longer knew Hebrew, but spoke colloquial Greek as their first or second language, the Hebrew scriptures were translated into Greek. A word had to be found for $Y\sim hw\sim h$, but the Name itself could not be spoken or translated. Instead, the translators chose *kyrios*, a term used "to denote respect for any male authority from a stranger to the emperor."[26]

In Christian faith the two histories of *kyrios* came together. From Judaism, it stood in place of, but did not translate, the enigmatic, personal, liberating name of the Living God—a name without overtones of human gender. In Jewish and Gentile Christian experience, it was a title of the Living Christ, the *kyrios*, once crucified by earthly *kyrioi*, now over and above them all.

Like the three terms in "Father, Son, and Holy Spirit," "Lord" and "LORD" are interlocking uses of language. "This double term LORD/Lord is shorthand for a fundamental formula of Christian faith: Jesus is titled with the name of God."[27] Unlike the Trinitarian use of "Father-Son," where the two belong inseparably together,[28] a liturgical alternative to "LORD" ($Y\sim hw\sim h$) would not necessarily require an alternative to "Lord" (meaning Jesus Christ). However, if one is replaced, a coherent alternative to the other is desirable.

It may be granted that, for Christians scarred by oppression and discrimination, the acclamation "Jesus is Lord" frequently retains its liberating power. "If Jesus is my Lord and master," says one African

---

24. The singular word, Adon, is pronounced with long vowels (Aah-thôn: the "d" is sounded "th" as in "that"); the plural form, Adonai, has a shortened initial "a," sounded like the "a" in "alone."

25. Duck, *What to Do about "Lord,"* p. 5. "[the] Eternal" was also James Moffatt's choice ("Introduction," *A New Translation of the Bible* [London: Hodder & Stoughton, 1935], pp. xx–xxi).

26. Ramshaw, *God beyond Gender,* p. 49.

27. Ibid., p. 47.

28. See p. 241 and p. 319.

American pastor, "then nobody else is. It subverts every other power structure and authority in the world and keeps me free."[29] Euro-American worship presents an ironic contrast: "Lord" applied to Jesus Christ has mostly been depoliticized, and downgraded to an intimate, personal name.

My focus here is on "LORD" in congregational chant, the psalms in particular. When I question its repeated use in worship, some say that male authority is an appropriate understanding of God and others opine that although God is neither male nor masculine, they find "LORD" untroubling. In the latter category is Kathryn Greene-McCreight, an ordained minister of the United Church of Christ and a research fellow at Yale University Divinity School. Noting that in English versions of the Bible "LORD" traditionally stands for $Y\sim hw\sim h$, she states, incorrectly, that LORD "translates" it, then adds:

> This is extremely important for us to know: every time we encounter the word "LORD" in the King James, Revised Standard, and New Revised Standard Versions, it points to the divine name, and not some generic person of important status.[30]

There are four problems with this argument. First, "LORD" only "works" as a pointer when in capitals. When it migrates from Bible readings to other liturgical forms, it almost always loses its capitalization. Second, "LORD" can only do what it's supposed to do if everyone knows what it's supposed to do. In practice, few worshipers today can be expected to know that "LORD" stands for $Y\sim hw\sim h$, and even fewer know that the word translates, not the divine name, but a substitution. The only people who know that "LORD" points to $Y\sim hw\sim h$ are people in the know. Relying on special, esoteric knowledge of God is not a mark of mainstream Christian faith, but of an early deviation called gnosticism. Third, the supposed pointer is merely typographical. It functions only when seen on a page or a screen. When spoken and heard, in Bible readings or prayers, "lord" carries its aural meanings and connotations, untouched by typographical capitalization. Finally, whatever "LORD" is intended to point to, it overwhelmingly evokes not I WILL BE WHO I AM, but a figure of male authority.

Some Americans, aware of my English origins, say, "It's not a

29. Quoted by Christensen, "The Language of Faith," in Christensen, ed., *How Shall We Sing the Lord's Song?* p. 27.

30. Greene-McCreight, "Our Pride Is in the Name of the Lord."

problem for us, because we don't have lords in the United States,"
occasionally mentioning King George III and the outcome of the Revolutionary War. Though the U.S.A. is a society without hereditary
titles, American usage of "lord" nevertheless retains prerevolutionary
meanings. When I invite Americans to brainstorm their associations of
the word, its liturgical meanings surface immediately, followed by current U.S. dictionary definitions: master and ruler; someone with
authority, control, or power over others; a feudal superior; lord of the
manor; titled nobleman; and House of Lords. Though my current
American dictionary carefully says *"person* with authority . . . ,*"* most
meanings cited are, in fact, male. Women with authority and control
over others are rarely, if ever, called "lords and masters," nor are
female financiers celebrated as "great lords of banking."[31] I conclude
that, even in lordless America, "lord" denotes a man with authority,
control, and power over others. Spoken liturgically, it projects these
meanings onto God. Because the psalms are peppered with the divine
name, LORD is said or sung repeatedly, over and over and over again.
The divine Name is cloaked by a man's title. The enigmatic, ungendered, liberating One is ousted by a masculinized deity clad in feudal
dominance.

Some argue that, if worshipers experience LORD incorrectly, the
solution is to teach them its "real meaning." If we let ourselves be
guided by the way people experience the word, they say, we are pro-
jecting our own experience onto God, not listening to what God has
revealed. One problem here is that LORD makes precisely this kind of

---

31. *Random House Webster's College Dictionary,* updated 2d ed, 1997, 1998, s.v.
"lord." Dictionary meanings—beginning with most important:

a person who has authority, control, or power over others; master or ruler

a person who exercises authority from property rights; an owner of land, houses,
    etc.

a person who is a leader or has great influence in a profession; *the great lords of
    banking*

a feudal superior; the proprietor of a manor

a titled nobleman or peer; person with title, Lord or higher title

Lords, UK usages: House of Lords, Lord Bishop, Lord Mayor

The Supreme Being, God

Jesus Christ

arch: husband

exclamation: Lord!

lord it

I recently met a distinguished female banker described in citations and news reports
    as a "dame" of banking.

false projection. Another is that, linguistically, usage determines meaning. Day by day, people cast their vote on word meanings by the way they use them. Pronouncements from "lordly" authorities cut no ice: majority meanings rule. Finally, from Pentecost onward, Christianity has been a religion of translation, recognizing that people need to hear the good news in their own language and thought forms. By analogy, if LORD now "mistranslates" God's name and nature, those who seek alternatives are following that tradition; the "real meaning" school is outside it.

As a label for God, or a substitute for God's Name, LORD is seriously misleading. Though God is not male, and divine sovereignty is not based on coercive domination, LORD has indelible meanings of maleness and male dominance. Because I have made my case, and others have argued it in detail,[32] I shall move on and ask how to replace LORD in worship, especially in the psalms.

When a psalm is read to a congregation, it comes to our culture from its own. If it asks $Y\sim hw\sim h$ to kill enemies, or applauds those who kill Babylon's children,[33] we can say, "That was then, and this is now." We can hear it, and wrestle with God through it, without ourselves having to pray it. When we take the same psalm and put it on our own lips, the lyric must meet a different standard: Is it an appropriate vehicle for our worship? From Isaac Watts onward, Christians have modified psalm texts, not only to avoid blatantly "unchristian" sentiments,[34] but to make the psalms more applicable to present conditions. Otherwise, as Watts explains, we find that, amid "sentences of the psalmist that are expressive of the temper of our own hearts and the circumstances of our lives," we stumble into "a following line which so peculiarly belongs but to one action or hour of the life of David or Asaph, that our song [breaks off] in the midst."[35] Changing psalm texts is a long-standing tradition.

One way around "LORD" is to change a text from third-person to second-person speech; from "The LORD is great, and greatly to be praised" to "You are great, and greatly to be praised." This procedure also avoids the masculine pronouns for $Y\sim hw\sim h$, which are more

32. Ramshaw, *God beyond Gender;* Johnson, *She Who Is;* also Wren, *What Language Shall I Borrow?*

33. See Psalms 58: 6–11; 69:19–28; and 137:8–9.

34. Watts's Preface to *Hymns and Spiritual Songs,* 1709 (ed. Bishop), pp. li–lii.

35. Ibid.

gender-laden in English than in Hebrew. But it has limitations. Because pronouns require an antecedent noun, an altered psalm must retain at least one "LORD," "God," or equivalent, so that it can say,"O God/LORD, you. . . ." And though Psalms 23:1 and 27:2 easily become, "LORD [?], you are my shepherd," and "O God [?], you are my light," the syntax of others resists alteration. In Psalm 2:10–12, the singer says:

> Now therefore, O kings, be wise;
>   be warned, O rulers of the earth.
> Serve the LORD with fear,
>   with trembling kiss his feet,
> or he will be angry, and you will perish in the way.

A rewrite would have to say something like:

> Version A: Now therefore, O kings, be wise; be warned, O
>   rulers of the earth.
> May they serve you, O LORD [?], with fear, with trembling kiss
>   your feet,
> or you will be angry, and they will perish in the way.

or:

> Version B: May kings be wise, and earth's rulers be warned.
> May they serve you, O LORD [?], with fear, with trembling kiss
>   your feet,
> or you will be angry, and they will perish in the way.

Version A switches from warning the kings to praying for them, a move both abrupt and implausible. In both versions, the kings no longer hear the threat against them, because it is redirected to God, who hardly needs to be told what "his" anger would do. Similar considerations apply (for example) to Psalms 20:1–3 and 24:7–10.

Another route, systematically adopted by *The New Century Hymnal,* is to replace "LORD" with "God." As a worshiper, I find this an improvement, but far from ideal. The word "God" itself has masculine overtones,[36] and becomes repetitious when it replaces its pronoun. A

---

36. Ramshaw, *God beyond Gender,* pp. 8–14.

generic noun, it calls up an array of religious longings, but cannot specify which "god" is being addressed. It lacks the specific connotations of $Y\sim hw\sim h$, the Name that comes with Israel's story. Replacing "LORD" with "God" is, at best, a stopgap measure.

Another possibility, popularized by the *Jerusalem Bible,* is to say "Yahweh," on the assumption that this was the original pronunciation. Advantage: it is clearly a name, not a title. Disadvantage: speaking God's Name is abhorrent to Orthodox Jews. Additional disadvantage: in English it sounds like a sheep's bleat. Conclusion: "Yahweh" is not an option.

Why not "Adonai," the ancient substitution for $Y\sim hw\sim h$? Popularized by songs like Amy Grant's "El Shaddai, El Shaddai, El Elyon, na Adonai," it is now quite widely known, and recognizably "biblical." Because its Hebrew meaning is not, I suspect, transparent to most English speakers, it sounds more like a name than a title. How might it sound to Orthodox Jews? Too familiar, perhaps; yet not, I submit, blasphemous—an epithet justified only when we say the Name that "Adonai" originally avoids. Italicized in the text, and sounding more like a name than a title, *Adonai* could do what "LORD" fails to do: remind us that God's Name is being intentionally avoided.[37] When reading Hebrew scripture (though not yet in congregational psalmody), I usually substitute Adonai for LORD. Needing only a one-sentence explanation, the substitution is seamless, because Adonai has the same grammatical function as the word it replaces.

A more radical reminder that the God of Moses has a Name would be to print "(NAME)*" wherever $Y\sim hw\sim h$ appears, with a footnote saying: "*God's Name is not spoken: use 'Adonai,' 'El Shaddai,' 'Living One,' or another reverent substitution." This procedure would be feasible, I think, for both scripture readings and chanted psalms. If worshipers and worship leaders choose a substitution, they are more likely to remember what "LORD" conspicuously fails to convey.

"Living One" is Gail Ramshaw's proposal. In Hebrew scripture, it points to a key theme in the burning bush story and later divine

---

37. The capitalization of "LORD" achieves its intended aim, if at all, only on the printed page. Aurally, when spoken and sung, it conveys only "lord," a title signifying maleness, and male dominance.

epiphanies: God *is*, God lives, God is active now as in the past, and will be "the Living One" in the future. In the Christian story, Christ is also "the Living One," risen from the dead, the same yesterday, today, and forever. If carefully varied grammatically, "(the) Living One" could substitute for $Y{\sim}hw{\sim}h$ in the First Testament, and identify Jesus Christ in the Second, linking the two as effectively, and more adequately, than "LORD/Lord."[38]

---

38. Ramshaw, *God beyond Gender,* pp. 54–57.

Chapter Eight

"Such a Feast as Mends in Length": Hymns as Poems of Faith

Come, my Light, my Feast, my Strength:
such a light as shows a feast;
such a feast as mends in length*;
such a strength as makes a guest.
——George Herbert, 1633

*improves as it goes on.

Earlier, I defined a hymn as a congregational song consisting of a sequence of units, called stanzas, with or without a repeated refrain. Such sequences have the capacity—not always realized—to develop a theme and reach a conclusion. A good hymn lyric has flow and direction, and keeps its quality as it unfolds. An outstanding lyric may even "mend in length," as Herbert puts it, meaning that it improves as it goes on. It takes us somewhere as it tells a story, paraphrases scripture, or develops a theme. There have always been exceptions to this rule. Many of Charles Wesley's hymns were written for evangelistic field preaching, where "line-by-line impact seems to have mattered most and the total weight of accumulated imagery was apparently more important than its overall pattern."[1] Today, our

---

1. Forell Marshall and Todd, *English Congregational Hymns in the Eighteenth Century,* p. 87. See also Forell Marshall, *Common Hymnsense.* She shows how, in some hymns, Wesley "tends to write single lines in isolation, each invoking powerful ideas but unrelated to the lines coming before and after" (p. 55). However, the "best of Wesley" (title of chap. 4) shows more coherence, as demonstrated in her analysis of "Come, Thou Long-Expected Jesus," "Love Divine, All Loves Excelling," and "Lo! He Comes with Clouds Descending," which show clear thought with logical progression, and have been less altered by editors.

postmodern, televisual age may have room for hymns that are not sequential. Even so, a hymn needs to consist of more than one fragment after another. Jaroslav Vajda's "God of the Sparrow" and "Now the Silence" break the mold of traditional syntax and sequence, yet are unified by carefully chosen metaphors and repetitions.[2] Though other genres can have poetic qualities, hymns are the most developed form of poetry in congregational song. I shall look first at their form and format, then at their function.

Poetic Meter

In form, then, a hymn lyric is a sequence of units, each of which has the same line length, rhythms, and rhyme scheme (if rhymed) as its predecessor. Such identical units are called *stanzas*, distinguishing them from units of varied form, which are called *strophes*. Thus, a hymn lyric is a piece of *stanzaic verse*. Because it is stanzaic, a hymn lyric can be sung, stanza by stanza, to the same tune. A lyric's pattern of rhyme and speech rhythms is known as its *meter*.[3] For the sake of accuracy, I call it *poetic meter*, because the word *meter* is also used to denote the pattern of rhythmic pulses, or "beat," in a given piece of music (often also called *time* or *time signature*). Though the rhythms of speech and music overlap, and speech can follow musical rhythms (as in rap, for example), their rhythmic systems are distinct.

A hymn's poetic meter has two major variants: the number of syllables in a line, and their speech rhythm, which in English is a pattern of loudness and softness, in which loudness is called *stress*. When a poem is spoken aloud, the stresses can be quite varied. Try speaking the hymn by Dan Damon, "A Parent's Heart Will Feel the Hurt" (for full text, see p. 98). Does it sound like this?

> A *par*-ent's *heart* will *feel* the *hurt*
> each *time* a *child* is *bruised*,
> and *God* was *weep*-ing *like* a *child*
> when *Je*-sus *was* a-*bused*.

---

2. See, for example, the *United Methodist Hymnal*, #122 and #619.

3. For a more detailed discussion of poetic meter, see, for example, Espy, *Words to Rhyme With;* Grindal, *Lessons in Hymnwriting;* Hollander, *Rhyme's Reason;* and Lovelace, *The Anatomy of Hymnody.*

> Which *one* of *us* would *give* a *child*
>   a *stone* in *place* of *bread?*
> What *kind* of God would *be* con-*tent*
>   as *Je*-sus *cried* and *bled?*

Or is it more like this?

> A *par*-ent's *heart* will *feel* the *hurt*
>   *each time* a *child* is *bruised,*
> and *God* was *weep*-ing like a *child*
>   when *Je*-sus was a-*bused.*

> *Which* one of *us* would *give* a *child*
>   a *stone* in *place* of *bread?*
> *What* kind of God would *be* con-*tent*
>   as *Je*-sus *cried* and *bled?*

The second example varies the stress for dramatic effect, and to prevent the speech rhythms from becoming too predictable. In dramatic speech, the stress pattern can be varied in many ways. To track them accurately we would need more subtle markers than my simple division between "stressed" or "unstressed." In rap, the stress can also be varied, but any rap rendering makes it more emphatic:

> *WHICH* one of *US* would *GIVE* a *CHILD*
>   a *STONE* in *PLACE* of *BREAD?*
> *WHAT* kind of *GOD* would *BE* con-*TENT*
>   as *JE*-sus *CRIED* and *BLED?*

Rap moves us closer to song by using the poem's spoken beat more emphatically. Sometimes—as here—the spoken beat coincides with the number of syllables in each line. Sometimes it doesn't. Try rapping the following, being sure to clap your hands to the beat:

> Our *God,* our *help* in *a*-ges *past,*
> our *hope* for *years* to *come,*
> our *shel*-ter *from* the *storm*-y *blast,*
> and *our* e-*ter*-nal *home.*

You will probably find that the "pull" of the first, four-beat line, is so strong that you automatically add an extra clap at the end of the second and fourth lines:

our *hope* for *years* to *come,* (CLAP)

To give a detailed analysis of speech rhythms, we would have to take account of such "unvoiced" or silent beats. I cannot do so here, but invite you to listen for them when poetry is spoken.

English verse has a variety of stress patterns. The couplet by Henry Williams Baker (1821–77),

> The *King* of *love* my *Shep*-herd *is,*
> whose *good*-ness *fail*-eth *nev*-er

has eight syllables followed by seven, in a pattern called *iambic,* where the stress, or emphasis, is on the second of every two syllables. By contrast, these lines of John Newton (1725–1807),

> *Glor*-ious *things* of *thee* are *spo*-ken,
> *Zi*-on, *ci*-ty of our *God*

have the same syllable count, but a different speech rhythm. The first line is *trochaic,* where the stress falls on the first of every two syllables, but in the second the author varies the stress by using the soft, or unstressed, syllable "of," so that three unstressed syllables come before, and highlight, the emphatic line-ending word, *"God."* Many hymn writers do what Newton does, and vary a hymn's basic speech rhythms, to prevent a "singsongy" effect. The stress patterns (speech rhythms) of English verse are described in terms borrowed from ancient Greek poetry. In English hymnody, the most common rhythms are:

Iambic: Two syllables, the second stressed—I *slip,* I *fall,* I *rise,* I *limp.*

Trochaic: Two syllables, the first stressed—*Chas*-ing, *pac*-ing, *run*-ning, *rac*-ing.

Dactylic: One stressed, two unstressed—*Fin*-gers are *wag*-ging and *beck*-on-ing.

Anapestic: Reverse of Dactylic—In a *hop* and a *skip* and a *jump.*

If derivations aid your memory, "trochaic" is from a Greek word meaning "running"; "dactyl" is Greek for finger, used because a finger has one long bone followed by two short bones; and "anapest" means "struck back, reversed," in other words the reverse of dactylic.

In hymnals, a hymn's poetic meter is indicated by numbers. In the examples above, Henry Baker's and John Newton's couplets would be marked "8.7." This describes the number of syllables but not their rhythm. Some hymnals add "Iambic," "Trochaic," and so on, for clarification. A complete description would have the following information on the page, and/or in an index:

> "Glorious Things of Thee Are Spoken"—Words: John Newton (1725–1807). Tune: ABBOT'S LEIGH, Cyril V. Taylor (1907–91). 8.7.8.7.D (Trochaic).

> "The King of Love My Shepherd Is"—Words: Henry Williams Baker (1821–77). Tune: ST. COLUMBA, Ancient Irish Hymn Melody. 8.7.8.7. (Iambic).

In the second example, the numbers "8.7.8.7." indicate that each stanza has four lines. By contrast, each stanza of Newton's hymn has eight lines. Because the syllable pattern of the first four is repeated, the meter is indicated as "8.7.8.7.D" (= Double), to save writing "8.7.8.7.8.7.8.7." Because several tunes can sometimes be sung to the same text, each tune has its own name, usually printed in capital letters.

Most hymnals have a "metrical index" somewhere near the back cover. Because the word "meter" is also used in music, a metrical index is sometimes perceived as purely musical information. It isn't. Instead, it lists all the tunes believed to fit a given *poetic meter*. Beware! Most metrical indexes give only partial information. To find out if a tune "goes with" a given text, it is essential to play it, *and sing all the stanzas of the hymn in question.* Failing this, one risks choosing a tune that doesn't fit the mood of the text; is designed for a different speech rhythm (trochaic instead of iambic, for example), or partially fits the rhythm but has a stanza or line "out of sync." Sometimes a hymn's poetic meter is described as "Irregular." The word is often used inaccurately to mean that the poetic meter, though consistent throughout, is so unusual that the editors can't be bothered to list it separately. What it ought to mean is that every stanza follows the same syllable count and speech rhythm except for a line in, say, stanza three, where an extra syllable must be fitted to the music, as in the following:

1. Be thou my *vis-ion*
2. Be thou my *wis-dom*
3. Be thou my *bat-tle-shield*[4]

---

4. From "Be Thou My Vision," ancient Irish poem, trans. Mary Elizabeth Byrne (1880–1931) and Eleanor Henrietta Hull (1860–1935), in *Congregational Praise* (London: Independent Press, 1951), #432. Recent hymnals often alter or omit the irregular stanza.

Meter and Meaning

English-language hymns mostly use rhyme. Unrhymed verse is sometimes appropriate, but no easier. Stanzas need to be metrically consistent; opening lines must convince the singer that there ain't gonna be no rhyme, nohow; and the remainder must avoid sound similarities close to rhyme—otherwise singers will think the writer wanted to use rhyme, but didn't know how.

Rhyming verse makes strict demands on the writer and sets limits to what can be said. The word "love," for example, is a strong "Christian" word, and sounds resonant at the end of a line. Unfortunately, its perfect rhymes are limited to "above," "dove," "glove," "guv," "of" (pronounced "uv"), and "shove."[5] "Guv" and "of" are too colloquial for most hymn lyrics. "Glove" and "shove" have few relevant contexts in a hymn. "Above" and "dove" have been worked and overworked. It is hard to use them with freshness and surprise. Some aspiring writers give up, frustrated by the restrictions of meter and rhyme, and hope for sympathy, as if to say, "I've been consistent in the first two stanzas—can't you give me the benefit of the doubt on this one?" However, as composer Carl Schalk pithily puts it, piety is no substitute for crafting.

On the other hand, a well-chosen rhyme enhances its lyric. Here, again, is Henry Williams Baker:

> Lord, thy word abideth
> and our footsteps guideth;
> who its truth believeth
> light and joy receiveth.

The short lines and two-syllable rhymes add impact to the message. As J. R. Watson observes, "The meaning is in the echoing sounds: it is a rhymer's way of seeing the gospel."[6] A longer line scheme, or prose rendering, would weaken it. Who would want to sing, "Lord, thine everlasting word guides our footsteps. Whoever believes its truth receives light and joy"?

---

5. Espy, *Words to Rhyme With,* p. 177, "UV," adds compounds, which do not significantly expand rhyming possibilities: hereof, whereof, thereof; mourning dove, ringdove, rock dove, turtledove; foxglove, unglove; lady love, light-o'love, puppy love, self-love, and true love.

6. For this and the following example, I am indebted to Watson, *The English Hymn,* p. 31. I have elaborated his discussion with prose renderings and the extended discussion of "wean."

Another example comes from Charles Wesley:

> Lord, that I may learn of thee,
> give me true simplicity;
> wean my soul, and keep it low,
> willing thee alone to know.

In other contexts, "simplicity" is usually a disappointing rhyme, because most tunes draw out its final, unstressed, syllable into an unnatural stress: from "sim-*plic*-i-ty" to "sim-*plic*-i-*tee*." Here, however, word choice reinforces meaning. The soul is like a toddler, weaned from mother's milk, who must spell out the word, saying (or especially, singing) "sim—plic—i—tee," as if learning to read. Moreover, the subject matter—what we are learning to read—is not trivial but something we need to remember and live by. The second couplet also gains strength from its rhyme. The last line's inverted word order (from "willing to know thee alone" to "willing thee alone to *know*") throws emphasis on the verb by placing it at the end of the line, and puts the rhyming words in close relationship: only by keeping "low" can the soul come to "know." Because the realm of God is given only to childlike openness (Mark 10:15), the soul must remain low in stature (like a young child), as well as in posture, in order to receive it.

The Freedom of Form

Though poetic meter is strict, it is freeing as well as constricting. Each metrical form has its own character, "which shapes the material and becomes part of the meaning."[7] A given meter empowers a writer in some directions, even as it prevents progress in others. Short meter, or SM (6.6.8.6.), occurs frequently in English hymnody. It steers the writer toward short opening phrases, followed by a longer statement leading to a conclusion, as in this stanza:

> Breathe on me, Breath of God,
> fill me with life anew,
> that I may love what thou dost love,
> and do what thou wouldst do.
>   Edwin Hatch, 1835–89

---

7. Ibid., p. 32.

The first two lines are a petition; the last two lines are the hoped-for action. After the brevity of the opening lines, the eight-syllable line feels spacious, even though it has only two more syllables. Internal repetitions (breathe/breath, and "what thou dost"/wouldst) further strengthen the lyric. John Wesley achieves a similar effect in his translation of Paul Gerhardt:

> Give to the winds thy fears,
>   hope and be undismayed:
> God hears thy sighs and counts thy tears,
>   God shall lift up thy head.
>   Paul Gerhardt, 1653,
>   trans. John Wesley, 1739

Three verbal imperatives (give, hope, be undismayed) are matched by three divine responses (hears thy sighs, counts thy tears, shall lift up thy head). Here also, after the pithy opening lines, the third line expands in parallel phrases conveying assurance. The final line is both development and summary.

Thus, short meter encourages the lyric to go "One, Two, Climax, Conclusion." A different treatment is possible, however. Here is an accomplished hymn writer and journalist, James Montgomery, using short meter to make the last two lines a single statement, building and expanding through fourteen syllables:

> Stand up and bless the Lord,
>   ye people of his choice,
> *stand up and bless the Lord your God*
>   *with heart and soul and voice.*
>
> God is our strength and song,
>   and his salvation ours;
> *then be his love in Christ proclaimed*
>   *with all our ransomed powers.*
>
> Stand up and bless the Lord,
>   the Lord your God adore;
> *stand up and bless his glorious name,*
>   *henceforth forevermore.*
>   James Montgomery, 1771–1854

In the first stanza, Montgomery uses the eight-syllable line to expand the opening statement, giving both repetition and emphasis.

The final stanza blends repetition of the first ("stand up, bless") with variety.

Common meter, or CM (8.6.8.6.), came into congregational song from the English ballad, which flows through several stanzas as it tells a story or elaborates a theme. Common meter was used first in metrical versions of the psalms, then in hymns. Compared with short meter, the extra two syllables in the opening line make a big difference, because both halves of the stanza can open out into fourteen syllables, or be broken into smaller units. Here is Isaac Watts, using several variations:

> Joy to the world! The Lord is come:
>   let earth receive its King;
> let every heart prepare him room,
>   and heaven and nature sing.

The first line is broken in half by an exclamation mark. The second half of the line stops at a semi-colon, from which hangs a six syllable sentence unit, followed by another of fourteen syllables, split by a comma. In the second stanza the last couplet sweeps on without interruption: While fields and floods, rocks, hills, and plains / repeat the sounding joy.

Dan Damon's hymn, "A Parent's Heart" (see above, p. 98), uses all fourteen syllables in every couplet except the last. Thus, sentences like:

> A parent's heart will feel the hurt / each time a child is bruised,
> Which one of us would give a child / a stone in place of bread?
> Rejected love endured the cross / and earth and heaven kept
>   still.

are followed by the conclusion, where a semicolon stops the flow, highlighting the importance of the final line:

> God's final will cannot be lost;
>   love rolls away the stone.

Long meter (8.8.8.8.) is more expansive still. Each line can be a complete sentence, either standing by itself or as part of a series. Here is Fred Pratt Green, with a stanza whose four phrases form one sentence:

The church of Christ in every age,
    beset by change, but Spirit led,
must claim and test its heritage
    and keep on rising from the dead.

By contrast, the final stanza of William Kethe's paraphrase of Psalm 100 has four lines, each containing a verb. All but the last are capable of standing on their own:

For why? The Lord our God is good,
    his mercy is forever sure;
his truth at all times firmly stood,
    and shall from age to age endure.[8]

Other meters have their own character, limits, and possibilities. A previously quoted hymn of mine (see pp. 171–72) reads, in part:

When love is found
    and hope comes home,
sing and be glad
    that two are one.
When love explodes
    and fills the sky,
praise God, and share
    our Maker's joy.

When love has flowered
    in trust and care,
build both each day,
    that love may dare
to reach beyond
    home's warmth and light,
to serve and strive
    for truth and right.

---

8. For the example, and my analytical framework, I am indebted to Watson, *The English Hymn,* p. 33. See also Forell Marshall and Todd, *English Congregational Hymns,* p. 13.

Praise God for love,
    praise God for life,
in age or youth,
    in calm or strife.
Lift up your hearts!
    Let love be fed
through death and life
    in broken bread.

This is sometimes cast as long meter (8.8.8.8.). In writing it, how-ever, I was thinking in terms of four-syllable lines, and prefer to cast it as: 4.4.4.4.D. Though some lines flow together in longer phrases, as in the second stanza, the decision to *think* in terms of four-sylla-ble units did, I think, mandate simple, mostly one-syllable, word choices and lead me to place "strong" words at the end of most four-syllable units: for example, *found, home, glad, one, explodes, sky, share, joy, flowered, care, day, dare, beyond, light, strive,* and *right.*

Among today's hymn writers, New Zealand's Shirley Murray has a notable gift of strong speech rhythms in economical, often unusual meters. In "Star Child," she uses 4.5.4.5., plus a refrain, and the same phrase-pattern in almost every stanza:

[Stanza 1]
Star-Child, earth-Child,
    go-between of God,
love-Child, Christ Child,
    heaven's lightning rod,
*Refrain: This year, this year,
    let the day arrive
    when Christmas comes for everyone,
    everyone alive!*

[Stanza 4]
Spared child, spoiled child,
    having, wanting more,
wise child, faith child,
    knowing joy in store,
Refrain

In the first four stanzas, the first and third lines divide into two, two-syllable phrases, while the second and fourth have single phrases, differently divided. In the final stanza, complete phrases vary the previous pattern, and closure is created by the emphatic three-syllable adjective, "stupendous," and by repeating the "star" and "earth" motifs of the opening stanza:

> [Stanza 5]
> Hope-for peace Child,
> God's stupendous sign,
> down-to-earth Child,
> star of stars that shine,
> *Refrain*

A final example comes from Dan Damon. Here is the first stanza of a hymn lyric in the poetic meter 3.3.3.3.3.3.3.D, cast so that it can be read in "skeins" of three, six, nine, or even twelve syllables. The lower case "l" at the beginning of the stanza, and the absence of punctuation at the end, are deliberate, because the concluding phrase begins the next stanza, and the final stanza returns us, as on a carousel, to the first.

> like a child
> love would send
> to reveal
> and to mend,
> like a child
> and a friend
> Jesus comes
> like a child
> we may find
> claiming heart,
> soul and mind,
> like a child
> strong and kind
> Jesus comes
> like a child . . . [and so on]

Visual Art

As a minor but complex art form, hymns are both aural (heard) and visual (seen). When read aloud as a poem, a hymn lyric is time art. It unfolds in a time sequence, however short. Each such experience, though it may be similar, is unrepeatable. When sung as a solo or choral item, a hymn affects a listener as other presentational songs do. When sung by a congregation, it becomes a communal utterance inviting commitment. When seen on the page, printed in its poetic form, a hymn is visual art.

Occasionally a hymn lyric visually coheres with its meaning. Look, for example, at two great hymns of the Reformation by Philipp Nicolai (1556–1608), "Wie schön leuchtet der Morgenstern" ("How Brightly Shines the Morning Star") and "Wachet auf!" ("Sleepers, Wake!"):

> Zion hört die Wächter singen,
> das Herz tut ihr vor Freude springen,
> sie wachet und steht eilend auf.
> Ihr Freund kommt vom Himmel prächtig,
> von Gnaden stark, von Wahrheit mächtig,
> ihr Licht wird hell, ihr Stern geht auf.
> Nun komm, du werte Kron,
> Herr Jesu, Gottes Sohn!
> Hosianna!
> Wir folgen all
> zum Freudensaal
> und halten mit das Abendmahl.

> Sion hears the watchmen shouting.
> Her heart leaps up with joy undoubting.
> She stands and waits with eager eyes;
> See her Friend from heaven descending,
> Adorned with truth and grace unending!
> Her light burns clear, her star doth rise.
> Now come, Thou precious Crown,
> Lord Jesu, God's own Son.
> Hosanna!
> Let us prepare
> To follow there,
> Where in thy supper we may share.[9]

---

9. "Wachet auf!" stanza 2; translation by Francis C. Burkitt (1864–1935). The chalice effect was pointed out to me by Robin Leaver in a personal communication, and is noted also by Young, *Companion to the United Methodist Hymnal*, p. 806. Such "pattern poems" reappear from time to time in the Hellenistic age, in the Renaissance, and in our own era (Hollander, *Rhyme's Reason*, p. 30). George Herbert crafted one of his poems to appear like a Hebrew altar made of unhewed stones.

Their poetic meter is such that, when centered on the page, each stanza takes the shape of a Communion chalice. I do not know if this can be proven as intentional, but Nicolai was a strong supporter of Lutheran sacramental orthodoxy, and the chalice shape is especially appropriate in "Sleepers, Wake!" which has explicit references to Communion, as in this second stanza, reproduced in German and English.

Though few hymn poets can do what Nicolai did, the visual appearance of hymns on the page makes a difference in how they are perceived and understood. In most of the English-speaking world, congregational hymnals print hymns as poems, sometimes with the melody line above. Choir members, pianists, and organists have a full music edition, with the poem printed either beneath the complete tune or between the staves of music, so that each syllable is matched to its corresponding musical note(s), a method known as "interlining."

In the United States, what is elsewhere limited to choirs is published for the whole congregation. Earlier (see p. 98) I quoted a hymn poem by Dan Damon, and printed it in poetic form. In an American hymnal, as indeed in Dan Damon's own hymn collection, interlining alters the lyric's visual appearance, so that the opening lines of each stanza appear together, like this:

| 1. | A | par | - | ent's | heart | will | feel |
| | | the | hurt | each | | | |

| 2. | Which | one | of | us | would | give | a |
| | | child | a | | | | |

| 3. | The | will | of | God | is | just | and |
| | | good | but | | | | |

| 4. | We | meet | our | Mak | - | er | at | the |
| | | wound ex | - | | | | | |

| 5. | Al - | though | we | miss | God's | first | de |
| | | - | sign | as | | | | |

(And so on down the page.)

In other words, most American worshipers see hymns printed not as poems, but interlined, as words-between-the-notes.

To form your own judgment of the difference this makes, if any, I invite you to try a reading experiment. In the Appendix is a hymn of mine, "Give Thanks for Music-Making Art," printed in two formats. Turn first to pp. 392–93, and read (not sing) the first two stanzas of the hymn in its interlined format. Then turn to pp. 394–95 and read the remaining three stanzas in poetic form.

I can't predict your response, so let me invite you to test it against responses from others. For the last decade, in well over a hundred settings all over the U.S.A., I have found a consistent pattern, irrespective of regional, denominational, and ethnic differences. Some 1–3 percent find interlined words easier to comprehend than their poetic form; 1–3 percent find no difference; and the overwhelming majority, 90–95 percent, find the poetic format easier to read and understand.

The reasons for these responses differ somewhat. People who read music commonly say they can't avoid trying to sing the tune as they read it; this moves them from the meaning of the text to the sound of the tune and which note goes with which syllable. If you know two different "languages" (in this case, English and music notation), it is hard to avoid using both when you see them on the same page. Both music readers and others report that the interlined format hinders comprehension because word spacing follows the music, in a typography full of hyphens, random gaps, and, sometimes, long dashes to help the eye skateboard across syllables. Line breaks also follow the music, whose bars (also called measures) do not always coincide with the syntax and line endings of poetic meter.

Since most people read in phrases rather than single words, the poetic format is easier to follow. It visually maps the relationship between what has gone before and what comes after, allowing the reader to scan up and down and check the syntactic, semantic, and alliterative connections between a given line and the lines above and below it. In an interlined format, such scanning is impossible, because—the___eye——must—move___slow——ly__ and___hori—zon- ___tal—ly, syl___—la—ble ——by——syl—la—ble, then— skip— a_____cross mu—sic and___ words to find the corresponding line of text in the next or previous system of music. The more stanzas in a hymn, the harder it is for the eye to jump from system to system and land in the right place, which gives lyricists the bleak new commandment: "Don't write more than four stanzas if you want to get published!"

I am not arguing for a return to the eighteenth century, when congregations knew only ten tunes and hymnals were published in words-only editions, often in six-point typefaces that strained the eye. *My argument is that we need both poetic and interlined formats to make the most of hymns and to do justice to hymns as poems of faith.* In my travels across the United States, I meet two responses to my hymn writing, frequent enough to be noticeable. When people like what I've written, they commonly say, "I like your *music*," though I have in fact written the lyric, not composed the tune. When I highlight the poetry of hymns, time after time people say, in surprise, "I never thought of hymns that way before." In Britain, where hymns are routinely printed as poetry, people recognize them as such and rarely equate "hymns" with "music." Most American worshipers encounter hymns only as words-between-the-notes, so the notion that hymns are poetry comes as a surprise. Because the dominant visual impression of an interlined hymn is its music, "I like your *music*" seems an appropriate response.[10]

Singing an interlined hymn entails going from syllable to syllable, not necessarily connecting the syllables into meaningful units. From time to time, when I'm visiting one of the great schools of American church music, I feel a strong temptation to have a room full of voice majors sight-read an interlined hymn, enjoy their glorious vocal sound, then ask them to close their books and tell me the sense of what they've sung. When I admit to this temptation, a frisson of horror ripples across the room, because the singers know they are paying more attention to music than to meaning.

Research backs my claim that the exclusive use of interlining diminishes the worshiper's comprehension of the text and appreciation of it as poetry. An article by James Rawlings Sydnor cites a doctoral dissertation whose author, Jack Renard Presseau, studied the effect of singing interlined hymns on people's comprehension. He concluded that "singing is a more complex exercise than oral speech. Hence, singing [in an interlined format] would seem to make poetry more difficult to comprehend than reading it."[11]

Anecdotal evidence supports Presseau's findings. At a memorial

---

10. Hustad writes that it is not easy to understand hymn words, especially when singing them. His discussion presupposes interlining: "In singing, *we utter one syllable at a time, concentrating on fittng each to its proper pitch;* as a result, often we do not identify the meaning of a phrase or a full sentence" (*True Worship*, pp. 63–64).

11. Sydnor, "The Hymn Society's New Hymnal."

service in an American Presbyterian church, someone copied the words of two familiar hymns from the 1990 denominational hymnal, and printed them in the worship order thus:

> Dear Lord, Creator good and kind, Forgive our foolish
> ways; Reclothe us in our rightful mind, In
> purer lives Thy service find, In deeper reverence, praise.
>
> In simple trust like theirs who heard, Beside the Syrian
> sea, The gracious calling of the Lord, Let
> us, like them, without a word Rise up and follow Thee.[12]
>
> . . . .
> Eternal Father, strong to save, Whose arm has bound the
> restless wave, Who bade the mighty ocean deep Its
> own appointed limits keep: O hear us when we
> cry to Thee For those in peril on the sea.[13]

The layout misses the proper line endings of the hymns as poems, but faithfully follows the *Presbyterian Hymnal,* where systems of music often end in midsentence. Evidently the person who transcribed these hymns had never seen them written as poetry, and did not realize that the oddly placed capital letters in this particular hymnal ("ways;/Reclothe us in our rightful mind, / In purer lives") are intended to indicate the beginnings of each new line of text. Using the capital letters as clues (but retaining them only when grammatically necessary) the verse can be poetically reconstructed, thus:

> Dear Lord, Creator good and kind,
>   forgive our foolish ways;
> reclothe us in our rightful mind,
> in purer lives Thy service find,
>   in deeper reverence, praise.

The exclusive use of interlining sometimes makes nonsense of a text, or makes it hard to follow. A hymn of mine has the couplet:

---

12. *Presbyterian Hymnal,* #345. The printed first line is, "Dear Lord and Father of mankind," but the person copying the hymn chose the alternative reading, given in a footnote at the bottom of the page ("Dear Lord, Creator good and kind").

13. *Presbyterian Hymnal,* #562. Examples supplied by Glenn A. Haynes, Minister of Music and Worship, Woodbrook Baptist Church, Baltimore, Md., in a personal communication, May 1996.

In great Calcutta Christ is known.
Soweto thunders at his voice.[14]

Whenever I use the hymn in an interlined version, I have to explain that the first word of the second line is the city in South Africa, not "So we to." In another hymn, the first five stanzas begin with the word "Wom-an." The sixth stanza changes to the plural, "Wom-en." Singers sight-reading it in the interlined form routinely misread the sixth stanza, because the first syllable of the interlined form, "Wom-," is typographically the same (though differently pronounced) in both plural and singular, and the clue provided by "-en" comes only after the first syllable has been misread. Unless the text is read beforehand, the singular is expected, and the shift to plural is missed.[15] In 1996, the United Church of Canada received a fine new hymnal. Alas, it takes the backward step, influenced by American practice, of relying exclusively on interlining. A stanza from one of my hymns reads, "At-tracted by life's deep-est claim / we wait, as-sem-bled in this place, / with needs and hopes we can-not name, / *a thirst* for healing, truth and grace." A hyphen has gone missing, so that instead of "athirst" (meaning "thirsty") we have "a thirst," which is nonsensical.[16] Further evidence of the baleful effect of interlining comes from a leaflet by the National Council of the Churches of Christ in the U.S.A., entitled *When a Church Wants to Commission a Work of Music.* The leaflet envisages a work that can be either instrumental or choral, yet speaks only about composers! It asks, "Why Commission a Piece *of Music?*"; "How Do We Begin?"; "How Do We Find *a Composer?*"; and "When Will It Be Ready?" The only reference to lyrics is in two incidental phrases: "indicate dates *for the approval of text*" and "*text selection* may take several weeks." The writer assumes either that text writers are dead and their work in public domain, or that the work of living writers can be had for free, or that composers write as skillfully as they compose (hardly ever

---

14. "In Great Calcutta Christ Is Known," *Piece Together Praise*, #104, and (interlined with music) in *Praising a Mystery*, #15.

15. Wren, "Woman in the Night," *United Methodist Hymnal*, #274.

16. From "How Great the Mystery of Faith," #390 in *Voices United*.

true!), so that, in general, words don't matter. It's the music that counts.[17]

I have argued that hymns are a threefold art form: poems that can be heard, seen, and read as such; music that can be heard as music; and the combination of both when a hymn is sung. The exclusive use of interlining privileges the second and third, and downgrades the first. When hymns are seen only as "music," their power and potential as theological poetry, expressing people's faith, are ignored, and their pastoral, homiletic, and educational possibilities diminished. Incoming mail announcing a conference on hymnody is passed, unopened, from pastor to musician—because hymns are perceived as "music," and so outside the province of the preacher, pastor, and theologian.

Perhaps the tide is turning. In the U.S.A., some hymnals are available in large-print editions which print the words as poetry, thus making their poetic form accessible again. Churches with screens for text projection usually show only words of the chorus or stanza being sung, accidentally or intentionally allowing worshipers to perceive it as poetry. The Hymn Society in the United States and Canada has recognized the value of hymns as poems by preparing an anthology of well-known hymns in poetic format, for devotional use. Its 252 hymn-poems are grouped under the headings "God," "Jesus Christ," "Holy Spirit," and "Christian Life," with the overall title *Amazing Grace*.[18]

If hymns are more easily comprehended and appreciated in poetic form, the poetic format is likely to enhance our appreciation of hymns as works of theology. I shall explore this theme in the next chapter. For the moment, having looked at a hymn's form and format, it is time to consider its purpose.

Poems of Faith

As I am using the word, "hymns" are a particular kind of Christian poetry, designed for congregational singing, as developed (as free compositions or metrical psalms) during the Protestant Reformation, but with many earlier precedents.[19] Viewed in terms of its purpose, a

---

17. 1994 leaflet produced by the Department of Worship and the Arts, National Council of Churches, 475 Riverside Drive, New York, NY 10115. Number 3 in a series on "When a Church Wants to Commission . . . "

18. Polman, Stulken, and Sydnor, *Amazing Grace*.

19. See, for example, the Latin hymns quoted in Chapter 1, which were in metered verse, and Routley's treatment of Greek and Latin hymns (*Panorama*, pp. 55–81).

hymn lyric can be described as a poem of faith, designed so that it can be sung by a group of people in a particular time and place. Hymns are poems. At their best, they contain memorable words, metaphors, and phrases: language that delights and inspires. Hymns are poems of faith. They express whatever a congregation may need to express in the presence of God, including praise, thanksgiving, prayers for others, confession of sin, affirmation of faith, adoration, grief, and lament. The stanzaic form of the hymn can be used in varied ways, but its genius is its ability to unfold a theme, tell a story, or take us on a journey, with or without repetitions and refrains.

Though it can also be read, studied as a poem, and heard as a song, a hymn lyric is designed to be corporately sung. Whether recent or ancient, hymns are sung by a group of people in a particular time and place. There are no timeless congregations, though some appear to wish they were. We do not inhabit Luther's Wittenberg or Calvin's Geneva. We cannot experience Isaac Watts's hymns as they were first sung, nor enter into Charles Wesley's hymns with the driven intensity of early Methodist revivalism. If we sing nineteenth-century words, we do so as people of the third millennium, from the specifics of our class, gender, color, and social location. "Who is singing this, and why?" is as important a question as "What hymn are we singing?"

What Kind of Poetry?

What follows are two hymns, one by Isaac Watts (1674–1748) and one by Shirley Murray (b. 1931), both taken from denominational hymnals in the Reformed tradition. The Watts hymn, "Nature with Open Volume Stands," is from *Congregational Praise,* published in 1951 by the Congregational Union of England and Wales.[20] Shirley Murray's hymn, "O God, We Bear the Imprint of Your Face," is from the *Presbyterian Hymnal,* published for the Presbyterian Church (U.S.A.) in 1990.[21] To appreciate these hymns as poems, let me offer my response, and invite you to compare it with your own.

---

20. The hymn is #129 in *Congregational Praise* and #219 in *Rejoice and Sing.* The United Reformed Church (UK) is a union of Congregational, Presbyterian and Churches of Christ (= Christian Church, or Disciples) traditions. The 1991 version replaces "man" with "us" and inverts the third line for the sake of rhyme ("'tis fairest drawn upon the cross"), but otherwise leaves the hymn unaltered.

21. "O God, We Bear the Imprint of Your Face" is #385 in the *Presbyterian Hymnal,* and is published as #54 in Shirley Murray's hymn collection, *In Every Corner Sing.*

Nature with Open Volume Stands

Isaac Watts (1674–1748)   Long Meter (8.8.8.8.)

Nature with open volume stands
  to spread her Maker's praise abroad;
and every labor of his hands
  shows something worthy of a God.

But in the grace that rescued man,
  his brightest form of glory shines;
here, on the cross, 'tis fairest drawn
  in precious blood, and crimson lines.

Here his whole Name appears complete,
  nor wit can guess, nor reason prove
which of the letters best is writ,
  the power, the wisdom, or the love.

O the sweet wonders of that cross
  where Christ my Savior loved, and died!
Her noblest life my spirit draws
  from his dear wounds, and bleeding side.

I would for ever speak his Name
  in sounds to mortal ears unknown,
with angels join to praise the Lamb,
  and worship at his Father's throne.

"Nature with Open Volume Stands" is quoted, unaltered, from *Congregational Praise.* Though less popular than Watts's other great hymn on the crucifixion, "When I Survey the Wondrous Cross," it was judged important enough to be selected in 1991 for *Rejoice and Sing,* the United Reformed Church's successor hymnal to *Congregational Praise.* In both cases the hymn was chosen, not as a museum piece, but because the compilers believed it can still express the faith and piety of their congregations.[22]

---

22. The compilers of *Congregational Praise* say that a hymn must have a subject worth singing about, and "should express the common faith of Christendom" (Preface, p. iv). The compilers of *Rejoice and Sing* speak in similar terms.

The poem makes statements about God, nature, Christ, and the crucifixion, then presents a believer's response. It functions as a kind of creed, stating and teaching Christian faith and expressing a viewpoint with which we are invited to identify. It affirms that God is revealed in all of creation, but most fully and clearly in Christ, and supremely on the cross.

When I first sang this hymn, in the early 1960s, I identified easily with its viewpoint and expressions. Nowadays, the word "man" grates on my ears, because it no longer unambiguously means humanity or humankind. The repeated masculine pronouns for God invoke a male image for the divine nature, which I believe is more truthfully prayed to as beyond male and female. In the third line of the fourth stanza, the inversion of normal word order (from "My spirit draws her noblest life" to "Her noblest life my spirit draws") trips me up, as I fumble to grasp what the pronoun refers to. But in the act of singing, I skim over this momentary puzzlement, and have little time to query Watts's characterizations of nature and the human spirit as female.

Besides its structure of statement and response, the poem is unified by a series of metaphors, understated but forming a connecting thread. In the first stanza, nature is pictured as an open book, where anyone can read God's wondrous works. In the second stanza, the book of grace presents us with a full-color portrait of the cross, "drawn in precious blood, and crimson lines." In stanza three, the focus narrows to the letters of God's name, written as in an illuminated manuscript. The believer's response culminates in speaking the Name that has been so vividly written, as when a reader goes to the lectern, opens the Bible, and declaims what is written therein.

When the hymn was first sung, it probably had a stronger impact than it does now, because it faced less competition from other media. TV and movies were far in the future, and Watts's congregations were supposed to avoid the theater, from which, however, Watts borrows some of his techniques. The first three stanzas paint tableaux, or scenes, with pointers like "Here!" which invite us to view what is presented. The closing stanzas give a scripted response, intended to instruct us in the role we should play as we watch the drama.[23]

It is hard for us to play the role Watts has scripted for us, because we probably hear "sweet wonders" through the sentimentality of nineteenth-century romanticism, and the word "I" as affirming our

23. Forell Marshall and Todd, *English Congregational Hymns*, pp. 34–35.

autonomy and freedom of choice. Watts, on the other hand, was trying to provide "poetic expression for familiar states of mind shared by
all believers and, as he articulated such feelings, [clarify] the correct
devotional attitude."[24] If we continue to sing such a hymn, it is
because it has been able to travel from Watts's assumptions to ours.

When I read or sing it today, the word choices still appeal. Watts is
direct, vivid, and economical. The word "wit" is a momentary puzzle,
because I equate it with humorous verbal dexterity while realizing
from the context that Watts meant something more profound. If we
assume it meant something like "intuition, shrewdness, imagination,"
Watts captures the whole activity of the human mind—both right and
left brain—in a single phrase balancing nouns and verbs (wit—guess /
reason—prove). The final line of the same stanza uses three nouns to
describe the letters of God's name, in a suggestive triad: power, wisdom, love. The word choices are inclusive: all can grasp their meaning, yet many will find new meaning as they ponder them afresh.

It is fair to assume that, when writing this hymn-poem, Isaac Watts
expressed his own viewpoint and beliefs. But this aim is secondary to
another. As a hymn writer, Isaac Watts's primary aim was to provide
Christian congregations with words they can say, pray, and sing together.

O God, We Bear the Imprint of Your Face

Shirley Erena Murray, 1987   Meter: 10.10.10.10.10.10

O God, we bear the imprint of your face:
    the colors of our skin are your design,
and what we have of beauty in our race
    as man or woman, you alone define,
        who stretched a living fabric on our frame
        and gave to each a language and a name.

Where we are torn and pulled apart by hate
    because our race, our skin is not the same;
while we are judged unequal by the state
    and victims made because we own our name,
        humanity reduced to little worth,
        dishonored is your living face on earth.

_____

24. Ibid., p. 33.

> O God, we share the image of your Son
>   whose flesh and blood are ours, whatever skin;
> in his humanity we find our own,
>   and in his family our proper kin:
>   Christ is the brother we still crucify,
>   his love the language we must learn, or die.

Shirley Murray's hymn has the same logic. Though it reveals its author's beliefs and sensitivities, its primary purpose is communal. Its opening phrase presupposes a group of people who identify with its viewpoint. By saying "O God, we bear the imprint of your face," we (the singers) place ourselves in the presence of God, then rehearse before God our status and role as creatures in God's image (Genesis 1:27), called to be in the image of Christ (2 Corinthians 3:18). This theme is developed with a metaphor of printed cloth. Women and men, we jointly bear the divine imprint in the living fabric of our flesh, whose variety of skin colors is God's design.

The second stanza echoes the metaphor, as the fabric of human life is painfully torn apart by racism, state-sponsored "ethnic cleansing," and anything else that degrades or disregards human dignity and worth. The final stanza is Christ-centered. As people renewed in Christ's image, we find our identity and kinship in Christ, rather than in the ties of biological family, ethnicity, or nation. The hymn ends with a new metaphor: *learning the language* of Christ's love is a life-or-death matter for humankind. The lyric is carefully constructed.[25] The word "face" links stanza one (first line) with stanza two (last line), and is supported by the word "skin" in the second line of each stanza. The word "language" suggests the mouth needed to speak it, in a human *face*. Its first use is ambiguous: there is an (implied) language of hate which contrasts with the explicit "language of love," further linking the second "negative" stanza to the third "positive" stanza. The word "imprint" carries evocative secondary associations: the "imprint" of a human face on the Turin Shroud, perhaps, or, more commonly, "imprinting" in animal behav-

---

25. For the remainder of this paragraph, I am indebted to Pat Harris, of Austin, Texas, in a personal communication on June 6, 1988.

ior, suggesting the deep, nonvolitional bonding of parent and off-spring.

As a series of faith statements, this hymn shares the necessary absurdity of all verbal prayer, telling God what God already knows in order to explore who we are, what we believe, and what we are called to say and do. Though Shirley Murray's concerns differ from those of Isaac Watts, she writes in the same tradition, whereby we rehearse who we are and what God has done for our own illumination and instruction. Though framed as a prayer, the hymn lacks overt prayer responses such as thanksgiving, wonder, penitence, and petition for ourselves and others. If its affirmations instruct and inspire us, they may evoke such responses in the act of saying or singing it. Worship can be enhanced if this hymn is followed by prayers responding to its themes.

As with Isaac Watts's hymn, some of Shirley Murray's phrases invite further thought. In the second stanza, we identify with people who are victimized, not in this case because they follow Christ, but because they claim their own, God-given, human identity ("because we own *our* name" [emphasis mine]). The third stanza affirms that the centrality of Jesus as God's embodied Word lies not in his maleness, but in qualities we can all aspire to and emulate ("in his *humanity* we find our own" [emphasis mine]).

Because the hymn makes a series of affirmations, our first singing tests whether we agree with it. If we agree sufficiently to sing it again, we know what to expect, and can entrust ourselves to its viewpoint. Who, then, are "we"? In this hymn, the first point of reference is the congregation—"we singers." In the first two stanzas, "we" also means any and all human beings. In stanza three, "we" is less clearly defined. "We Christians" are certainly included. And perhaps it also implies that, as such, we believe all humans need to learn, with us, the language of Christlike love.

Classical and Public

As the above examples illustrate, hymn lyrics are communal poetry with a public purpose. As such, their poetic genre is most accurately described as classical, meaning that, unlike romantic and much modern poetry, the hymn poet is not preoccupied with her own, unique vision. In classical poetry, wisdom has primacy over inspiration, and the focus is more on the human condition than on the author's self-expression. As Thomas Troeger observes, when "classical" poets draw on their feelings and experience, it is from the viewpoint of their likeness to the feelings and experience of others, rather than their difference or particularity.[26] This understanding of poetry is well expressed by Alexander Pope, a contemporary of Isaac Watts:

> True Wit is Nature to advantage dressed,
> What oft was thought, but ne'er so well expressed,
> Something, whose truth convinced at sight we find,
> That gives us back the image of our mind.[27]

What Pope hoped to do for his readers, Isaac Watts aimed to do for congregations. From their shared understanding of poetry, it was easy for Watts to take the further step of writing lyrics that were communal, expressing the faith, experience, and aspirations of their singers.

As a communal utterance, a hymn cannot give free rein to the poet's imagination. It is poetry in the service of its singers, and the feelings and experiences it expresses must be familiar—the "frequent tempers and changes of the spirit and conditions of our life," as Isaac Watts puts it.[28] Singers of hymns need poetry that will express their faith and enable them to be truthfully themselves in the presence of God. The greatest compliment to a hymn poet is the unspoken "yes" from singers who grasp, delight in, and identify with the hymn in the act of singing it, yet rarely know or care who wrote the words or composed the tune. Years before I found Alexander Pope's elegant expression of this theme, I expressed it colloquially as follows:

> Yes—that's what I mean, though I couldn't have said it;
> that's what I believe, though I couldn't express it;
> that's what I feel, though I couldn't explain it;
> that's true for me, though it wasn't till I read it.
>   Brian Wren, 1976

---

26. Troeger, *Borrowed Light,* pp. 183–85, following T. S. Eliot. Troeger rejects the sharp contrast between poems and hymns often made by modern hymn writers, arguing that it springs from identifying poetry with romantic and postromantic poetry.

27. Pope, *Essay on Criticism,* 1711, quoted by Carl P. Daw Jr., in "Approaches to Hymn Writing" (Clarkson, Daw, and Pratt Green).

28. Watts, Preface to *Hymns and Spiritual Songs* (1707), quoted by Forell Marshall and Todd, *English Congregational Hymns,* p. 33. Watts added that hymns must be directed by devotional purpose and reach out to weaker Christians, involving them in a process of spiritual development and pious understanding.

Because of its communal purpose, a good hymn is a poem under three monastic vows: clarity, simplicity, and obedience to strict rhythm. Though I have previously discussed all three,[29] it is worth underlining the value of clarity and simplicity. The imagery, vocabulary, and syntax of a hymn lyric must be clear enough to grasp immediately. Singers can't stop to consult a dictionary, and it is hard to identify with sentiments imperfectly understood. Thus, as Isaac Watts puts it, hymn writers need "a clear and distinct idea . . . which represents the object with full evidence and strength, and plainly distinguishes it from all other objects whatsoever."[30] On the other hand, a lyric must be deep enough to give inspiration through life's changes, allow multiple significance, suggest new associations, and reveal new meanings through repeated singing. Simplicity is the opposite of triviality. For most lyricists, most of the time, simplicity is not an effortless habit, but a hard-won achievement. Isaac Watts describes it well: "I have endeavoured at ease of numbers and smoothness of sound," he writes, "and to make the sense plain and obvious." If cultured minds find it "so gentle and flowing as to incur the censure of feebleness, I may honestly affirm that sometimes it cost me labour to make it so." To achieve the simplicity of public, communal poetry, he avoids erudite and allusive language, attention-getting metaphors, and many of the rhetorical devices expected in the poetic literature of his day, and confides that he has thrown out lines deemed "too sonorous."[31]

New Songs for Old

Because hymn lyrics are communal, designed to be sung by a group of people in a particular time and place, three things happen over time. As faith communities change, new lyrics are written and old ones drop out of use or get altered. New lyric writing seems to happen in spurts, not evenly. Though all types of congregational song go through such changes, textual alterations and the emergence of groundbreaking lyrics are especially noticeable in hymnody, because hymn lyrics have a longer tradition, carry more detailed faith expression than, say,

---

29. On clarity and simplicity, see Chapter 5. On speech rhythms, see the beginning of the present chapter.

30. Watts, quoted in Watson, *The English Hymn*, p. 138.

31. Watts, in Bishop, ed., *Isaac Watts, "Hymns and Spiritual Songs,"* Preface, p. liv.

choruses; and have been more sensitive to the deeper currents of cultural and theological change. Alterations in hymn lyrics need a separate chapter (see below). I shall close this chapter by looking at the outpouring of new, English-language hymn lyrics in the second half of the twentieth century.

In 1950s Britain, when people talked about "new hymns," they meant, not new lyrics, but Victorian texts sung to 1940s pantomime and ballroom tunes.[32] In the early 1960s, new lyrics began to be written, passed around, and published. Beginning in Britain, the "hymn explosion" spread through Canada, the United States, Australia, and New Zealand. Thousands of new lyrics have been written, and hundreds published, not only in speculative commercial ventures but in a stream of revised, improved, and newly revised denominational hymnals. Of today's most widely published hymn writers, the largest group comes from the "balancer" or "silent" generation (born 1925–42), and the smallest groups are from the "builder" (or "civic") and "boomer" generations (born 1901–24 and 1943–60).[33] With the exception of

---

32. An example is Patrick Appleford's skip-and-shuffle tune for "The Church's One Foundation." His "Lord Jesus Christ, You Have Come to Us" has proved more enduring.

33. Data from Miller, "Contemporary Hymn Authors and Hymns as Represented in Ten Recent Hymnals," analyzed with generational models drawn indirectly from Strauss and Howe, *Generations* (New York: Morrow, 1991), as discussed by Hudson, "The Thirteenth Generation: Demographics and Worship," and Scifres, *Searching for Seekers: Ministry with a New Generation of the Unchurched,* p. 35. Miller lists the twenty-four English-language writers most frequently published in recent American hymnals (the twenty-fifth is a Spanish author). Of these twenty-four, five were born between 1901 and 1924 (Albert Bayly, 1901–84; Margaret Clarkson, b. 1915; Fred Pratt Green, b. 1903; James Quinn, b. 1919; and Jaroslav Vajda, b. 1919); thirteen between 1925 and 1942 (Tom Colvin, 1925–2000; Timothy Dudley-Smith, b. 1926; William [b. 1936] and Gloria [b. 1942] Gaither—counted as one because they work as a team; Jane Parker Huber, b. 1926; Christopher Idle, b. 1938; Fred Kaan, b. 1929; Bryan Jeffery Leech, b. 1931; Shirley Murray, b. 1931; Michael Perry, 1942–96; Jeffrey Rowthorn, b. 1934; Michael Saward, b. 1932; Miriam Therese Winter, b. 1938; and Brian Wren, b. 1936); and six between 1943 and 1960 (Andraé Crouch, b. 1945; Carl P. Daw Jr, b. 1944; Ruth Duck, b. 1947; Sylvia Dunstan, 1955–93; Marty Haugen, b. 1952; and Thomas Troeger, b. 1945). Other authors published more recently, or in hymnals other than American, include "balancers" Herbert O'Driscoll (b. 1928), Walter Farquharson (b. 1936), Alan Gaunt (b. 1935), and Bill Wallace (b. 1933); and "boomers" Marnie Barrell (b. 1952—New Zealand), John Bell (b. 1949), Daniel C. Damon (b. 1955), Richard D. Leach (b. 1953), and Rusty Edwards (b. 1955). The other two generations are the "thirteenth" or "buster" (b. 1961–1981) and the "millennials" or "birthers" (b. 1982–2003).

Albert Bayly, an influential forerunner of the British hymn renaissance,[34] the "builder" generation authors mostly began hymn writing in the 1960s, concurrently with their younger counterparts. This suggests that the start of the hymn explosion had more to do with the times in which the writers lived than with their chronological age. If one asks representatives of the two older groups why they began writing hymns when they did, they typically say that the time was ripe, and that in their congregations there was a felt need for new words to sing.

Liturgy and Bible

Liturgical and theological developments were an important stimulus. A growing use, or rediscovery, of the psalms prompted new metrical versions.[35] A renewed emphasis on the humanity of Jesus and the seasons of the Christian year, combined with the increased use of lectionaries, prompted new hymns for Advent, Epiphany, the Baptism of Jesus, the Transfiguration, and Lent (or, more accurately, Jesus' life and ministry). New hymnals also reflect a wider and deeper understanding of the Holy Spirit (active in the world and cosmos, not merely in the church and individual believers); a greater need for adult baptism; and the centrality—though not usually frequency—of Communion / the Eucharist / the Lord's Supper as a joyful celebration.

The 1960s also saw a return to the Puritan axiom that congregational song should reflect, and speak to, the particular situation of its singers.[36] Many older hymns began to feel unsatisfyingly generic. If "timely" means "in touch with our time, and in tune with God's timing," and "topical" means "designed for the present time, using metaphors, slogans, and allusions current at the time of writing," it is

---

34. Albert F. Bayly (1901–84) was an English Congregational minister who published four collections of "hymns and verse" (see Bibliography). Theologically able, socially aware, pastorally sensitive, and with a keen ear for the rhythms of verse and the sound of words, his hymns were cast in the idioms and vocabulary of his generation, yet inspired others by demonstrating that good new hymns could still be written. Thus, "forerunner" is an apt compliment. "What Does the Lord Require?" is one of his enduring legacies, and appears in several recent hymnals.

35. In the United States, see, for example, the *Presbyterian Hymnal* (1990), #158–#258, and the *Psalter Hymnal* (Grand Rapids: CRC Publications, 1987), #1–#150.

36. Isaac Watts held and applied this conviction. See Stackhouse, *The Language of the Psalms in Worship*, p. 38, and in my next chapter, p. 308.

fair to say that most recent hymn lyricists have tried to be timely, top-ical, or both. By contrast, evangelical choruses often have topical music, but most of their lyrics are merely "recent." Though the hymn is a traditional, even archaic, form of congregational song, recent hymn writing is markedly more timely than most "contemporary" wor-ship songs.

New Bible translations were another stimulus to new hymn writing. Published in 1961, the *New English Bible* (NEB) was the first scholarly and officially sponsored Bible translation since 1611 to "start over," by rendering the New Testament, then in 1970 the whole Bible, into "the English of the present day, that is . . . the natural vocabulary, con-structions and rhythms of contemporary speech," untrameled by the cadences and vocabulary of the King James Version.[37] For some, it was a sacrilegious departure from the obscure beauty of the KJV. For many, it was a breath of fresh air, following the Holy Spirit's Pentecostal mandate to speak the good news to people, "each . . . in [their] own native language" (Acts 2:8). For the remainder of the century, it was followed by a stream of translations, from a variety of theological and ecclesiastical perspectives, such as the *Jerusalem Bible;* the *Good News Bible* (Today's English Version), the *New International Version,* the *Contemporary English Bible,* and revisions such as the *Revised English Bible,* the *New King James Bible* and the *New Jerusalem Bible.*

The *New English Bible* was itself a response to growing dissatisfac-tion with the archaic conventions of early-twentieth-century worship language. Looking back, it seems odd that English-speaking Chris-tians clung for so long to a mode of discourse best described as Imita-tion Cranmer or Fake Elizabethan, full of thees, thous, hasts, dosts, wouldests, vouchsafests, beseechings, bewailings, and supplications. The Anglican *Book of Common Prayer* (BCP), crafted in lean, clear language from sixteenth-century colloquial, though elegant, English, had been weathered by the passage of time into a moss-covered mon-ument. Anglicans memorized its liturgies; non-Anglicans imitated its cadences. Together, the KJV and BCP sanctioned prayers, hymns, and

---

37. *The New English Bible* (Oxford and Cambridge: Oxford and Cambridge Uni-versity Presses, 1961), Introduction, p. xiii. Though the *Revised Standard Version* (1946–1957) preceded the NEB, it was, as its title indicates, a blend of translation and revision, following wherever possible the syntax and vocabulary of the King James Version.

liturgies set apart from everyday speech, so that English-speaking worshipers prayed and sang in a semiforeign language.

The NEB was both product and catalyst of change. First conceived by the Church of Scotland in 1946, out of a conviction that the KJV, "already archaic when it was made, had now become even more definitely archaic and less generally understood,"[38] its publication coincided with early attempts at contemporary-language prayers, and prompted the writing of new hymns. While reading a review copy, Timothy Dudley-Smith realized that the NEB translation of Mary's Song (Luke 1:46–55) began with a line of iambic pentameter (five iambs), striking enough to be the first line of a hymn:

Tell *out*, my *soul*, the *great*ness *of* the *Lord*.

His paraphrase of the NEB passage was one of the first, and most widely sung, contributions to the hymn-writing renaissance. The NEB's influence on other hymnists was equally important, though indirect: it showed what could be done, and gave encouragement to do more.[39] Language changes have continued to stimulate the writing of new lyrics. The ambiguous and tendentious double meanings of "man" and "men" led many writers to modify their early work, and prompted new texts making women and children linguistically visible. The language debate broadened out to include the claims of different ethnic groups and of people "differently abled." These debates continue, as does the debate about God-language, which has prompted most recent denominational hymnals to include a modest proportion of texts naming God in more varied ways.

Cultural Changes

An unforeseen result of the *New English Bible* was that, instead of creating one new, accepted English version, it opened the door to a

---

38. Preface to the *New English Bible*, p. v.

39. In speech, the "of" in the NEB line quoted is more lightly stressed than when the hymn is sung, but still counts, I think, as an iambic stress. "Tell Out My Soul" is widely published. For the author's account of the writing of this hymn, see the *Companion to the United Methodist Hymnal*, p. 618. J. R. Watson surmises that Dudley-Smith's hymn may have been the "detonator" for the hymn explosion (*The English Hymn*, p. 28), but others who began writing then or later (Wren, 1961, 1962, and Kaan, 1963) were not at the time aware of it, or of each other.

multitude. The consequent array of Bibles reminds us that "the Bible" is not "the Bible as Saint Paul wrote it," but a translation. Varied renderings sometimes yield insight and warn against hanging too much weight on minor differences. On the other hand, today's hymn writers, unlike their predecessors, cannot quote from a single, accepted version of the Bible. When our hymns tell the old, old story, they tell a story that many people no longer know and can no longer use or evoke a common translation vocabulary.

In other words, the lyrics of many new hymns, like the music of contemporary worship songs, respond to social and cultural changes that have made formerly "churched" societies a mission field. Because worship gatherings are the most common entry or enquiry point for seekers and lapsed churchgoers, new lyrics must *tell* the story of Jesus, not simply evoke it. As we move more and more into a visual, electronic, multimedia culture, hymn lyrics that survive will be those that memorably tell biblical stories; appeal to the eye as well as the ear, and can be mimed, signed, danced to, or partnered with still photos, drawings, and video. Lyricists also have to decide how far to reject or accept "postmodernist" assumptions: for example, that the self is not a trustworthy observer; that our role in life is to be consumers whose identity is vested in what we possess; that there are no universal principles and stories true for everyone everywhere; and that life has no reliable order, structure, and meaning.

Decolonization

By the early 1960s, African and Asian colonies of European powers were gaining their independence. Political decolonization was followed by a decolonization of Christian mission and theology, as Asia, Africa, and Latin America produced outstanding theologians and church leaders. Missionary societies changed their name and function, and churches formerly "senders" and "receivers" moved slowly toward equal partnership. New English-language hymnals have responded in three ways: by dropping a host of older "mission" hymns; by publishing new ones; and by including a growing number of songs from other Christian cultures.

The extent to which older "mission" hymns have been discarded, and Christian mission rethought, can be illustrated from two British hymnals in the same tradition: *Congregational Praise*, published in

1951 for the Congregational Union of England and Wales, and *Rejoice and Sing*, published in 1991 by its successor, the United Reformed Church.

Congregational Praise had a section on "The Church," with subdivisions on worship and prayer, the sacraments, "The Church Militant on Earth—Home and Foreign Missions," and "The Church Triumphant in Heaven—the Communion of Saints." The wording suggests that the church's outward-going work is focused mainly on evangelism. However, though the relevant section is titled "Home and Foreign Missions," the adjective "home" was by the 1950s a pious fiction. In practice, England and Wales were not actively treated as mission fields. Evangelism was what Billy Graham did, and we didn't do that sort of thing, thank you. "Mission" meant sending people to Africa and Asia as doctors, teachers, nurses, and pastors, certainly to serve (which many did magnificently), but to do so by giving the blessings of health and education as much as by sharing the gospel. The focus was wide, and socially aware: the London Missionary Society, the "overseas mission" agency most closely connected with Congregational churches, pioneered British church awareness of third-world poverty by a 1955 conference on world hunger. Nonetheless, whether we were thinking about evangelism, health, education, or poverty, our mind-set at the time (including my youthful self in the equation) was that "foreign" neighbors were to be fed, loved, and respected, because Christ loved them *and because we had something to give them.* Returning missionaries tried to convey how much they *received* from overseas Christians, but the "we give, you take" missionary mind-set took decades to dislodge. The hymnal had, for its time, some excellent hymns on peace and justice, but in a separate section, titled "Social and National." The implication was that action for peace and justice is a matter of individual choice, not the direct concern of the church.

Rejoice and Sing is very differently organized. Gone are the "militant / triumphant" language and a world divided into "home" and "foreign" territories. All Christian life and work come under the heading "Creation's Response to God's Love," with three subheadings: "The Gospel" (our need for God, hearing, and response); "The Church's Life and Witness" (worship, sacraments, growth in faith, discipleship, pilgrimage, unity, proclaiming the gospel, and Christian hope); and "The Gospel in the World" (Christ for the world, plus love in action, justice, and peace, and healing and reconciliation). Church life is understood as giving equal emphasis to evangelism, service, healing, reconciliation, peacemaking, and action for social justice.[40]

In *Congregational Praise,* "Home and Foreign Missions" was a substantial section, containing thirty-three hymns, fifteen from nineteenth-century authors, and eight from authors born in that century and living into the twentieth.[41] *Rejoice and Sing* has twenty-four comparable hymns, divided between "Proclaiming the Gospel" (fifteen) and "Christ for the World" (nine). Half are from the twentieth century, and none before the nineteenth.[42] *Two-thirds of the "mission" hymns in Congregational Praise were discarded by its successor.*[43] Some were simply too archaic, but many were dropped because their viewpoints are no longer acceptable. In a world church, distant partners should not be word-painted as exotic foreigners living in "strange and lovely cities" or in "sultry forests where apes swing to and fro." When Christians in Asia and Africa far outnumber their European, Australasian, and North American counterparts, it is inaccurate and

---

40. For publication details, see Bibliography. *Congregational Praise* has: "The Church": Its Fellowship; At Worship and Prayer; The Sacraments—Baptism; The Sacraments—The Lord's Supper; "The Church Militant on Earth—Home and Foreign Missions"; "The Church Triumphant in Heaven—the Communion of Saints." *Rejoice and Sing* has: "Creation's Response to God's Love: The Gospel": The Need for God; Hearing and Responding; "The Church's Life and Witness": Worship, Baptism, and Confirmation; The Lord's Supper; The People of God; Growing in Faith; Discipleship; Pilgrimage; Unity; Proclaiming the Gospel; The Continuing Hope; "The Gospel in the World": Christ for the World; Love in Action; Justice and Peace; Healing and Reconciliation.

41. The full tally is : Seventeenth century—one (German source, nineteenth-century translation); eighteenth century—six; nineteenth century—fifteen; nineteenth living into twentieth—eight; twentieth century (authors born in 1897 and 1901)—two; and a hymn with no date.

42. The full tally is: Nineteenth century—five; nineteenth living into twentieth—seven; twentieth century—twelve.

43. Most of the hymns on "mission" themes are in the "Home and Foreign Missions" section of *Congregational Praise,* and in the "Proclaiming the Gospel" and "Christ for the World" sections of *Rejoice and Sing.* In *Rejoice and Sing,* twelve hymns are retained from the "Home and Foreign Missions" section of *Congregational Praise,* but only four are in one of its comparable sections, "Christ for the World." The other eight are reassigned to theological and liturgical categories (Christ's Coming—three; The Coming of the Holy Spirit—one; One God in Trinity—one; The Word and the Spirit—one) and social action categories (Healing and Reconciliation—one; Justice and Peace—one). In *Rejoice and Sing,* "Proclaiming the Gospel" and "Christ for the World" take nine hymns from *Congregational Praise* (Home and Foreign Missions—four; Communion of Saints—one; Christ's Coming in Power—one; The Love and Service of Man—two; and Evening Hymns—one).

offensive to characterize their territories as "heathen lands" wrapped in slumber. Describing them as "the Gentiles" casts "us" as God's chosen people, a designation both arrogant and inaccurate because, except for Jews, all of us are Gentiles by definition. Imperial arrogance also painted "us" as enlightened givers to "them," seen as deluded recipients, as in Reginald Heber's "From Greenland's Icy Mountains":

> From many an ancient river,
>   from many a palmy plain,
> they call us to deliver
>   their land from error's chain.
> Can we, whose souls are lighted
>   with wisdom from on high,
> can we to men benighted
>   the lamp of life deny?

Similarly, the last thing today's British (and kindred) worshipers need is an imperialist mind-set that puts the singer at the center of Christendom, looking north, south, east, and west, as in Charles Edward Oakley's "Hills of the North, Rejoice!" Since the risen Christ is equidistant from every time and place, and the Holy Spirit inhabits all creation, it is untrue to say that Christ has been "absent long" from "the north," that Western lands have been "unvisited, unblest," and that Eastern lands have been wrapped in "the sleep of ages"—even if the singer is willing to accept the obvious but usually unrecognized corollary that he or she belongs by definition to someone else's "west," "east," "south," and "north"![44]

By contrast, new hymns in *Rejoice and Sing* do not set their singers apart from other lands and other Christians, but include them in the whole church. We join the church's "glorious company," and recall how the Christian message has been both given and received, going first from (the singer's) east to west, then by God's "later voice" returned to sender, now heard in every land. "East" and "west" are still

---

44. Quotations and examples (all in *Congregational Praise*) are, in the order given, Percy Dearmer (1867–1936), "Remember All the People," #344; George Washington Doane (1799–1859),"Fling Out the Banner!" #331; Arnold Brooks (1870–1933), "Trumpet of God, Sound High!" #338; Arthur Cleveland Coxe (1818–96), "Saviour, Quicken Many Nations," #33 ("By thy pains and consolations / draw the Gentiles unto thee"); Reginald Heber (1783–1826), "From Greenland's Icy Mountains," #329; and Charles Edward Oakley (1832–65), "Hills of the North, Rejoice!" #337.

relative to the singer, but there is an emphasis on receiving as well as giving, as God tries to reach us all "in more global ways." All who sing now accept Christ's "great commission" to "go now into every place," and strive "to make effective God's good news." Specifically, we are called to "give the message to the people we meet," and take God's saving news to all nations—including our own. The saving news is holistic: we tell others that God's kingdom is here by giving good news to the poor, setting the downtrodden free, and giving prisoners the news of Christ's liberating love.[45]

Though these examples show new English-language "mission" hymns being published, the emphasis in recent hymnals falls elsewhere. While it is good to sing "our own" new hymns of global mission awareness, they should not be the main focus. For paleface congregations, singing about mission only from a white, Western perspective—however enlightened—is a kind of hymnological neocolonialism. Better by far to hear, welcome, and sing songs from our global neighbors themselves. This trend can be illustrated from two North American hymnals, the *United Methodist Hymnal* (1989) and the *Presbyterian Hymnal* (1990). The *United Methodist Hymnal* includes eighteen "Hispanic" items, in Spanish and English; two hymns from mainland China; one from Taiwan; two from Japan; three from Korea; and one each from Laos, Vietnam, India, and Pakistan. The *Presbyterian Hymnal* has twelve "Hispanic" hymns; five from mainland China; one from Taiwan; three from Japan; three from Korea; three from different parts of Africa; and one from the Philippines. Both hymnals have a selection of Native American tunes and texts. The *Presbyterian Hymnal* has twenty-three African American "spirituals," while the *United Methodist Hymnal* has thirty, plus at least twelve black gospel songs.[46] Hymnals published since 1990 continue this trend and carry it farther.[47]

---

45. Examples taken, in the order given, from *Rejoice and Sing:* Albert F. Bayly (1901–84), "A Glorious Company We Sing," #570; Caryl Micklem (b. 1925), "Thanks Be to God, Whose Church on Earth," #582; Hugh Sherlock (b. 1905), "Lord, Thy Church on Earth Is Seeking," #579; Jeffery Rowthorn (b. 1934), "Lord, You Give the Great Commission," #580; Fred Pratt Green (b. 1903), "Sing, One and All, a Song of Celebration," #581; Sue McClellan, John Pac, and Keith Rycroft, 1974, "Colours of Day Dawn on the Mind," #572; James C. Seddon (1915–83), "Go Forth and Tell," #574; and Hubert Richards (b. 1921), "God's Spirit Is Deep in My Heart," #576.

46. See also Hawn, "A Survey of Trends in Recent Protestant Hymnals."

47. See, for example, the *Chalice Hymnal* and *New Century Hymnal* (U.S.A.), and *Voices United* (Canada).

Expanding Knowledge

New hymns have also been inspired by advancing knowledge of the universe, the human past, and the global present. The big bang theory seems well established as a description of how the universe began, but even if it is superseded, recent discoveries paint a universe vast, evolving, and in some respects downright weird. Archaeology and paleontology have immeasurably increased our knowledge of the human past and the story of our planet. Space flight, computers, electronic communication, biotechnology, and genetics shift our mental landscapes, raising hopes, thanksgivings, laments, and questions, which at some point need to be expressed in song. Social-action movements of the 1960s each focused on one particular cause. Nowadays, even the most ardent single-issue activist is aware of the interconnectedness of all life on earth, and of social, ecological, political, and economic issues.

Most new hymnals make some response to these developments. Creation hymns speak more about caring for the earth, and less about conquering it. Thus, we thank God for water, soil, and air, "large gifts supporting everything that lives"; "pray for the wilderness, vanishing fast," and for our planet "brought down by degrees"; and affirm that we cannot own the sky, the moon, and the flowers—a conviction needing active guardianship as space-flight planners muse about turning Mars into real estate and global agribusiness files patents for genetically modified seeds.[48] In 1961, some were scandalized when Sydney Carter speculated about how God might be revealed to sentient creatures on other planets; his musings now seem more prophetic than far-fetched.[49] As early as the 1940s, Albert Bayly praised God for "the boundless curves of space," "the atom's hidden forces," and the awakening and agelong unfolding of life in cell and tissue.[50] In 1967, Catherine Cameron wrote "God, Who Stretched the Spangled Heavens," joining cosmological awareness with concern about urban dehumanization and the ambiguities of nuclear power.[51]

---

48. See Brian Wren, "Thank You, God, for Water, Soil, and Air" (*Presbyterian Hymnal*, #266; *New Century Hymnal*, #559); Dan Damon, "Pray for the Wilderness" (*New Century Hymnal*, #557); and Ruth Duck, "We Cannot Own the Sunlit Sky" (*New Century Hymnal*, #563).

49. Sydney Carter, "Every Star Shall Sing a Carol," *Songs of Sydney Carter*, p. 7.

50. Bayly, "O Lord of Every Shining Constellation" and "Lord of the Boundless Curves of Space," #4 and #19 in *Rejoice, O People: Hymns and Verse*.

51. For the text, see, for example, the *United Methodist Hymnal*, #150, and *Rejoice and Sing* (to a better tune), #86.

Evil and Injustice

Catherine Cameron's hymn joins thanksgiving for new knowledge with concern about human suffering and evil. The nuclear age began on August 6, 1945, when a "small" (by today's standards) nuclear fission bomb devastated Hiroshima. Allied propaganda reported it as an attack on a Japanese naval base. By the 1950s it was clear that we had entered a new era. Henceforth forever, by explosion or pollution, the human race can end its collective life. Newsreels of living human skeletons in Belsen and Buchenwald concentration camps led to full awareness of the Nazi Holocaust: the state-sponsored, systematic extermination of six million Jews, and many thousands of gypsies, mentally handicapped, and others deemed expendable. Henceforth forever we know, or should know, that radical evil has happened, and happened again: as in Cambodia, Uganda, Rwanda, and the Balkans.

Social justice is another central theme of recent hymnody.[52] Christian concern about social injustice waxes and wanes; actual injustice shifts, and mutates into new complexity. Globalization brings world economic integration, global tourism, a global Internet for the few with access to it—and global economic inequality. In a world market dominated by corporations, opportunities for improvement and exploitation go hand in hand. What Karl Marx called fetishism has greater power than ever, namely, the symbolic significance of products, from cars to trainer shoes, as markers of social status, cultural identity, and economic power. In some economies average living standards have risen. In others, such as the United States, middle and lower-class incomes have been static or declining in real terms, while income differentials between top CEOs and minimum-wage workers have grown (to use an exact adverb) astronomically.

Hymn writers have responded to these themes, and recent hymnals increasingly represent them. As "weapons grow more lethal, and only hope stands proud," we become "weary of all trumpeting, weary of all killing," and cry, "When will people cease their fighting?" We pray that Christ will "rid the earth of torture's terror, / you whose hands were nailed to wood." Nearer home, our cities wear "shrouds of pain," as poor and homeless people cry out for health and strength; but "indif-

---

52. A useful survey of the sources is Westermeyer, *Let Justice Sing*.

ference walks unheeding by / as hunger stretches out its hand." As the hope of the poor "fades to depression, [and] despair erodes the soul," we pray for the healing of the nations, deliverance from despair, and "for a just and equal sharing" of earth's goods and gifts. Christ meets us through hungry people, and through those who sleep beneath the bridges of our cities. Natural disasters fill the world "with awesome ill" but are less horrific than human-ignited warfare. The human race suffers from collective greed as "we reach to take what is not ours, and then defend our claim with force." Injustice is not merely personal, but systemic, as "vested power stands firm entrenched" and "waste and want live side by side."[53]

To exemplify some of the best new writing, I shall conclude with a closer look at two recently published hymns. Summarizing and partially paraphrasing Psalm 10, Ruth Duck sounds a rare note of lament in today's hymnody. She begins with blunt, perennial questions, followed by a deft description of abusive power:

> Why stand so far away, my God?
>   Why hide in times of need?
> The proud, unbridled, chase the poor,
>   and curse you in their greed.

The opening line gives the hymn its title and theme, and grabs attention, because the first line of a stanza always has the power to be emphatic. In the second couplet, the adjective "unbridled" cannot be ignored. Straddling the middle of the line, it delays, and thus highlights, the verb "chase," which suggests energetic, relentless, almost gleeful pursuit. The choice and placing of "unbridled" is exact: it is *deregulated* power that becomes relentlessly greedy and knows no

---

53. See Constance Cherry, "When Will People Cease Their Fighting?" PH #401, VU #687; Walter Farquharson, "Though Ancient Walls," VU #691; Martin Franzmann, "Weary of All Trumpeting," UMH #442; Fred Kaan, "For the Healing of the Nations," TCH #668, NCH #576, UMH #428, VU #678; Joy Patterson, "O Lord, You Gave Your Servant John," PH #431; Shirley Murray, "God of Freedom, God of Justice," PH #700; "Great God of Earth and Heaven," NCH #579; "O God, We Bear the Imprint of Your Face," PH #385, NCH #585; "Through All the World a Hungry Christ," NCH #587; Thomas H. Troeger, "God Marked the Line and Told the Sea," NCH #568, PH #283; and Brian Wren, "Here Am I," TCH #654; "Thank You, God, for Water, Soil, and Air," PH #266, NCH #559. Abbreviations: TCH = *The Chalice Hymnal;* NCH = *New Century Hymnal;* PH = *Presbyterian Hymnal;* UMH = *United Methodist Hymnal;* and VU = *Voices United.*

bounds. The sound of the words supports their meaning: in the first half of the couplet, the dental and labial plosive sounds ("p," "d," "b," "d," "d," and "p"—the prou*d*, un*b*ri*dl*e*d*, chase the *p*oor) strengthen the sense with unobtrusive alliteration, paralleled by the guttural sounds ("k"—curse, and "g") in the concluding line. The sound pattern of both is staccato: a drumbeat followed by throaty expletives.

The second stanza repeats the question, then describes the "chase" of the poor in a metaphor drawn from the psalm:

> Why do you hide when, full of lies,
>   they murder and betray?
> They wait to pounce upon the weak
>   as lions stalk their prey.

The repetition is doubly effective: it states the opening theme in different language, and thus rings true as lament, because lament says, "Why?" not once, politely, but again and again, insistently: "Why, O why, O why, O why?"

The third stanza again repeats question and comment, but in reverse order, varying the pattern and putting the question in the other most emphatic part of the stanza, at the end:

> The weak are crushed and fall to earth;
>   the wicked strut and preen.
> Why, in these cruel, chaotic times,
>   cannot your face be seen?

Previously, the word "why" was followed immediately by its verb. This time the verb is delayed, and the "why?" reverberates, like a note struck on a piano and held, instead of immediately being superseded by a following note. Once more, the word choices and sound patterns fill out the portrait of the powerful as arrogant and self-centered: they "strut" and "preen," as proud as peacocks, while in the second couplet the guttural "k"—sounds (*c*ruel, *c*haotic, *c*annot) match the ugliness of their meaning.

Four times the question has been asked, and three times the situation described. Now the hymnist follows the psalmist, and turns for hope in the only possible direction: the memory of God's love in times past:

> In ages past you heard the voice
>   of those the proud oppress.

Remember those who suffer now,
     who cry in deep distress.

Following the psalmist, our memory of God's love allows us to ask
God, also, to remember. The verb is used in its full, biblical meaning:
when God remembers, God acts on the memory. As the question was
reiterated, so now is the prayer, in a logical action sequence: first,
"Remember," then "Arise," then having arisen, "Come!" The hymn
ends with two vivid images. The bleeding wounds of the oppressed
depict both individual suffering and social devastation: the blood flow
is not a trickle but a hemorrhage, enfeebling and life-threatening. The
final line reminds us (and God) that the problem is not a headache but
a migraine, not anxiety, but intimidation:

Arise, O God, and lift your hand;
     bring justice to the poor.
Come, help us stop the flow of blood!
     Let terror reign no more!

Ruth Duck, from Psalm 10, in Common Meter, *Chalice Hymnal,* #671.
© 1992 G.I.A. Publications, Inc. All rights reserved. Used by permission.

Ruth Duck's hymn shows the resilience of one of the oldest metrical forms, common meter. By contrast, Shirley Murray makes effective use of an unusual meter, 5.5.10.D, in an already-well-accepted
hymn on ecological responsibility:

Touch the earth lightly,
     use the earth gently,
nourish the life of the world in our care:
     gift of great wonder,
     ours to surrender,
trust for the children tomorrow will bear.

The metrical rhythm is also unusual: the first two, five-syllable, lines
are dactyls each followed by an iamb, giving a feeling of something
said, but only half complete. They are followed by a ten-syllable line
which brings completion by uncurling in three dactyls stopped by a
final stressed syllable. If "/" denotes a loud (stressed) syllable, and "x"
a softer (unstressed) syllable, the rhythmic pattern sounds like this:

/ x x / x,
/ x x / x,
/ x x / x x / x x /.

The opening line is taken from an Australian aboriginal saying.[54] Like all good hymnic first lines, it claims attention, states the hymn's theme, and sets the tone for what follows. The "light" unstressed endings of the four five-syllable lines (by some sexist grammarians still chauvinistically called "weak" or "feminine" endings), give gentle sounds as well as gentle meanings (lightly, gently, wonder, surrender). In mid-stanza comes a paradox: the "gift of great wonder" is "ours"—not, however, to keep, but to *surrender,* a word suggesting that we let go of it, as much reluctantly as willingly, for the sake of our children. The first stanza was couched in imperatives: "Do this!" The second is a confession of the human race's failure as planetary guardians:

> We who endanger,
>   who create hunger,
> agents of death for all creatures that live,
>   we who would foster
>   clouds of disaster,
> God of our planet, forestall and forgive!

The first two lines now use their rhythms more insistently, as the dactyls (Greek: fingers) are pointed in accusation. The fourth and fifth lines vary the pattern by becoming, in effect and rhythm, an extra ten-syllable line, building a long petition that climaxes in the final line with the alliterative, and dramatic, *"forestall* and *forgive."* The closing stanzas continue the prayer, mostly reverting to the light, gentle endings of the first (greening, garden, children, living, loving), reinforced by other word choices (blesses, sweet, health, hope, seedling, snow, sun):

> Let there be greening,
>   birth from the burning,
> water that blesses and air that is sweet,
>   health in God's garden,
>   hope in God's children,
> regeneration that peace will complete.

---

54. Shirley Murray, *In Every Corner Sing,* in her explanatory note on this hymn ("Notes on the Hymns," end of book, no page number).

God of all living,
God of all loving,
God of the seedling, the snow, and the sun,
     teach us, deflect us,
     Christ, reconnect us,
using us gently, and making us one.

Shirley Murray, 5.5.10.D, *Chalice Hymnal*, #693; *New Century Hymnal*, #569; *Voices United*, #307. Copyright © 1992 by Hope Publishing Company. All rights reserved. Used by permission.

Other word choices are worth noting. In the third stanza, the word "birth" has overtones of Christian "new birth" language. It is followed and paralleled by "regeneration," a technical term whose five-syllable length also suggests that the process takes time. The opening stanzas also invite us to play with the related meanings of "trust," "agents," and "foster": parenting, legal guardianship, financial management, and stewardship, for example. In the second and final stanzas God in Christ opposes our destructive mismanagement, not violently, but as a skilled judo instructor who "forestalls" and "deflects" us. The phrase "using . . . gently" links the opening and closing stanzas. As we are called to use the earth gently, so we can trust Jesus to use us gently, and make us one.

As Ruth Duck and Shirley Murray use their poetic skills, they are also, I think, doing theology. In the final chapter I elaborate on this conviction. Before doing so, I shall investigate how hymn texts come to be altered, for reasons only partly theological.

Chapter Nine

"To Me, to All, Thy Bowels Move": Why Do They Keep Changing the Good Old Hymns?

> *To me, to all, thy bowels move,*
> *Thy nature, and thy name is love.*
> —Charles Wesley, 1742

> *To me, to all, thy mercies move—*
> *Thy nature, and thy name is Love.*
> —Charles Wesley, 1893 alteration[1]

I have shown that congregational song lyrics are communal. Though they usually originate from particular authors, their primary purpose is to give shared expression to shared experience, not parade the author's personality. Because they are communal a faith community may, in principle, amend them. This principle often gets in a tug-of-war with another: the importance of familiarity (see Chapters 1, 2, and 4 above). When a lyric is well known, changes disturb the singer's memory bank. People have to think twice about what they are singing, and are apt to dislike both the disturbance and the change that causes it. In this chapter I shall show why the need for change sometimes overrides the need for familiarity, and suggest guidelines for alteration. The founder of English hymnody, Isaac Watts, was aware of both needs. In the Preface to his *Hymns and Spiritual Songs*, he says that "what is provided for public worship should give to sincere

---

1. From "Come, O Thou Traveler Unknown." For the full text, see *United Methodist Hymnal*, #387. For commentary, see *Companion to "Hymns and Psalms,"* pp. 264–265.

consciences as little vexation and disturbance as possible." However (or perhaps we should say "therefore"), "where any unpleasing word is found, he that leads the worship may substitute a better; for (Blessed be God) we are not confined to the words of any Man in our public solemnities."[2] Because Watts was writing lyrics for congregational use, he accepted alteration in principle, though he may not have expected it to happen very often.

Isaac Watts wrote for his own time, so that seventeenth-century congregations could sing their faith with conviction, clarity, and joy. He wrote new hymns because worship then, as now, was not a museum, but an expression of the day's faith and hope. We could, of course, decide to worship one Sunday in the style of our forebears a hundred, two hundred, or five hundred years ago. For churches in Watts's tradition this could mean hearing long prayers and closely argued fifty-minute sermons, singing eight- to eighteen-stanza hymns and metrical psalms without accompaniment to unfamiliar original tunes, and "lining them out" (repeating them line by line after a song leader), a slow and not always tuneful process. While it may be instructive, it is unlikely that we would want to do it very often: we are too remote from our forebears' culture for the experience to be inspirational. However much we value our past, our present interest in congregational song is not antiquarian, but immediate. We sing to God from today, in lyrics which—whether ancient or recent—express today's faith. When a lyric from the past gets too archaic to be understood, or too out of sync with today's hope, faith, and issues to speak for us, it will eventually cease to be sung, or amended to keep it singable.

Traditional Change

Altering hymn lyrics is not a modern fad, but the latest development of an old tradition. In English hymnody, Matthew Prior, Joseph Addison, and Isaac Watts make quite varied paraphrases of Psalm 19, as does a modern hymn writer, Thomas Troeger.[3] The psalm declares that God has pitched a tent for the sun, which comes out each day like

---

2. Watts, "The Preface," in Bishop, ed., *Isaac Watts' Hymns and Spiritual Songs,* p. liii.

3. Troeger, "Personal, Cultural and Theological Influences on the Language of Hymns and Worship."

a bridegroom leaving his chamber, and runs its course across the sky like a strong man running a race. Prior turns this statement into questions, asking why the sun "orders the diurnal hours / to leave Earth's other part, and rise in ours." Addison sees the movement of sun, moon, and other heavenly bodies as evidence of rational order and divine creation. Silently, they all proclaim, "The hand that made us is divine." Watts contrasts the way the heavens declare God's glory with the surer revelation of God's Word. Troeger develops the classic metaphor of celestial orbits as silent music, inviting us to give "glory to God for the song of the stars, / music so deep that the silence is sound" (first couplet of hymn, © Oxford University Press, 1987). All four writers base their work, closely or loosely, on the psalm; each interprets it differently.

With closer attention to the words of scripture, successive new versions of English-language metrical paraphrases have been written for at least three hundred years, and each in turn has been repeatedly modified, to make the psalms more applicable to current conditions and remove sentiments seen as unchristian.

Isaac Watts allowed for the possibility of his hymns' being altered. John Wesley altered them. Though convinced that nobody else could "mend" (improve) what he and his brother Charles had written,[4] John Wesley edited Charles's work, omitted some of Watts's stanzas, and altered or rearranged what he retained. He popularized "Our God, Our Help in Ages Past," one of Watts's greatest psalm paraphrases, but reduced its nine stanzas to seven and changed the first words to "O God." The alteration is small, but significant. Watts uses the word "our" five times, to express the joyful faith that the eternal, transcendent God is loving and reliable:

> *Our* God, *our* help in ages past,
>   *our* hope for years to come,
> *our* shelter from the stormy blast,
>   and *our* eternal home.

John Wesley's alteration blunts Watts's repetition, but can be defended on the ground that it shows our trust by addressing God directly at the start, instead of making statements about God. Both versions have merit. Methodist hymnals generally follow Wesley's

---

4. Charles, of course, was by far the more prolific hymn writer.

alteration, while churches in Watts's tradition often prefer the original. No one, however, sings all nine original stanzas.

Another Isaac Watts hymn altered by John Wesley is "Eternal Power, whose high abode / becomes the grandeur of a God." First published by Watts in 1709, in a book of poems intended for a more literary audience,[5] it began to be used in hymnals. Watts's second and third stanzas read as follows:

> The lowest step beneath thy seat
> Rises too high for Gabriel's feet,
> In vain the tall archangel tries
> To reach thine height with wond'ring eyes.
>
> Thy dazzling beauties whilst he sings,
> He hides his face behind his wings;
> And ranks of shining thrones around
> Fall worshipping, and spread the ground.

John Wesley omitted the second stanza, obliterating the striking picture of the "tall archangel" Gabriel failing to reach the first step beneath God's throne. Perhaps because the first line of the second stanza is grammatically puzzling, Wesley alters it, changes "behind" to "beneath," and "ranks" to the more alliterative "throngs":

> Thee while the first archangel sings,
> He hides his face beneath his wings,
> And throngs of shining thrones around
> Fall worshipping, and spread the ground.

In a later stanza, Isaac Watts writes:

> Earth from afar has heard the fame,
> And worms have learnt to lisp thy name;

"Worms" (probably then pronounced to rhyme with "storms") was a seventeenth-century metaphor of human creatureliness and unworthiness. Wesley changes "the" to the more personal "thy," and draws on Psalm 8:2, changing "worms" to "babes":

---

5. Watts, in *Horae Lyricae and Divine Songs*. The poem concludes Book I, and is titled "God Exalted above All Praise."

Earth from afar has heard thy fame,
And babes have learnt to lisp thy name;

Some of Wesley's changes seem improvements, others less so. However we judge them, both authors wanted Watts's hymns to be sung by congregations (though Watts did not originally envisage this use of "Eternal Power"). For this purpose, the lyric must be able to express a congregation's faith. Both Watts and the Wesleys gave first priority to this aim, over and above any claims of "authorial integrity."

A classic example of textual alteration is found in a popular Christmas hymn. What could be more quintessentially Charles Wesley than "Hark! The herald angels sing / glory to the newborn King"? Except that this is not what he wrote. Below are Charles's original poem, written in 1739, and a late-twentieth-century version (*United Methodist Hymnal*, 1989).

Changes in a Wesley Hymn

Charles Wesley, *Hymns and Sacred Poems*, 1739

Original Text: "Hymn for Christmas Day"

Hark how all the welkin rings!
"Glory to the King of kings,
Peace on earth and mercy mild,
God and sinners reconciled."

Joyful, all ye nations, rise,
Join the triumph of the skies;
Universal nature say:
"Christ the Lord is born today."

Christ by highest heaven adored,
Christ the everlasting Lord,
Late in time behold him come,
Offspring of a Virgin's womb.

Veiled in flesh the Godhead see!
Hail the incarnate Deity!
Pleased as man with men to appear,
Jesus, our Immanuel here!

Hail the heavenly Prince of Peace!
Hail the Sun of Righteousness!
Light and life to all he brings,
Risen with healing in his wings.

Mild he lays his glory by,
Born that man no more may die,
Born to raise the sons of earth,
Born to give them second birth.

Come, Desire of Nations, come.
Fix in us thy humble home;
Rise, the woman's conquering seed,
Bruise in us the serpent's head.

Now display thy saving power,
Ruined nature now restore,
Now in mystic union join
Thine to ours, and ours to thine.

Adam's likeness, Lord, efface;
Stamp thy image in its place;
Second Adam from above,
Reinstate us in thy love.

Let us Thee, though lost, regain,
Thee the Life, the heavenly Man;
O! to all thyself impart,
formed in each believing heart.

Typical Twentieth-Century Version

United Methodist Hymnal, 1989, # 240

(*Italics* = alterations from original)

Hark! *the herald angels sing,* (1)
"Glory to the *newborn King;* (2)
peace on earth, and mercy mild,
God and sinners reconciled!"
Joyful, all ye nations rise,
join the triumph of the skies;
with th' angelic host proclaim,
"Christ is born in Bethlehem!" (3)
Hark! the herald angels sing,
"Glory to the newborn King!" (4) (5)

Christ, by highest heaven adored;
Christ, the everlasting Lord;
Late in time behold him come,
Offspring of a virgin's womb.
Veiled in flesh the Godhead see;
Hail, th' incarnate Deity,
Pleased *with us in flesh* (8) *to dwell,*
Jesus, *our Emmanuel.* (6)
Hark! the herald angels sing,
"Glory to the newborn King!"

Hail the *heaven-born* Prince of Peace! (7)
Hail the Sun of Righteousness!
Light and life to all he brings,
risen with healing in his wings.
Mild he lays his glory by,
born that *we* no more may die, (9)
born to raise *us from the* earth, (10)
born to give *us* second birth: (11)
Hark, the herald angels sing,
"Glory to the newborn King!"

Editions in which the numbered changes appeared (for
explanation, see text below)
(1), (2), (7)   George Whitefield, *Collection* (1753).
(3)   Martin Madan, *A Collection of Hymns and Psalms
     Extracted from Various Authors* (1760).
(4), (5)   Tate and Brady, *New Version of the Psalms of David*
     (1782).
(6)   John Kempthorne, *Select Portions of Psalms* (1810).
(8), (9), (10), and (11)   *United Methodist Hymnal* (1989).
1857: first use of today's well-known tune, MENDELSSOHN.

In 1739, Charles Wesley wrote the ten four-line stanzas found on
pp. 301–2. Though his hymn is a Christmas poem, its central theme is
the theological meaning of Christmas, not the Christmas story. In 1753,
George Whitefield, the Wesleys' evangelistic counterpart and Calvinist disputant, amended "Hark how all the welkin rings! / 'Glory to the
King of kings' " to "Hark! *the herald angels sing* / 'Glory to the *newborn*
King,' " omitted stanzas eight and ten, and changed "heavenly Prince"
to "heaven-*born* Prince." The changes relate the poem more vividly to
the Christmas story, and have a pleasing sound pattern (Hark—herald). For modern singers, Whitefield's alterations advantageously

dispense with the now-archaic word "welkin" (the visible regions of the air; the vault of heaven; the sky). It was frequently used in eighteenth-century poetry, and the phrase "the welkin rings" occurs in a poem, "The Chase" (about hunting), published just before Wesley's poem. Here, as elsewhere, he may have been taking a topical phrase and appropriating it for Christian purposes.[6]

In 1760, Martin Madan related the hymn yet more closely to the Christmas story by altering Wesley's original couplet,

> Universal nature say:
> "Christ the Lord is born today."

to:

> *With the angelic host* proclaim,
> "Christ is born *in Bethlehem.*"

In 1782, still within Charles Wesley's lifetime, the hymn was added to an edition of Tate and Brady's *New Version of the Psalms of David.* At this point, Whitefield's amended opening couplet was added to the end of each stanza to make the now-familiar refrain, and the first six stanzas were doubled up to form three stanzas of eight lines each. One consequence of turning the opening couplet into a refrain was that the last four stanzas became out of place. As a series of requests or petitions, looking beyond Christmas, they do not expect the conclusion, "Hark! the herald angels sing," even if revised to remove obscurities and end with an affirmation of faith:

> Come, Desire of Nations, come,
> fix in us thy humble home.
> Formed in each believing heart,
> Now to all thyself impart;
> Life, descending from above,
> Reinstates us now in Love,
> And, abounding more and more,

---

6. J. R. Watson, e-mail communication, May 1999. In dictionaries, "welkin" is found from the thirteenth to the nineteenth centuries. Examples include "On the welkne shoon the sterres lyght" (Chaucer), "The fair welkin foully overcast" (Spenser), and "When storms the welkin rend" (Wordsworth). In the United States, the best experience of the welkin is a starry night on the high plains of eastern Montana or the Dakotas, when the vault of heaven spreads unclouded overhead.

> Ruined nature shall restore:
> *Hark, the herald angels sing*
> *Glory to the newborn King.*

I made this revision as an exercise, to see if it could be done. Even if it is a reasonable revision, the transition to the refrain remains awkward. Another result of turning the first couplet into a refrain is that "newborn" is emphasized by repetition, and in the first stanza now comes directly after "Bethlehem," further strengthening the hymn's relationship with the biblical nativity stories.

In the nineteenth century the hymn went through two more developments. In his 1810 collection, *Select Portions of Psalms,* John Kempthorne changed "Jesus, our Immanuel here" to "Jesus, our Immanuel." The alteration allows "Immanuel" to be pronounced as four syllables. Instead of singing *"our* Im*manu'l here,"* the line now reads, and sings, "Jesus, *our* Im-*man*-u-*el* [or Em-*man*-u-*el*]." Placed emphatically, at the end of the line, the word invites the refrain's glad response, so that the Christmas story and its meaning ("Immanuel" = "God with us") are further emphasized. In 1857, 118 years after the hymn was first written, Mendelssohn's magnificent tune, composed in 1840, was arranged by W. H. Cummings and matched with this text. Text and tune have remained inseparable ever since.

By the mid–twentieth century, Charles Wesley's use of "man," "men," and "sons" no longer conveyed their original meanings. "Sons of earth," an idiom meaning "of the earth, earthbound," and based on a literal translation from biblical Hebrew, is now either puzzling (How can the earth have sons?), or misleading (Will God resurrect only male offspring?). The words "man" and "men," intended to convey the news that Jesus Christ became a fully human being, able to free all humankind from death, now refer unambiguously only to the male half of our species.

In response, "pleased as man with men to dwell" has been revised to read, "pleased as man with us to dwell," "pleased with us in flesh to dwell," and "pleased on earth with us to dwell."[7] In the last three lines of the final stanza, most alterations read, "born that we no

---

7. See, respectively, *Rejoice and Sing,* #159; *United Methodist Hymnal,* #240, *Presbyterian Hymnal,* #31, *Chalice Hymnal,* #150, and *Voices United,* #48; and the *New Century Hymnal,* #144.

more may die" and "born to give us second birth." The middle line has been variously rendered as "born to raise the things of earth," "born to raise us from the earth," and "born to raise us all from earth."[8]

The evolution of "Hark! the Herald Angels Sing" illustrates how almost any hymn that stands the test of time receives alteration. If your favorite hymns are more than fifty years old, they were almost certainly altered before you first sang them. Among the most common alterations to a hymn are: leaving out stanzas, changing the tune, updating archaic words, improving a hymn's focus, and responding to theological, political, and cultural changes.

Acceptable Change

Individual reactions to lyric changes depend on how far they disturb the singer's memory bank, how far the reason for change is understood and accepted, and how elegantly the changes are made. The degree of disturbance varies from person to person, but we can assume that, the more popular a hymn, the greater the number of people who will be disturbed by change, and the more disturbed they are likely to be.

Crucially important, however, is how far the reason for change is understood and accepted. Most of the alterations in "Hark! the Herald Angels Sing" have long been accepted, because they gave it a progressively more direct reference to the Christmas story. Whether or not eighteenth-century Wesleyans objected to losing the word "welkin," arguments for its reinstatement now find few takers.

Over time, words change their meanings. In the year 1710, Queen Anne visited the nearly completed St. Paul's Cathedral in London, in the company of its architect, Sir Christopher Wren. At the end of the tour, she reportedly turned to my namesake and said, "It is awful. It is artificial. It is amusing." Sir Christopher was delighted, because the

---

8. Of six recent hymnals, *Rejoice and Sing, Presbyterian Hymnal, United Methodist Hymnal, Chalice Hymnal, New Century Hymnal,* and *Voices United,* all read "born that we no more may die" and "born to give us second birth." Variant versions of the middle line are: "born to raise the things of earth" (*Rejoice and Sing*); "born to raise us from the earth" (*Presbyterian Hymnal, United Methodist Hymnal, Chalice Hymnal,* and *Voices United*) and "born to raise us all from earth" (*New Century Hymnal*).

queen was telling him that the cathedral was awe-inspiring, artistic, and amazing.[9] When people first sang Isaac Watts's hymn "Jesus Shall Reign Where'er the Sun," they began the final stanza with the words,

> Let every creature rise and bring
> *peculiar* honors to our King,

meaning "special" or "particular" honors. Most hymnals have altered the hymn, because nowadays "peculiar" means "weirdly strange." When Richard Baxter wrote, "He *wants not friends* that hath thy love," he meant that those whom God loves will never lack friends, not that they can get along without them (see p. 373). When Isaac Watts described human beings as "worms," and Charles Wesley spoke of God's "bowels" moving, they were using words and phrases whose meaning has changed radically since the seventeenth century. The meaning of the latter phrase is easily illustrated. The King James Version translates the Song of Solomon 5:4 thus:

> My beloved put his hand by the hole of the door, and my bowels were moved for him.

The New Revised Standard Version reads, perhaps more erotically:

> My beloved thrust his hand into the opening, and my inmost being yearned for him.

Clearly, "moving bowels" originally meant what today we might call "gut feelings" of yearning, or compassion, as in Philippians 1:8 and 2:1:

- "For God is my record, how greatly I long after you all in the bowels of Jesus Christ." (KJV)
- "For God is my witness, how I long for all of you with the compassion of Christ Jesus." (NRSV)
- "If there be therefore any consolation in Christ, if any comfort of love, if any fellowship of the Spirit, if any bowels and mercies." (KJV)
- "If then there is any encouragement in Christ, any consolation from love, any sharing in the Spirit, any compassion and sympathy." (NRSV)

---

9. Anecdote from John Claypool, in a public lecture. I have not been able to find a printed source, so as to check the details of this story. Sir Christopher Wren may conceivably be a (remote) ancestor of mine, but no connection has been found.

Take a straw poll of any group of worshipers, and you will find an overwhelming majority in favor of changing such outdated words. Why? Because we implicitly realize that the lyric is for communal use, and that it does no service to yesterday's author or today's congregation to leave misleading or unintelligible lyrics unchanged.

Social and Political

Political and cultural changes prompt hymn alterations, often requested and accepted. I have already shown how, since the 1950s, many hymns on Christian mission dropped out of use as interchurch relationships changed.Their mind-set was no longer acceptable; if retained, they would certainly have been altered. Looking back at the late eighteenth century, Rochelle Stackhouse shows how Isaac Watts's hymns were successively altered, for reasons mostly political.[10]

By the time of the Revolutionary War against the British Crown, Isaac Watts's metrical version of the psalms was becoming widely used in the New England colonies.[11] Because Watts held the Puritan belief that prayer and praise should be particular and relevant, reflecting the situation of its singers, his metrical psalms included specific references to Britain, its monarch, and its "islands." As Stackhouse observes, "setting this model of the Psalms sung in worship reflecting the situation of the people who sing them practically requires that subsequent generations would revise Watts to make sense in their own times and places, or even write new hymns themselves."[12]

Already, in 1737, John Wesley had revised Watts for North American use, for example amending a line in Watts's Psalm 19, "Ye British lands rejoice," to "Ye happy lands rejoice."[13] In post-Revolutionary New England, the process continued. Three people in succession made

---

10. Stackhouse, *The Language of the Psalms in Worship*. This and following paragraphs are drawn from Stackhouse's book. See also her article "Changing the Language of the Church's Song Circa 1785."

11. Watts, *The Psalms of David Imitated in the Language of the New Testament* (London: 1719). Watts held correspondence with the New England puritan, Cotton Mather, and sent him samples of this work, but they did not become widely used until just before the Revolutionary War.

12. Stackhouse, *Language of the Psalms*, p. 38.

13. John Wesley, *A Collection of Psalms and Hymns* (Charleston, S.C.: Lewis Timothy, 1737). Wesley used fourteen of Watts's psalms and many of his hymns. His revisions of Watts include omission, adding other stanzas, and textual alteration. See Stackhouse, *Language of the Psalms*, p. 39.

extensive alterations to Watts's psalms: John Mycall, Joel Barlow, and Timothy Dwight. Mycall and Barlow were in printing and publishing, and both Barlow and Dwight were prolific writers. All three lived in a literate culture, where pamphleteering flourished and the printed word was the only—but effective—way of reaching a wider audience.

John Mycall was born in Worcester, England. At some point he emigrated to Massachusetts, where he ran a school in Newburyport and also taught in Amesbury. By 1776 he had begun a printing business, then edited a newspaper, *The Essex Journal and Merrimack Packet.* In 1781, in the immediate aftermath of the American Revolution, he published a revision of Watts's *Psalms,* in which he amended the "British" references but also made other changes. Little else is known about him. In the changed political situation, he perhaps saw both a need and a commercial opportunity.

Joel Barlow and Timothy Dwight were contemporaries, and, for a time, colleagues. Barlow was born in 1754, the fourth child of Samuel and Esther Barlow, farmers at Redding, Connecticut. An able scholar, he went to Yale, where he studied literature and poetry. He served briefly in the war, then returned to Yale. His epic poem, *The Vision of Columbus,* remained popular throughout his lifetime. In 1784 he joined Elisha Babcock in publishing a newspaper, *The American Mercury.* In that year, the General Association of Connecticut commissioned him to produce a revision of Watts's *Psalms.* The Association, by which Congregational churches in Connecticut organized themselves more tightly than their Massachusetts counterparts, no doubt saw the need for a "post-Revolutionary" revision. The immediate stimulus was, however, that some churches were using Mycall's revisions, tending, as they put it, "to destroy that uniformity in the use of Psalmody, so desirable in religious assemblies."[14]

Barlow's revision of Watts was published in 1785. Later, he left the printing business and opened a store. To promote his land speculation ventures in Ohio, he visited France and England, where he met Mary Wollstonecraft and other radicals, and moved increasingly away from Calvinist orthodoxy. He became a close associate of Thomas Jefferson, and was Jefferson's envoy to Napoleon Bonaparte.

Most commentators agree that it was Barlow's perceived association with radicals and atheists, rather than purely literary considera-

---

14. General Association of Connecticut, as quoted on the first page of Barlow's first edition (1785), quoted by Stackhouse, *Language of the Psalms,* p. 46.

tions, that prompted the General Association to commission a further revision, published in 1801, from Timothy Dwight.

Born in 1752, Dwight entered Yale in 1765, and was appointed as a tutor in 1771. He served as a chaplain in the Revolutionary War, then went home to Northampton, Massachusetts, to run the family farm. He founded a coeducational school (a radical move), but otherwise became progressively more conservative, both theologically and politically. From 1783 to 1795 he was pastor of the Greenfield Hill Congregational Church, Connecticut, then president of Yale. During this timespan he came to see the church in America—and in particular the Congregational churches in Connecticut—as God's instrument to save the United States from what he regarded as growing moral degeneration. Once Barlow's colleague and friend, Dwight's animosity to Barlow deepened as his own views grew more conservative.[15]

The Mycall, Barlow, and Dwight revisions illustrate changes made both in response to changing times, and to reflect the views of the revisers.[16] When he paraphrased Psalm 21, Isaac Watts revised the psalmist's point of reference, transferring it from ancient Israel to seventeenth-century Britain. He titled it, "Our King Is in the Care of Heaven," and began his version thus:

> The King, O Lord, with songs of praise
>   shall in thy strength rejoice,
> and, blest with thy salvation, raise
>   to heaven his cheerful voice.

The first reviser, Mycall, changed the title to "America the Care of Heaven," and altered the first couplet to read, "Our States, O Lord, with songs of praise, / shall in thy strength rejoice." Joel Barlow, seeing American independence as an act of divine providence, changed the title to "National Blessings," and rewrote the first stanza thus:

> In thee, great God, with songs of praise,
>   *our favoured realms* rejoice;
> and blest with thy salvation, raise
>   to heaven their cheerful voice. [Emphasis mine]

---

15. On Mycall, Barlow, and Dwight, see Stackhouse, *Language of the Psalms*, chap. 4.

16. For what follows, see ibid., chap. 5, pp. 71–96, and her Appendix 2, pp. 141–49.

Fifteen years later, the Revolution was less in the forefront of national consciousness. Dwight's revision reflects this, and returns more closely to Watts:

> Our Rulers, Lord, with songs of praise
>> shall in thy strength rejoice,
> and blest with thy salvation, raise
>> to heaven their cheerful voice.

In the third and fourth stanzas of the psalm, Barlow's revision makes explicit reference to what was still a recent and climactic war. His stanza three reads:

> In deep distress our injured land
>> implored thy power to save;
> for life we prayed; thy bounteous hand
>> the timely blessing gave.

In stanza four, Watts's original referred to enemies of the British king:

> But righteous Lord, his stubborn foes
>> shall feel thy dreadful hand;
> thy vengeful arm shall find out those
>> that hate his mild commands.

Barlow rewrites the stanza to celebrate America's defeat of British forces, the navy in particular:

> Thy mighty arm, eternal Power,
>> opposed their deadly aim,
> in mercy swept them from our shore,
>> and spread their sails in shame.

Dwight discards Barlow's no-longer-topical reference, and again returns more closely to Watts's original, with one significant change. The enemies now become God's enemies, anywhere (including by implication sinners in the United States), an amendment reflecting Dwight's concern about America's perceived moral degeneracy:

> But, righteous Lord, *thy* stubborn foes
>> shall quake through all their bands;
> thy vengeful arm shall find out those
>> that hate thy mild commands.

Some of Barlow's and Dwight's changes are theologically moti-vated. Watts's version of Psalm 68, part two, shows Jesus suffering at God's command, and for God's benefit:

> 'Twas for *thy sake,* eternal God,
> thy Son sustained that heavy load
> of base reproach, and sore disgrace,
> while shame defiled his sacred face.

Both Barlow and Dwight object to this view, substituting "our sake" and "my sake" respectively. In Psalm 2, Watts is at his most forbidding:

> With humble love address the Son,
>   lest he grow angry, and ye die.
> His wrath shall burn to worlds unknown
>   if ye provoke his jealousy.

Mycall and Dwight leave the stanza unchanged. Barlow steers it in a more gracious direction, as the last couplet becomes:

> His wrath shall burn to worlds unknown;
>   His love gives life above the sky.

On the whole, however, the most striking changes are made in response to the changing political and social situation, differently viewed by each reviser. In the first line of Psalm 67, revision goes in three directions:

Watts: Shine, mighty God, on Britain shine.
Mycall: Shine, mighty God, on all the land.
Barlow: Shine, mighty God, on Zion shine.
Dwight: Shine on our land, Jehovah, shine.

In stanza 8 of Psalm 124, Watts summons Britain to know the liv-ing God. Mycall says "New England," while Barlow widens it to "Ye nations." Dwight narrows the perspective to the New England churches, described metaphorically as "Zion," seen as "a fortress in the conflict with change."[17] In Psalm 67 (stanza 4, lines 1, 3, and 4) Watts summons all nations, including his own:

---

17. Ibid., p. 123.

> Sing to the Lord, ye distant lands . . .
> while British tongues exalt his praise
> and British hearts rejoice.

In the immediate aftermath of a hard-won war, Mycall urges his compatriots to thank God for their deliverance:

> Sing to the Lord, ye rescued States . . .
> while thankful tongues exalt his praise,
> and grateful hearts rejoice.

A few years later, in more peaceful times, Barlow makes the summons universal:

> Sing to the Lord, ye distant lands . . .
> Let every tongue exalt his praise
> and every heart rejoice.

Dwight follows suit, but emphasizes gratitude as the appropriate response:

> Sing to the Lord, ye distant lands . . .
> Let thankful tongues exalt his praise
> and thankful hearts rejoice.

Each of the three "New England" revisions of Watts was well received. Mycall's version evidently sold well enough to annoy the Connecticut church authorities. Barlow's version sold well enough for him to pay his bills, read law, and (possibly) capitalize other business ventures. Reprinted several times in New England, it was wholeheartedly adopted by Presbyterians in New York and Pennsylvania. Rochelle Stackhouse lists eleven printings in New England between 1785 and 1801, twenty-three Presbyterian printings between 1787 and 1817, sixty-one probably unofficial printings between 1793 and 1827, and eight more "corrected" editions between 1801 and 1830.[18]

Like all revisions, Barlow's had its detractors. A contemporaneous verse, circulating in Norwich, Connecticut, said:

> You've proved yourself a sinful cre'tur; ["creeter"?]
> You've murdered Watts, and spoilt the meter;

---

18. Ibid., pp. 55–56, and Appendix 1, pp. 133–38.

You've tried the Word of God to alter,
And for your pains deserve a halter.[19]

Overwhelmingly, however, newly independent Americans could no longer honestly sing about God's special favor to the British king and the British Isles. If Watts had been expressing his own vision, for people to hear and read as entertainment and edification, his work might have been treated differently. As poetic art, it could be heard with a mixture of immediacy and distance, its British references either discounted or seen as part of its charm. As congregational song lyrics, his work was inevitably subject to a different standard. Though the author's integrity is important, it is always subject to what congregations can sing with integrity.

The title of Dwight's revision precisely reflects the difference between "poetry as art" and "poetry for congregational song." It begins with Watts's title: "The Psalms of David, Imitated in the Language of the New Testament, and Applied to the Christian Use and Worship." The phrase "imitated . . . and applied" remind us that Watts himself was not simply versifying the psalms, but reworking them from a Christian perspective. Dwight's title then sets out the aims of his revision, which are also the aims of the Connecticut church authorities: to include psalms Watts had omitted, rework some of Watts's versifications, and make sure that "local passages are altered"—in other words, that topical and particular references (especially Watts's "Britishisms") were brought up to date.[20]

Dwight's revision was also well received, and sold well enough for him to contribute the considerable sum (in those times) of over a thousand dollars to help establish the Missionary Society of Connecticut. It was printed at least twenty-two times between 1801 and 1819.[21] By the middle of the nineteenth century, hymn alteration was such an established practice that it prompted Austin Phelps and others to publish a book showing how to do it, including guidance on archaisms, grammatical changes, stanza order, and poetic meter.[22]

---

19. Stackhouse, "Changing the Language," p. 18.

20. Dwight's full title is *The Psalms of David, Imitated in the Language of the New Testament, and Applied to the Christian Use and Worship, by I. Watts, D.D. A New Edition, in which the Psalms, Omitted by Dr. Watts, are Versified, Local Passages are Altered, and a Number of Psalms are Versified Anew, in Proper Meters* (Hartford, Conn.: Hudson and Goodwin, 1801). See Stackhouse, *Language of the Psalms*, p. 137.

21. Stackhouse, *Language of the Psalms*, pp. 69 and 137.

22. Austin Phelps et al., *Hymns and Choirs* (Andover, Mass.: Warren Draper, 1860), cited by Stackhouse, "Changing the Language of the Church's Song," p. 18.

I have shown that altering congregational song lyrics, and hymn lyrics in particular, is a long and well-established tradition, that many changes have been readily accepted, and that though the author's integrity is important, it is subject to what congregations can sing with integrity.

Few people are aware of this tradition, or its logic. When the *New Century Hymnal* was published in 1996, *Newsweek* ran a three-column one-page review, focusing on the hymnal's wholesale inclusive-language alterations and citing their numerous critics. Its author, *Newsweek* religion editor Kenneth L. Woodward, is articulate, well read, and acquainted with some aspects of early Christian tradition. Surprisingly, the burden of his critique is not the extent of this hymnal's alterations (an arguable case), but the mere fact that alterations were made. For many American Protestants, he claims, the hymnal is their most beloved book, over and above the Bible, because "a hymn from an inspired writer *speaks directly to the soul. At least it used to.* . . . Good hymns are works of art, not ideology. *Their integrity deserves respect,* and so do the traditions from which they spring." Later, in a letter to United Church of Christ staff writer Andrew Lang, Woodward reiterates his criticism. "Many ask, . . . why not write new hymns that incorporate the canon of linguistic inclusiveness? Why *violate the integrity of the old hymns?* . . . Does their faith witness make no claims on those who come after?" The last question is rhetorical. In context, it expects the answer, "No." From these quotations, and their contexts, it is clear that, for Woodward, violating the integrity of a hymn means changing it from its original form, and that only in its original form can it "speak directly to the soul." Because he is unaware of the tradition of alteration, and its logic, Woodward makes no distinction between poetry as art and poetry as lyrics for congregational song.[23] Logically, he would prefer the original version of "Hark! the Herald Angels Sing."

Though historically uninformed, Kenneth Woodward's critique raises an important question: How far should revision go? In all the revisions instanced above, the revisers had two aims: to preserve the integrity of the congregation's song and, subject only to this, the integrity of the original author's work. Thus, one criterion for evaluating

---

23. Woodward, "Hymns, Hers, and Theirs" and "Reply to Andrew Lang," emphasis mine. In his reply to Lang, Woodward cites historian Caroline Walker Bynum, St. John of the Cross, Julian of Norwich, and the Bible.

changes is whether they obscure and distort the original, or let it shine through.

Linguistic Assumptions

User response to language changes also depends on how elegantly they are made. Our perception of what constitutes "elegance" is partly subjective, but can be analyzed by considering the sound of words, and their meaning. I shall explore these questions as an amateur linguist, hoping to stimulate, or discover, more professional treatments.

Every alteration in a lyric arises from a mixture of church politics (Barlow and Dwight, for example); theological, cultural, and personal motivations; and linguistic assumptions. I list these ingredients in descending order of probable clarity: revisers tend to be more aware of the church politics of their work than the linguistic theory on which their revision operates. In recent revisions, I detect five linguistic theories, or perhaps I should say attitudes, overlapping and competing with one another.

The Soothing Sounds theory (my labels are not academically respectable) is that if it sounds nice, it must be OK, even if the meaning is obscure or objectionable. In practice, this is usually an argument *against* revision. I reject this theory, and have already argued that "we cannot be beguiled by pleasant sounds" (above, p. 183). As a colleague observes, defending obscurity on aesthetic grounds is an elitist error:

> If we say that the beauty of the language is worth preserving, even it requires some explanation, we may be saying that the only people who are truly welcome at our table are those who have acquired some specialized literary skill. We cannot wait for everyone to learn to understand us before we proclaim God's love.[24]

By contrast, the Ugly Truth theory is that if the change is theologically and ideologically correct (as perceived by the reviser) it doesn't matter how ugly it sounds, or how hard it is to say and sing. In 1834, Henry Francis Lyte wrote, "Praise, My Soul, the King of Heaven," a paraphrase of Psalm 103. When sung to LAUDA ANIMA, its most popular tune, one of the stanzas goes:

---

24. Bill Doggett, course paper on "Emancipatory Worship," Pacific School of Religion, Berkeley, Calif., January 1995.

> Father-like, he tends and spares us;
>> well our feeble frame he knows;
> in his hands he gently bears us,
>> rescues us from all our foes:
>> Praise him! Praise him! (Praise him! Praise him!)
>> widely as his mercy flows.

Believing that God is neither male nor female, recent revisions try to reduce or eliminate the masculine pronouns; some replace, or alternate, "Father" with "Mother." I agree with the diagnosis, but not with the Ugly Truth solution, which at its worst might read:

> Parent-like, God tends and spares us,
>> Well our feeble frame God knows.
> In God's hands God gently bears us,
>> rescues us from all our foes.
>> Praise God, praise God, praise God, praise God,
>> widely as God's mercy flows.

Frankly, this has too many Gods for comfort. To be sure, British hymnals would—if they were less conservative—have more of a problem than American, which replaced "Praise him" with "Alleluia" more than a century ago. Even so, the *United Methodist Hymnal* (#66) sounds awkward:

> Father-like, God tends and spares us;
>> well our feeble frame God knows;
> mother-like, God gently bears us,
>> rescues us from all our foes.
>> Alleluia! Alleluia!
>> widely yet God's mercy flows.

One reason for the awkwardness is that "God" is almost inevitably a stressed word, while its pronouns are stressed only in certain contexts. In the original, the pronouns are unstressed, and the stress pattern is:

> *Fa*-ther-*like*, he *tends* and *spares* us;   8
>> *well* our *fee*-ble *frame* he *knows*;   7
> *in* his *hands* he *gen*-tly *bears* us,   8

The meter is trochaic, with the stress falling on the first syllable of each pair, completed by a stressed final syllable in the seven-syllable line. In the revision, the stress pattern is:

Fa-ther-like, *God tends* and *spares* us;
well our *fee*-ble *frame God knows.*
*m*oth-er-like, *God gen*-tly *bears* us,

In two of the three lines, the substitution of "God" for "he" creates a juxtaposition of two guttural sounds in the sequence, "-li*k*e, *G*od" (unvoiced 'k' and voiced 'g'), which do not, I think, flow well in speech and song (try it for yourself). In all three, it creates two, sometimes three,[25] stressed syllables, one after the other, a pattern known as spondaic meter. Used deliberately and occasionally, spondaic meter can be very effective, as in these two examples:

"*Fields, streams, skies* I know; Death not yet."

"We hear the Christmas angels
the *great glad ti*-dings tell."[26]

Used in three successive lines, it becomes tedious: the accidental by-product of replacing "he" with "God." As a result, the emphasis falls in the wrong place, where no emphasis is needed. Better is the recent revision in the *Chalice Hymnal* (#23), by the Ecumenical Women's Center and Ruth Duck, which uses the phrase "feeble frame" to make the rhyme:

Mother-like, God tends and spares us,
    knowing well our feeble frame.
Father-like, God gently bears us,
    tenderhearted, slow to blame.

Here the spondees are less obtrusive, occurring only in the first and third lines. This revision retains much of the original vocabulary, and deletes the dubiously truthful fourth line (Does God really rescue us from all our foes?). "Knowing well our feeble frame" has a pleasing sound pattern and firm trochaic rhythm, while "tenderhearted, slow to blame" is a coherent elaboration of "gently bears."

A variant of Ugly Truth is the Stone in the Shoe theory, which is not so much a theory as it is a clueless reflex. A Stone in the Shoe revision

---

25. *"Frame God knows"* is a succession of three spondees; "-like God tends" and its counterpart may be three, two, or two and a half spondees: to my ear, the word "like," when overshadowed by "God," loses some, though not all, of its emphasis.

26. The first example is from Espy, *Words to Rhyme With*, p. 3. The second is from "O Little Town of Bethlehem," Phillips Brooks, 1868.

conveys the message, albeit unintentionally, that "we've changed this in such a way that you won't like it and are bound to notice it." An example is this rendering of Thomas Ken's 1674 doxology, found in a church's worship order:

> Praise God from whom all blessings flow.
> Praise God all creatures here below.   [originally "him"]
> Praise God above, ye heavenly host,   [originally "him"]
> Creator, Son, and Holy Ghost.   [originally, "Father, Son," etc.]

Of all traditional ritual songs, Ken's original is one of the most widely known. Even if the singer doesn't know it, the revision is a jolt. Presumably the reviser found "Father" problematic, and substituted "Creator." The problem is that "Father" and "Son" are not unrelated nouns, but a relational metaphor, whose two terms go together "like a horse and carriage," as a 1950s' pop song puts it. In this case, "Father" is the horse, and "Son" the carriage. Standing on its own, in the middle of the street, the abandoned carriage draws attention to itself. What's it doing? *Where's the horse?* Why is "Father" missing? And, now that "Father" is gone, do we hear "Son" as "Sun"?

The creator of this stranded carriage probably operates on the Construction Site theory of hymn revision. In this approach, the reviser looks at a line of words as if they were bricks in a wall. One of the bricks is faulty—a divine masculine pronoun, perhaps, or the word "men" or "mankind." So the reviser starts up the crane of linguistic rectitude, swings it over the site, extracts the faulty brick, drops it in the landfill of discarded words, picks up a clean, new word of exactly the same size and shape, and slots it neatly into place.

The problem is that words in a sentence are not like bricks in a wall, but parts of speech organically related to one another, just as in the "dry bones" song the bones belong together: "The toe-bone connected to the foot-bone, the foot-bone connected to the ankle-bone, the ankle-bone connected to the leg-bone." Remove one of the bones, and the skeleton wobbles or collapses. In 1969 I wrote a Communion hymn, "I come with joy," using "he/man" language uncritically absorbed. It read, in part:

> I come with Christians far and near
>   to find, as all are fed,
> man's true community of love
>   in Christ's communion bread.   [Second stanza]

As Christ breaks bread for men to share
    each proud division ends.   [Third stanza]

Later, I considered how to revise these lines. Using the Construction Site theory, "man" could be replaced by "our" and "men" by "us," or "all." This would have two drawbacks. First, the pronouns are limited in meaning and, in these contexts, colorless. Second, the hymn begins with a first-person statement ("I come with joy") and moves steadily from the individual to the corporate, ending with the plural, "we'll go." Introducing "our" and "us" at this early point would destroy that progression, while "for all to share" would be a repetitious, rather than emphatic, reiteration of "all" in the second line of the quotation. Therefore, instead of trying to replace individual words, I looked at the lines as a whole, and rewrote:

to find, as all are fed,
the new community of love . . .
        [and:]
As Christ breaks bread and bids us share
    each proud division ends.

This and the preceding quotation copyright © 1971 by Hope Publishing Company for the U.S.A., Canada, Australia, and New Zealand, and by Stainer & Bell Ltd., London, England, for all other territories. All rights reserved. Used by permission.

The contrast between "man" (meaning humankind) and "Christ" is lost, but it was irredeemable. In its place is an emphasis on new creation, new birth ("the new community of love"), and the actions of Jesus at the Last Supper, not only taking and breaking the bread, but giving it to the disciples and directing them to share it among themselves. Hymn revisions often require such a trade-off; something is lost, but hopefully replaced with something as good, or better.

Lastly, and preferably, comes the Invisible Mending theory, where the reviser makes alterations close to the metaphors, vocabulary, and meaning of the original, so that the congregation can sing with integrity while the author's light still shines through. The 1985 Reformed Church in America hymnal, *Rejoice in the Lord,* tried to follow this principle, in order to "release the author's true meaning." God-language was left untouched, but obscure phrases and exclusive language were amended, as far as the committee thought possible. "We have done our best," said the editor, "to stay close to each author's original text, and the occasional archaism has not deterred us from doing that." However, decreasing use of the King James Version makes phrases like "If thou but suffer God to guide thee" hard to understand, and it is amended to "If thou but trust in God to guide thee."[27] Most "man/men" references are also amended. In "Jesus, Thou Joy of Loving Hearts" (#273), the first stanza of the traditional text reads:

> Jesus, thou joy of loving hearts,
> thou fount of life, thou light of men,
> from the best bliss that earth imparts
> we turn, unfilled, to thee again.

This is altered to:

> Jesus, thou joy of loving hearts,
>   thou fount of life, thou light of all,
> from the best bliss that earth imparts
>   we turn, unfilled, to heed thy call.

The meter is preserved (no intrusive spondees), with long vowel sounds for the two stressed end-of-line rhymes ("all" / "call"). In this context, "all" is an accurate replacement of "men," while "call" leads neatly into the traditional, unaltered second stanza:

> Thy truth, unchanged, hath ever stood,
> thou savest those that on thee call.

Another example is this hymnal's revision of #244, "Nature with Open Volume Stands," Isaac Watts's great hymn on the crucifixion (see pp. 273–75). The original version of stanza two reads:

> But in the grace that rescued man
>   His brightest form of glory shines.
> Here, on the cross, 'tis fairest drawn
>   in precious blood and crimson lines.

To avoid the misleading word "man," the simplest move might be to substitute "us" in the first line, and invert the third to read, "'tis

---

27. Quotations and example from Erik Routley, "Editor's Introduction," *Rejoice in the Lord: A Hymn Companion to the Scriptures* (Grand Rapids: Eerdmans, 1985), p. 9. "If Thou But Trust in God to Guide Thee" is #151.

fairest drawn upon the cross," a choice made by the 1991 British hymnal, *Rejoice and Sing* (#219). This revision has two weaknesses: the word "us" narrows the scope of salvation from the human race to a particular group of singers; and its short vowel sound cannot adequately fit the second, stressed half of an iamb at the end of the line, unless it is (mistakenly) emphasized as "res-cued *us*," suggesting that somewhere out there is a "them" who are not so fortunate.

Rejoice in the Lord avoids this problem thus:

> But in the grace that saved the world
>> His brightest form of glory shines.
> See, on the cross, the tale unfold
>> in precious blood and crimson lines.

Though the divine pronoun remains masculine, the global scope of salvation is preserved; "world" and "-fold" fit their stressed positions; and Watts's metaphor-sequence (nature's volume, the book of grace, the handwritten name of God) is retained, though slightly modified, as "tale unfold" replaces "fairest drawn." Though not a perfect rhyme, "world" / "unfold" does not disappoint the modern ear, for two reasons. First, it is not the concluding rhyme of the stanza, where the ear comes to rest ("shines" / "lines"). Second, changes in pronunciation have accustomed English-speaking ears to a range of "half-rhymes" not originally intended. We know this with certainty from Shakespeare, who rhymed "unkind" with "wind" ("Blow, blow, thou winter wind; / thou art not so unkind / as man's ingratitude"), because both were pronounced "wined" as in the verb "to wind [a clock]." Shakespeare also rhymed "eats" with "gets," both pronounced "-aytes." His couplet in *As You Like It*, "seeking the food he eats, / and pleased with what he gets," was pronounced something like this: "saykin' the food 'e ayts, an' playzed with what 'e gayts."[28] Similarly, in Watts's day, as in this hymn, we may assume that in stanza one "God" ("Gawd"?) rhymed with "abroad," and that in the above stanza "man" rhymed with "drawn."

A final example of invisible mending is the first stanza of G. W. Briggs's hymn, "Christ Is the World's True Light," whose traditional wording is:

> Christ is the world's true light,
>> its captain of salvation,

---

28. Scull, "Rhyme and Reason."

> the Daystar clear and bright
>> of every man and nation.[29]

In the Construction Site theory, the word "man" would be replaced by a single-syllable equivalent. Of the most likely candidates, "person" has too many syllables, "folk" is too folksy, and "one" is doubly incorrect. Metrically, it would have to be stressed ("every *one*"), which sounds odd. Semantically, the words "every" and "one" are mostly used together, meaning "everybody," seldom apart to mean "each individual." In this context, the only possible usage is "everyone and nation," which would make no sense.

Instead of pursuing the futile quest for a single-syllable substitute, the reviser, Norman Kansfield (a member of the hymnal committee) looked back to "daystar" in the previous line, a Christ-image drawn from the King James Version of Isaiah 14:12 and 2 Peter 1:19. Matching this with a parallel image in the KJV of Haggai 2:7, he amended the stanza to read:

> Christ is the world's true light,
>> its captain of salvation,
> our Daystar clear and bright,
>> Desire of every nation.

The revision loses the (irredeemable) "man/nation" contrast, but replaces it with a second, biblical Christ-image; both metaphors have two syllables, and their initial "d" gives a pleasing alliteration.

Sound and Meaning

One mark of elegance (or otherwise) is whether the language is euphonic—in other words, whether it "flows smoothly," "sounds good," and is easily enunciated. Our perception of how language sounds is affected by our response to what it means. For someone who regards "Father" as essential to Trinitarian doctrine, a substituted "God" may always sound ugly; for someone who hears "Father" as distant, angry, and cold, "God" may always be a pleasing alternative.

Despite these difficulties, I shall try, for a moment, to listen for the sound of words in some recent revisions. Professionally, such work is

---

29. G. W. Briggs, "Christ Is the World's True Light," *Rejoice in the Lord*, #181.

the province of a linguist skilled in English phonetics. Because I have only a smattering of phonetics, I shall listen as best I can, in a non-technical way, and invite you to listen with me.

At a commonsense level, tongue twisters remind us that some sequences of spoken sound are difficult to enunciate.[30] Try speaking these examples aloud two or three times:

> A skunk sat on a stump and thunk the stump stunk, but the stump
>   thunk the skunk stunk.
> Tim was a thin twin tinsmith.

In both cases, the difficulty of the consonants ("t," "sk," "th," "k," "tw," etc.) is compounded by the similarity or repetition of some of the vowels (the "ung" sound in the first example, and the "in/im" sounds in the second). In the next example, a classic Scottish sobriety test, I suspect that its particular vowel sequence also contributes to the difficulty of saying the correct "th" (unvoiced as in "brea*th*") and "ss" sounds:

> The Leith police dismisseth us.

In the next three examples, the first joins the voiced guttural, "g," with three vowels, including a diphthong ("oy"); the second plays with four or five different vowel sounds; while the third pairs several different vowels with "b" (a staccato sound made with the lips, using the voice, and known as a labial plosive):

> Girl gargoyle, guy gargoyle.
> Old oily Ollie oils old oily autos.
> Brad's big black bath brush broke.

Finally, some examples which look innocuous on the printed page, but can spring a trap when spoken or sung:

> Unique New York.
> Truly rural.
> Preshrunk silk shirts.
> Strategic statistics.
> A frost-free refrigerator-freezer.

---

30. "While tongue-twisters have a dominant consonant, the place of articulation for the vowels is different and requires tongue gymnastics in order to produce the sounds. Most people, given ample time, can say a tongue-twister, but if you throw in the idea of saying the words faster, people stumble because their tongues just can't move that quickly." Dee Allen, e-mail communication, 24 June 1999.

With the above as preparation, consider these extracts from the revision of "Hark! the Herald Angels Sing" in the *New Century Hymnal* (#144):[31]

> Hark! the herald angels sing,
> "Glory to the Christ-child bring:
> peace on earth and mercy mild,
> God and sinner reconciled!"
> Joyful, all you saints arise,
> join the triumph of the skies. . . .
>
> Hail the Bearer of God's peace!
> Hail the Sun of righteousness!
> Light and life our Savior brings,
> risen with radiant, healing wings,
> mildly laying glory by,
> born that we no more may die.

In making these alterations, the revisers follow policies applied to every lyric in the hymnal. The aims of their thoroughgoing revision include: removing archaic language (ye, thee, thine, etc.); removing archaic cosmological and other references (God up above in heaven, for example); eliminating male titles (e.g., Father, Son) and pronouns for God, Jesus Christ, and the Holy Spirit; avoiding language thought to deal unjustly with people on the basis of gender, ethnicity, or mental and physical conditions (blind, lame, etc.); and drawing a distinction between Jesus during his earthly life (a male human being) and Christ (beyond and/or including both male and female), risen from the dead, alive in the world, and known through female, male, older, and younger members of the international community of faith. Because the theology and rationale of its revisions have been extensively discussed elsewhere, I shall consider only their phonic and metrical quality.

From this viewpoint, "light and life our Savior brings" is a successful revision: a balanced, trochaic line with no misplaced emphases, whose revised phrase has a sound sequence easy to articulate ("Sayv'ya'brings"). The same goes, soundwise, for "*ris'n* with *ra*-diant,

---

31. Jean Whitcomb, Minister of Music and Education at First Congregational Church, Paxton, Mass., made this analysis possible by providing me with comparisons between entries in the *New Century Hymnal* and its *Pilgrim Hymnal* predecessor.

heal-ing *wings*," but the metaphor is incoherent: it is unclear what sort of wings they are, how they heal, and what they radiate. "Mi*ldly lay*-ing glory by" (replacing "mild, he lays his glory by") opens with a tricky sequence of labial and dental sounds ("l"-"d"-"l"-"l") and the alteration leaves intact the archaism of the whole construction. (What does it mean, today, to "lay glory by"?) "Joyful, all you saints arise" has a smooth sound sequence, but the same archaism. The original phrase, "joyful, all ye nations rise" is obvious oldspeak; "joyful, all you saints arise" is an uneasy mix of old and new. Where do we hear anyone say, today, "Arise, *all you* saints"? Even in the American South, the phrasing might be different: "Saints, y'all rise!" "Hail the Bearer of God's peace" has an appropriate metaphor ("Bearer") but the word "God," here as elsewhere, creates a pointless spondaic meter—"*Bear*-er of *God's peace.*" "Glory to the *Christ-child bring*" has the same problem. At the end of a line, the double-emphasis of "Christ-child" can be effective:

> Bring to the Christ-child
> 　　honor and glory;
> sing for the Christ-child,
> 　　telling his story.

or else at the beginning of a line:

> Christ-child, God with us,
> friend of earth and friend of all
> Song lyric, © Praise Partners Publications, 1995.

In the *New Century Hymnal* revision, however, the threefold emphasis has no rationale. The substitution of "bring" for "King" also creates a grammatical problem. The received text has the angels making a triple announcement: glory to the newborn, peace to all the earth, and mercy for all sinners. The substituted "bring" either leaves the next two lines hanging, or commands *us*, nonsensically, to bring world peace and mild mercy to the Christ-child.

Other alterations show a similar mix of the good, the bad, and the ugly. When the *New Century Hymnal* amends this passage:

> Rapt in reverence we adore thee, marvelling at thy mystic ways

to read:

> Rapt in reverence we adore you, marveling at your mystic
> ways.[32]

there is a slight phonic improvement: "marveling-at-your-mystic" flows more easily than "marvelling-at-thy-mystic." In the same hymn, "man's" dominion over nature is replaced by "our" communion with nature:

Old: Thou hast given man dominion o'er the wonders of thy hand.
New: You have set us in communion with the wonders of your
        hand.

This is a good idea, but the retention of the archaic phrase "wonders of [God's] hand" leaves the meaning incoherent: what are these wonders, and what does it mean to be *set in communion* with them?

In the Easter hymn, "Come, Ye Faithful, Raise the Strain,"[33] the revision reads, in part (older text in brackets):

Come, you faithful, raise the strain   [Come, ye faithful]
  of triumphant gladness.
God has brought all Israel   [his Israel]
  into joy from sadness.
. . . .
All the winter of our sins,
long and gray, is flying   [long and dark]
from the Light, to whom we give   [his light]
laud and praise undying.

As a replacement for "his Israel," the line "God has brought all Israel" flows quite well. Judged as an attempt at modernization, the revision as a whole is unsuccessful: the archaic "laud" (a redundant synonym for "praise") is untouched, and "Come, *you* faithful" is not a modern colloquial construction.

In "Joy to the World,"[34] the line "let *earth* its *prais*-es *bring*" successfully replaces "let earth receive her King," but "let *ev*-ery *heart* pre-*pare* him *room*" is replaced with "let *ev*-ery *heart* pre-*pare Christ room*," another clunker.

---

32. From "O How Glorious, Full of Wonder," *Pilgrim Hymnal*, #74, *New Century Hymnal*, #558.

33. *Pilgrim Hymnal*, #185, *New Century Hymnal*, #230.

34. "Joy to the World," *Pilgrim Hymnal*, #130, *New Century Hymnal*, #132.

The revision of "O Come, All Ye Faithful," reads, in part:

O come, all you faithful,	[all ye faithful,]
joyful and triumphant	
O come now, O come now	[O come ye, O come ye]
to Bethlehem.	
Come and behold the	[Come and behold him]
ruler of all angels.	[born the King of angels.]
. . . .	
Word of our Go-od,	[Word of the Fa-ther]
now in flesh appearing[35]	

The word "God" is written as it now has to be sung. Though the meter of the received text is irregular, making "God" stretch musically across two syllables is awkward. "Come and behold the / ruler of all angels" looks as if it was written from an interlined version; it follows the tune, and ends a line of verse limply with "the." Here, as elsewhere, patchy modernizations underline the archaism of the whole. In archaic English, "Come ye!" is as acceptable as the town crier's "Hear ye!" Replacing "ye" with "you" does not produce a contemporary colloquial phrase: "O come all you" is not a summons frequently heard in the pulpit, the schoolyard, or the street, and "Come now!" is nowadays more a reproof than a summons.

My final example is, "O Little Town of Bethlehem," which reads, in part:

O little town of Bethlehem,	
how still we see you lie.	[thee]
Above your deep and dreamless sleep	[thy]
the silent stars go by;	
yet in your *dark streets shines forth*	[thy dark streets shin-eth]
the everlasting light.	
The hopes and fears of all the years	
are met in you tonight.	
. . . .	
O morning stars, together	
proclaim the holy birth,	

---

35. "O Come, All Ye Faithful," *Pilgrim Hymnal*, #132, *New Century Hymnal*, #135.

| and praises sing, and voices ring | [to God the King] |
| with peace to all on earth. | [and peace to men on earth.] |

Once again, a partial makeover highlights the archaism of the whole. In the phrase "how still we see thee lie," the archaism is as much in semantics as vocabulary; it is not commonplace today to address remarks to a town, whether as "thee" or "you," and the concluding phrase, "are met in you tonight," is equally stilted. The revision even adds a new archaism, in a double spondaic sequence (see emphasis above): When did you last hear a weather forecaster say, "Good morning, folks. It's a clear sky, and the sun is shining *forth?*" In the last couplet quoted, "and voices ring" is a euphonic alternative to "to God the King," but "voices ring with peace to all on earth" is incoherent. In the received text, the morning stars are summoned to proclaim the holy birth, sing praise to the divine king, and (proclaim and sing the news of) peace to all humankind. In the revision, the morning stars proclaim the birth and sing praises to an unspecified recipient, and it remains unclear whose voices are singing and how they "ring with peace."

In attempting such a thorough revision, the *New Century Hymnal* performs a useful service. Some changes sound good; many sound awkward; *everywhere it is clear that the archaism of traditional hymnody resides, not merely in individual word choices like "O," "Ye," "thou," and "shineth," but in syntax, sentence structure, stylistic habits, and rhetorical conventions.* I don't know how far this deeper level of archaism can be revised: the *New Century Hymnal* shows that wholesale revision is hard to do well.

Principles for Lyric Alteration

From the above exploration, I offer the following principles for lyric alteration, assuming that, for whatever reason, alteration has become necessary. Though I have hymnal committees especially in mind, the same principles apply to local, and informal, changes.

1. Think ecumenically. At present, there are too many variant revisions of hymns widely sung across denominations. In an era when people migrate from place to place, and from one denomination to another, too much textual variation reduces familiarity and detracts from the worship experience. Those who prepare the next generation

of hymnals (if there is one) should consult one another, and strive for more widely agreed revisions.

2. Clarify your policy on archaisms, God-language, and human-language, and openly explain it. Though revisions always evoke resistance, timely explanation makes change more acceptable.

3. Don't be doctrinaire and sectarian. Respect, and reflect, the diversity of theology, culture, and ethnicity in the constituency you hope will sing your revisions.

4. Consult living authors early. It is bad professional ethics to make your changes in their texts and expect them to roll over and say "OK" at proof stage. Respect their integrity by explaining the problem as you see it, and asking them to make their own changes. Many authors willingly do this, and are better able to change their work than your committee.

5. Closely read each text you revise. At a regional church assembly in the early 1980s, hymns for worship were printed in a booklet, revised to avoid sexist language. A zealous revisionist, on the lookout for masculine pronouns, changed some occurrences of "his" to "God's." Unfortunately, one of the hymns was Martin Luther's "A Mighty Fortress," where the pronoun in question refers not to God, but to Satan. So it was that several hundred delegates found themselves singing:

> *God's* craft and power are great,
> and armed with cruel hate,
> on earth is not his equal (!)[36]

6. Have each text formatted as poetry, and read it as such. Weigh the poetic merits of each alteration, and attend to the stresses of poetic meter, before singing the text with its tune.

7. Don't alter a text simply to fit the music of a given tune. Print it out as a poem, and make it prosodically right.

8. Respect stress patterns as well as the syllable count; don't sow a field of spondees.

9. Respect metaphor as well as meter. If the original sees nature as an open book, either preserve the allusion or find a suitable alternative.

10. Speak and hear each proposed revision aloud. What looks OK on the printed page may sound ugly when spoken or sung. Get advice

---

36. Leaver, "Opinion: Playing Scrabble with Hymns."

from speech professionals with no theological ax to grind, and feedback from listeners with no emotional investment in your project.

11. Don't alter first lines unless you are as skillful as George Whitefield (see above, pp. 302–6). The first line of a hymn is what most people remember. Alterations will be noticed. Make them only if essential, and make them persuasively good.

12. Don't alter rhymes unless you have replacement rhymes of like quality, and that smoothly fit the stress pattern.

13. Respect the style and vocabulary of the original. Don't import twenty-first-century psychobabble into a seventeenth-century hymn.

14. Don't change some archaisms in a way that highlights others.

15. Avoid liturgical dissonance. In a congregation, don't ask people to look at one thing on the page and sing another: they are there to worship, not play word games. Print the revised hymn in its entirety, so that worshipers can concentrate on worshiping. In a hymnal, never use asterisked alternatives. Hardly anyone reads them, and they are distracting to the few who do.

16. Don't copyright textual revisions to classic hymns!! You are subediting someone else's work, not building our own intellectual property. If the hymn was in public domain before you came along, leave it there.

17. *In all things, let the original author shine through.* Don't create a hybrid of your work and the author's. I did this once, with a hymn of Albert Bayly's. He was gracious enough to accept the change, but looking back, I realize it was poor professional ethics to graft my work onto his. Similarly, don't set the classic author straight by keeping two or three of the best-known phrases, and rewriting everything else. If the original text seems unusable but the original theme inspires you, use it as a model, and write something new.

I conclude this chapter with case studies of four widely used hymns—"Rise Up, O Men of God," "At the Name of Jesus," "It Came Upon the Midnight Clear," and "I'll Praise My Maker While I've Breath"—whose lyrics have been variously altered.[37]

---

37. Unless otherwise indicated, information on these four hymns is drawn from the *Companion to "Hymns and Psalms"* and the *Companion to the United Methodist Hymnal.*

Rise Up, O Men of God

William P. Merill, 1867–1954   Short Meter

Rise up, O men of God!
  Have done with lesser things:
give heart and soul and mind and strength
  to serve the King of kings.

Rise up, O men of God!
  His kingdom tarries long:
bring in the day of brotherhood
  and end the night of wrong.

Rise up, O men of God!
  The Church for you doth wait;
her strength unequal to her task;
  rise up, and make her great.

Lift high the cross of Christ!
  Tread where his feet have trod;
as brothers of the Son of Man
  rise up, O men of God!

Merrill's hymn was prompted by a suggestion that the Presbyterian Brotherhood Movement needed a hymn, and inspired by a magazine article entitled "The Church of the Strong Men." Leaving aside its content, this is an effective piece of hymnic verse. It uses short meter to advantage, as for example the third line of the first stanza, "give heart and soul and mind and strength," and has a single, insistent message, reinforced by the fivefold repetition of "Rise up!" In the British 1951 hymnal *Congregational Praise* it was in a section entitled "The Love and Service of Man," understood by implication as a clarion call to all Christians, male or female, a usage that made it more sexist than was perhaps originally intended.

The 1989 *United Methodist Hymnal* (U.S.A.) retains the hymn, because of its popularity as a theme song of United Methodist Men, and offers the feeble, asterisked alternative, "Rise up, ye saints." Even if restricted to men's meetings, the lyric, though stirring, is theologically questionable. Whether we regard God's sovereignty ("kingdom") as already established in Jesus Christ, or more plausibly as revealed yet not universally recognized, biblical sources reject the notion that men (or women) can bring it in if they use a bit of extra muscle. Throughout the New Testament, it is God who decides when to intervene in history to end or transform it. Equally problematic is the image of the church as a languishing female heroine, "her strength unequal to her task," waiting for brawny men to "rise up and make her great," a phrase laced with phallic ambiguity. Because these problems run right through the hymn, most recent hymnals have adopted the simplest form of amendment: deletion.

Faithful to the Last

Carolina Maria Noel's hymn "At the Name of Jesus" was first published in 1870, as the leading item in an enlarged edition of her poems, *The Name of Jesus, and Other Verses for the Sick and Lonely* (for the text, see pp. 334–35). This title aptly reflects both the subordinate status of Victorian middle-class women, marked by "timidity, sadness, pain and sorrow," and the circumstances of Noel's own life. It was said of her that she endured a twenty-year illness before the end came, and thus "learned in suffering what she taught in song."[38] To a sufferer from chronic illness, the hymn's "perfect rest," free from pain and tiredness—from which the incarnate Word descends, and to which the risen Christ returns—has obvious appeal. So does the triumphant language of the poem as a whole: the sufferer does not dwell on suffering, but is uplifted and inspired by Christ's glorious ascent to the heart of God, where death is no more, neither is there mourning, nor crying, nor pain anymore, for the former things have passed away (Revelation 21:4).

Since its first appearance in the second edition of *Hymns Ancient and Modern in 1875*, "At the Name of Jesus" has been included in hymnals of all traditions, with decreasing numbers of stanzas. I shall summarize the revisions and selections made by a selection of recent hymnals, using abbreviations for simplicity: Hymns and Psalms, Methodist, U.K., 1986 (H&P); Rejoice and Sing, United Reformed Church, U.K., 1991 (R&S); The United Methodist Hymnal, U.S.A., 1989 (UMH); The Baptist Hymnal, Southern Baptist, U.S.A., 1991 (SBH); The Presbyterian Hymnal, U.S.A., 1990 (PH); A New Hymnal for Colleges and Schools, Yale University Press, 1991 (HCS); Voices United, United Church of Canada, 1996 (VU); and The Book of Praise, Presbyterian Church in Canada, 1997 (BOP).

---

38. Watson, *The English Hymn,* p. 424. The first quotation is Watson's comment. He takes the second from Mrs. E. R. Pitman, *Lady Hymn Writers* (London, 1892).

At the Name of Jesus (Original Version)

Carolina Maria Noel, 1817–77   Poetic Meter: 6.5.6.5.D

1. At the name of Jesus
       every knee shall bow,
   every tongue confess him
       King of glory now;
   'tis the Father's pleasure
       we should call him Lord,
   who from the beginning
       was the mighty Word.

2. Mighty and mysterious
       in the highest height,
   God from everlasting,
       Very Light of Light,
   in the Father's bosom,
       with the Spirit blest,
   Love, in Love eternal,
       rest, in perfect rest.

3. At his voice creation
       sprang at once to sight,
   all the angel faces,
       all the hosts of light,
   thrones and dominations,
       stars upon their way,
   all the heavenly orders
       in their great array.

4. Humbled for a season
       to receive a name
   from the lips of sinners
       among whom he came,
   faithfully he bore it
       spotless to the last,
   brought it back victorious
       when through death he passed.

5. Bore it up triumphant
    with its human light,
through all ranks of creatures
    to the central height,
to the throne of Godhead,
    to the Father's breast;
filled it with the glory
    of that perfect rest.

6. Name him, brothers, name him,
    with love as strong as death,   (6 syllables, instead of 5))
but humbly and with wonder,   (7 syllables, instead of 6)
    and with bated breath;
he is God the Savior,
    he is Christ the Lord,
ever to be worshipped,
    trusted, and adored.

7. In your hearts enthrone him,
    there let him subdue
all that is not holy,
    all that is not true.
Crown him as your captain
    in temptation's hour;
let his will enfold you
    in its light and power.

8. Brothers, this Lord Jesus
    shall return again,
with his Father's glory,
    with his angel-train;
for all wreaths of empire
    meet upon his brow
and our hearts confess him
    King of glory now.

At the Name of Jesus
(Revision in *Rejoice and Sing,* #261)

Carolina Maria Noel, 1817–77   Poetic Meter: 6.5.6.5.D

1. At the name of Jesus
     every knee shall bow,
   every tongue confess him
     King of glory now;
   'tis the Father's pleasure
     we should call him Lord,
   who from the beginning
     was the mighty Word.

2. Humbled for a season
     to receive a Name
   from the lips of sinners
     unto whom he came,
   he became a witness
     faithful to the last
   and returned victorious
     when from death he passed.

3. In your hearts enthrone him;
     there let him make new
   all that is not holy,
     all that is not true.
   He is God the Saviour,
     he is Christ the Lord,
   ever to be worshipped,
     trusted and adored.

4. When this same Lord Jesus
     shall appear again
   in his Father's glory
     there with him to reign,
   then may we adore him,
     all before him bow,
   as our hearts confess him
     King of glory now.

The hymnals and p. 333 all select four or five stanzas from the original eight.[39] Two recent U.S. publications, *The New Century Hymnal* (NCH) and the *Chalice Hymnal* (TCH) omit the hymn. All the hymnals change "among whom he came" (stanza 4) to "unto whom he came," and alter "when *through* death he passed" (stanza 4) to "when *from* death he passed" (see further below). Hymnals that include the last stanza (omitted by UMH) drop the word "Brothers," and try various amendments showing slight, but interesting, differences in theology: "For this same Lord Jesus / shall return again" (H&P); "When this same Lord Jesus / shall appear again" (R&S); "Watch, for this Lord Jesus shall return again" (SBH), and "Christians, this Lord Jesus / shall return again" (PH and VU).

Noel's poem, written as a processional hymn for Ascension Day, begins with a quotation from the King James Version of Philippians 2: 9–11: "Wherefore God also hath highly exalted him, and given him a name which is above every name; that at the name of Jesus every knee should bow, of things in heaven, and things in earth, and things under the earth; and that every tongue should confess that Jesus Christ is Lord, to the glory of God the Father." This is followed (stanzas 1–2) by language drawn from John 1:1–18 (the Word . . . with God in the beginning . . . in the bosom of the Father). The third stanza draws on the KJV of Colossians 1:16: "For by him were all things created, that are in heaven, and that are in earth, visible and invisible, whether they be thrones, or dominions, or principalities, or powers: all things were created by him, and for him."

The second stanza quotes the Nicene Creed ("light of light"), and the hymn as a whole follows the creed's "story line": "Light of Light, Very God of Very God, . . . being of one substance with the Father by whom all things were made, . . . came down from heaven, . . . was crucified . . . rose again . . . and ascended into heaven, and sitteth on the right hand of the Father. And he shall come again with glory to judge both the quick and the dead, whose kingdom shall have no end." As I have already noted, the creed's story is followed selectively, with an emphasis on the Word's imperial majesty. Every knee shall bow to him, the Lord, the King of glory. Twice hailed as "mighty," he is

---

39. Numbers indicate which stanzas are selected from Noel's eight: *Hymns and Psalms*—1, 4, 5, 7, 8; *Rejoice and Sing*—1, 4, 7, 8; *United Methodist*—1, 4, 5, 7; *Baptist*—1, 4, 7, 8; *Presbyterian*—1, 4, 5, 8; *Hymnal for Colleges and Schools*—1, 3, 4, 5, 6, 7; *Book of Praise*—1, 4, 6, 7, 8; *Voices United*—1, 4, 6, 7, 8.

"victorious" and "triumphant." If we "crown" him as our captain-prince, he will be "enthroned" in our hearts, "subduing" everything unholy and wrapping us in his light and power. When he comes again in glory, he will be crowned with all the "wreaths of empire," and hailed as the glorious King.

Only one stanza of the eight refers to Jesus' life, suffering, and death: "humbled for a season . . . spotless to the last . . . victorious when through death he passed." The reference is brief and indirect. There are no crosses on a hill, no nails hammered into wood, merely a "name" carried—like a silver trophy—"spotless to the last," and an execution transmuted into a subway ride: "when *through* death he *passed*" (which is why recent hymnals change "through" to "from"). Noel's treatment is several times removed from the creed's specificity: "came down from heaven, and was incarnate by the Holy Ghost of the Virgin Mary, and was made man, and was crucified also for us under Pontius Pilate. He suffered and was buried."

In its original context, as a poem to inspire "the Sick and Lonely," the hymn's selective viewpoint makes sense. Removed from that context, its triumphalism becomes open to question. As a lifeboat moored to suffering, its bright colors lift the spirit. Released from its moorings into the mainstream of Christian worship, it glides downstream, transmuted into a royal barge playing music for the king's fireworks.

Aware of the hymn's problematic triumphalism, *Rejoice and Sing* makes several amendments. Its first stanza (also Noel's stanza 1, as shown) is retained unchanged. Its second stanza (Noel's stanza 4) is amended, in part, to read:

> Humbled for a season
>   to receive a Name
> from the lips of sinners
>   unto whom he came,
> *he became a witness,*
>   *faithful to* the last,
> *and returned* victorious
>   when *from* death he passed.

Though there is still no cross, the revision nudges the hymn closer to the story, and Christ is now God's faithful witness in the face of death. Gone also is the peculiar metaphor "faithfully he bore it . . . bore it up triumphant," which treats the Name of Jesus as a family heirloom, safely transported home, "Christ carrying his own name up to heaven as a sort of exhibit," as an English hymnologist puts it.[40] The third stanza (Noel's 7) replaces "subdue" with "make new," and the crowned captain with these lines from Noel's stanza 6:

> He is God the Saviour,
>   he is Christ the Lord,
> ever to be worshipped,
>   trusted and adored.

In the final stanza, the Lord Jesus "appears" rather than "returns," a verb more in keeping, perhaps, with our space/time universe. Kingship language is retained ("in his Father's glory / there with him to reign" as "all before him bow"), but imperial "wreaths of empire" are cast aside. The only loss is that instead of confessing Christ as King of glory *now*, in anticipation of our final destiny, that "now" is delayed until his return: *"then* may we adore him . . . as our hearts confess him / King of glory now."

Having looked at this hymn in some detail, I have two suggestions for using it in worship: critique its relationship to Philippians 2:5–11, and reconnect it with the story of Jesus' betrayal, suffering, and death. In Philippians, more than half of the "Christ hymn" Paul quotes is about Jesus' humility, humiliation, and death:

> Let the same mind be in you that was in Christ Jesus,
> *who, though he was in the form of God,*
>   *did not regard equality with God*
>   *as something to be exploited,*
> *but emptied himself,*
>   *taking the form of a slave,*
>   *being born in human likeness.*
> *And being found in human form,*
>   *he humbled himself*
>   *and became obedient to the point of death—*
>   *even death on a cross.*
> Therefore God also highly exalted him
>   and gave him the name
>   that is above every name,
> so that at the name of Jesus

---

40. John Wilson, of Guildford, Surrey, quoted in *Companion to the United Methodist Hymnal*, "At the Name of Jesus," p. 221.

> every knee should bend,
>   in heaven and on earth and under the earth,
> and every tongue should confess
>   that Jesus Christ is Lord,
>   to the glory of God the Father.

For reasons already explained, Noel's hymn begins where Paul ends. Because this hymn and scripture reading are commonly linked in hymnals and lectionary notes, preachers and worship leaders should "be aware of the very different emphases found in Scripture and in the hymn."[41] Using the version in *Rejoice and Sing* (see p. 336), the hymn could be sung meditatively, rather than triumphantly, in counterpoint with Paul's hymn, or with extracts from the Gospel narratives of Jesus' betrayal, suffering, and death. Here, as a stimulus to creativity, are biblical passages that could be heard in counterpoint with this version of the hymn. There are three "tracks": one from Philippians (for any time of year), and two others, from the Gospel of John and the Gospel of Mark (for Palm/Passion Sunday, Good Friday, and "The Reign of Christ" Sunday):

Hear:	Phil. 5:4–7a ("likeness") / or John 12:20–26 / or Mark 14: 32–36
Sing:	At the name of Jesus / every knee shall bow . . .
Hear:	Phil. 5:7b–8 / or John 13:2b–5 (i.e., from "And during supper") / or Mark 15: 12–15
Sing:	Humbled for a season / to receive a Name . . .
Hear:	Phil. 5:1–5 / or John 19:16b–19 / or Mark 15:16–20
Sing:	In your hearts enthrone him; / there let him make new . . .
Hear:	Phil. 4:4–7; or John 19:28–30 / or Mark 15:33–39
Sing:	When this same Lord Jesus / shall appear again . . .

That Glorious Song of Old

Sometime around Christmas, in the year 1849, Edmund H. Sears, a Unitarian minister in Wayland, Massachusetts, wrote a poem entitled "Christmas Carol," published on December 29 in the *Christian Register,* Boston (for the text, see p. 341). Its five stanzas develop the theme of the angel song of peace on earth (Luke 1:8–14), with a recurring emphasis on whether or not people listen to the song:

---

41. Smith, "From Scripture to Congregational Song," p. 14.

1. On Christmas night, the angels announced God's gift of peace on earth and goodwill to all human-kind.
2. The world is weary and sad, yet still today the angels sing their song.
3. Sin and conflict roll on, and warring nations won't heed the angel song of peace.
4. Yet there is hope for weary and burdened people who listen to the song.
5. The golden age will return, and all the earth will sing the angel song of peace.

It Came Upon the Midnight Clear (Original Version)

Christmas Carol
Edmund H. Sears, 1849   Common Meter Double

1. It came upon the midnight clear,
     that glorious song of old,
   from angels bending near the earth
     to touch their harps of gold;
   "Peace on the earth, goodwill to men,
     From heaven's all-glorious King."
   The world in solemn stillness lay
     to hear the angels sing.

2. Still through the cloven skies they come
     with peaceful wings unfurled,
   and still their heavenly music floats
     o'er all the weary world;
   above its sad and lowly plains
     they bend on hovering wing,
   and ever o'er its Babel sounds
     the blessed angels sing.

3. But with the woes of sin and strife
     the world has suffered long;
   beneath the angel-strain have rolled
     two thousand years of wrong;
   and man, at war with man, hears not
     the love song which they bring:
   O hush the noise, ye men of strife,
     and hear the angels sing!

4. And ye, beneath life's crushing load,
    whose forms are bending low,
who toil along the climbing way
    with painful steps and slow,
look now! for glad and golden hours
    come swiftly on the wing.
O rest beside the weary road,
    and hear the angels sing!

5. For lo! the days are hastening on
    by prophet-bards foretold,
when with the ever-circling years
    comes round the age of gold;
when peace shall over all the earth
    its ancient splendors fling,
and the whole world give back the song
    which now the angels sing.

It Came Upon the Midnight Clear (Proposed Revision)

Revised by Brian Wren, 1997   Common Meter Double

Suggestions from various hymnals, with additions, respectfully revised, and left in the public domain. The bracketed stanza, stanza 4, should be omitted if four stanzas are selected.

1. It came upon the midnight clear,
    that glorious song of old,
from angels bending near the earth
    to touch their harps of gold;
"Goodwill to all, and peace on earth:
    great news of joy we bring!"
The world in solemn stillness lay
    to hear the angels sing.

2. Still through the clouds of time they come
    with peaceful wings unfurled,
and still their heavenly music floats
    through all the weary world;
above its sad and lonely plains
    they bend on hovering wing,
and still, through all its babbled sounds,
    the blessed angels sing.

3. But with the woes of sin and strife
      the world has suffered long.
   Beneath the angel-hymn have rolled
      two thousand years of wrong
   as warring armies clash, and drown
      the love song which they bring:
   O hush your noise, lay down your arms,
      and hear the angels sing!

4. [Let all who bear a crushing load
      and stagger, bending low
   to toil along life's climbing way,
      with painful steps and slow,
   take heart, for every winter wild
      shall blossom into spring,
   and rest beside the weary road
      to hear the angels sing!]

5. For still the days are hastening on
      by prophets seen of old,
   when in our planet's circling years
      shall come a time foretold,
   when peace shall over all the earth
      its newborn splendors fling,
   as all the world sends back the song
      which now the angels sing.

The poem was written in the aftermath of the 1845–48 Mexican-American war, which ended with the defeat of Mexico after an American invasion and fierce fighting around the capital city. Following its defeat, Mexico ceded most of what is now California, New Mexico, and Texas to the United States. I read somewhere that Sears was strongly against the war, but have no documentary evidence. The California gold rush, begun in 1848, was at its height, accompanied by frontier lawlessness. Throughout the previous year, Europe had been swept by revolutionary movements. Nearer home, leaders of the anti-slavery movement had entered politics during the 1840s, and slavery was becoming a hot issue. In New England and elsewhere, there was growing concern and agitation at the low wages, long hours, poor safety, and grinding poverty of industrial workers and child laborers.

Whether or not these events prompted the hymn, it comes from the pen of a minister whose church had an active social conscience, and its theme of war and peace is insistent, and unmistakable.

Set to different tunes, and with different stanza selections, the hymn is well loved and widely sung.[42] During its 150-year journey, several issues have prompted revision. Because Christian hope is in God's purpose, not a recurrent "golden age," and "bards" is a word not now in common use, the second and fourth lines of stanza five have been amended to "by prophets seen of old" / "shall come the time foretold" (UMH, HCS, BOP), or "by prophet seen of old" / "shall come the time foretold" (TCH). The archaism of "lowly" and its juxtaposition with "sad" led one hymnal to make a minor, but useful change to "sad and *lonely* plains" (HCS). The archaism of "angel-*strain*" (stanza 3) prompted the same hymnal to replace it with "heavenly hymn." In the opening stanza, "good will to men" was retained by the *United Methodist Hymnal*, with the footnote, " 'all' may be substituted," a rarely accepted invitation to liturgical dissonance. Other hymnals try "goodwill to all" (PH, #38; TCH, #153; HCS, # 229 & 230, VU, #44); "goodwill to all, great news of joy we bring" (NCH); "To all the earth goodwill and peace" (BOP #148); "Glory to God! On earth be peace" (R&S). Hymnals using the third stanza change its "man/men" language. "And man, at war with man, hears not" becomes "and we, through din of war, hear not" (BOP); "and warring humankind hears not" (VU); "and we, at bitter war, hear not" (R&S); or "and warring humankind hears not the tidings which they bring" (HCS). "O hush your noise, ye men of strife" is amended to "O hush your noise and cease your strife" (HCS, VU); "Oh hush the noise, O still the strife" (BOP); " O hush the noise, and end the strife" (R&S).

Two major issues receive less attention. Sears's fourth stanza opens with a picture of people carrying a load, apparently up a mountain ("climbing way"). Whatever it may originally have signified, the image vaguely suggests a hike on the Appalachian Trail, and the assurance that "glad and golden hours" are soon coming is closer to pollyanna optimism than Christian faith. In a four-stanza selection, this stanza is the most suitable candidate for omission. If retained, my amendments may prove helpful.

The most serious alteration in Sears's hymn is the widespread omission of its third stanza in American hymnals (British and Canadian hym-

---

42. In the hymnals surveyed, the hymn occurs as follows: BH, # 93; PH, #38; TCH, #153; HCS, # 229 and #230; VU, #44; NCH, #131; BOP, #148; H&P, #87; R&S, #144; UMH, #218.

nals retain it).[43] As the editor of the 1989 *United Methodist Hymnal* observes, "The hymn's central theme contrasts the scourge of war with the song of the angels' 'peace to God's people on earth.' "[44] In spite of this, the hymnal omits stanza three, where the scourge of war is most clearly addressed! It is time to reinstate this stanza, and think again about the customary American tune (though I focus on lyrics, the tune choice affects their interpretation). In the U.S.A., the usual tune is CAROL, by Richard Willis, composed for Philip Doddridge's hymn "See Israel's Gentle Shepherd Stand." A gently waltzing lullaby, it is a good match for Doddridge's text, but utterly unsuited to the impassioned prophecy of "It Came Upon the Midnight Clear." People who worry about hymn alterations should worry more about this one. In American congregations, the omission of stanza three and choice of a lullaby tune (also chosen in Canada) take the hymn in a direction totally at variance with the author's intention. A more suitable tune is Arthur Sullivan's NOEL, long in public domain. The standard choice in British collections, it is available in the U.S.A. in *The Hymnal for Colleges and Schools* (#229 and #230), which uses both NOEL and CAROL for Sears's text, and (to a different text) in the *New Century Hymnal* (#401). My revision updates the hymn's man/men language and repairs some of its archaisms. I offer it for consideration, hoping that it allows the author's light to shine through.

My Days of Praise Shall Ne'er Be Past

Finally, I shall look at Isaac Watts's superb paraphrase of Psalm 146, and offer a revision. The original text has six stanzas (for the full text, compared with the KJV of Psalm 146, see the Appendix). Watts follows the psalm and its line of argument, stanza by stanza:

1. I will praise God "with my breath," and then for all eternity.
2. Why should I put my trust in human rulers? They will die, and cannot "make their promise good."
3. Rely instead on God, who created all things and intervenes to feed the poor and save the oppressed.
4. God gives eyesight, forgiveness, and comfort, and helps the most vulnerable members of society.

---

43. An exception is *Hymnal for Colleges and Schools* (#229 and #230). In earlier times the stanza seems to have been used more widely. The full text appears, for example, at #194 in *Hymnal of the Methodist Episcopal Church, with Tunes* (New York: Phillips & Hunt and Cincinnati: Cranston & Stowe, 1888), next to another (and greatly inferior) poem by Edmund Sears, in the same meter, entitled "Christmas Anthem."

44. Young, *Companion to the United Methodist Hymnal*, p. 434.

5. God loves the saints, and turns the wicked down to hell.
   Let everyone praise God.
6. I will praise God, who "lends me breath," throughout
   earthly life, then for all eternity.

Stanzas two and five are now usually omitted. I shall consider the remainder in their original wording, and ask what needs revision and why, hoping to let the author shine through.

> I'll praise my Maker with my breath;
> and when my voice is lost in death,
>   praise shall employ my nobler powers:
> my days of praise shall ne'er be past
> while life and thought and being last
>   or immortality endures.

Here, as in all six stanzas, Watts writes for a Genevan tune, first composed for a metrical version of Psalm 113. Now usually known as OLD 113th, the tune is in two sections, each covering three lines of the six, so indicated metrically as 888.888. Watts likewise breaks his stanzas in the middle, at the end of each third line. John Wesley made a neat revision of "with my breath" to "while I've breath," which I shall retain.

> Happy the man whose hopes rely
> on Israel's God! He made the sky
>   and earth and seas, with all their train:
> his truth for ever stands secure;
> he saves the oppressed, he feeds the poor,
>   and none shall find his promise vain.

Issues here are the masculine pronoun, which nowadays irretrievably casts the divine in a male mold, and the word "man." Recent revisions of the first line include: "Happy are they" (UMH); "How happy they" (PH, TCH), and "Happy are those" (VU). The last option is a nonstarter, awkward to say in itself and disastrous in the resultant mouth-mangler, "those whose hopes." "How happy they" is attractive, but can be guaranteed to work only with the tune OLD 113th, whose long starting note holds the first half of the spondee, and sounds something like: "Ho—w hap-py." I therefore opt for "Happy are they." In replacing divine masculine pronouns, I avoid repeating "God" where possible. Here, one can say, "Israel's God, who . . . ; whose truth . . . who saves . . . who feeds [using "who" emphatically] . . . for none shall find the promise vain." ("The promise" is, in context, construable only as God's promise.) The plural, "seas," is precise, but awkward to enunciate when followed by "with"; I shall follow British revisions and use "sea."

> The Lord hath eyes to give the blind;
> the Lord supports the sinking mind;
>   he sends the laboring conscience peace;
> he helps the stranger in distress,
> the widow and the fatherless,
>   and grants the prisoner sweet release.

I shall retain Wesley's inspired revisions, "pours eyesight on the blind," and "fainting mind." Since Watts famously uses the phrase "Our God" elsewhere (see above, p. 299), it can replace both occurrences of "the Lord," preserving the author's emphatic repetition. I shall say "gives" instead of "sends," because it is simpler, and clearer. Extra "Gods" can be avoided by using "*and* gives," and by substituting "defends" for "he helps." The penultimate line raises tricky questions. The psalm does indeed say "widow" and "fatherless," because it was composed in a society where a widow was often made destitute when her husband died (he being the property owner), whereas a widower could easily remarry. A motherless child would be bereft, but not without support while its father was alive. On the other hand, a *fatherless* child was as vulnerable as a widow. Two options present themselves: stay with the biblical language, on the grounds that (a) it's biblical and (b) many children in our society are indeed fatherless; or seek a revision that follows the spirit of the psalm and names some of our society's vulnerable people. This, I think, is what Isaac Watts meant by "imitation," so I shall follow his method, and try "the orphan and the comfortless."

> I'll praise him while he lends me breath;
> and when my voice is lost in death,
>   praise shall employ my nobler powers:
> my days of praise shall ne'er be past,
> while life and thought and being last,
>   or immortality endures.

Amazingly, some revisions replace the superb "lends me breath" with a tame repetition of the initial "while I've." Another recent revision has the tongue twister "I'll praise you while you. . . ."[45] I shall read, simply, "I'll praise my God, who lends me breath."

I'll Praise My Maker While I've Breath

Isaac Watts (1674–1748)   Poetic Meter: 888.888.
                                           Best tune: OLD 113th

Respectfully revised and left in the public domain by Brian Wren, 1997.

I'll praise my Maker while I've breath,
and when my voice is lost in death
    praise shall employ my nobler powers.
My days of praise shall ne'er be past
while life and thought and being last,
    or immortality endures.

Happy are they whose hopes rely
on Israel's God, who made the sky
    and earth and sea, with all their train;
whose truth forever stands secure,
who saves the oppressed, who feeds the poor;
    for none shall find the promise vain.

Our God pours eyesight on the blind,
our God supports the fainting mind
    and gives the laboring conscience peace,
defends the stranger in distress,
the orphan and the comfortless,
    and grants the prisoner sweet release.

I'll praise my God, who lends me breath,
and when my voice is lost in death,
    praise shall employ my nobler powers.
My days of praise shall ne'er be past
while life and thought and being last,
    or immortality endures.

---

45. "While I've" is adopted by the *United Methodist, Presbyterian,* and *Chalice* hymnals. *Voices United* perpetrates "you while you."

Chapter Ten

"Echoes of the Gospel": How Hymns Do Theology

Harmony of ages, God of listening ear
thank you for composers tuning us to hear
echoes of the Gospel in the songs we sing,
sounds of love and longing from the deepest spring.
— Ruth Duck

Periodically, professional theologians show an interest in the lyrics of congregational song, especially hymn lyrics.[1] Whether the approach is descriptive, appreciative, or critical, a theologian studying hymns is in the position of an American visiting Australia. The language is familiar, yet foreign. Though the Christian story is told, doctrines elaborated, and theological viewpoints expressed, a hymn lyric's theological work—if any—is done within the syllable count, stress patterns, and rhyming options of English verse, and the limits and possibilities of rhetorical devices such as epigram, simile, antithesis, and metaphor. To avoid sounding silly or off the point, the theological visitor needs to understand the possibilities and limits of the medium, treat lyricists as partners rather than suspects, and have a wider definition of "theology" than the tradi-

---

1. Schilling, *The Faith We Sing*, is thorough, informed, and (though inevitably dated) still valuable. Gabriel Fackre has critiqued "inclusive language" changes in recent hymnals, especially *The New Century Hymnal* (Fackre, "Christian Teaching and Inclusive Language Hymnody" and his contributions to Christensen, ed., *How Shall We Sing the Lord's Song?*

tional. In this chapter I aim to show that the best hymn lyrics can justly be said to "do theology." To do this, I must first argue for a wider definition of "theology" than the dominant paradigm. Though I focus on hymns, much of what follows applies to other genres of congregational song.

Theology as Reasoned Enquiry

Punctually at eleven o'clock in the morning, Dr. Caird enters the room, his academic gown swishing quietly as he walks to the front and ascends the platform. He arranges his lecture notes on the podium, adjusts his spectacles, and begins.

For fifty-five minutes, he leads us through a verse-by-verse commentary on the Gospel of Mark. He varies the pace, allowing ample time for note-taking. He analyzes the Greek text, lucidly, wittily, and with helpful illustrations. He discusses issues of interpretation, reviewing the major viewpoints and adding his own.

At five minutes to twelve, he piques our interest by raising an intriguing question he will deal with next time, adjusts his spectacles, picks up his notes, descends from the platform, and leaves the room at twelve noon precisely.

George Caird was my tutor and doctoral supervisor. He was a superb lecturer and teacher, who understood and exemplified "theology" as an ordered, reasoned account of Christian faith. A skilled communicator, he knew the importance of humor, story, and metaphor, and how to integrate them into a presentation that offered information, weighed evidence, and drew conclusions. But ordering information, weighing evidence, making a reasoned argument, and drawing conclusions were central to his theological endeavor.

Caird exemplified the predominant understanding of Christian theology, as a form of *reasoned enquiry*. With variations and nuances, most definitions follow suit. Thus, a theological dictionary defines "theology" as "the rational account given of Christian faith,"[2] while an introduction to Christian theology defines it as "the systematic study of the fundamental ideas of the Christian faith."[3] Roman Catholic theologian Karl Rahner defines theology as "the conscious and methodical explanation and explication of the divine revelation received and grasped in faith."[4] Paul Schilling, a Protestant theologian exploring

2. Sykes, "Theology," *Westminster Dictionary of Christian Theology.*
3. McGrath, *Christian Theology: An Introduction,* p. 119.
4. Karl Rahner, quoted in ibid.

"how the message of hymns can enhance Christian belief," argues that "any exploration of the meaning of God for any aspect of our experience is theological," but adds that, "more precisely, Christian theology is the *thoughtful enquiry* into the meaning of the faith called forth by God's self-disclosing activity, especially in Jesus Christ. It seeks through *critical examination* to discover the truths implied in the history and experience of the Christian community and to interpret them in the most intelligible and persuasive manner."[5]

On the basis of these definitions, hymns cannot do theology, even when the meaning of "reasoned enquiry" is broadened and qualified.[6] Their brevity and form are ill suited to systematic reasoning, and, though not lacking in rationality, a hymn invites us, not to step back from faith and examine it, but to step into faith and worship God.

Hymns are typically said or sung in public worship, and the authors of a worship textbook reflect a widely held opinion when they say that "worship in all its forms and elements is laden with theological insights." In worship, "theology is acted out, expressed in practice." So "worship is the vehicle of theology, communicating far more effectively than learned treatises ever can."[7] Perhaps we should simply accept the implication that hymn lyrics, as elements in worship, can be "vehicles" of theology, putting in memorable language "what oft was thought, but ne'er so well expressed."[8]

This view is not as straightforward as it sounds. The "vehicle" metaphor is attractive, but limited. Accidents aside, passengers expect to occupy a vehicle without being reshaped by the experience. But expressing a theological concept in verse entails moving from concept

---

5. Schilling, *The Faith We Sing*, p. 30.

6. Stephen Sykes notes "the comparatively recent discovery that there is a diversity of forms of rational argument in different disciplines," which obliges theologians to attend to the fact that "Christianity exists in liturgies, rituals, art forms and other forms of cultural expression" (Sykes, "Theology"). John Macquarrie defines theology as "the study which, *through participation in* and reflection upon a religious faith, seeks to express the content of this faith in the clearest and most coherent language available" (quoted by McGrath, *Christian Theology: An Introduction*, p. 118, emphasis mine). Macquarrie broadens the definition from "systematic reasoning" to "clearest and most coherent language," and adds the dimension of participation. In an American Protestant milieu, for example, this implies that theological reasoning is inadequate without a faith-commitment expressed in such activities as prayer, public worship, going to church potlucks, and serving on the Board of Trustees.

7. Forrester, McDonald, and Tellini, *Encounter with God*, p. 7.

8. See p. 278. It is widely agreed that hymns *communicate* theological beliefs, as for example in Paul Schilling's axiom that "theology, good, bad, or indifferent, is present in all hymns" (*The Faith We Sing*, p. 25).

to metaphor, from elaboration to epigram, and from balanced prose
to the energy of rhyme and rhythm, any or all of which can make sub-
stantive, and not merely stylistic, alterations to what is being expressed
(I shall give examples later in this chapter). Moreover, because a hymn
has a limited word length and time frame, a poet must be selective,
highlighting some themes and omitting others. For these reasons, it is
unlikely that a hymn lyric can "carry" theological concepts without also
interpreting them, and thus in its own way doing theology.[9]

Nonverbal Theology

Before I elaborate this claim, let me make a case for a wider definition of "theology." Christian theology as reasoned enquiry hopes not
merely to *express* and *convey* the faith called forth by God's self-disclosure in Jesus Christ, but to explore, discover, and know more about
it. If there are communicable ways of exploring, discovering, and
knowing more about God's self-disclosure in Christ other than verbal
reasoning, they are *doing* theology, not merely expressing it, conveying it, or doing nontheological work with theological implications.

The human brain has two, largely symmetrical, left and right cerebral hemispheres, independently able to process and store information.
The hemispheres are connected by a bundle of two hundred million
nerve fibers, the *corpus callosum,* and are psychologically distinct. The
left hemisphere is normally dominant for language functions, while the
right is better equipped for handling spatial and other nonverbal relations. Some variations in this pattern correlate with left-handedness
and right-handedness. Visually, in right-handed persons, the left hemisphere has been shown as specialized to recognize printed words or
numbers, while the right hemisphere processes complex nonverbal
material such as geometric figures, faces, and road maps. Aurally, the
left hemisphere analyzes words, while its counterpart analyzes tone of
voice and certain aspects of music.[10] The following elaboration invites
comparison with the definitions of "theology" above:[11]

---

9. To test this hypothesis would involve analyzing the contents of a representative
group of hymnals to evaluate what happens when particular theological concepts are
expressed in hymn lyrics, but that is a large project, beyond the scope of this work.

10. "Brain Bilateralism" and "Brain (ii)", *The 1997 Grolier Multimedia Encyclopedia,* CD-ROM, citing V. Bianki, *The Mechanisms of Brain Lateralization* (1993); R.
Dean, and C. Reynolds, *Assessment of Laterality* (1994); and J. Ward, and W. Hopkins, eds., *Primate Laterality* (1993).

11. Adapted from Lusser Rico, *Writing the Natural Way,* chap. 4.

Left: *verbal,* knowing grammar and syntax, deploying words; *sequential* (a-b-c), producing linear, rule-governed thinking; *makes distinctions,* splitting the world into identifiable, name-able bits and pieces; *logical,* seeing cause and effect, receptive to what is verifiable; *charts the informational aspects of thought;* draws on *fixed codes and accumulated, organized information*	**Right:** *nonverbal,* uses pictures, not words, or responds to words as images; *nonlinear,* producing analogic, imagistic thinking; *makes connections,* seeing cor-respondences and resemblances; *imaginative and holistic,* looking at the whole and remembering complex images; *charts emotional nuances of thought;* draws on *unbounded, qualitative patterns in clusters rather than sequences.*

I believe that the best work of systematic, biblical, and other the-ologians necessarily draws on both hemispheres, integrating reasoning and imagination and making connections that are then tested ratio-nally. With that proviso, it is clear that "theology as reasoned enquiry" prioritizes left-brain functions of verbal articulation, sequential and linear thinking, marshaling information, making precise distinctions, reasoning logically, weighing evidence, establishing cause and effect, clarifying, codifying, and concluding.

By contrast, right-brain ways of knowing prioritize nonverbal cog-nition, using pictures, sounds, and/or movement rather than words. Verbal or nonverbal, they are analogical and holistic, often nonlinear. They prioritize connections, correspondences, and resemblances.

Nonverbal Knowing

Some acts of knowing are nonverbal. When learning phonetics, the primary mode is aural; when learning to dance or drive a car it is bod-ily, kinesthetic. In these processes, verbal reasoning and description are auxiliary to, and geared toward, kinesthetic and aural learning. One does not learn how to dance, drive, or recognize and articulate Xhosa and Zulu click-sounds merely by reading a textbook. Learning proceeds through practice and feedback, aided (but not achieved) by written theory. One year in high school I was second in the class in woodwork theory, and bottom of the class in woodwork practice: the-oretical knowledge could not teach me how to make a mortise and tenon joint, and I would not have gained employment as a carpenter.

A teacher, John Holt, gives a striking example of visual learning. Visiting a school of arts and crafts with some friends, he saw, for the first time, a hand loom. All the parts were clearly visible. As his friends talked knowledgeably about weaving, he puzzled over it and tried to reason how it worked. All such left-brain activity proved fruitless. His friends' repeated explanations were unhelpful, as was the niggling feeling that a moderately intelligent person ought to be able to work it out for himself. In the end he shut out the explanations, silenced his verbal, rational self, and contented himself with looking wordlessly at the machine.

Hours later, after demonstrations of pottery, printmaking and glass-blowing, the group began the long drive home. The conversation was about pottery, and Holt was not consciously thinking about the loom. But "as we talked, a loom began to put itself together in my mind. There is no other way to describe it. Suddenly, for no reason, the image of a particular part would appear in my consciousness, but in such a way that I understood what that part was for." The under-standing was visual (right-brain), not verbal (left-brain). Holt could not *say* what the part did but could *see* it doing its work. "By the end of the day," he continues, "a loom had made itself in my mind." There was much he didn't yet understand, but he knew where knowledge left off and ignorance began, what questions to ask and how to make sense of the answers.[12]

John Holt was able to communicate his nonverbal experience in words, or more precisely, communicate enough of the experience for it to be understood. A theologian of the arts asks, "In what fashion can we speak of a theology that relies fundamentally on vision or sound or the organization of space rather than words?"[13] Nonverbal art (such as sculpture and dance) and mixed-media art (drama, movies) are noto-riously hard to "put into words." Art and drama critics sometimes sound obscure and pretentious, not necessarily because they *are* pre-tentious, but because media and message are hard to capture in lan-guage.

Nonverbal does not mean unthinking. Whether or not their art form uses language, most artists "know what they are doing," and can artic-ulate it verbally: their degree of verbal clarity varies according to their personality, verbal skills, the medium they are working in, and, some-

---

12. Holt, *How Children Learn*, pp. 161–64.
13. Yates, "Issues for Discussion," p. 2.

times, whether it is worth the bother of trying to put their intent into words. Painting, sculpture, drama, and dance attract extensive bodies of theory and description from artists, critics, and thinkers concerning what is done and discovered. Yet verbalization cannot play the lead, only a supporting role. Theory and description can point us toward the meaning of nonverbal and mixed-media art, but we grasp their meanings inadequately, if at all, unless and until we encounter them directly. The same applies to nonverbal and mixed-media theology.

Since this book is a verbal medium, I cannot present paintings, videos, and recorded sound with words as pointers to interpretation. I shall discuss music, drama, and painting, limiting myself to examples capable of sufficient, though inadequate, verbal description.[14]

Musical Theology

Mozart's opera *Don Giovanni* communicates a terrifying choice: repent or be damned. Mozart explores this theme not only dramatically, but musically. His "musical definition of the Don himself opens a window onto the emptiness of a godless life." The Don's music has no originality, no personality of its own. In every aria but one, his music is derivative. "It takes its character not from some inner integrity or strength, but rather from the person with whom the Don is double-dealing." There is one exception, a drinking song, whose short musical phrases are repeated over and over again, with no change in harmonic or rhythmic detail. "By the time we have heard this silly tune twenty times, we are well aware of the biting truth of Mozart's description of the person inside the Don: no one, a void, a person emptied of all that makes human relationships have meaning."[15] The musical argument, like verbal reasoning, may not be grasped or accepted by everyone who hears it. But to those who "get it," Mozart's musical exploration of a theological theme brings new insight, new knowledge. Here is theology through music, a gift given and received through "the lively interplay of intelligence and feeling."[16]

On a smaller scale, it is conceivable that a congregational song tune can express and generate theological insights. In an article exploring

---

14. For dance theology, see Rock and Mealy, *Performer as Priest and Prophet*, chap. 4, pp. 29–44.
15. Ibid., p. 25.
16. Ibid., p. 29.

"music as theology," Victoria Sirota discusses two tunes commonly matched with the hymn lyric "O Little Town of Bethlehem": FOREST GREEN, and English folk-melody harmonized by R. Vaughan Williams (1872–1958), and ST. LOUIS, by Lewis H. Redner (1813–1908). Sirota argues persuasively that FOREST GREEN, though bright and singable, is better able to depict the joy of Christ's birth than the profound silence of which the lyric also speaks. Through its harmonies, melodic construction, and shift between major and minor keys, ST. LOUIS, is more successful in setting "the conflicting human feelings of fear, awe, and yearning that would be present for those actually witnessing the entrance of Christ on earth." Its music "knows the darkness well, and yet is able to reach out to the light."[17]

Dramatic Theology

Culture of Desire is a multimedia drama, conceived and directed by Ann Bogart. Performed by the Saratoga International Theater Institute, it received its world premiere in Portland, Maine, in March 1998. The seven-member cast has two central characters. One is artist Andy Warhol, whose art gave, and gives, a witty, sardonic, playful, and painful critique of modern consumer culture. Ann Bogart writes that "Andy Warhol made art from the present moment. He fetishized our culture and our desire and created art from it. Warhol became our metaphor and central figure because he projected the vast emptiness that reflects us profoundly."[18]

The other central role is a Woman. She has black hair, in a hairstyle that mimics Jackie Kennedy, and wears a black dress. When she beckons, Warhol follows. Strong and compelling, our interpreter and guide, she is played by a man. The Woman is an analogue of the Roman poet Virgil, who was Dante's guide through hell in his dramatic poem, "The Inferno."

---

17. Sirota, "An Exploration of Music as Theology," p. 22. Her discussion could profitably include the tune CHRISTMAS CAROL, by Walford Davies (1869–1941), as found, for example, in *Hymns Ancient and Modern New Standard* (Norwich, England: Hymns Ancient and Modern Limited, 1983), #90. For FOREST GREEN see, for example, BOP #164, HCS #236, PH #43 and R&S #145. For ST. LOUIS see BH #86, BOP #165, PH #43 UMH #230, and VU #64. On music's power to give meaningful progression, mimic the flow of emotion, and satisfy intellect and emotion, see above, pp. 57–67.

18. Bogart, "Director's Notes."

Dante's "Inferno" (written ca. 1307–21) begins with the poet in midlife, lost and disoriented in a dark wood at the bottom of a deep, dreadful valley. At the beginning of *Culture of Desire,* Andy Warhol comes to his own valley of the shadow, when he is shot and seriously wounded by playwright Valerie Solanas on June 3, 1968. As he lies semiconscious, groaning in pain, in a timeless zone between shooting and hospitalization, he hears the opening lines of the "Inferno." The Woman appears and guides him through hell here and now, created by our culture's empty, accursed drive to buy, sell, accumulate, and possess. An airport departure gate represents the gates of hell ("Abandon hope, all who enter here"). A fast-talking line of consumers, volubly narrating their desire to buy, buy more, own, and possess, is stopped, one by one, frozen into silence, and pulled backward through the gate by invisible hands. In a supermarket ballet, three couples go round and round on shopping carts, pushing and pulling, leaping, reaching, and taking, in an endless, mindless spending spree that is both Temptation Waltz and Dance of Death.

Short, pungent scenes succeed each other, each seizing attention, each rapidly displaced by the next. The drama grabs the audience by the ears, makes us laugh, then gets under our guard with an epigram. In real life, advertisements (misleadingly called "messages") interrupt the "real program." In *Culture of Desire,* the message slips in between scenes satirizing advertisements. We learn that though advertisements cannot create desire, they channel it. Advertisements carry our culture, in images and definitions of what we are. Supermarkets put produce at one end, dairy products at the other, and meat at the back, so that shoppers must trek through the entire store to buy necessities, cajoled and enticed to load the cart with other goods on the way. Warhol's paintings of dollar bills depict our idolatry of money. A Bag Lady leans over her shopping cart, babbling in slogans: "New, Improved, BargainBargainBargain! Startling, Fresh" and finally, pointedly, "These prices are *insane!*" In one scene, Warhol shines a spotlight on the audience, then on the characters. "Talk to me!" he says. They respond with slogans and clichés. In another scene, the Woman questions Warhol: Why do you do what you do? Would you do it as well if you were stupid? "Yes." Who are you? "I don't know." What did you learn last year? "Nothing, that's why I'm wiser."

The dialogue is humorous and pungent: a barrage and collage of slogans and jingles, mixed with satirized snippets of corporate philosophy. Uprooted from their persuasive contexts, advertising slogans seem ludicrous and manipulative. The audience is bombarded by words, high-decibel music, flashing lights, rapid movement, and insistent "messages," theatrically exaggerated yet startling in their familiarity. The inhabitants of "consumerhell" are stylized caricatures, posturing, hilarious, empty-headed, aggrieved, anguished, and lost: emptied of "character." Yet they are not aliens—they are us. We smile, laugh, and sigh as in them we see ourselves.

In brief interludes, the Woman summarizes the social critique in Warhol's art. Warhol is the connecting thread and most developed character, in appearance, speech, and body language. He traverses the circles of hell in a waking dream, periodically collapsing and curling up in pain from his wounds.

The creator-director of *Culture of Desire* may, or may not, view it as relevant to Christian theology. It is a multidimensional work with its own integrity. In assessing it theologically, I am highlighting a motif in its tapestry, not shrinking the tapestry to fit a church wall.

By drawing on Dante, who stands at the intersection of theology and literature, *Culture of Desire* inevitably raises theological questions. In the final scene, the Woman faces the audience from a shadowed stage. Steadily, relentlessly, she questions us, all humor gone. As if mimicking a quiz show, her questions blend profundity with trivia. Yet the mood is serious and intense, her speech sharp and clear, as she taps out question after question, like a snare drum beating retreat.

Why do you do what you do? Would you do it as well if you were stupid? Should you be compensated if your work makes you happy? Should you be compensated if your work makes you unhappy? Who are you? Do you feel a fraud? How much is enough? What do you love? What do you believe in? Are my seams on straight? What *will* the well-dressed woman be wearing next year? What did you learn last year? You mean you don't get wiser as you grow up? Are you human? What *is* this? What do you know? Why do you answer what you answer?

The "Director's Notes" raise similar questions more quietly, in measured prose:

> Many of us live in a constant state of desire for things: objects, wealth, fame. . . . What does it mean personally, politically and spiritually to be treated as a lifetime consumer? How does it affect us to be born into a culture where the fulfillment of desire

through the abnegation of individuality and responsibility is the norm?[19]

Here is a work exploring theological themes. What does it mean to be human? What is our destiny as human beings (on earth? hereafter? Is there a hereafter?)? Is "hell" a convenient, if antiquated image ("We don't believe in it, but it's a useful metaphor"), or is there a fearsome truth in it, when reinterpreted this way? The "useful metaphor" interpretation risks trivializing the drama. On the "fearsome truth" interpretation, *Culture of Desire* portrays a culture empty, alienated, and sinful (separated from God and true humanness), and in consequence permeated with sins causing spiritual death (the "seven deadly sins"): avarice (greed), envy, gluttony, and lust ("a constant state of desire for things"); sloth (apathy) ("abnegation of individuality and responsibility"); anger (when the dream of having more is denied or unfulfilled); and pride (idolizing objects, wealth, and fame in place of God).

Culture of Desire has a strong "left-brain" element. Research, planning, theory, and thought have partnered intuition, imagination, and a variety of performance skills in its creation. Language can describe *Culture of Desire,* but cannot do what it does, or fully explain it. Ann Bogart's "Director's Notes" give us a jump start, but can only frame our approach to the drama. To know it, one must experience it.

Culture of Desire uses drama to *problematize* reality, meaning that it reorganizes and *re*-presents the everyday reality in which we are immersed in such a way that we are bounced out of it, and can see it as a problem for inspection, thought, and investigation.[20] The bombardment of words, music, light, and movement is theatrical, yet familiar, prompting the response, "Yes, this is what it's like every day: *how come I don't notice it?*" Though it treats advertising slogans with humor, it reveals them as no longer amusing and clever, but ludicrous, deceitful, and manipulative. The inhabitants of consumerhell are caricatures, and deliberately characterless. Why then do we see ourselves in some of them? Are we more empty than we know, less human than we realize, already in danger, already being pulled through Hopeless Gates by invisible hands? These are discoveries, cognitions, knowings—a sufficient case for arguing that *Culture of*

---

19. Ibid.

20. Problematization is developed, as educational theory and practice, in Freire, *Education for Critical Consciousness, Cultural Action for Freedom,* and *Pedagogy of the Oppressed.*

Desire is not merely expressing theological issues, but in its own way doing theology.

Visual Theology

In a well-researched article, Mary Charles Murray discusses visual theology,[21] beginning with the observation that Christian theology has always been at home with words. Because Christianity began as an announcement of good news, it was bound to be verbal in expression, both orally and in writing. Shaping this good news, it gave the world a new literary form, called "Gospels." Later, Christian theology drew on the Platonic view of language as therapeutic: by constantly refining language, the Socratic method hoped to arrive at true knowledge and the healthful condition that was believed to be its result. From the idea that goodness and health can be conveyed by speech came another new literary form, the sermon.

Visual communication, and reflection on the visual, came later. Christian art did not appear before 200 C.E. Not until the ninth century was the essentially Christian nature of the visual, and of visual art, clearly established. After bitter controversy, they were recognized as sanctioned and demanded by the doctrines of creation and incarnation. "But because it came late and was a post New-Testament development, the visual has always remained relatively undeveloped, and the tension between the verbal and the visual within Christianity, rather than their complementarity and integration, has always marked their history, particularly in the West."[22]

Problems arise from modern theology's perception of the visual as having to do with symbolism: the terminology is confused; there are no agreed-upon definitions; psychological, linguistic, cultural, and philosophical critiques put all symbols in question; and in any case, most theological discussions of symbol have centered on language (e.g., "In what way is language symbolic?"), not on the visual. Particularly problematic is the belief that the divine can be encountered, and perhaps best be encountered, through beauty and our response to it.[23] A preoc-

---

21. Murray, "Art and the Tradition: Theology." This and following paragraphs are drawn from her article.

22. Ibid., p. 11.

23. Ibid., p. 12. Murray adds that Hans Urs von Balthasar and Paul Tillich follow this track and that their work "is still a philosophical and therefore a verbal approach to the question. Theology still remains verbal despite the topic of discussion."

cupation with aesthetics ignores the fact that a major tradition of visual theology, namely Orthodox iconography, is based not on beauty but on holiness. A further problem is that aesthetic arguments stand or fall on whether there is such a thing as a *theological* category of the beautiful. Yet the scriptures have no reflection on the nature of the beautiful, and Christian theology would need an aesthetic embracing suffering (crucifixion), which is not normally considered beautiful. One may add that making Christ's suffering "beautiful" all too often means making it nice: turning the gallows-tree into ornaments, and replacing blood and death with gold and jewels, thus nullifying the scandal of the cross.

In view of the above problems, Mary Charles Murray calls for a visual theology not of the symbol, but of the image. From the second century, Irenaeus provides a starting point, in his dispute with the Gnostics. Though gnosticism had a visual element (an iconography) and their secret knowledge (*gnosis*) was mystical in nature, it was communicated in words. Gnostics went to the extreme in verbalism. In their view, words were crucially important, because knowledge of God could be obtained only by knowing the right words, the correct verbal formulae. This is an "essentialist" mistake, namely, the assumption that Christianity, or any other belief system, has an inner essence that can be encapsulated in the "essential meaning" of certain words.

In reply, Irenaeus argued that meaning cannot be reduced to words. One reason is that words do not function in isolation, but form parts of a language. More important, the truth of Christianity is not found in words, but in Jesus Christ, who is not a disembodied Utterance but the Word made flesh, God's living image. Thus, for Irenaeus, "it is the material which conveys meaning primarily, not the verbal. Meaning is revealed in the incarnation of the divine word."[24] Irenaeus's understanding of God's image revealed in Jesus Christ is a starting point for an image-based theology of the visual.[25]

To do visual theology, theologians have to consult artists, "since they alone have the skill to develop the image, which is also a medium

---

24. Ibid., p. 13.

25. Ibid. Murray also cites Wittgenstein's *Lectures and Conversations on Aesthetics, Psychology and Religious Belief,* where Wittgenstein sees religious language as a picture that regulates the believer's life. For example, language about the last judgment paints images in words, and those images are intended to function, not as descriptors of some strange future event, but as motivators for life now. It is wrong to set up a disjunction between word and image. No disjunction is possible; there is bound to be an interrelation.

as well as a visual construct."[26] Having made this point, Mary Charles Murray consults, as it were, three painters: Paolo Veronese (ca. 1528–88); Caravaggio (1573–1610), and Paula Rego (1935–). I shall focus on her discussion of one of Caravaggio's works, because it can be rendered sufficiently, though not adequately, in words.

Caravaggio's *Supper at Emmaus* exists in two versions. In the earlier version, which hangs in the National Gallery, London, Caravaggio does some important visual theology.[27]

Looking at the painting, we see a square table, covered with a tablecloth and set with a modest meal: a basket of apples and grapes; a roasted fowl; two loaves of bread; a decanter of wine, a jug, and a wine cup. There are four figures, three of them seated at table. Facing us across the table is someone whose long, dark hair flows shoulder length on either side of an oval face. The face has neither line nor wrinkle, and is a smooth face: hairless, not clean-shaven. The eyes are veiled by lowered eyelids; they are either closed or looking down. The right hand is raised in a gesture of blessing; the left hovers over a piece of bread, with fingers delicately outstretched. Hands, face, and body are unmarked, showing neither bruises, scars, nor wounds.

The other characters have eyes open, as a crucial part of the facial pattern that makes them recognizable to friends and acquaintances. Standing on the right, looking down at the man with veiled eyes, is the innkeeper, holding a jug, in the act of serving the guests. He is an onlooker, with little more than an expression of professional attentiveness. He has a short, trim mustache and a narrow strip of beard-stubble.

In the left foreground, seated in a chair half turned away from us, angled toward the central figure, is a man, black-haired and full-bearded. He leans forward, caught in a sudden, startled movement, shoulders tense, arms bent, elbows jutting backward, hands gripping the arms of his chair. The semiprofile of his face shows him staring, eyes wide open, eyebrows raised.

On the right, facing left across the table, is an older man, gray-bearded, with a steeply receding hairline. He sits upright, with a hint of forward inclination, eyes intent but in shadow, his arms stretched wide in welcome, horizontally, like the twin arms of a cross. His left

---

26. Ibid.
27. The later version hangs in the Brera Gallery, Milan, and depicts Christ more conventionally, with a beard.

hand reaches toward us, half out of the picture; his right hand hovers by the shoulder of the one who blesses the bread.

When first painted, the *Supper at Emmaus* was fiercely criticized by church authorities, and dismissed as unsuitable, low and vulgar. A late-seventeenth-century critic, Gian Pietro Bellori, gives an important clue to this reaction. He criticized several elements, but was particularly critical of Christ's beardlessness. Apparently convention and tradition decreed that Christ had a beard. To paint Christ without a beard was unseemly, because it made him unrecognizable.

This was precisely Caravaggio's point. The painting is based on two scripture passages, Luke 24:13–55 and Mark 16:12. Luke tells the story of the Emmaus walk, and how the risen Christ was recognized in the breaking of bread, but does not explain why recognition was so long delayed. Mark 16:12 puts the story in a sentence, but includes an explanation of the disciples' nonrecognition: "After this he appeared *in another form* to two of them, as they were walking in the country." [Emphasis mine.] Caravaggio puts the passages together, letting Mark interpret Luke. In this first version of the *Supper at Emmaus,* Christ is not recognized visually, because he does not look like himself. Even in this moment of recognition, the disciples do not identify Christ visually in this "other form": a smooth, oval, unlined face, eyes hidden and unseen. The risen Christ is recognized only by his gesture, which the first viewers of Caravaggio's painting would also have been able to recognize. It is the gesture of a priest at the Eucharist. Thus, "in the picture the disciples' recognition is dependent wholly on the meal—all clues to Christ's identity, such as his wounds, have been removed, and his face is not that of the crucified. . . .Only in the Eucharist does Christ reveal himself to his faithful." The doctrine is traditional, but Caravaggio offers a new, and compelling, interpretation of the biblical texts.[28]

Today's viewers of the painting are unlikely to grasp Caravaggio's visual "argument," unless they have the helping hand of historical, verbal interpretation. Even so, that interpretation, and my verbal description, cannot substitute for the painting itself. Intriguingly, it appears that many in Caravaggio's time didn't "get" the argument either: they were looking for conventional representations to stir their devotion, not visual theology to startle them into insight. Just as one sometimes has to read and reread an unfamiliar chain of reasoning, or presentation of evidence, until insight comes, so one must look and look again, or listen and listen again until a

---

28. Murray, "Art and the Tradition," p. 16.

work of art reveals itself. "The only way to know an art-form is to wait: to wait with, wait for, wait on the intuitive truth it has to tell. This process of waiting, watching, listening creates in the one who waits an empty space into which some new perception of the truth can come."[29]

A Wider Definition

I have argued that theology can be done through music, drama, and the visual arts. By extension, theology that can also be done through verbal art that draws more on metaphor, narrative, and description than on reasoned argument. If my analysis is correct, "theology" needs a wider definition; I offer the following as a starting point, and will then explore how a hymn lyric does theology:

> Christian theology is done when anyone attempts, by artistic skill and creativity, the interplay of intellect and imagination, and/or the methods of reasoned enquiry, to grasp, know, and understand the meaning of God's creating, self-disclosing, and liberating activity centered and uniquely focused in Jesus Christ.

When I meet a hymn for the first time, I find myself asking questions as I sing or read it. Putting them roughly in reverse order of priority, my questions include: How well does the tune express the viewpoint and rhythms of the text (the complete text, not just the first stanza)? Is the tune well crafted and appealing? Is the text well crafted, beautiful, and memorable, so that I'll want to read or sing it again? Does it enlarge my understanding, illuminate what I know, affirm or contradict what I believe, and depress or uplift my spirit? What viewpoint is the writer expressing, and how far can I identify with it?

If the task of theology is, "by artistic skill and creativity, the interplay of intellect and imagination, and/or the methods of reasoned enquiry, to grasp, know, and understand the meaning of God's creating, self-disclosing and liberating activity centered and uniquely focused in Jesus Christ," most of these questions have theological implications. If I identify with a hymn's viewpoint, it will express my belief and orient me in relationship to God. If I sing it often enough to memorize it, the hymn will help to shape what I believe, and so either develop or distort my faith. The more I sing and enjoy it, the more it will encourage me to emphasize what it highlights and overlook what it hides. If I acquire a

---

29. Rock and Mealy, *Performer as Priest and Prophet*, p. 44.

repertoire limited to devotional hymns about me and Jesus, in a worship setting with like limitations, it will not be surprising if I do not prioritize, or cannot express, a joyful awareness of the Trinity, the Holy Spirit, God as wonderful creator, and the cosmic, social, and historical scope of God's love. Conversely, if my repertoire is varied, one hymn's individual piety will be balanced by another's social conscience, and I can entrust myself to the viewpoint of the hymn I'm singing now, confident that it will be enriched, corrected, and supplemented by the next hymn I sing and by the hymns I sing next Sunday.

Hymns are a particular way of using words, a specific genre of verbal theology, different from narrative, history, parable, sermon, lecture, and reasoned treatise.[30] Hymns are a particular genre of theological song. Like other theological work, they need to be appraised and tested for coherence, truthfulness, and practicality. "If a hymn appears to have no theology at all, what purpose does it fulfil in the context in which it is being sung? Does it enable the community to have a deeper relationship with God, within itself, with the world? Does it add another dimension to faith?"[31]

Hymn Viewpoints

Whether by default or design, every hymn expresses a theological viewpoint. When Charles Wesley writes:

> Forth in thy name, O Lord, I go,
>   my daily labor to pursue,
> thee, only thee, resolved to know
>   in all I think or speak or do.[32]

he expresses the belief that daily work is a divine vocation and that God can be known, and should be sought, in the events of everyday life. A hymn by F. W. Faber expresses the belief that God's holiness is both majestic and intimidating:

> My God, how wonderful thou art,
>   thy majesty how bright,

---

30. For a useful discussion of theological literary genres, and their contexts, see Castle, *Sing a New Song to the Lord,* pp. 22–26.

31. Ibid., p. 31.

32. See, for example, the *United Methodist Hymnal,* #438.

how beautiful thy mercy-seat
   in depths of burning light!

How dread are thine eternal years,
   O everlasting Lord,
by prostrate spirits day and night
   incessantly adored!

How beautiful, how beautiful,
   the sight of thee must be,
thine endless wisdom, boundless power,
   and aweful purity![33]

Though both viewpoints are theological, they are not "purely" so. As poems of faith designed to be sung by a group of people in a particular time and place, both hymns also reveal the social location of their writers and their assumptions concerning the appropriate social attitudes of potential singers. In the original version of his hymn, Charles Wesley continues by inviting us to pray, "*Give me to bear thine easy yoke,/* and every moment watch and pray,/ and still to things eternal look, / and hasten to thy glorious day." When he speaks of daily work as Christ's "easy yoke," he is quoting scripture, but writing from the experience and viewpoint of "a university-educated clergyman who would have had some control over his timetable." Agricultural laborers in Wesley's time found their yoke much harder to bear. Even today, someone using that stanza may want to ask how far working life is an "easy yoke" for their particular congregation.[34]

---

33. *Hymns Ancient & Modern Revised* (Beccles, Suffolk, England: Hymns Ancient and Modern Limited, 1972,) #169. F. W. Faber lived from 1814 to 1863.

34. For these hymn examples, and the quoted comment, I am indebted again to Castle, *Sing a New Song to the Lord*, pp. 15 and 36–37. British hymnals include the "easy yoke" stanza; the *United Methodist Hymnal* (U.S.A.) omits it. The social conservatism of the Wesleys is well known. One of Charles's hymns, dated 1780 and titled "For Masters," shows his belief in a hierarchical society where employers, owners, and aristocrats keep their distance from those beneath them: "*Inferiors, as a sacred trust/I from the Sovereign Lord receive,/*that what is suitable and just,/impartial I to all may give. /O'erlook them with a guardian eye;/from vice and wickedness restrain;/mistakes and lesser faults pass by,/and govern with a looser rein. . . . / *Yet let me not my place forsake,/*the occasion of his stumbling prove,/*the servant to my bosom take,/or mar him by familiar love.*" Quoted by Brian Castle, p. 58; emphasis mine.

Frederick Faber's hymn reflects an English Victorian upper-middle-class viewpoint on the social order, though not as overtly as the oft-quoted, mostly omitted, original third stanza of Cecil Frances Alexander's "All Things Bright and Beautiful":

> The rich man in his castle,
>   the poor man at his gate,
> God made them, high or lowly,
>   and ordered their estate.
> *All things bright and beautiful,*
>   *all creatures great and small,*
> *all things wise and wonderful:*
>   *the Lord God made them all.*

The social viewpoint of "My God, How Wonderful Thou Art" becomes clearer in its continuation:

> O how I fear thee, living God,
>   with deepest, tenderest fears,
> and worship thee with trembling hope
>   and penitential tears.
>
> Yet I may love thee too, O Lord,
>   Almighty as thou art,
> for thou hast stooped to ask of me
>   the love of my poor heart.
>
> No earthly father loves like thee,
>   no mother, e'er so mild,
> bears and forbears as thou hast done
>   with me thy sinful child.
>
> Father of Jesus, love's reward,
>   what rapture will it be,
> prostrate before thy throne to lie,
>   and gaze and gaze at thee!

The hymn has scriptural roots and classic theological statements, "but the way in which they have been combined encourages the singer to have a low self-opinion in the face of God who is overbearing yet benign and whose authority and power are absolute." To the extent that such attitudes are also encouraged in everyday life, the singer is being encouraged to react to secular authority figures with like deference.[35] We may add that our choice of congregational songs, and the context in which they are used, also reflect our theological and social viewpoint.

Hymn Lyrics and Systematic Theology

Until quite recently, theology as reasoned enquiry has taken precedence over other theological genres, while academic ways of theological reasoning, European in origin, have held sway over the perspectives and methods of other cultures. Though times are changing,[36] there is still a widespread belief that the lecture, sermon, reasoned enquiry, or systematic treatise is a superior, more *theological* way of doing theology than the painting, poem, drama, dance, or hymn. Because of this, it is important to inquire how hymns relate to systematic theology.

By default or design, every hymn expresses a theological viewpoint. In a comprehensive systematic theology, or systematic inquiry into a particular theme, such viewpoints would have to be explained, elaborated, questioned, argued, and set alongside other viewpoints past and present in a sustained attempt to develop a reasoned exposition of Christian faith. A hymn text cannot do this kind of theology, and though a hymn poet's work can sometimes be quite comprehensive, it can never be complete. Hymn poets share the common human characteristic of being gendered, class-bound, and time-bound (a limitation which the revision process partially reveals even to the writer). We also write within a collegial community whose work complements our own, so that when someone else says something well, we typically say "Amen," instead of trying to duplicate or outdo it.

Although hymns cannot do systematic theology, many hymns offer condensed arguments, as in, " 'Take up thy cross,' the Savior said, 'if thou wouldst my disciple be,' "[37] where the implied argument, drawn

---

35. Castle, *Sing a New Song to the Lord*, p. 37.

36. Liberation and feminist theologies have shaken the hegemony of "Western" academic theology; the theological validity of art forms other than verbal is increasingly recognized; and the electronic media revolution is bypassing, and therefore relativizing, the formerly privileged methods of print culture.

37. First line of a hymn by Charles W. Everest, 1833, drawing on Matthew 16:24–25 and parallels.

from scripture, is that discipleship entails being ready to bear the cross, or in

> Though I may speak with bravest fire,
> and have the gift to all inspire,
> and have not love, my words are vain
> as sounding brass, and hopeless gain.

where the underlying argument is that since love is the supreme gift and virtue described by Paul in 1 Corinthians 13:4–8, it follows that other gifts are, for a Christian, valueless without it.

In most cases, however, a hymn's viewpoint will convince us only if we already accept it or have heard it argued convincingly elsewhere. A four-stanza verse lyric gives barely enough space for reasoned argument, and even in a longer format only a Milton, Donne, or Shakespeare can rise above the singsong pitfalls of the medium and craft arguments that are weighty without being dull.

Epigram and Economy

Nevertheless, precisely because it has few words to play with, one way in which a hymn can do theology is to state, pithily and vividly, theological viewpoints whose claims are argued elsewhere, or to frame praise, thanksgiving, longing, lament, trust, commitment, and other God-centered responses based on such viewpoints.[38] In doing so, a hymn poet uses the techniques of prosody (verse writing) and the tools of epigram and metaphor. By "epigram" I mean the economy of phrase already noted in Isaac Watts ("nor wit can guess, nor reason prove"), Shirley Murray ("in his humanity we find our own"), and Dan Damon ("love rolls away the stone"). Before looking at metaphor, consider the poetic skills in Thomas Troeger's hymn on Christ and "Doubting Thomas." In four short stanzas, the hymn tells the story,

---

38. The hymn writer herself may be such a theologian or, more commonly, someone with a passion for theology who draws on the work of the best theologians of her time. Even the person who writes one great hymn and nothing thereafter, does so by expressing a viewpoint that has been discussed, articulated, argued, preached, prayed, and sung by many others before being distilled into hymnic form.

interprets it, and involves us in the action. The opening stanza uses descriptive imagery of touch and sight to evoke the crucifixion and portray Thomas's perception of reality:

> These things did Thomas count as real:
> the warmth of blood, the chill of steel,
> the grain of wood, the heft of stone,
> the last frail twitch of flesh and bone.

Notice the musicality in the sound of the words (here and throughout), the contrast in the second line ("warmth"/"chill"), the freshness of the first rhyme scheme ("steel" is not a predictable rhyme for "real"), and the structure, where the opening and closing lines are complete phrases, wrapped around four short, almost urgent, four-syllable phrases in the two middle lines.

The second stanza moves from accumulated phrases to a smooth sentence, and from descriptive imagery to an analysis of Thomas's doubt, interpreted in terms of a mind that demands tangible evidence and framed in ironic contrasts between vision and blindness, large and small:

> The vision of his skeptic mind
> was keen enough to make him blind
> to any unexpected act
> too large for his small world of fact.

Once again, the rhymes are sound, uncontrived, and in the case of act/fact, fresh yet seemingly inevitable, while the short, "flat" sound of "fact," emphasized by its position as the final, stressed, syllable of the iambic line, perfectly reinforces its meaning and drops us abruptly into the sterility of Thomas's worldview.

The third stanza lulls us with an opening couplet in the same style, then plunges into a startling simile to describe Thomas's encounter with the risen Christ:

> His reasoned certainties denied
> that one could live when one had died,
> until his fingers read like Braille
> the markings of the spear and nail.

Because it brings together two radically dissimilar images (an unsighted person reading Braille dots with fingertips, and the wound marks of crucifixion), the simile ("read like Braille") is as powerful as any metaphor (on simile and metaphor, see further below). It combines a description of what it might be like to touch those wounds with the suggestion that Thomas, though able to see, had an impervious mind-set, "blind to [this] unexpected act," so had to be convinced by touch rather than sight. The unprecedented rhyme, "Braille"/"nail," is a perfect choice, while the position of the rhyming words, as stressed line endings, gives them an impact hard to achieve in prose (compare, for example: "Thomas stretched out his hand and touched the wounds with his fingertips, like a blind man reading Braille").

The first couplet of the final stanza is a simple petition giving a breathing space from astonishment, followed by a closing couplet that ends the story and clinches its interpretation:

> May we, O God, by grace believe,
> and thus the risen Christ receive,
> whose raw, imprinted palms reached out
> and beckoned Thomas from his doubt.[39]

The closing couplet presents us with two metaphors, and invites us to make a third. The raw wounds of the risen Christ are described as "imprinted," encouraging us to see them as marks conveying meaning, as (for example) in a visa stamp on a passport or a watermark in a sheet of paper. In the second metaphor, Christ's outstretched hands not only beckon Thomas to approach, but invite him to believe—a double invitation condensed into one phrase, "beckoned Thomas *from his doubt*." Harking back to the opening couplet, if we pray that we may "thus . . . receive" the risen Christ, the outstretched hands in the Gospel story become a metaphor for the ways in which Christ's unseen presence impinges on us and questions our own assumptions about life, death, and reality.

Metaphor

By "metaphor" I mean "that figure of speech whereby we speak about one thing in terms that are seen to be suggestive of another." This careful definition comes from Janet Martin Soskice, who uses

---

39. Originally published in Troeger (texts) and Doran (music), *To Glorify the Maker's Name.*

the word "metaphor" to describe this particular use of language in speech or writing.[40] Though the word is often bandied about more loosely, it is more useful, because more precise, to reserve it for the particular trick of language (or, more accurately, trope) under discussion.[41]

Consider the following lines from a widely published hymn by Walter Russell Bowie:

> O holy city, seen of John,
>   where Christ, the Lamb, doth reign,
> within whose foursquare walls shall come
>   no night, nor need, nor pain.[42]

The *subject*—what the writer is talking about—is a set of conditions where God's gracious love is fully accepted, or prevails, among human beings, within and beyond the continuum of space and time. Because we have not experienced this, and it is beyond our capacity to describe it, we can either grope for abstract precision, as I have just done, or use images, word pictures drawn from human experience. Two common ways of doing this, known classically as tropes, are the simile, which compares one thing with the other ("God's new reality will be like a beautiful, safe, well-ordered city") and the metaphor, where we speak of one thing (God's new reality) in terms that suggest the other (a safe, well-ordered city), *so that the image of the city fuses or "intersects" linguistically with the subject.*

Walter Russell Bowie begins with a biblical image of an ancient walled city, idealized and surrealistically conceived as cube-shaped in Revelation 21:10–27.[43] In the following stanzas his hymn describes the harsh realities of poverty and exploitation in the modern city, and prays for strength "to build the city that hath stood too long a dream,"

---

40. Soskice, *Metaphor and Religious Language*, p. 215.

41. Metaphors are not mental events. We may connect different situations wordlessly in our heads, but the word "metaphor" is best used for any language that results. Similarly, metaphors are not physical objects. To say that daffodils are metaphors of rebirth is to use the word in a vague and wide sense, where "symbol" will do perfectly well. For a more complete discussion of metaphor and religious language, see Soskice's book and my own exploration in *What Language Shall I Borrow?* pp. 85–110.

42. "O Holy City, Seen of John," by Walter Russell Bowie, 1909. See, for example, the *United Methodist Hymnal*, #726; *Presbyterian Hymnal*, #453; *New Century Hymnal*, #613.

43. For "foursquare," see Revelation 21:16: "Its length and width and height are equal."

believing that God's new reality is not an otherworldly hope, but can come near, and come true, in human life:

> Already in the mind of God
>   that city rises fair:
> lo, how its splendor challenges
>   the souls that greatly dare;
> yea, bids us seize the whole of life
>   and build its glory there.

Here is a different metaphor on a similar subject, from the sixteenth-century Puritan pastor and spiritual leader Richard Baxter:

> As for my friends, they are not lost:
>   the several vessels of thy fleet,
> though parted now, by tempests tossed,
>   shall safely in the haven meet.[44]

Baxter's theme is the communion of saints on earth and in heaven. Death and other trials separate us, but we shall be reunited. The intersecting image is of a fleet, perhaps a fishing fleet, which puts out to sea from a coastal town and is scattered by a storm. In real life some of the boats might well founder, but Baxter uses the image to affirm that the storms of life and death will not divide us: all the boats will meet again in the harbor.

If we accept them, both metaphors organize our thinking and encourage us to transfer the associations and feelings evoked by the intersecting image to the main subject, so that we respond to both in the same way. Bowie's metaphor encourages us to think of city life at its best, and transfer those positive associations to our understanding of God's new reality. Through the image of the holy city, we may understand God's new reality as, for example: social, ordered, diverse, cosmopolitan, peaceful, and exciting; having varied options, possibilities, and levels of relationship; growing, developing, and evolving; a delightful, beautiful place where we shall live, grow, and flourish. Baxter's metaphor invites us to think of the Christian community as individuals or small groups, each making separate life

---

44. Stanza 3 of "He wants [= lacks] not friends that hath thy love," *Congregational Praise*, #355. For an analysis of the whole hymn, and its original typography, see Watson, *The English Hymn*, pp. 119–20.

journeys, but with a common purpose. The play of chance, circumstance, trouble, and death separate us from our friends, relatives, and partners in Christ, but the metaphor enables us to make sense of those separations and see beyond them to an eventual reunion. The trials and anxieties of living and dying may terrify us and make us feel as helpless as in a storm at sea, but our fears will not overwhelm us if we are inspired and persuaded by the image of the fleet coming safely home.

Not all writers have the skill of Baxter, Troeger, and Bowie, but at their best, hymnic metaphors organize our thinking, generate insights as we transfer ideas and associations from intersecting image to main subject, help us express and make sense of powerful feelings, and move us at a deep level by their appeal to the senses and the imagination. In doing so, the hymn-poem does theological work as valid and important as the reasoned article, lecture, or book. Naturally, both genres have limitations. Reasoning can be manipulative and perverse. As metaphors highlight some themes, they screen out others. The image of the city speaks more of human interaction than of our devotion to God. Though it is said that the Lamb reigns there, we may need the equally powerful metaphors of thousands singing in adoration before the throne to highlight God's new reality as a set of conditions in which we encounter God's presence in all its fullness, and respond, as creatures, with praise and adoration. Moreover, though the city image includes some references to nonhuman life (trees, and a river), neither it nor the throne image is able to highlight the equally important conviction that all life on earth, and the whole of the cosmos, are included in God's new creation.

Janet Martin Soskice also shows that metaphor can be cognitive, meaning that sometimes a metaphor can say something inexpressible in any other way, "not as an ornament to what we already know, but as an embodiment of a new insight."[45] Skeptics can consult her analysis. For minds open to such possibilities, let me offer a poem of my own for consideration:

> We are the music angels sing:
>   short or long,
>   each life a song,
>   a treasured offering.

---

45. Soskice, *Metaphor and Religious Language,* pp. 47–48.

A child, brief skylark, soaring young,
   fell from sight,
   yet all that flight
by Gabriel is sung.

The melody, though short it seems,
   deeper grows:
   heav'n's music flows,
developing its themes.

Discordant grief and aching night,
   love-transposed,
   will be composed
in symphonies of light,

And every human pain and wrong
   shall be healed,
   for Christ revealed
a new and better song.

We are the music angels sing:
   short or long,
   each life a song,
a treasured offering.

The poem commemorates a child who died at the age of eight. Though life spans vary widely, and have no guaranteed duration, our knowledge of potential life span and assumptions about life quality dispose us to say of one person that their death is "untimely," of another that "they had a full life and it was their time," and of a child or youth that their life was "cut short." Such beliefs jostle uneasily with the conviction that the length or brevity of a life does not determine its value in the sight of God. What happens to a life that is cut short? How can we express a conviction that, in some way, God receives it and brings it to fulfillment? Thomas's parents, for whom the poem was written, have a knowledge and love of music, so it was appropriate to look for musical metaphors. Musing on this, I got the idea of the human life span as a melody, augmented with a companion image of the short, soaring, singing flight of a skylark, whose song ceases abruptly when the lark dives on its prey. In music, a melody is defined as a coherent succession of pitches, where "pitch means a stretch of sound whose frequency is clear and stable enough to be heard as not noise; succession means that several pitches occur; and coherent means that the succession of pitches is accepted as belonging together."[46] By calling someone's life a melody, we claim it as music, not noise, and as a meaningful sequence of events.

Some melodies are short, others extended, but a succession of pitches needs a certain minimum length to be apprehended as melodic, and its maximum is determined by what the human ear can encompass as complete. Unlike a melody, the human life span cannot be extended once it has ended. Yet even a short melody can be treated in many ways. It can be sung or played on a solo instrument, and every instrument and rendition will interpret it differently. It can be harmonized, orchestrated, played at different tempi, set in different time schemes, and transposed into different keys. It can be made into a theme with variations, each faithful to the melody yet yielding new insight. A classic example is Ralph Vaughan Williams's *Variations on a Theme by Thomas Tallis.* My poem draws on some of these possibilities, to celebrate a life cut short, express the conviction that every life is eternally valid, and suggest how the divine purpose might elaborate and develop a life span we might regard as incomplete. Since a melody needs singers and instrumentalists, my poem summons angels to perform it. I have an open mind about angels, but if you can't accept them, even as metaphors, the saints in heaven can step into their role.

How far the theme and metaphors in the poem can be expressed conceptually is for the reader to decide. Even if the theme can be fully expressed in nonmetaphorical language, the metaphor still has value as it organizes thinking, articulates belief, presents its theme in twenty-four short lines, and views one human life in terms of the complexity, variety, beauty, enjoyment, and inspiration associated with music. If the poem's subject matter resists full conceptual articulation, then some aspects of the metaphor are cognitive, yielding insights unattainable in other modes of discourse. The relationship between theological metaphor and theological concept is neatly expressed by Sallie McFague:

> Images feed concepts; concepts discipline images.

---

46. *New Harvard Dictionary of Music,* s.v. "melody."

> Images without concepts are blind; concepts without images are sterile.[47]

Not surprisingly, she articulates her viewpoint with metaphors (feed, discipline, blind, sterile), which themselves invite critique, or prompt further elaboration.

I conclude that, besides giving memorable, liturgical expression to theological themes elaborated more systematically elsewhere, the best hymns act as worthy partners to other theological work by expressing Christian faith in metaphor, epigram, and descriptive imagery which combine impact with economy, and whose metaphors may sometimes be cognitive, expanding our knowledge in ways inaccessible to reasoned exposition.

---

47. McFague, *Metaphorical Theology.* p. 26, developing a sentence in Immanuel Kant's *Critique of Pure Reason,* trans. Norman Kemp Smith (New York: St. Martin's Press, 1929), p. 93: "Thoughts without content are empty, intuitions without concepts are blind. . . . The understanding can intuit nothing, the senses can think nothing. Only through their union can knowledge arise."

Epilogue: Findings

The first English settlers in Australia found a landscape familiar, yet strange. Though the beaches were larger than those back home, the bays, inlets, and estuaries around Sydney had been sculpted by tidal mechanisms familiar to island dwellers. Clouds gathered, rain fell, and rivers cut through rock, formed valleys, and flowed down to the sea, as rivers do everywhere else on earth.

The flora and fauna were different. Kangaroos, wombats, and koalas have no analogues in either hemisphere, and eucalpyti are unique. Their dusty green is distinctive, and some shed their bark, rather than their leaves. The Blue Mountains, so-called because of the haze given off by gum trees, look different from English hills.

Early settler paintings, however, show an Australia remarkably like the English countryside. Years elapsed before the new arrivals could see the landscape differently and put their perceptions on canvas.

Writing this book, I have explored the terrain of congregational song. Some features are as expected. Others I have learned to see anew.

Every valley, and every vantage point, reaffirms the *theological* value of congregational song. It is important to facilitate strong congregational singing, especially where group singing is so little done as to be countercultural.

A wordsmith myself, I have come to recognize the musical autonomy of the tunes we sing. However, I have found little published work accessible to a nonspecialist that describes *how* particular tunes express and validate meaningful progression through time, or beautify and dignify emotional flow. It would be good to have more work of this kind, or have it more widely available.

Similarly, it would be good to see, in work accessible to a nonspecialist, more attention to the following issues: how and why melodies get modified over time; how and why new harmonizations replace older ones; how and why lyrics are matched with new and different tunes; or how and why hymnal music committees exercise their freedom to make large-scale editorial decisions on such matters. I would also like to see more work, accessible to a nonspecialist, discussing how the music of congregational song expresses theology or does theological work.

By "nonspecialist," I mean someone who wants to know more about music, but does not read music well enough to "hear" or "decode" printed score, and does not play keyboard well enough to play printed-score examples. New work on the above issues should be published on CD-ROMs, or in book form with an audio CD in the back cover, so that musical examples can be easily heard.

I have revisited the importance of familiarity. A song becomes familiar when sung repeatedly over a period of time. Many congregational songs also have repetition built into their use on a given occasion. As the lyric of a hymn unfolds over two or more stanzas, its tune is repeated twice, thrice, sometimes six or seven times. When choruses are repeated, the tune is repeated along with the lyric. Critics of this procedure can logically object only to the repetition of the lyric: the tune is repeated no more, and sometimes less, than the tune of a hymn. The tune and words of a refrain are also, by definition, repeated twice or more as their song unfolds.

Repetition stores music-with-words differently in the memory from speech alone, in such a way that the music recalls the words it voices. When the repeated tune is familiar and loved, singers look forward to the expected surprise of its development, emotional flow, and completion. Because repeated lyrics are so likely to be memorized, my initial questions are sharpened: What ideas, doctrines, God-images, social postures, and attitudes to other people are thus, by repetition, imprinted in memory? On the other hand, language revisers face a warning sign: PROCEED WITH CAUTION! When a lyric is theologically objectionable, obscure, or unjust, it should be revised as little as necessary, not as much as possible.

My exploration has mapped some of the cultural and class dimensions of congregational song tunes and lyrics. What counts as "musical" varies over time and differs according to culture. What counts as enjoyable, meaningful, or inspiring music varies according to our generational cohort, social class, ethnic experience, and the acuteness of our inherited or acquired sonic perception. What counts as an enjoyable, meaningful, and inspiring lyric varies according to our verbal perception, ethnic experience, generational cohort, and social class. We need to take more account of differences such as these.

Music makes the body want to move, even when the muscular movements it evokes are infinitesimal. Perhaps music with a strong, marked beat appeals so widely because it suggests a meaningful progression and flow of emotion which are energetic, joyful, and get the body moving (often literally). If so, music with a marked beat is doing what all music does, only more viscerally, more immediately. This would explain why, for a great many people, the sound of music with a marked beat, especially in a style they identify with, is a compelling nonverbal signal that *"something interesting is happening here!"* The belief that "something interesting is happening here" is, surely, what we hope to signal at the beginning of any worship service. Music with a marked beat can function as a nonverbal summons to worship the living God, who lives and moves, and in whom we move and live.

I have found it hard to track the appeal, in some worship services, of trite, forgettable lyrics to trite, forgettable music—and the advocacy of both by some proponents of contemporary worship. Everything we do sends messages about what we are doing, and about us. One message of "instant-forgettable" worship song is immediacy: "The Spirit is among us now." Another message, however, is that in song, at least, we live in the moment, and for the moment. The past is unimportant: we need no musical or lyrical connection with it. Since anything we repeat soon becomes a tradition, the *"instant-forgettable" worship tradition* is that congregational song is moment-ary, a means of getting us moving and feeling, but nothing more. Other worship elements may show continuity with the past, or draw on memory, or offer something worth thinking about and remembering, but not the people's song.

If this is so, the theological power of congregational song is being squandered. Memorable music has unique power to store memorable lyrics in memory—for sustenance, spiritual growth, and recall in time of need. Memorable music has unique power to mimic the meaningful progression of God's work over time, in history, in the life of Jesus, and in us today. To ignore such divine gifts seems daft or perverse.

Perhaps instant-forgettable song springs from unthinking imitation of the instant-consumption aspects of fast-food, microwave culture. Or perhaps it represents a confusion between difficulty and depth. My exploration shows that it is possible to craft music and lyrics that speak immediately, but stay in memory. Examples include gospel song refrains, some evangelical and Taizé choruses, African songs, ritual music, and hymn lyrics.

Isaac Watts could combine simplicity and depth. It was not his temperament or historical calling to be a fundamental reformer, like Martin Luther, or an evangelical revivalist, like Charles Wesley. But he did think carefully about how to craft congregational lyrics with simplicity, epigram, word painting, elegant structure, and theological depth. He knew, also, how to serve the congregational practice of his day. Though he apparently disliked lining out, he thought the practice was irreformable, so commonly crafted each line of lyric as a complete unit of meaning, either with a grammatical end point (nowadays marked by a semicolon or full point) or as a self-sufficient thought within a larger syntactical structure.

I have gained a clearer view of the appeal and importance of vocal sound: whether textless (only to a limited extent, I think, in Christian song); or where linguistic meaning is present but distant (Latin, and some "foreign" languages); or in the flow of lyrics in the singer's own tongue. Because vocal sound contributes to vocal meaning, revisers of congregational song lyrics should give more weight to it, and be better informed about the phonetics of vocal euphony.

I have reaffirmed the importance of the words we sing. Because lyrics are indelibly stored with their tunes, they help to shape our belief, worship, and action. Thus, our lyrics need to be devout, just, frugal, and within those boundaries, beautiful. Revision of lyrics over time is normal, and is entailed by their function as *congregational* song.

My journey has shown me how hard it is to avoid the nonverbal arts in worship. When Reformation traditions banished paintings, carvings, and banners, their architecture, pulpit, table, and seating still conveyed powerful nonverbal messages. The most determinedly word-centered congregations are heavily engaged in nonverbal art whenever they sing. The music they sing has its own inescapable autonomy: even unaccompanied unison song needs strong, memorable melodies to be singable for any length of time.

Today, words still matter, but in different ways from even the recent past. In emerging electronic culture, whether or not we have the desire or resources to create worship spectaculars, we need to use our worship speech (including song lyrics) more economically and more vividly, in a seamless unity of words, visual images, drama, dance, and music.

It is a TV cliché for interviewers to demand a sound bite to conclude the program:

"OK, Brian, in fifteen seconds: What's your message about congregational song?"

"Thank you, Jill. My message is this: To word-conscious worriers—Lighten up! And to music-loving musicians—Listen up! And above all, sing when the Spirit says sing!"

Endpiece

Surprise us by the words we sing,
    dear Christ, and as we praise,
break through each warm, familiar shell
and use the songs we know so well
    to challenge and amaze.

Surprise us by the crowds you call
    to join us, when your grace
gives us, through them, your sovereign choice,
enlive'ning echoes of your voice
    and glimpses of your face.

Fulfilled and cherished by your love,
    we'll trace your wider ways;
beyond our safe and local view
we'll gladly go, expecting you
    to challenge and amaze.

Appendix: Selected Hymns

"The True Use of Musick"

Charles Wesley (1707–1788)

Written for the tune Nancy Dawson, whose melody was related to "Here We Go Round the Mulberry Bush" and "I Saw Three Ships Come Sailing In," the hymn was sung in response to a company of intoxicated sailors who had interrupted Charles's open-air preaching service in Plymouth, England, in 1746. It was printed in 1749 with the above title. Here is the full version as it appeared originally.

> Listed into the Cause of Sin,
>   Why should a Good be Evil?
> Musick, alas! Too long has been
>   Prest to obey the Devil:
> Drunken, or lewd, or light the Lay
>   Flow'd to the Soul's Undoing,
> Widen'd, and strew'd with Flowers the Way
>   Down to Eternal Ruin.
>
> Who on the Part of God will rise,
>   *Innocent Sound* recover,
> Fly on the Prey, and take the Prize,
>   Plunder the Carnal Lover,
> Strip him of every moving Stain,
>   Every melting Measure,
> Musick in Virtue's Cause retain,
>   Rescue the Holy Pleasure?
>
> Come let us try if JESU'S Love
>   Will not as well inspire us:
> This is the Theme of Those above,
>   This upon Earth shall fire us.
> Say, if your Hearts are tun'd to sing,
>   Is there a Subject greater?
> Harmony, all its Strains can bring,
>   JESUS'S Name is sweeter.

JESUS the Soul of Musick is;
　　His is the Noblest Passion;
JESUS'S Name is Joy and Peace,
　　Happiness and Salvation:
JESUS'S Name the dead can raise,
　　Shew us our Sins forgiven,
Fill us with all the Life of Grace,
　　Carry us up to Heaven.

Who hath a Right like Us to sing,
　　Us whom his Mercy raises?
Merry our Hearts, for Christ is King,
　　Cheerful are all our Faces:
Who of his Love doth once partake
　　He evermore rejoices;
Melody in our Hearts we make,
　　Echoing to our Voices.

He that a sprinkled Conscience hath,
　　He that in God is merry,
Let him sing Psalms, the Spirit saith,
　　Joyful, and never weary,
Offer the Sacrifice of Praise,
　　Hearty, and never ceasing
Spiritual Songs and Anthems raise,
　　Honour, and Thanks, and Blessing.

Then let us in his Praises join,
　　Triumph in his Salvation,
Glory ascribe to Grace Divine,
　　Worship, and Adoration:
Heaven already is begun,
　　Open'd in Each Believer;
Only believe, and still sing on,
　　Heaven is ours forever.

Quoted in Young, *Music of the Heart*, pp. 170–71, and Leaver, "Hymnody and the Reality of God."

"Psalm 146 For the Tune, Psalm 113 (Genevan)"

Isaac Watts (1674–1748)

Praise to God for His Goodness and Truth

Here is Watts's full text, each stanza prefaced by the relevant verses from the King James Version, for comparison:

Psalm 146:1–2. "Praise ye the LORD. Praise the LORD, O my soul. While I live will I praise the LORD: I will sing praises unto my God while I have any being."

> I'll praise my Maker with my breath;
> and when my voice is lost in death,
> praise shall employ my nobler powers:
> my days of praise shall ne'er be past
> while life and thought and being last
> or immortality endures.

Psalm 146:3–4. "Put not your trust in princes, *nor* in the son of man, in whom *there is* no help. His breath goeth forth, he returneth to his earth; in that very day his thoughts perish."

> Why should I make a man my trust?
> Princes must die and turn to dust;
> vain is the help of flesh and blood:
> their breath departs, their pomp and power
> and thoughts, all vanish in an hour.
> Nor can they make their promise good.

Psalm 146:5–7a. "Happy *is he* that *hath* the God of Jacob for his help, whose hope *is* in the LORD his God: Which made heaven, and earth, the sea, and all that therein *is:* Which keepeth truth for ever: Which executeth judgment for the oppressed: Which giveth food to the hungry."

> Happy the man whose hopes rely
> on Israel's God! He made the sky
> and earth and seas, with all their train:
> his truth for ever stands secure;
> he saves the oppressed, he feeds the poor,
> and none shall find his promise vain.

Psalm 146:7b–9a. "The LORD looseth the prisoners: the LORD openeth *the eyes of* the blind: the LORD raiseth them that are bowed down: the LORD loveth the righteous: The LORD preserveth the strangers; he relieveth the fatherless and widow:"

> The Lord hath eyes to give the blind;
> > the Lord supports the sinking mind;
> > he sends the laboring conscience peace;
> he helps the stranger in distress,
> > the widow and the fatherless,
> > and grants the prisoner sweet release.

Psalm 146:9b–10. "But the way of the wicked, he turneth upside down. The LORD shall reign for ever, *even* thy God, O Zion, unto all generations. Praise ye the LORD." (END OF PSALM)

> He loves his saints; he knows them well,
> > but turns the wicked down to hell;
> > thy God, O Sion, ever reigns:
> let every tongue, let every age
> > in this exalted work engage;
> > praise him in everlasting strains.

Psalm 146:1 (reprise—see above)

> I'll praise him while he lends me breath;
> > and when my voice is lost in death,
> > praise shall employ my nobler powers:
> my days of praise shall ne'er be past,
> > while life and thought and being last,
> > or immortality endures.

"Directions for Singing"

From John Wesley's *Select Hymns*, 1761

   I. Learn these tunes before you learn any others; afterwards learn as many as you please.

  II. Sing them exactly as they are printed here, without altering or mending them at all; and if you have learned to sing them otherwise, unlearn it as soon as you can.

 III. Sing all. See that you join with the congregation as frequently as you can. Let not a slight degree of weakness or weariness hinder you. If it is a cross to you, take it up, and you will find it a blessing.

 IV. Sing lustily and with a good courage. Beware of singing as if you were half dead, or half asleep; but lift up your voice with strength. Be no more afraid of your voice now, nor more ashamed of its being heard, than when you sung the songs of Satan.

  V. Sing modestly. Do not bawl, so as to be heard above and distinct from the rest of the congregation, that you may not destroy the harmony; but strive to unite your voices together, so as to make one clear melodious sound.

 VI. Sing in time. Whatever time is sung, be sure to keep with it. Do not run before nor stay behind it; but attend close to the leading voices, and move therewith as exactly as you can; and take care not to sing too slow. This drawling way naturally steals on all who are lazy; and it is high time to drive it out from us, and sing all our tunes as quick as we did at first.

VII. Above all sing spiritually. Have an eye to God in every word you sing. Aim at pleasing God more than yourself, or any other creature. In order to do this, attend strictly to the sense of what you sing, and see that your heart is not carried away with the sound, but offered to God continually; so shall your singing be such as the Lord will approve here, and reward you when he cometh in the clouds of heaven.

Give Thanks for Music-Making Art

Words: Brian Wren
Music: *Gesangbuch der H.W.K. Hofkapelle, 1784*

ELLACOMBE
C.M.D.

1. Give thanks for __ mu - sic - mak - ing __ art, and
2. Through years of __ train - ing they ac - crue the
3. With mu - sic, __ mov - ing on through __ time in
4. Then let us __ reach for ex - cel - lence to
5. God, give us __ mu - sic to ex - press and

1. praise __ the Spir - it's choice of mem - bers __ called and
2. skills __ of mind and hand, which hours of __ prac - tice
3. se - quen - ces of sound, we show and __ tell God's
4. sing __ and sym - pho - nize for God, our __ ut - most
5. rich - ly in - ter - weave our yearn - ing __ with our

1. set a - part with in - stru - ment and voice.
2. must re - new, en - liv - en, __ and ex - pand.
3. sto - ry - line of how __ the __ lost are found:
4. au - di - ence, with joy __ our __ high - est prize.
5. thank - ful - ness, and sing __ what __ we be - lieve,

1. With __ work and wis - dom, skills hard - won, life -
2. With __ Spir - it - grace they tune our __ hopes; to __
3. the __ old, un - fold - ing cov - e - nant of __
4. When __ kind - ly skill our spir - it __ lifts and __
5. till __ glo - rious in the realms of __ grace, with __

1. giv - ing and life - long, they cel - e - brate what
2. Christ their hearts be - long; for love of __ God must
3. jus - tice right-ing wrong, re - sounds through __ word and
4. makes the hum - ble strong, give thanks and __ praise the
5. new cre - a - tion's throng, our Sav - ior __ meets us

1. God has __ done, and lead __ the __ peo - ple's song.
2. guide the __ arts that lead __ the __ peo - ple's song.
3. sac - ra - ment, and leads __ the __ peo - ple's song.
4. grace - ful __ gifts that lead __ the __ peo - ple's song.
5. face to __ face and leads __ the __ peo - ple's song.

"Give Thanks for Music-Making Art"

Brian Wren   Common Meter Double

Give thanks for music-making art,
 and praise the Spirit's choice
of members called and set apart
 with instrument and voice.
With work and wisdom, skills hard-won,
 life-giving and life-long,
they celebrate what God has done,
 and lead the people's song.

Through years of training they accrue
 the skills of mind and hand,
which hours of practice must renew,
 enliven, and expand.
With Spirit-grace they tune our hopes;
 to Christ their hearts belong;
for love of God must guide the arts
 that lead the people's song.

With music, moving on through time
 in sequences of sound,
we show and tell God's story-line
 of how the lost are found:
the old, unfolding covenant
 of justice righting wrong
resounds through word and sacrament,
 and leads the people's song.

Then let us reach for excellence
 to sing and symphonize
for God, our utmost audience,
 with joy our highest prize.
When kindly skill our spirit lifts
 and makes the humble strong,
give thanks and praise the graceful gifts
 that lead the people's song.

God, give us music to express
      and richly interweave
our yearning with our thankfulness,
      and sing what we believe,
till glorious in the realms of grace,
      with new creation's throng,
our Savior meets us face to face
      and leads the people's song.

Bibliography

Hymnals (arranged by title)

The Baptist Hymnal. Nashville: Convention Press, 1991. Southern Baptist.

Chalice Hymnal. St. Louis: Chalice Press, 1995. Disciples of Christ.

Congregational Praise. London: Independent Press, 1951. Congregational Union of England and Wales.

Hymnal 21. Tokyo: United Church of Christ in Japan, 1997. The United Church of Christ in Japan (*Kyodan* in Japanese) unites a range of Protestant traditions, and has a history different from that of the United Church of Christ (U.S.A.).

Hymns and Psalms: A Methodist and Ecumenical Hymn Book. London: Methodist Publishing House, 1983. British Methodist.

The New Century Hymnal. Cleveland: Pilgrim Press, 1995. United Church of Christ.

A New Hymnal for Colleges and Schools. Jeffery Rowthorn and Russell Schulz-Widmar, eds. New Haven and London: Yale University Press in association with the Yale Institute of Sacred Music, 1992. An independent publishing venture.

The Presbyterian Hymnal: Hymns, Psalms, and Spiritual Songs. Louisville, Ky.: Westminster/John Knox Press, 1990. Presbyterian Church (U.S.A.).

Rejoice and Sing. Oxford: Oxford University Press, 1991. United Reformed Church in the UK.

Rejoice in the Lord: A Hymn Companion to the Scriptures. Grand Rapids: Eerdmans, 1985. Reformed Church in America.

Together in Song: Australian Hymn Book II. Sydney, Australia: Harper-CollinsReligious, 1998.

The United Methodist Hymnal: Book of United Methodist Worship. Nashville: The United Methodist Publishing House, 1989. United Methodist Church, U.S.A., with overseas offshoots.

Voices United: The Hymn and Worship Book of the United Church of Canada. Etobicoke, Ontario: The United Church Publishing House, 1996. United Church of Canada.

Works of Reference

Espy, Willard R. *Words to Rhyme With: For Poets and Song Writers.* New York: Facts on File, 1986.

Grolier Multimedia Encyclopedia. Novaka, Calif.: Mindscape, 1997.

Harvard Dictionary of Music. 2d ed., rev. and enl., edited by Willi Apel. Cambridge: Harvard University Press, Belknap Press, 1986.

Keck, Leander E., ed. *The New Interpreter's Bible.* 12 vols. Nashville: Abingdon Press, 1994– . Cited with volume number, and the particular commentary or article referenced.

Randel, Don Michael, ed. *The New Harvard Dictionary of Music.* Cambridge, Mass., 1986.

Random House Webster's College Dictionary. 2d ed. Revised 1997, 1998.

Richardson, Alan, and John Bowden, eds. *The Westminster Dictionary of Christian Theology.* Philadelphia: Westminster Press, 1983.

Watson, Richard, and Kenneth Trickett, eds. *Companion to "Hymns and Psalms."* Peterborough, England: Methodist Publishing House, 1988.

Wren, Brian. *Piece Together Praise: A Theological Journey—Poems and Collected Hymns Thematically Arranged.* Carol Stream, Ill.: Hope Publishing Company; London: Stainer & Bell, 1996. ISBN 0-916642-62-3 in U.S.A., Canada, Australia, and New Zealand, and 0-85249-835-7 in rest of world.

Young, Carlton R. *Companion to the United Methodist Hymnal.* Nashville: Abingdon Press, 1993.

Sources

Acoustics of Liturgy: A Collection of Articles of the Hymn Society in the U.S. and Canada. Chicago: Liturgy Training Publications, 1991. Contains articles by Dennis Fleisher ("Acoustics for Congregational Singing"), Austin C. Lovelace ("Good Acoustics for Music and Word"), George Taylor ("Acoustics and Organs"), Walter R. Bouman ("Acoustics for the Church"), Terry K. Boggs ("The Relationship between Acoustics and the Creation of Meaningful Worship Spaces"), and Scott R. Riedel ("Worship Space Acoustics: An Annotated Bibliography").

Bell, John, and Graham Maule. *Heaven Shall Not Wait.* Vol. 1, *Songs of Creation, the Incarnation, and the Life of Jesus.* Chicago: G.I.A. Publications; Glasgow: Wild Goose Publications, 1987.

Benedict, Daniel C., and Craig Kennet Miller. *Contemporary Worship for the 21st Century: Worship or Evangelism?* Nashville: Discipleship Resources, 1995.

Berthier, Jacques. *Music from Taizé: Responses, Litanies, Acclamations, Canons.* Chicago: G.I.A. Publications, 1981(?).

———. *Music from Taizé.* Vol. 2. Conceived and edited by Brother Robert. Chicago: G.I.A. Publications, 1984(?).

Bishop, Selma L., ed. *Isaac Watts' Hymns and Spiritual Songs, 1707–1748: A Study in Early Eighteenth Century Language Changes.* London: Faith Press, 1962.

Bogart, Ann. "Director's Notes." Theater Program for *Culture of Desire, Conceived and Directed by Ann Bogart.* Saratoga International Theater Institute, Portland Stage Company, Portland, Maine. March 1998, presented in cooperation with the Andy Warhol Museum.

Bouwsma, William J. *John Calvin: A Sixteenth Century Portrait.* New York and Oxford: Oxford University Press, 1988.

Brueggemann, Walter. "The Psalms as Prayer." *Reformed Liturgy and Worship* 33/1 (1999): 9–27.

Bryan, J. Michael, M. Anne Burnette Hook, Andy Langford, and Brian McSwain, eds. *Abingdon Chorus Book 1: Praise and Worship Music for Today's Church.* Nashville: Abingdon Press, 1996. (Also available as the *Cokesbury Chorus Book 1*—identical publication, different title.)

Calta, Marialisa. "Singing in Groups Becoming a Thing of the Past in This Country." *New York Times,* 30 April 1991.

Campbell, Don. *The Mozart Effect: Tapping the Power of Music to Heal the Body, Strengthen the Mind, and Unlock the Creative Spirit.* New York: Avon Books, 1997.

Carson, Tim, and Kathy Carson. *So You're Thinking about Contemporary Worship.* St. Louis: Chalice Press, 1997.

Castle, Brian. *Sing a New Song to the Lord: The Power and Potential of Hymns.* London: Darton, Longman & Todd, 1994.

Christensen, Richard L., ed. *How Shall We Sing the Lord's Song? An Assessment of The New Century Hymnal.* Centerville, Mass.: Confessing Christ, 1997.

Christenson, Donald E. "A History of the Early Shakers and Their Music." *The Hymn* 39/1 (January 1988): 17–22.

Chupungco, Anscar J. *Liturgical Inculturation: Sacramentals, Religiosity, and Catechesis.* Collegeville, Minn.: Liturgical Press, 1992.

Clark, Linda J. *Music in Churches: Nourishing Your Congregation's Musical Life.* Bethesda, Md.: Alban Institute, 1994.

———. "From Inner, Material Necessity." *NewSong—Brian Wren Newsletter,* no. 9 (May 1993). Carol Stream, Ill.: Hope Publishing Company.

Clarkson, E. Margaret, Carl P. Daw Jr., and Fred Pratt Green. "Approaches to Hymn Writing." *The Hymn* 35/2 (April 1984): 78–82.

Cole, David. "Hymns and Meaning." *St. Mark's Review* (Canberra, Australia), Autumn 1991: 14–17.

Collins, Clayton S. "Doctor of the Soul." *Profiles.* Continental Airlines In-Flight Magazine, February 1994.

Collins, Dori Erwin, and Scott C. Weidler. *Sound Decisions: Evaluating Contemporary Music for Lutheran Worship.* Minneapolis: Augsburg Fortress, 1997.

Davis, Sheila. *Successful Lyric Writing: A Step-by-Step Course and Workbook.* Cincinnati: Writer's Digest Books, 1988.

Dawn, Marva. *Reaching Out without Dumbing Down: A Theology of Worship for the Turn-of-the-Century Culture.* Grand Rapids: Eerdmans, 1995.

Day, Thomas. *Why Catholics Can't Sing: The Culture of Catholicism and the Triumph of Bad Taste.* New York: Crossroad Books, 1990.

Doran, Carol, and Thomas H. Troeger. *Trouble at the Table: Gathering the Tribes for Worship.* Nashville: Abingdon Press, 1992.

Duck, Ruth C. *Gender and the Name of God: The Trinitarian Baptismal Formula.* New York: Pilgrim Press, 1991.

Duck, Ruth C., and Patricia Wilson-Kastner. *Praising God: The Trinity in Christian Worship.* Louisville, Ky.: Westminster John Knox Press, 1999.

Duncan, Larry T. "Music among Early Pentecostals." *The Hymn* 38/1 (January 1987): 11–15.

Dunfee, Susan Nelson. *Beyond Servanthood: Christianity and the Liberation of Women.* Lanham, Md.: University Press of America, 1989.

Ellerton, John. "John Ellerton on Good Hymnody." *Bulletin of the Hymn Society of Great Britain and Ireland* 14/6 (April 1995): 150–51.

Everett, William Johnson. *God's Federal Republic: Reconstructing Our Governing Symbol.* Mahwah, N.J.: Paulist Press, 1988.

Fackre, Gabriel. "Christian Teaching and Inclusive Language Hymnody." *The Hymn* 50/2 (April 1999): 26–32.

Farlee, Robert Buckley, ed. *Leading the Church's Song.* Minneapolis: Augsburg Fortress, 1998.

Foley, Edward. *Foundations of Christian Music: The Music of Pre-Constantinian Christianity.* Collegeville, Minn.: Liturgical Press, 1996.

———. *From Age to Age: How Christians Celebrated the Eucharist.* Chicago: Liturgy Training Publications, 1991.

Forrester, Duncan B., J. Ian H. McDonald, and Gian Tellini. *Encounter with God: An Introduction to Christian Worship and Practice.* 2d ed. Edinburgh: T. & T. Clark, 1996.

Freire, Paulo. *Cultural Action for Freedom.* London: Penguin Books, 1972.

———. *Education for Critical Consciousness.* London: Sheed & Ward, 1974.

———. *Pedagogy of the Oppressed.* London: Herder & Herder, 1970.

Gottwald, Norman K. *The Tribes of Yahweh: A Sociology of the Religion of Liberated Israel, 1250–1050 BC.* London: SCM Press, 1980.

Greene-McCreight, Kathryn. "Our Pride Is in the Name of the Lord." In *How Shall We Sing the Lord's Song? An Assessment of the New Century Hymnal,* ed. Richard L. Christensen, pp. 133–38. Centerville, Mass.: Confessing Christ, 1997.

Grey, Mary. *Feminist Redemption and the Christian Tradition.* Mystic, Conn.: Twenty-Third Publications, 1990.

Grindal, Gracia. *Lessons in Hymnwriting.* Boston: Hymn Society in the U.S.A. and Canada, 1986, 1991.

Harvey, Arthur W. "An Active Process of Responding to God: Response to 'Praise Singing.'" *The Hymn* 38/1 (January 1987): 24–25.

Hawn, C. Michael. "A Survey of Trends in Recent Protestant Hymnals: International Hymnody." *The Hymn* 42/4 (October 1991): 24–32.

Hollander, John. *Rhyme's Reason.* New Haven, Conn.: Yale University Press, 1989.

Holt, John. *How Children Learn.* London: Penguin Books, 1970.

Hopson, Hal H. *The Creative Use of Handbells in Worship.* Carol Stream, Ill.: Hope Publishing Company, 1997.

Hudson, Jay. "The Thirteenth Generation: Demographics and Worship." *Reformed Liturgy & Music* 30/2 (1996): 43–47.

Hunter, Tom. "Thoughts While Singing: During the Hymn." *The Christian Century,* 22 February 1995, 197–98.

Hustad, Donald P. *Jubilate II: Church Music in Worship and Renewal.* Carol Stream, Ill.: Hope Publishing Company, 1993.

———. *True Worship: Reclaiming the Wonder and the Mystery.* Wheaton and Carol Stream, Ill.: Harold Shaw Publishers and Hope Publishing Company, 1998.

———. "The Historical Roots of Music in the Pentecostal and Neo-Pentecostal Movements." *The Hymn* 38/1 (January 1987): 7–11.

———. "Let's Not Just Praise the Lord." *Christianity Today,* 6 November 1987, 28–31.

Idle, Christopher. "The Language of Hymnody." *The Hymn* 34/4 (October 1983): 214–16.

Jenkins, Karl. Cover Notes to *Adiemus: Songs of Sanctuary.* London Philharmonic, Karl Jenkins. Miriam Stockley, vocals; Mike Ratledge, additional percussion. Virgin Records, compact sound disc CDVE 925, 1995.

Jennings, Carolyn. "Why Are You Walking Away?" *Creator Magazine,* November/December 1991, 12–16.

Jensen, Richard A. *Thinking in Story: Preaching in a Post-Literate Age.* Lima, Ohio: CSS Publishing Co., 1993.

Johansson, Calvin M. *Discipling Music Ministry: Twenty-First Century Directions.* Peabody, Mass.: Hendrickson Publishers, 1992.

———. *Music and Ministry: A Biblical Counterpoint.* Peabody, Mass.: Hendrickson Publishers, 1984.

———. "Singing in the Spirit: The Music of Pentecostals." *The Hymn* 38/1 (January 1987): 25–29.

Johnson, Elizabeth A. *She Who Is: The Mystery of God in Feminist Theological Discourse.* New York: Crossroad Books, 1993.

Jourdain, Robert. *Music, the Brain, and Ecstasy: How Music Captures Our Imagination.* New York: Avon Books, 1997.

Kallestad, Walt. *Entertainment Evangelism: Taking the Church Public.* Nashville: Abingdon Press, 1996.

Kaufman, Gordon. *Theology for a Nuclear Age.* Philadelphia: Westminster Press, 1985.

LaCugna, Catherine Mowry. *God for Us: The Trinity and Christian Life.* San Francisco: HarperColllins, 1991.

Larson, L. B. "We Have Come a Long Way . . . Response to Larry Duncan's Article." *The Hymn* 38/1 (January 1987): 16–17.

Leach, John. *Hymns and Spiritual Songs: The Use of Traditional and Modern in Worship.* Worship Series No. 132. Cambridge, England: Grove Books, 1995.

Leaver, Robin A. "The Failure That Succeeded: The *New Version* of Tate and Brady." *The Hymn* 48/4 (October 1997): 22–31.

———. "Hymnody and the Reality of God." *The Hymn* 44/3 (July 1993): 16–21.

———. "Opinion: Playing Scrabble with Hymns." *The Hymn* 35/2 (April 1984): 114–15.

Lorenz, Ellen Jane. "Chorus, Refrain, Burden." *The Hymn* 45/1 (January 1994): 18–20.

Lovelace, Austin C. *The Anatomy of Hymnody.* Chicago: G.I.A. Publications, 1965, 1982.

Lusser Rico, Gabriele. *Writing the Natural Way: Using Right-Brain Techniques to Release Your Expressive Powers.* Los Angeles: J. P. Tarcher, 1983.

Marshall, Madeleine Forell. *Common Hymnsense.* Chicago: G.I.A. Publications, 1995.

Marshall, Madeleine Forell, and Janet Todd. *English Congregational Hymns in the Eighteenth Century.* Lexington: University Press of Kentucky, 1982.

McFague, Sallie. *Metaphorical Theology.* Philadelphia: Fortress Press, 1982.

McGrath, Alister E. *Christian Theology: An Introduction.* Oxford, England, and Cambridge, Mass.: Blackwell, 1994.

Meeks, M. Douglas. *God the Economist: The Doctrine of God and Political Economy.* Minneapolis: Fortress Press, 1989.

Meyer, Leonard. *Meaning and Emotion in Music.* Chicago: University of Chicago Press, 1956.

Miller, Ronald L. "Contemporary Hymn Authors and Hymns as Represented in Ten Recent Hymnals." *The Hymn* 48/2 (April 1997): 39–42.

Miller, Sarah S. "Below the Frost Line: Hymns of Faith." *The Christian Century,* 12 December 1990.

Mitchell, Robert H. *I Don't Like That Music.* Carol Stream, Ill.: Hope Publishing Company, 1993.

Mitchell-Wallace, Sue. "The Composer's Connection." *NewSong—Brian Wren Newsletter,* no. 2 (January 1991). Carol Stream, Ill.: Hope Publishing Company.

Moger, Peter. *Music and Worship: Principles to Practice.* Worship Series No. 127. Cambridge, England: Grove Books, 1994.

Mountain, Charles M. " 'Glory and Honor and Blessing': The Hymns of the Apocalypse." *The Hymn* 47/1 (January 1996): 41–47.

———. "The New Testament Christ-Hymn." *The Hymn* 44/1 (January 1993): 20–28.

———. "The New Testament Epiphany-Hymn." *The Hymn* 45/2 (April 1994): 9–17.

Murray, Mary Charles. "Art and the Tradition: Theology, Art and Meaning." *ARTS: The Arts in Religious and Theological Studies* 5/3 (summer 1993): 10–17.

Music, David W. "Getting Luther out of the Barroom." *The Hymn* 45/4 (October 1994): 51.

Noth, Martin. *Exodus, A Commentary.* Philadelphia: Westminster Press, 1962.

Parker, Alice. *Melodious Accord: Good Singing in Church.* Chicago: Liturgy Training Publications, 1991.

———. "How Can We Sing without the Organ?" *NewSong—Brian Wren Newsletter,* no. 10 (September 1993). Carol Stream, Ill.: Hope Publishing Company.

———. "Mus. Ed. 2001." *Melodious Accord Newsletter* 13/1 (August 1997).

Pelikan, Jaroslav. *The Illustrated Jesus Through the Centuries.* New Haven and London: Yale University Press, 1997.

Polman, Bert, Marilyn Kay Stulken, and James R. Sydnor, eds. *Amazing*

Grace: Hymn Texts for Devotional Use. Boston, Mass.: Hymn Society Book Service, 1995. Boston University School of Theology, 745 Commonwealth Ave., Boston MA 02215-1401; phone 1-800-843-4966 / 617-353-6493; fax 617-373-7322; e-mail <hymnsoc@bu.edu>.

Price, Milburn. "The Impact of Popular Culture on Congregational Song." *The Hymn* 44/1 (January 1993): 11–19.

Ramshaw, Gail. *God beyond Gender: Feminist Christian God Language.* Minneapolis: Augsburg Fortress, 1995.

————. "Words Worth Singing." *The Hymn* 46/2 (April 1995): 16–19.

Reagon, Bernice Johnson, ed. *We'll Understand It Better By and By: Pioneering African American Gospel Composers.* Washington, D.C.: Smithsonian Institution Press, 1992.

Reynolds, William J., and Milburn Price. *A Survey of Christian Hymnody.* 4th ed., rev. and enl. by David W. Music and Milburn Price. Carol Stream, Ill.: Hope Publishing Company, 1999.

Rice, Howard. *Reformed Spirituality.* Louisville, Ky.: Westminster/John Knox Press, 1991.

Rock, Judith, and Norman Mealy. *Performer as Priest and Prophet: Restoring the Intuitive in Worship through Music and Dance.* San Francisco: Harper & Row, 1988.

Roof, Wade Clark. *A Generation of Seekers: The Spiritual Journeys of the Baby Boom Generation.* New York: HarperCollins, 1993.

Routley, Erik. *Hymns Today and Tomorrow.* London: Darton, Longman & Todd, Libra Books, 1964.

————. *A Panorama of Christian Hymnody.* Chicago: G.I.A. Publications, 1979.

Sacks, Oliver. *The Man Who Mistook His Wife for a Hat, and Other Clinical Tales.* New York: Touchstone, 1998.

Saiving, Valerie. "The Human Situation: A Feminine View." In *Womanspirit Rising: A Feminist Reader in Religion,* ed. Carol P. Christ and Judith Plaskow, pp. 25–42. New York: Harper & Row, 1979.

Sample, Tex. *The Spectacle of Worship in a Wired World: Electronic Culture and the Gathered People of God.* Nashville: Abingdon Press, 1998.

Sankey, Ira D. *Sacred Songs and Solos: Revised and Enlarged with Standard Hymns.* London and Edinburgh: Marshall, Morgan and Scott, early 1900s.

Schilling, S. Paul. *The Faith We Sing.* Philadelphia: Westminster Press, 1983.

Scifres, Mary J. *Searching for Seekers: Ministry with a New Generation of the Unchurched.* Nashville: Abingdon Press, 1998.

Scull, Tony. "Rhyme and Reason." *The Guardian* (London), 15 April 1989.

Shorter, Aylward. *Toward a Theology of Inculturation.* Maryknoll, N.Y.: Orbis Books, 1988.

Sirota, Victoria. "An Exploration of Music as Theology." *ARTS: The Arts in Religious and Theological Studies* 11/2 (1999): 18–23.

Smith, William Farley. *Songs of Deliverance: Organ Arrangements and Congregational Acts of Worship for the Church Year Based on African-American Spirituals.* Nashville: Abingdon Press, 1996.

Smith, William S. "From Scripture to Congregational Song." *The Hymn* 50/2 (April 1999): 12–16.

Soskice, Janet Martin. *Metaphor and Religious Language.* Oxford: Clarendon Press, 1985.

Sövik, Edward Anders. "Architecture for Hymn Singing." *The Hymn* 41/3 (July 1990): 10–14.

Spencer, Jon Michael. *Protest and Praise: Sacred Music of Black Religion.* Minneapolis: Fortress Press, 1990.

———. "Hymns of the Social Awakening: Walter Rauschenbusch and Social Gospel Hymnody." *The Hymn* 40/2 (April 1989): 18–23.

Stackhouse, Rochelle. *The Language of the Psalms in Worship: American Revisions of Watts's Psalter.* Lanham, Md., and London: Scarecrow Press, 1997.

———. "Changing the Language of the Church's Song Circa 1785." *The Hymn* 45/3 (July 1994): 16–18.

Sternhold, Thomas, John Hopkins, and others. *The Whole Book of Psalmes: Collected into English Meter.* London, 1639 ed.

Storr, Anthony. *Music and the Mind.* New York: Ballantine Books, 1993.

Studdert-Kennedy, G. A. *The Hardest Part.* London: Wm. Heinemann, 1918.

Sydnor, James Rawlings. "Dietrich Bonhoeffer and Hymns." *The Hymn* 46/4 (October 1995): 20–21.

———. "The Hymn Society's New Hymnal." *The Hymn* 44/3 (July 1993): 7–9.

Tamblyn, Bill. "Has the Hymn Had Its Day? A Composer's Viewpoint." *The Hymn Society of Great Britain and Ireland Bulletin* 13/5, no. 190 (January 1992): 90–95.

Teuscher, Gerhart. "'Jesus, Still Lead On': Count von Zinzendorf (1700–1760)—Poet and Master-Singer of the Moravian Church." *The Hymn* 47/3 (July 1996): 32–43.

Troeger, Thomas H. "Hymns as Midrashim: Congregational Song as Biblical Interpretation." *The Hymn* 49/3 (July 1998): 13–16.

———. "Personal, Cultural and Theological Influences on the Language of Hymns and Worship." *The Hymn* 38/4 (October 1987): 7–16.

VanDyke, Mary Louise. "Closing the Case on 'Kum ba Yah.'" *The Hymn* 47/3 (July 1996): 60.

Walker, Wyatt Tee. *"Somebody's Calling My Name": Black Sacred Music and Social Change.* Valley Forge: Judson Press, 1979.

Watson, J. R. *The English Hymn: A Critical and Historical Study.* Oxford: Clarendon Press, 1997.

———. "The Victorian Hymn: An Inaugural Lecture." Durham, England: University of Durham, 1981.

Watts, Isaac. *Horae Lyricae and Divine Songs.* London, 1709. (See also under Bishop, Selma.)

———. *The Psalms of David Imitated in the Language of the New Testament.* London, 1719.

Webb, Richard. "Contemporary." Chap. 7 in *Leading the Church's Song,* ed. Robert Buckley Farlee, pp. 82–95. Minneapolis: Augsburg Fortress, 1998.

Webber, Robert. *Blended Worship: Achieving Substance and Relevance in Worship.* Peabody, Mass.: Hendrickson Publishers, 1994, 1996.

———. *Planning Blended Worship: The Creative Mixture of Old and New.* Nashville: Abingdon Press, 1998.

———. *Renew: Songs and Hymns for Blended Worship.* Carol Stream, Ill.: Hope Publishing Company, 1995.

Westermeyer, Paul. *The Church Musician.* San Francisco: Harper & Row, 1988.

———. *Let Justice Sing: Hymnody and Justice.* Collegeville, Minn.: Liturgical Press, 1998.

———. *Te Deum: The Church and Music—A Textbook, a Reference, a History, an Essay.* Minneapolis: Fortress Press, 1998.

———. "The Breach Repair'd." *The Hymn* 47/1 (January 1996): 10–16.

———. "The Future of Congregational Song." *The Hymn* 46/1 (January 1995): 4–9.

White, Susan J. *Christian Worship and Technological Change.* Nashville: Abingdon Press, 1994.

Whittle, D. W., ed. *Memoirs of Philip P. Bliss.* New York: A. S Barnes & Co., 1877.

Wilhoit, Mel R. "The Music of Urban Revivalism." *The Hymn* 35/4 (October 1984): 219–21.

———. " 'Sing Me a Sankey': Ira D. Sankey and Congregational Song." *The Hymn* 42/1 (January 1991): 13–19.

Wilson-Dickson, Andrew. *The Story of Christian Music: From Gregorian Chant to Black Gospel. An Authoritative Illustrated Guide to All the Major Traditions of Music for Worship.* Minneapolis: Fortress Press, 1996.

Witvliet, John D. "The Blessing and Bane of the North American Megachurch: Implications for Twenty-First Century Congregational Song." *The Hymn* 50/1 (January 1999): 6–14.

Wohlgemuth, Paul W. "Praise Singing." *The Hymn* 38/1 (January 1987): 18–23.

Woodward, Kenneth L. "Hymns, Hers, and Theirs: Is Nothing Sacred? A New Hymnal Keeps the Music but Changes the Words to Fit Some Modern Sensibilities." *Newsweek,* 12 February 1996. Reprinted in *How Shall We Sing the Lord's Song? An Assessment of The New Century Hymnal,* ed. Richard L. Christensen, 41–43. Centerville, Mass.: Confessing Christ, 1997.

———. "Reply to Andrew Lang." In *How Shall We Sing the Lord's Song? An Assessment of The New Century Hymnal,* ed. Richard L. Christensen, 53–60. Centerville, Mass.: Confessing Christ, 1997.

Wren, Brian. *What Language Shall I Borrow? God-Talk in Worship: A Male Response to Feminist Theology.* New York: Crossroad Books, 1989.

Wright, Timothy. *A Community of Joy: How to Create Contemporary Worship.* Nashville: Abingdon Press, 1994.

Yates, Wilson. "Issues for Discussion." *ARTS: The Arts in Religious and Theological Studies* 5/3 (summer 1993): 2.

Yee, Russell M. "Shared Meaning and Significance in Congregational Singing." *The Hymn* 48/2 (April 1997): 7–11.

Young, Carlton R. *Music of the Heart: John and Charles Wesley on Music and Musicians.* Carol Stream, Ill.: Hope Publishing Company, 1995.

————. *My Great Redeemer's Praise: An Introduction to Christian Hymns.* Akron, Ohio: OSL Publications, 1995.

Hymnody (Single-Author Collections Cited)

Bayly, Albert F. (1901–84). Self-published:
————. *Again I Say Rejoice* (87 items, 1967)
————. *Rejoice in God* (25 items, 1977)
————. *Rejoice, O People* (54 items, 1950)
————. *Rejoice Together* (26 new items and 45 revisions, 1982)
Carter, Sydney. *Songs of Sydney Carter.* New York: Galaxy Music, 1969.
Damon, Dan C. *Faith Will Sing.* Carol Stream, Ill.: Hope Publishing Company, 1994.
Murray, Shirley. *Every Day in Your Spirit: 41 New Hymns from 1992–1996,* Carol Stream, Ill.: Hope Publishing Company, 1996.
————. *In Every Corner Sing.* Carol Stream, Ill.: Hope Publishing Company, 1992.
Troeger, Thomas H. *Borrowed Light: Hymn Texts, Prayers and Poems.* New York and Oxford: Oxford University Press, 1994.
————. *New Hymns for the Life of the Church: To Make Our Prayer and Music One.* Music by Carol Doran and Words by Thomas H. Troeger. New York: OUP, 1992. 25 hymns and tunes, with indexes.
————. *To Glorify the Maker's Name: New Hymns for the Ecumenical Lectionary.* With Carol Doran, composer. New York: OUP, 1986.
Wren, Brian. *Bring Many Names: 35 New Hymns and 3 Doxologies.* Carol Stream, Ill.: Hope Publishing Company, 1989.
————. *Faith Renewed: 33 Hymns Revisioned and Revised.* Carol Stream, Ill.: Hope Publishing Company, 1995.
————. *New Beginnings: 30 New Hymns for the 90s.* Carol Stream, Ill.: Hope Publishing Company, 1993.
————. *Praising a Mystery: 30 New Hymns.* Carol Stream, Ill.: Hope Publishing Company, 1986.
————. *Visions and Revisions: 33 New Hymns and 7 Reissues.* Carol Stream, Ill.: Hope Publishing Company, 1998.

Index of Scripture

Index of Names

Index of Subjects

Index of Titles

Lyrics, non-English

Tunes